Transforming Women's Work

Transforming Women's Work

Copyright © 1994 by Thomas Dublin

First published 1994 by Cornell University Press
First printing, Cornell Paperbacks, 1995

Library of Congress Cataloging-in-Publication Data
Dublin, Thomas, 1946–
    Transforming women's work : New England lives in the industrial
revolution / Thomas Dublin.
        p.   cm.
    Includes bibliographical references and index.
    ISBN 0-8014-2844-0 (cloth : alk. paper).
    ISBN 0-8014-8090-6 (pbk. : alk. paper)
    1. Women—Employment—New England—History. 2. Wages—Women—
New England—History. 3. New England—Economic conditions. I. Title
HD6096.A11D83   1994
331.4'0974—dc20   93-40054

Printed in the United States of America

Cornell University Press strives to use environmentally responsible suppliers and materials to the fullest extent possible in the publishing of its books. Such materials include vegetable-based, low-VOC inks, and acid-free papers that are recycled, totally chlorine-free, or partly composed of nonwood fibers. Books that bear the logo of the FSC (Forest Stewardship Council) use paper taken from forests that have been inspected and certified as meeting the highest standards for environmental and social responsibility. For further information, visit our website at www.cornellpress.cornell.edu.

Paperback printing   10 9 8 7 6 5 4 3 2

To Kitty

Contents

List of Figures

List of Figures

List of Tables

List of Tables

List of Tables

Preface

The issue of women's wage work in the industrial revolution has engaged social theorists and historians since Friedrich Engels wrote his account, *The Condition of the Working Class in England*, in the mid-1840s. In the intervening century and a half the debate has focused on the relative weight of the liberating and exploitative elements involved in women's paid employment under capitalism. I first addressed these issues in 1979, in *Women at Work: The Transformation of Work and Community in Lowell, Massachusetts, 1826–1860*, a case study of women workers in the early cotton textile mills of Lowell. Unwilling to generalize from the experience of a single occupational group in an unusual working and living setting, I began in 1983 a broader collective biographical study of New England women workers in five occupational groups. Out of that initial study, with numerous detours, emerged this book. Here I explore the work and family lives of rural and urban New Englanders across the industrial revolution of the nineteenth century. I see women's integration into industrial capitalism as a two-step process that involves first the penetration of market practices into farming households with the emergence of rural outwork, followed by massive rural-urban migration and foreign immigration to create a female urban industrial workforce in the years between 1830 and 1900.

During the nineteenth century the character of female wage labor underwent a major shift, and work that initially offered women a degree of social and economic independence became more fully integrated within an urban family wage economy. The promise of economic independence, so evident for Lowell's early Yankee millworkers, gave way to the realities of a struggle for survival among urban immigrant working-class families at the turn of the twentieth century. Out of this nineteenth-century history we see the emergence of social patterns and practices that remain very much with us almost a century later.

Preface

It is a pleasure to acknowledge the support I have received in the decade I have worked on the research and writing of this book. Archivists, librarians, local historians, and owners of manuscripts have been unstinting in their assistance as I roamed across New England and occasionally other regions in search of relevant sources. I'd like especially to thank Robert Bristol, Walter Collins, William Copeley, Peter Drummey, Richard Fyffe, Florence Lathrop, Martha Mayo, Eva Moseley, Dorothy Sanborn, Clare Sheridan, and the late Mildred Tunis. I am also grateful to the late Joel Whittemore. For permission to quote from manuscript materials in their collections, I thank the American Antiquarian Society, University of Vermont Library, Baker Library of Harvard Graduate School of Business Administration, Center for Lowell History, Essex Institute, Huntington Library, Massachusetts Historical Society, Museum of American Textile History, New Hampshire Historical Society, New Hampshire State Library, Rhode Island Historical Society, Vermont Historical Society, and Wheaton College.

In my search for illustrations to enrich the analysis offered here, I have incurred another set of debts. For permission to reprint engravings, photographs, and maps, I thank the Baker Library of Harvard Graduate School of Business Administration, Boston Public Library, Bostonian Society, Robert Bristol, Center for Lowell History, Essex Institute, Library of Congress, Lowell Historical Society, Lowell Museum, Lynn Historical Society, Museum of American Textile History, National Survey, New Hampshire Historical Society, Smithsonian Institution, and Vermont Historical Society.

I presented earlier versions of portions of this work at the Tocqueville Society Seminar in Arc-et-Senans, France; at "The Future of American Labor History" conference at Northern Illinois University; at the Rockefeller Foundation conference "Gender, Technology, and Education" in Bellagio, Italy; at the 1987 Berkshire Conference on the History of Women; and in talks at the University of Massachusetts, the University of Pennsylvania, Syracuse University, Stanford University, and the State University of New York at Binghamton. Comments and criticism offered in each of those forums have forced me to rethink and sharpen my analysis.

Earlier versions of portions of this book have appeared in print, and I acknowledge permission to reprint that material here and thank the journal editors and readers of those articles for helpful criticism. I developed the arguments offered in Chapter 2 in "Women's Work and the Family Economy," *Tocqueville Review* 5 (1983): 297–316; "Women and Outwork in a Nineteenth-Century New England Town," in Steven Hahn and Jonathan Prude, eds., *The Countryside in the Age of Capitalist Transformation* (Chapel Hill: University of North Carolina Press, 1985); and "Rural Putting-Out Work in Early Nineteenth-Century New England," *New England Quarterly* 64 (1991): 531–73. Early ideas for Chapter 4 appeared in "Rural-Urban Migrants in Industrial New England," *Journal of American History* 73 (1986): 623–44.

My ideas have evolved in a constant dialogue with friends and colleagues. Mary Blewett, Richard Brown, Anna Davin, Sarah Deutsch, Ileen DeVault, Melvyn Dubofsky, Estelle Freedman, Wendy Gamber, James Henretta, Adrienne Hood, Gary Kulik, Michael Merrill, Gail Fowler Mohanty, Joan Scott, Caroline Sloat, Philip Taylor, Louise Tilly, Laurel Ulrich, and Helena Wright read and commented on portions of this work at various stages, and their comments helped me sharpen the argument presented here. Susan Porter Benson, Mari Jo Buhle, Paul Faler, Steven Hahn, Gary Kornblith, Carol Lasser, Nancy Grey Osterud, Richard Oestreicher, Kathryn Kish Sklar, Judith E. Smith, and Carole Turbin read the whole manuscript at different stages and offered helpful comments and criticism. I have not always followed their advice, and they are not responsible for the argument I make, but the work is much improved for their collegial criticism.

I have had wonderful technical support as the work has progressed. Librarians and computer center staff at the University of California, San Diego, and the State University of New York at Binghamton have made innumerable contributions to the research behind this book. My special thanks to Susannah Galloway, Diane Geraci, Mary Hogue, and Ed Shephard. On the computer front, Jay Cummings, Jerry Fitzsimmons, Bill Hanrahan, and Rose Sherick taught me what I needed to know. For work on the two maps that appear in the book, I acknowledge the good work of Anne Gibson and Margaret Pearce of the Cartography Lab at Clark University.

I also acknowledge the intelligence, patience, and perseverance of a legion of research assistants who made it possible to carry out the incredibly labor-intensive work that is at the heart of this study. I could not possibly have completed this work entirely on my own, and I have learned a great deal from those who have assisted along the way. My thanks go to Barbara Bean, Deborah Bruns, Ingrid Brydolf, Victoria Bynum, Hannah Davidson, Yvette Huginnie, Richard Hunt, Seth Kreisberg, Benedict McTernan, Paul Miller, Kimberly Pellow, David Ruell, Jean Sherlock, Deborah Simmons, Patrizia Sione, Suzanne Toller, Colleen Wood, Kristin Webb, and Chloë Wurr.

Research and writing for this book were supported by sabbaticals, grants, and fellowships from the State University of New York at Binghamton, the University of California, San Diego, the Charles Warren Center for Studies in American History at Harvard University, the Henry A. Murray Center of Radcliffe College, the American Philosophical Society, the National Endowment for the Humanities, and the Museum of American Textile History.

Finally, my greatest thanks go to my family—to my wife and fellow historian, Kathryn Kish Sklar, and my daughters, Sascha and Sonya Dublin—whose support, encouragement, and timely impatience have spurred me on during the decade that I have pursued the work and family lives of New England wage-earning women.

THOMAS DUBLIN

Brackney, Pennsylvania

Abbreviations

Manuscript repositories frequently cited and their locations:

AAS   American Antiquarian Society, Worcester, Massachusetts

BL   Baker Library, Harvard Graduate School of Business
         Administration, Boston, Massachusetts

EI   Essex Institute, Salem, Massachusetts

MATH   Museum of American Textile History, North Andover,
         Massachusetts

MHS   Massachusetts Historical Society, Boston, Massachusetts

NHHS   New Hampshire Historical Society, Concord, New Hampshire

VHS   Vermont Historical Society, Montpelier, Vermont

1. *Introduction*

The industrial revolution that transformed Western Europe and the United States during the course of the nineteenth century had its origins in the introduction of power-driven machinery in the English and Scottish textile industries in the second half of the eighteenth century. It is no exaggeration to claim, as E. J. Hobsbawm did, that "whoever says Industrial Revolution says cotton."[1] And yet far more than the cotton textile industry was transformed in the course of capitalist industrialization; the growth of canal and railroad networks, the tremendous increase in coal production, and the emergence of iron and steel all owe their development to the changes we call the industrial revolution. Moreover, the revolution was not narrowly "industrial" but entailed a huge growth in nonindustrial wage labor as well. The appearance of urban centers contributed to the skyrocketing growth of domestic service and unskilled laboring jobs in commercial cities. In farming areas the growth of outwork occupations and commercial agriculture transformed the rural labor market. Finally, these economic developments coincided with dramatic changes in family life, particularly declining family size and increasing life expectancy. We have to look at more than factories and machine production to understand the broader consequences of this great watershed in human history.

Central to the changes in work associated with the industrial revolution was the emergence of new social relations of production—what Marx and subsequent social theorists termed "class relations." The growth of a capitalist employing class and of a working class relying on the sale of its labor power to earn its subsistence had profound economic, cultural,

---

1. E. J. Hobsbawm, *Industry and Empire: The Making of Modern English Society*, vol. 2, *1750 to the Present Day* (New York: Pantheon, 1968), p. 40.

and political implications in both British and American societies. Following the lead of English Marxists, American labor historians in the past two decades have devoted considerable energy to exploring the social consequences of the nineteenth-century industrial revolution in the United States. Herbert Gutman, Bruce Laurie, Paul Faler, Alan Dawley, and David Montgomery—to name only a few of those who have contributed to the transformation of our understanding of this period— have explored in detail the impact of the industrial revolution on artisans and factory workers and on the native-born and immigrants. Their writings have enriched our appreciation of the revolutionary character of developments over the course of the nineteenth century and have clarified the specific story that emerged in the United States.[2]

Despite this outpouring of scholarship, one is left with a strong sense that the industrial revolution is primarily a men's story. The transformation of artisan crafts, the growth of railroads, the emergence of iron and steel and later of mass-production industries—these are developments that primarily affected men's work. Although women workers were drawn in large numbers into the first factories in the United States—into the textile mills and early shoe factories of New England, for instance—one finds their stories at the margins of many of the studies that examine the nineteenth-century industrial revolution in the United States. Thus Paul Faler's and Alan Dawley's accounts of Lynn shoemakers are, in fact, studies of male shoemakers. Bruce Laurie's

2. For the English historiography, see E. P. Thompson, *The Making of the English Working Class* (New York: Pantheon, 1966); Hobsbawm, *Industry and Empire*; Raphael Samuel, "Workshop of the World: Steam Power and Hand Technology in Mid-Victorian Britain," *History Workshop*, no. 3 (Spring 1977): 6–72; and Patrick Joyce, *Work, Society, and Politics: The Culture of the Factory in Later Victorian England* (New Brunswick, N.J.: Rutgers University Press, 1980). On the American side, see Herbert G. Gutman, *Work, Culture, and Society in Industrializing America: Essays in American Working-Class and Social History* (New York: Pantheon, 1977); Bruce Laurie, *Working People of Philadelphia, 1800–1850* (Philadelphia: Temple University Press, 1980); Paul G. Faler, *Mechanics and Manufacturers in the Early Industrial Revolution: Lynn, Massachusetts, 1780–1860* (Albany: State University of New York Press, 1981); Alan Dawley, *Class and Community: The Industrial Revolution in Lynn* (Cambridge: Harvard University Press, 1976); and David Montgomery, *The Fall of the House of Labor: The Workplace, the State, and American Labor Activism, 1865–1925* (Cambridge: Cambridge University Press, 1987). For discussion of political and ideological developments that accompanied the early industrial revolution, see Sean Wilentz, *Chants Democratic: New York City and the Rise of the American Working Class, 1788–1850* (New York: Oxford University Press, 1984).

Introduction

Working People of Philadelphia begins with a disclaimer that the thinness of the historical record prevented him from systematically including accounts of women and African Americans in his story of that city's working people. The underlying conceptual framework of David Montgomery's fine study draws primarily on the shopfloor experiences of skilled male workers. Workingwomen find places in all these studies, but they are at the margins of the analysis.[3] Their experiences are apparently not central to an understanding of the industrial revolution in the United States; nor do we learn a great deal about women's experiences or attitudes in the course of these momentous changes.

We can move beyond these present limitations. This book is guided by a concern to understand how women's wage work and family lives in the United States were affected by the industrial revolution. Implicit in this focus is an expectation that gender influenced the ways that men and women experienced the changes it brought. Finally, this approach raises the question as to how our view of the industrial revolution is changed when we consciously introduce gender into the analysis. This work thus offers an opportunity both to illuminate important elements in women's lives—the growth of wage labor and changing family relations during the nineteenth century—and to rethink our basic understanding of the industrial revolution in the United States.[4]

Let us begin, however, at a more concrete level—that of individual women in New England who experienced the industrial revolution. The

3. Laurie, *Working People of Philadelphia*, p. xiii. For a fine study that explicitly introduces women into the story of New England shoemaking, see Mary H. Blewett, *Men, Women, and Work: Class, Gender, and Protest in the Nineteenth-Century New England Shoe Industry* (Urbana: University of Illinois Press, 1988). For a perceptive call for the integration of women into our understanding of labor history, see Sue Benson, "The 1920's through the Looking Glass of Gender: A Response to David Montgomery," *International Labor and Working-Class History*, no. 32 (Fall 1987): 25–30.

4. Two essays whose arguments have influenced the approach I have taken are Gerda Lerner, "The Challenge of Women's History," in her *The Majority Finds Its Past: Placing Women in History* (New York: Oxford University Press, 1979), pp. 175–77, and Joan Wallach Scott, "Gender: A Useful Category of Historical Analysis," in her *Gender and the Politics of History* (New York: Columbia University Press, 1988), pp. 28–50. A collection of articles that demonstrates the distance scholarship on women's history has come in recent years to meet the challenges posed by Lerner and Scott is Ava Baron, ed., *Work Engendered: Toward a New History of American Labor* (Ithaca: Cornell University Press, 1991). See especially Baron's introduction.

lives of four women in one New Hampshire family—great-grandmother, grandmother, mother, and daughter—span more than a century and offer a microscopic view of the broader experiences of women of their generations.[5]

Judith Rand was born in Barnstead, New Hampshire, in July 1795, the daughter of Moses, a farmer, and Mary Rand. In 1813 she married Edward Leighton and moved to nearby Northfield. Also a farmer, Edward was taxed for eighty-seven acres of land, seven horses, oxen, and cattle, and twenty-two sheep in 1840. His property holdings placed him in the top half of taxpayers in this farming community. Judith Rand Leighton had eight children, seven of whom survived into adulthood. She probably milked the family cows, made butter and cheese, tended the family's garden plot, and sewed the children's clothes as they outgrew one set after another. She may also have spun woolen or linen yarn and woven cloth for her growing family, for the local historian remarks on the common appearance of spinning wheels and looms in the "homes of over-worked farmers' wives" before the coming of textile factories.[6] She may also have woven cloth or braided palm-leaf hats for local storekeepers or middlemen, for members of New Hampshire families in this period commonly pursued these outwork occupations to earn credits toward necessary store purchases.

The Leightons lived for sixty years in the adjoining towns of Northfield and Franklin.[7] Edward Leighton continued to work his farm into his eighties and lived to see four sons become farmers in their own right.

5. The following paragraphs are based on linkage in a variety of sources: published genealogies, Northfield, N.H., tax lists, Concord and Lowell city directories, Massachusetts vital records, federal manuscript censuses of population, and the wills of Edward Leighton (file 8409) and Winthrop Ford (file 8614), Merrimack County Registry of Probate, Concord, N.H. The key published sources are Lucy R. H. Cross, *History of the Town of Northfield, New Hampshire* (Concord: Rumford Press, 1905); James Otis Lyford, *History of the Town of Canterbury, New Hampshire, 1727–1912*, vol. 2 (Concord: Rumford Press, 1912); Moses T. Runnels, *History of Sanbornton, New Hampshire*, vol. 2 (Boston: Alfred Mudge, 1881); and Perley M. Leighton, comp., *A Leighton Genealogy: Descendents of Thomas Leighton of Dover, New Hampshire* (Boston: New England Historic Genealogical Society, 1989).

6. Cross, *History of the Town of Northfield*, pp. 101–2.

7. Actually, the Leightons did not move off the home farm in these years. Franklin was formed out of Northfield in 1830. Initially it included the Leighton farm, but the land was soon returned to the jurisdiction of Northfield. Then, in 1858, a group of Northfield residents—including Edward Leighton—successfully petitioned to be annexed into Franklin.

By 1870 he had retired from active farming, and he and his wife lived out their final years on the home farm supported by their son John and his family.

In the experiences of the Leighton daughters we see the first evidence of the impact of the industrial revolution on this rural family. Mary Leighton, the second daughter and third child, was born in 1821 and worked five years in the mills of the Hamilton Company in Lowell, Massachusetts between 1844 and 1849. She married a machinist she met in Lowell, and the couple lived there for another twenty years. Her younger sister, Judith, joined her at the Hamilton Company and worked in Lowell between 1847 and 1850. Judith returned to Northfield in May 1850 and eight months later married Winthrop Ford, a neighbor of her married brother Moses.

Ford was a farmer and lived with his widowed mother and two siblings in nearby Sanbornton. After the marriage the young couple moved to the city of Concord, where Winthrop Ford became a stove mounter and co-owner with his brothers of a foundry. Although the Fords moved only fifteen miles to Concord, they led a life that differed significantly from that of Edward and Judith Leighton. First, they lived in a city, although with fewer than eleven thousand residents in 1860, Concord was hardly a metropolis.[8] Furthermore, Winthrop Ford exchanged farming for work in an iron foundry. In addition, the Fords had only five children in contrast to the eight in the Leighton family.

In the arrangements that Edward Leighton and his son-in-law Winthrop Ford made for their wives in their wills, we gain a further sense of the ways that industrialization changed women's lives. Edward Leighton was 70 when he drew up his final will and testament in May 1852. He had already made provision for most of his children, and in this document he focused on his wife and his two youngest sons, Loraine and John. He assured his wife the "use and occupation of the southeast room, the kitchen and bed room which we now occupy." After providing her access to the cellar and use of a horse and carriage, he also willed her "all of my furniture of every description and the one fourth part of the income of my home farm . . . and also the one fourth

---

8. U.S. Bureau of the Census, *Population of the United States in 1860* (Washington: GPO, 1864), p. 308.

part of my provisions on hand." Edward Leighton was following the common nineteenth-century practice of providing for his wife's shelter and maintenance after his death. He willed the farm itself to his son John, enjoining him to provide for his mother "according to the foregoing provisions." For his remaining son, Loraine, Edward Leighton provided "home and board at my present dwelling" and five hundred dollars when he turned 21.

Several aspects of the will's provisions are worth highlighting. Except for the two sons mentioned in the will, Leighton's other children were married and had already received whatever portions were coming to them. Edward Leighton stated as much explicitly, perhaps to ensure that no legal disputes arose. This settled, he proceeded to outline the measures intended to assure continued financial support for his surviving widow. Leighton had productive property to dispose of and saw that it was used in such a way as to provide for his widow and to permit at least one son to earn his living in the future as a farmer.

Leighton's son-in-law Winthrop Ford lived in a very different world, and his will, drawn up in 1873, reflected those changes. He had no farm to pass on to his heirs; instead, he offered his four surviving children payments of five dollars each. He willed his Concord "house and premises" to his wife, Judith. He could assure his wife a place to live in her widowhood, but he could not assure her a livelihood. Perhaps the couple had saved something for old age. Perhaps one of their married children would help provide for her, but there was nothing Ford could do in his will to assure that care. Ford and his children lived in an urban world in which wages and salaries provided families the means of their livelihood.

This development was as true for the Ford daughters as for the sons. Clara and Emma Ford grew up in Concord, and like their mother, they worked only briefly before marriage. They found paid work as teachers in the district schools of neighboring Canterbury. Clara Ford taught between 1875 and 1877, giving up employment to marry Fred C. Jenney, a railroad engineer, in September 1877. The new couple remained in New Hampshire for a period, and Clara Ford Jenney gave birth to two daughters and a son in the next seven years. By 1900, however, the Jenneys had moved to Toledo, Ohio, where Fred Jenney worked for the New York and Ohio Railroad. Clara does not appear to have worked for wages after her marriage, but her older daughter, Eva, continued to live at home and worked as a stenographer at the age of 30 in 1910. As the wife of a skilled railroad worker and the mother of a white-collar daughter, Clara Jenney had moved some distance from the farming world of her grandmother.

The broad influences of industrialization and urbanization are evident across the lives of the women in the Rand, Leighton, Ford, and Jenney families. Judith Rand was born and appears to have lived all her life within the farming communities of Barnstead, Northfield, and Franklin. Her daughter Judith Leighton lived primarily within the only slightly broader world of Northfield and Concord. She did, however, work for almost three years in Lowell, Massachusetts, and she lived for more than twenty years in the city of Concord, where her husband earned his living as a skilled artisan. Judith Leighton Ford's daughter Clara worked for three years as a teacher in Canterbury but after her marriage moved to Ohio, where her husband's work as a railroad engineer took the family. Finally, Clara's daughter Eva Jenney found employment in the new white-collar world of clerical work in the first decade of the twentieth century.

In the differences in women's experiences across these four generations, we anticipate the ways that the industrial revolution affected women's lives in the nineteenth century. The shifts in residence of these women from rural New Hampshire to the cities of Concord, Lowell, and Toledo were common across the century. In the shifts from farming to mill employment, teaching, and white-collar work, the occupations of these women reflected broader changes in women's wage work over these years. Finally, the family sizes of these women declined from one generation to the next, with the number of children going from eight to five to three. In the transitions from rural to urban residences, from farming to wage earning, from large families to small ones, these women's lives, like those of women in the United States more generally, underwent profound change.

Although early studies of the industrial revolution in the United States tended to focus entirely on male experience, recent years have witnessed considerable scholarship on the changing contours of women's lives in this process. Such work has helped to frame this book. Jeanne Boydston, in her recent study *Home and Work*, has examined the transformation in the

nature and perception of women's housework that accompanied industrialization in the early nineteenth century. She makes a strong case for
the economic value of women's unwaged domestic labor, which nonetheless became devalued as male employment shifted out of the home
into the workshop and factory. Hers is an important story that helps us
understand the emergence of notions concerning "separate spheres" in
the antebellum decades.[9] Nonetheless, industrialization also transformed
women's work in the home and their roles within the family by turning
much of women's work into wage labor. By understanding the changing
character of women's wage work in the nineteenth century, as well as the
interconnections of wage work and family life, we explore crucial dimensions of economic and social change in the lives of women in that
period.

Two historians, Louise Tilly and Joan Scott, have offered a conceptual framework for understanding women and early industrialization
within the European context and have influenced how others have examined the impact of the industrial revolution on women.[10] In *Women,
Work, and Family*, Tilly and Scott trace the evolving connections of
work and family life for women in England and France between the
eighteenth and twentieth centuries. Of particular interest is their view
of women's work in the early industrial period. They argue that before
industrialization all members of peasant and artisanal families contributed their labor to family economic activities controlled principally by
male household heads. Under early industrial capitalism, however, in
Tilly and Scott's view, much of the work of family members moved
away from the rural homestead or urban home. Increasingly, sons and
daughters went out to work—or may even have migrated to find work—
but they continued to contribute to family needs by sharing their wages
with their families; hence the shift, as the authors see it, from a "family

9. Jeanne Boydston, *Home and Work: Housework, Wages, and the Ideology of Labor in the
Early Republic* (New York: Oxford University Press, 1990).

10. Louise A. Tilly and Joan W. Scott, *Women, Work, and Family* (New York: Holt,
Rinehart, and Winston, 1978). See also Tilly, Scott, and Miriam Cohen, "Women's Work and
European Fertility Patterns," *Journal of Interdisciplinary History* 6 (1976): 447–76, and Scott
and Tilly, "Women's Work and the Family in Nineteenth-Century Europe," *Comparative
Studies in Society and History* 17 (1975): 36–64.

economy" in the preindustrial period to a "family wage economy" with early industrial capitalism.

The nature of women's contributions to the family economy in this period was dependent on their place in the family. Daughters were likely to go out to work for wages as family economic needs dictated. Tilly and Scott write: "A daughter's departure served not only to relieve the family of the burden of supporting her, but it might help support the family as well. A daughter working as a servant, seamstress, or factory operative became an arm of the family economy, and arrangements were made to ensure her contribution even though she did not live at home."[11]

Wage work for married women was influenced by a number of factors, particularly the nature of opportunities for such work in a given locale and the number and ages of children in a family. Married women integrated their wage earning with domestic responsibilities. They might work for wages outside the home before the birth of children, and they often took work into their homes during periods when the demands of raising a family kept them at home. As time passed, children's wages often made up the difference between a father's earnings and family needs, and married women were less likely to work for wages.[12] Women's paid employment outside the home was thus confined principally, in Tilly and Scott's view, to the work of young women in the years before marriage. Subsumed as it was within a family wage economy, this work served primarily familial rather than individual purposes.

Tilly and Scott advance a model to explain the significance of women's increased participation in the paid labor force in nineteenth-century Europe. Their model stresses elements of continuity between the preindustrial and early industrial periods. In both eras, women's work served larger familial needs. Tilly and Scott take strong exception to historians who have argued that paid employment outside of the home contributed to a new individualism among women.[13] Rather, they argue

11. Tilly and Scott, *Women, Work, and Family*, p. 109.

12. Tilly and Scott, *Women, Work, and Family*, pp. 134–36.

13. In particular, they offer a strong critique of the work of Edward Shorter, "Female Emancipation, Birth Control, and Fertility in European History," *American Historical Review* 78 (1973): 605–40. See also Tilly, Scott, and Cohen, "Women's Work and European Fertility Patterns."

that women's paid employment represented a novel familial strategy intended to serve quite traditional familial purposes. They acknowledge that with outside income and migration, young women may have gained leverage within their families of origin. Still, on balance, they find that continuities with the early industrial period outweigh discontinuities as far as women's work is concerned.

The perspective offered by Tilly and Scott has influenced interpretations of women's wage labor in the United States. Historians offering similar views include Carol Groneman, Virginia Yans-McLaughlin, and Tamara Hareven. Groneman focuses on the Irish in New York City during the 1850s, arguing that "Irish peasant women adapted to the economic pressures of urban life in such a way as to preserve their traditional role in the family." She finds that married Irish women consciously chose employment that permitted them to combine wage work and family responsibilities. They eschewed factory and shopwork for alternatives—sewing and keeping boarders, in particular—that allowed them to work within their homes.[14]

Examining Italian workingwomen in Buffalo in the early twentieth century, Virginia Yans-McLaughlin finds a similar concern that paid employment be consistent with unpaid domestic responsibilities. She argues that seasonal food-processing work outside the city particularly appealed to married Italian women over urban alternatives because it enabled family members to work and live together. Although Italian men often left their families to follow job opportunities, women remained very much within the family as they combined duties at home with efforts to increase family income.[15]

Tamara Hareven, studying French-Canadian workers in the cotton textile mills of Manchester, New Hampshire, at the turn of the twentieth century, argues that young single women were also operating within a familial perspective. Family and kin connections enabled workers to get jobs and advance within the mills. Such workers, in turn, "habitually"

14. Carol Groneman, "'She Works as a Child; She Pays as a Man': Women Workers in a Mid-Nineteenth-Century New York City Community," in Milton Cantor and Bruce Laurie, eds., *Class, Sex, and the Woman Worker* (Westport, Conn.: Greenwood Press, 1977), p. 90.

15. Virginia Yans-McLaughlin, *Family and Community: Italian Immigrants in Buffalo, 1880–1930* (Ithaca: Cornell University Press, 1977), pp. 170, 187, 200–202.

turned their wages over to their families, thus demonstrating a continuing "commitment to a collective family economy."[16]

The findings of these focused case studies are reinforced by a broader, synthetic study by Leslie Woodcock Tentler. In *Wage-Earning Women*, Tentler argues that American women in the early twentieth century entered paid employment primarily to serve broad family needs. Moreover, she contends that discrimination against women in paid employment was severe enough to discourage women from serious thoughts of any long-term commitment to work outside the domestic sphere.

Tentler's evaluation of paid employment in the lives of working daughters situates that experience within the framework employed by Tilly and Scott. "For most young women," she writes, "wage earning was an essentially domestic obligation; their wages belonged to the family. Neither the emotional nor the economic realities of working-class life prepared them to assume a role independent of this loyalty." Similarly, "When a working-class girl left school, then, and ventured into work, she did so more in the service of family and home than in search of personal independence."[17] Finally, in examining workingwomen who lived in boarding or lodging houses, Tentler stresses the precariousness of the economic status of women who supported themselves, arguing that marriage offered for most women the only reliable means of long-term support. Tentler offers an overall picture of extreme dependency of working-class women, whether as daughters or wives, which confined women to the domestic and familial sphere.

Although the writings of historians exploring the wage work of women in the United States do focus on the place of women in the industrial revolution, there is a tendency in these studies to view families rather than individuals as historical actors in human events. The very titles of the works—*Family and Community* and *Family Time and Industrial Time*, for instance—are indicative of an inclination to view women entirely within families rather than within a variety of relationships.

16. Tamara K. Hareven, *Family Time and Industrial Time: The Relationship between the Family and Work in a New England Industrial Community* (Cambridge: Cambridge University Press, 1982), p. 75.

17. Leslie Woodcock Tentler, *Wage-Earning Women: Industrial Work and Family Life in the United States, 1900–1930* (New York: Oxford University Press, 1979), pp. 86, 93.

More critical, this perspective can reify the family into an active historical subject that feels, thinks, and acts to promote its own interests. The very framing questions that Hareven poses in her introduction express this problem: "The crucial historical question is not merely whether the family was an active or passive agent, but rather under what historical conditions was it able to control its environment and under what circumstances did its control diminish? How did the family reorder its priorities to respond to new conditions, and how did this reordering affect internal family relations?"[18] Obviously, a "family" does not reorder its priorities, but individual family members may do so. Furthermore, some family members may have more to say than others when individual priorities do not mesh smoothly. To attribute an overarching authority to the "family" is to lose a clear sense of agency of individuals in this process. Rather than viewing the family as a unified group pursuing strategies agreed on and beneficial to all, we need to see the family as an arena in which individuals struggle, in which strategies are hammered out through cooperation and conflict.[19]

A family perspective also neglects the gendered identities of family members and the way power relations in the larger society affect relationships within the family. Women and men (and parents and children, for that matter) are apt to have conflicting interests, and power differences in the broader society favor men (and parents) in these conflicts. We lose any sense of these relations and of power dynamics within families by identifying the family unit as dominant in an analysis of the industrializing process.

Not all historians of workingwomen have viewed them exclusively within a familial context. Christine Stansell and Mary Blewett have written nuanced accounts that situate workingwomen more variously. In *City of Women*, for instance, Stansell examines the differences for New York sewing women between employment in factory and shop settings and work in one's own home. The former opened up opportunities for workingwomen to interact with one another at the workplace, to develop a social life of their own after working hours, and to exercise a

---

18. Hareven, *Family Time and Industrial Time*, p. 4.

19. See Amartya Sen, "Gender and Cooperative Conflicts," in Irene Tinker, ed., *Persistent Inequalities: Women and World Development* (New York: Oxford University Press, 1990), pp. 123–49. I thank Susan Porter Benson for pointing out the relevance of this work.

measure of independence in how they spent their earnings. Daughters, wives, and widows providing sweated labor sewing in their own homes were more closely bound by patriarchal authority and economic need. Contemporary observers, Stansell shows, reacted very differently to the "impudent" factory girls and the "timid" exploited seamstresses, demonstrating a range of circumstances for New York's needlewomen at mid-century.[20]

Similarly, Mary Blewett found that differing work settings and familial circumstances became sources of conflict between men and women shoeworkers and among women shoeworkers during the 1860 strike in Lynn, Massachusetts. Male strike leaders initially sought to have women shoeworkers lend their moral support to men's wage demands. Younger, single women workers, however, organized on their own behalf and demanded that male strike leaders take their needs into account in negotiating wages with shoe manufacturers. Older, homebound women shoeworkers were more inclined to subordinate their own demands to those of the men, ostensibly because the men had families to support. The tension between women's desire for self-support and women's subordination within working-class families is a recurrent theme in Blewett's analysis of New England shoemaking in the second half of the nineteenth century. Like Stansell, Blewett does not privilege women's familial commitments but explores the shifting interaction of gender, family, and class in the lives of men and women workers.[21]

Following the examples of Stansell and Blewett, in this book I explore women's experience of the industrial revolution by placing women at the center of analysis. The selection of specific groups of women in specific locales and at specific moments in time permits an exploration of the process of industrialization in women's lives at a level that focuses on concrete individuals. Generalizations, in turn, emerge out of a synthesis of the experiences of various groups of women situated differently in relation to unfolding developments. Finally, focusing on the broader lives of different occupational groups of women provides a means to examine the interplay of paid employment and family life for women during the transition to industrial capitalism.

20. Christine Stansell, *City of Women: Sex and Class in New York, 1789–1860* (New York: Alfred A. Knopf, 1986), p. 125.
21. Blewett, *Men, Women, and Work*, especially chap. 5.

The first region in the United States to undergo significant industrialization was New England in the years after 1790. There the application first of waterpower and later of steam power enabled manufacturers to substitute machines for hand labor. The rise, in turn, of textile mills, shoe factories, and urban garment manufacture drew large numbers of women into paid employment. Finally, New England also urbanized, saw a marked decline in fertility, and had an influx of immigrants earlier than did most other regions.

A focus on nineteenth-century New England permits a finely tuned analysis of the *process* of industrialization. The focus is well suited to speak to broader developments across the nation. Developments in New England often anticipated those in the Middle Atlantic states and other regions in subsequent decades. Furthermore, the range of employment opportunities in New England mirrored those evident elsewhere. Textiles and shoe manufacturing dominated female employment in New England, and they were of almost equal importance in the Philadelphia region. Domestic service and garment trades were particularly significant in the city of Boston, as they were in New York, Philadelphia, and Baltimore in the middle decades of the nineteenth century. Finally, schoolteaching was an important occupational choice for rural women as common schools expanded across New England and the nation. The precise mix of jobs differed across regions, but with thoughtful selection at the outset, a study of the varieties of female wage labor in New England may be of far more than regional interest.

At one level, then, the perspective here is that of a case study in which the experiences of New England wage-earning women provide a basis for understanding the impact of early industrialization on women in the United States more generally. At another level, the research is itself a series of discrete case studies. This approach offers both depth in its study of specific occupational groups of women and breadth in terms of the range of groups examined. Ultimately it addresses a series of questions that remain unanswered despite the increasing interest in women's wage labor in recent years: Who worked for wages? From what backgrounds did workingwomen come? How did women's paid employment fit within the larger pattern of the female life cycle? How did patterns of female employment change during the nineteenth century? And how did changes in women's wage work affect women's positions and power relations within their families?

These are the broad questions that tie together the accounts of separate occupational groups of women. More focused questions emerge in the respective case studies. The book begins with an analysis of the penetration of wage labor into the New England countryside with the emergence of rural putting-out work in the years between 1820 and 1850. Chapter 2 examines the growth of outwork weaving and palm-leaf hat making in the neighboring towns of Richmond and Fitzwilliam in southern New Hampshire and the ways that such work was integrated within the broader farming economy (see Figure 1.1). The analysis explores the place of this early form of wage work in the rural economy: Who engaged in rural outwork, and what purposes did this new employment serve? How did outwork accommodate the rural economy, and how did it challenge existing practices? Phrased somewhat differently, to what extent did outwork permit women to meet individual as well as familial needs?

Succeeding chapters trace the emergence of additional waged occupations for women in the years after 1830, focusing on five distinct groups of workingwomen in New England—textile, shoe, and garment workers, domestic servants, and teachers. A fuller understanding of women's place in early industrialization comes from an interweaving of the divergent experiences of these separate groups.

Women operatives in the early textile mills have long dominated our view of early industrialization in New England, and they rightfully constitute one group of women wage earners examined here. The new water-powered mills of rural New England were wondrous novelties for contemporaries and attracted considerable attention in their own times. By 1860, they employed more than sixty-two thousand women workers across New England.[22] The work and family lives of a group of women

22. U.S. Bureau of the Census, *Manufactures of the United States in 1860; Compiled from the Original Returns of the Eighth Census* (Washington: GPO, 1865), pp. xxi, xxxv. For a fuller picture of the development and transformation of textile manufacturing in New England, see Thomas Dublin, *Women at Work: The Transformation of Work and Community in Lowell, Massachusetts, 1826–1860* (New York: Columbia University Press, 1979), and Jonathan Prude, *The Coming of Industrial Order: Town and Factory Life in Rural Massachusetts, 1810–1860* (Cambridge: Cambridge University Press, 1983).

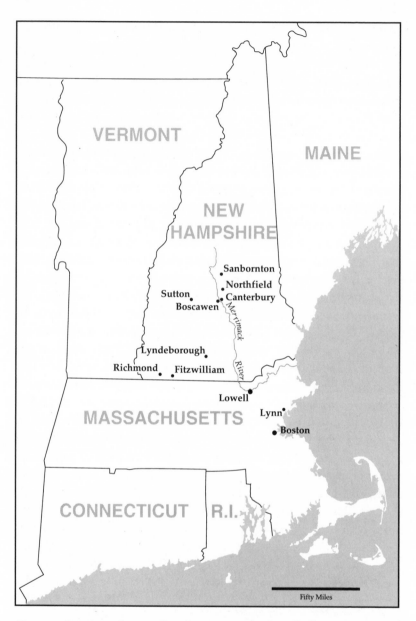

Figure 1.1. Locations of case studies of women wage workers. Outline map courtesy of the National Survey, Chester, Vt.

textile operatives from Lowell provide the focus for Chapter 3. By following these women from their rural homes to mill employment and into their subsequent marriages, we can address a number of important questions: What motivated rural women to leave their farming homes and work in urban factories? To what extent did their mill employment serve familial needs? And what impact did this wage labor have on women's later lives? [23]

Along with mill employment, shoebinding constituted the leading manufacturing occupation for women in New England at mid-century. Between 1830 and 1850, women in the boot and shoe industries toiled largely in their homes, stitching by hand (or binding, in the language of the day) the cloth or thin leather uppers of ladies' boots and children's shoes to be completed by the labor of male shoemakers. Between 1850 and 1870, however, the application of sewing machines to the stitching of shoe uppers created a new class of female factory workers— termed "shoe fitters" or "stitchers." The work and family lives of Lynn shoe stitchers offer distinct contrasts with the experiences of Lowell textile operatives in the antebellum decades and provide the focus of Chapter 4. [24] The very different setting of a shoe town in which factory production emerged slowly within an artisan community prompts somewhat different questions: How did family needs shape patterns of women's work in Lynn? What patterns of employment, marriage, and childbearing appeared over time? Although some thirty years separate the experiences of the Lowell millhands and Lynn shoeworkers who are studied in detail, the analysis focuses on each group of women at roughly comparable points in the industrialization process. Both groups of workingwomen were drawn into mechanized factory settings, which permits consideration of the impact of women on the industrializing process and the effects of factory employment on workingwomen. The striking differences in the family situations of mill operatives and

23. The analysis here differs from that offered in *Women at Work* by focusing entirely on the social origins and career patterns of Lowell millworkers and by expanding the size of the population of operatives studied from 175 to 410.

24. Recent studies of shoemaking in nineteenth-century New England provide a broader context for the more narrow focus here. See Dawley, *Class and Community*; Faler, *Mechanics and Manufacturers*; and Blewett, *Men, Women, and Work*.

shoeworkers reveal the range of possibilities for wage-earning women in early industrialization.

The mill town of Lowell and the shoe city of Lynn were two of the many single-industry manufacturing towns that developed across the nation in the nineteenth century. Although much female employment was concentrated in these new urban centers, they did not have a monopoly on women's wage work. Older seaport cities were transformed in the course of the century and offered considerable employment to women in their own right. New York and Philadelphia provided prominent examples of this change; within New England, Boston emerged as a major center of female employment.[25] Chapter 5 explores the nature of women's work in that city between 1845 and 1880. In Boston, domestic service and the needle trades dominated the female labor market and offered very different opportunities from employment in the textile and shoe industries of outlying cities. Examination of samples of Boston servants and garment workers in 1860 and 1880 provides the basis for the analysis presented in this chapter. The greater heterogeneity of the city and its labor force poses questions that did not arise in the study of earlier groups of workingwomen. How, for instance, were immigrant, black, and Yankee women situated in the city's occupational structure? Moreover, how did the character of women's wage labor change over time as native-born children of immigrants came of age? In addition, the richness of Boston census evidence permits the use of considerable cross-sectional data from various points of time to supplement the tracing of specific samples of workingwomen.

Most of women's wage labor was confined to urban centers in the mid-nineteenth century, either commercial centers like Boston or single-industry towns like Lowell or Lynn. Still, some employment was available in thoroughly rural areas, and women from farming families could remain close to home while earning wages. A common employment for women in the second quarter of the nineteenth century, one that expanded dramatically in subsequent years, was teaching. With the growth of common schools in the countryside in the 1830s and 1840s, towns

25. For a comparative view of New York City, see Stansell, *City of Women*, especially chaps. 6 and 8. Philadelphia women have yet to receive due treatment.

came increasingly to rely on women teachers. The final case study, offered in Chapter 6, focuses on female schoolteachers employed by three rural communities in central New Hampshire between 1860 and 1880.[26] Tracing these women in the years before and after their teaching permits comparison of the work and family lives of teachers with the experiences of the other groups of workingwomen examined earlier. Two significant findings emerge from the analysis: that women teachers had careers substantially longer than those of other New England workingwomen and that a sizable minority of women teachers—fully 30 percent—remained single all their lives. The implications of these findings for an understanding of women's paid employment more generally provide the final focus of the chapter.

Following the exploration of each of these separate groups of native-born workingwomen, the final chapter examines the changing ethnic makeup and family status of New England's female wage earners in the last decades of the nineteenth century. This chapter places the experiences of native-born women within the larger transformation of the female work force at the turn of the twentieth century. The discussion illuminates the legacy of nineteenth-century, native-born workingwomen in the shaping of twentieth-century patterns of women's work that remain significant today.

Rural outworkers, textile, shoe, and garment workers, domestic servants, and teachers made up the vast majority of New England women employed for wages in the nineteenth century. Before focusing on the work and family lives of specific groups of women, we do well to place these occupational groups within the larger world of women's paid employment in the nineteenth century.

Aggregate national statistics of women's occupations are not available before 1870, but an unusual Massachusetts census of industry in 1837

---

26. The literature on women teachers in the nineteenth century is not as developed as that on women in other occupational groups. But two useful sources that set a framework for viewing the teacher career study are Carl F. Kaestle, *Pillars of the Republic: Common Schools and American Society, 1780–1860* (New York: Hill and Wang, 1983), and Richard M. Bernard and Maris Vinovskis, "The Female School Teacher in Antebellum Massachusetts," *Journal of Social History* 10 (Spring 1977): 332–45.

Table 1.1. Occupational distribution of
wage-earning women in Massachusetts, 1837

Occupational group	Percentage
Palm-leaf hats and straw bonnets	48.6
Textiles	17.3
Boots and shoes	14.4
Domestic service	11.6
Teaching	3.6
Garments	3.0
Miscellaneous other	1.4
Total women employed	105,977

Sources: Mass. Secretary of the Commonwealth, *Statistical Tables Exhibiting the Condition and Products of Certain Branches of Industry in Massachusetts . . . 1837*, pp. 169–70, 172, 181, 187; and Kaestle and Vinovskis, *Education and Social Change*, p. 285. Domestic service employment is estimated from Boston figures for 1845–1880 and state figures for 1860–1880.

Note: Percentages may not add up to 100.0 because of rounding.

offers an early view of women's employment in that state.[27] Table 1.1 summarizes that evidence. What is most striking about the picture that emerges here is the predominance of rural outwork as a source of women's wage labor in the 1830s. These figures indicate that fully 63 percent of wage-earning women probably performed their work on a part-time basis braiding straw or palm leaf or binding boots and shoes in rural homes. Initially, rural women did not leave their farming homes to engage in limited wage earning.

This picture changed dramatically in the years between 1837 and 1870. Palm-leaf hat making and straw braiding declined, and shoe employment for women shifted from binding in farm kitchens to stitching in mechanized urban workshops. With the rise of the factory produc-

27. Total employment figures for females in specific occupational groups are available for workers in textiles, and boots and shoes, teachers, and other occupations. Estimates for available data have been required for the other groups noted in the table.

For straw and palm-leaf hat workers—the largest group in the table—I assumed that females made ¹⁵⁄₁₆ of all hats and on average made 104 hats a year, figures based on a detailed study of hat makers in Fitzwilliam, N.H. (reported in Chapter 2 below). This is a high estimate for annual production as it is based on the output of single women, the most prolific hat makers; this procedure, in estimating 29,767 palm-leaf hat braiders, thus probably understates the number of women employed in hat making at some point in 1837. For straw braiders, see

tion of shoes, women's wage work shifted from part-time to full-time employment, and the total number of female shoeworkers declined accordingly.

As women's employment in rural outwork declined in absolute numbers, domestic service, textiles, and the needle trades emerged as the leading wage-earning occupations for women in Massachusetts. The proportion of wage-earning women employed as domestic servants almost tripled over three decades, growing from 12 to 34 percent, the proportion of women employed in textile manufacturing increased more modestly, and the share composed of women in the needle trades skyrocketed. Overall, the total number of women wage earners in Massachusetts increased only slightly over this period, but their overall earnings increased more substantially as urban, full-time domestic servants and factory and shop employees replaced part-time rural outworkers in the female labor force.

The 1870 federal census of population provides evidence for these changes within Massachusetts and also the earliest picture of female

Caroline Sloat, "'A Great Help to Many Families': Strawbraiding in Massachusetts before 1825," in Peter Benes, ed., *House and Home*, Proceedings of the Dublin Seminar for New England Folklore, Dublin, N.H., 1988, pp. 89–100. Sloat notes an average of twenty-five yards of braid per hat and a price paid to braiders of two cents a yard. These figures suggest that there was about fifty cents of braiding labor in each hat. The overall figure of the 889,000 straw bonnets produced in 1837 comes from Mass. Secretary of the Commonwealth, *Statistical Tables Exhibiting the Condition and Products of Certain Branches of Industry in Massachusetts . . . 1837* (Boston: Dutton and Wentworth, 1838), p. 181. Assuming that straw braiders made annual earnings comparable with those of palm-leaf hat braiders (a mean of $20.48 in Fitzwilliam in 1830) led to an estimate of 21,704 female straw braiders across the state in 1837.

Mass. Secretary of the Commonwealth, *Statistical Tables*, pp. 4, 187, noted 3,939 employees in clothing manufacture in the state in 1837 but gave the male-female breakdown only for Boston. Applying the same proportion for the state as a whole as for Boston led to an estimate of 3,214 female garment workers in 1837.

Estimating the number of female domestic servants across the state required extrapolating from more complete data for other years. Accurate figures survive for the number of female servants in Boston in 1845, 1860, 1870, and 1880. For these four years, female servants constituted 5.4 percent of the overall Boston population on average. There was no trend in this proportion over time. I extrapolated backward to 1837, applying this same proportion to the city's overall population, and estimated 4,320 servants in Boston. For 1860, 1865, and 1880, I knew the proportion of Boston servants to all servants in the state, a figure that averaged 35 percent. Assuming that the same proportion held in 1837, I estimated 12,343 female servants in Massachusetts in that year.

Table 1.2. Occupational distribution of wage-earning women,
1870, for the United States and Massachusetts

Sector	United States		Massachusetts	
Agriculture	21.6%		0.04%	
Professional[a]	5.2		5.8	
Teaching		4.6		4.9
Domestic and personal service[a]	52.9		37.4	
Domestic service		47.2		33.9
Trade and transportation	1.0		1.6	
Manufacturing[a]	19.3		55.2	
Textiles		5.6		26.2
Boots and shoes		0.5		4.6
Garments		10.8		17.9
Total women employed	1,836,000		128,000	

Source: *Ninth Census*, vol. 1, pp. 686–95. Includes all females, 10 years of age and over.

[a] The sums of the percentages of women employed in the subgroups of professional, domestic and personal service, and manufacturing do not add up to the total percentages for those sectors because a number of smaller occupations have been excluded from the table. Percentages for major sectors may not add up to 100.0% because of rounding.

occupations in the nation as a whole.[28] Table 1.2 summarizes evidence on the leading female occupations in Massachusetts and the United States at that date. Domestic service provided the largest single occupation for wage-earning women in the nation as a whole and in Massachusetts in 1870. Almost half of all employed women in the United States and a third within the state of Massachusetts worked as domestic servants. After that group, the occupational distributions for women in the nation and the state differed dramatically. Nationally, agriculture employed the next largest group of women, whereas in Massachusetts the textile industry proved far more important.[29] The needle trades constituted the third leading employer of women in both the nation and Massachusetts, accounting for almost 11 percent of all wage-earning

28. U.S. Census Office, *The Statistics of the Population of the United States . . . from the Original Returns of the Ninth Census*, vol. 1 (Washington: GPO, 1872), pp. 686–95.

29. Agricultural workers among wage-earning women included farm laborers (both those working out and those working on family farms) and self-employed farmers and wives of farmers. Joseph A. Hill, *Women in Gainful Occupations, 1870 to 1920* (Washington: GPO, 1929), census monograph 9, pp. 18–20.

women nationally and 18 percent within Massachusetts. Finally, teaching proved the most important professional occupation for women, employing almost 5 percent of wage-earning women in Massachusetts and nationwide. Altogether, textile, shoe, and garment work, domestic service, and teaching employed 69 percent of all workingwomen in the United States in 1870; within Massachusetts, these same occupations accounted for more than 87 percent of workingwomen. Clearly, these groups provide a solid core for generalizations concerning all wage-earning women in the nineteenth century.

Between 1870 and 1900 the number of wage-earning women increased dramatically, accompanied by significant shifts in the particular occupations within which they were concentrated. For the nation as a whole, the number of gainfully employed women increased from 1.8 to 4.8 million over the thirty-year period.[30] Moreover, the proportions of workingwomen employed in agriculture and domestic service declined markedly, while garment workers, teachers, and sales and clerical workers all showed gains relative to other female occupations (see Table 1.3)

Clearly, the nineteenth century saw a dramatic quantitative expansion and qualitative shift in the nature of women's wage labor in the United States. The aggregate evidence from successive census enumerations makes this point most graphically. For women in the nation as a whole, domestic service, agriculture, and manufacturing employment predominated across the nineteenth century, with clerical and sales occupations making a strong showing at the end of the period. Were we to trace these aggregate statistics into the twentieth century, we would find women's employment in manufacturing, sales, and clerical

30. Figures based on counts of the censuses of population undoubtedly underestimate the proportion of employed women in the United States. Wives and daughters of farmers, female boardinghouse keepers, and women employed part-time or seasonally were not recorded as fully as were men in similar employment situations. Returns from censuses of manufacturing commonly reported more workers than counts from censuses of populations for the same locations. For examples of such discrepancies for female shoeworkers in Lynn, see Blewett, *Men, Women, and Work*, pp. 334, 338–39, and 343. For a useful discussion of census underenumeration, see Marjorie Abel and Nancy Folbre, "A Methodology for Revising Estimates: Female Market Participation in the U.S. before 1940," *Historical Methods* 23 (Fall 1990): 167–76. For a consideration of census occupational statistics, see Margo Conk, *The United States Census and Labor Force Change: A History of Occupation Statistics, 1870–1940* (Ann Arbor, Mich.: UMI Research Press, 1980).

Table 1.3. Occupational distribution of wage-earning women
in the United States, 1870 and 1900

Sector	1870		1900	
Agriculture	21.6%		15.9%	
Professional[a]	5.2		8.9	
Teaching		4.6		6.8
Domestic and personal service[a]	52.9		40.4	
Domestic service		47.2		24.1
Trade and transportation	1.0		10.0	
Manufacturing[a]	19.3		24.8	
Textiles		5.6		4.8
Boots and shoes		0.5		0.8
Garments		10.8		14.0
Total women employed	1,836,000		4,843,000	

Source: *Ninth Census*, vol. 1, pp. 686–95; and *Statistics of Women at Work*, p. 32.
The 1870 data are based on females 10 years of age and older; the 1900 data, on females 16 and older.

[a] The sums of the percentages of women workers employed in subgroups of professional, domestic and personal service, and manufacturing do not add up to the total percentages for those sectors because a number of smaller occupations have been excluded from the table.

occupations expanding still further at the expense of agriculture and domestic service.[31]

Aggregate evidence is important, for it reveals the overall structure of women's wage labor and permits a discussion of changing patterns over time. Aggregate statistics do not, however, in themselves speak to the broader meaning of wage labor in the lives of individuals. These figures may permit an economic historian to discuss the changing gender composition of the work force and explore the implications of that development for overall wage rates, but we still cannot know from such structural data how women perceived the experience of paid employment or

31. For useful twentieth-century evidence, see Valerie Kincade Oppenheimer, *The Female Labor Force in the United States: Demographic and Economic Factors Governing Its Growth and Changing Composition* (Westport, Conn.: Greenwood Press, 1976; originally published in 1970); Robert L. Daniel, *American Women in the 20th Century: The Festival of Life* (San Diego: Harcourt Brace Jovanovich, 1987); Claudia Goldin, *Understanding the Gender Gap: An Economic History of American Women* (New York: Oxford University Press, 1990); and Sarah E. Rix, ed., *The American Woman, 1990–91: A Status Report* (New York: W. W. Norton, 1990), especially pp. 349–97.

what motivated their actions. By shifting our focus to groups of women within each of the major female occupational categories, we can construct a more concrete and more nuanced view of women's paid employment in the nineteenth century. In this way we will explore the changing nature of women's wage labor in New England—the families workingwomen came from, the ages at which they worked, the lengths of their periods of employment, the connections between their work and family lives, and the place of paid employment in the broader female life cycle.

Much of the evidence presented in subsequent chapters is based on tracing these groups of wage-earning women in a variety of contemporary New England sources—genealogies, vital records, census enumerations, city directories, local tax records, and employment records. In all, evidence based on the experiences of about fifteen hundred outwork families and more than twenty-one hundred wage-earning women is brought together to permit generalizations about women's wage work in nineteenth-century New England.[32]

Admittedly, the focus on the native-born has meant the exclusion of immigrant workingwomen from much of the discussion that follows. This practice entails limitations regarding the findings but at the same time offers some strengths as well. It reflects the fact that New England's first female wage workers—rural outworkers and urban textile operatives—were overwhelmingly drawn from Yankee farming families. So, too, were Lynn shoeworkers and rural teachers after the Civil War. To compare these groups of women with immigrant workingwomen in Boston would entail so many cultural, economic, and occupational differences as to render their experiences almost incommensurable. Practical considerations reinforced concerns about comparability. Tracing immigrant women across censuses and into local vital records would have been even more difficult than for native-born women with results that would have raised serious questions of representativeness. Ultimately,

---

32. In some cases—shoeworkers, domestic servants, and garment workers—I have relied on random sampling; in other cases I have drawn nonrandom populations—outworkers, textile operatives, and teachers—from particularly rich surviving records. For a discussion of how these samples and populations were generated, see Appendix 2.

For discussion of the methods employed in linking women in a variety of contemporary records, see Appendixes 3–7.

the study of native-born women in a wide range of occupations seemed to promise the greatest returns for a deeper understanding of women and the industrial revolution in nineteenth-century New England.

To bring ethnicity into the analysis, we can link the detailed cases studies with broader changes transforming New England in these years. After examining the experiences of successive groups of native-born workingwomen between 1820 and 1880, I shift the focus in the concluding chapter to delineating fundamental changes in the identities of workingwomen in New England in the final decades of the \century. That discussion permits one to view the experiences of native-born women workers within the transformations wrought by the intersecting processes of industrialization, urbanization, and immigration. Particularly in the analysis of Lowell textile workers and Boston's domestic servants and garment workers, the influence of large-scale immigration becomes evident at numerous points.

The entry of repeated waves of European, Asian, and Latin American immigrants has transformed working-class life in the United States.[33] The occupational and demographic profiles of wage-earning women in the 1990s differ markedly from those of the mid-nineteenth century. Similarly, as early as 1900 a very different working class had emerged in American society than had been evident fifty or sixty years earlier. As we examine the story of native-born workingwomen in nineteenth-century New England, glimpses of this broader transformation emerge. In the shifting nature of the family wage economy among workingwomen in Lowell and Boston, we see a preview of working-class life in larger American cities at the turn of the twentieth century.

This study locates the origins of female wage labor in the cottage industries of weaving and palm-leaf hat making in farming families in the 1820s and 1830s. In that setting wage labor was well integrated within the economy of the family farm, although there are also early signs of the ways that rural women could turn outwork income to personal purposes. With the growth of urban female employment in the textile mills of Lowell and in domestic service in the Boston metropolis, women's

---

33. For a rich treatment of this transformation, primarily as it affected the lives of workingmen, see Herbert G. Gutman, "Work, Culture, and Society in Industrializing America, 1815–1919," *American Historical Review* 78 (1973): 531–68.

wage labor in the middle of the nineteenth century offered young single Yankee women a degree of economic independence unknown to rural women of earlier generations. Much of urban wage labor for women initially required that young women leave their families of origin and work and live on their own.

The economic and social independence of early female wage earners was short-lived in two senses. First, women typically worked for wages for only a brief period of time before marriage, at which point they were reincorporated into a family economy. Second, the decades after the Civil War saw a marked decline in the independent wage earning of single women. Among Yankee women, growing employment in the boot and shoe industry of Lynn contributed to the emergence of an urban family wage economy. There, female shoeworkers were drawn either from families permanently resident in Lynn or from families that had recently migrated to the city. Moreover, with the passage of time, we see the decline in both Lowell and Boston of a transient Yankee work force of recent rural-urban migrants and the appearance of a permanent work force composed primarily of the daughters of immigrants. This shift in the ethnic composition of the female work force coincided with a growing subordination of women's wage labor within a family economy. Wage labor, which appeared to increase women's independence in the first half of the nineteenth century, became a major constitutive element in the dependence of women within patriarchal families by century's end. Although much has changed over the course of the twentieth century, we live with this legacy still.

2. Women and Rural Outwork

Opportunities for wage work expanded steadily for rural women in New England in the first third of the nineteenth century. Yet there was something quite unconscious about this process; women continued to work at home as they shifted from production for family consumption to production for wider markets without realizing the full implications of the new activity. The handweaving of machine-spun cotton yarn into cloth and the braiding of split palm leaf into men's and children's hats became important economic activities for farm women in the years after 1810. Organized by local merchants, manufacturers, or middlemen, this work represented a significant departure from previous rural practice. No longer did farm families work up materials they produced on the farm; rather, they relied on outsiders who distributed or "put out" the yarn or split palm leaf into the countryside. Members of farm families performed the "outwork"—weaving cloth or braiding hats—and typically received credit toward store purchases for their labors.

The years after 1800 saw a significant proliferation of putting-out industries in New England. In their rural homes, young women integrated outwork into the fabric of their daily lives. Unmarried daughters in their teenage years attended district school about a third of the year, typically concentrated in the winter months.[1] In summer and fall they assisted their mothers in the cultivation of home gardens; throughout the year they tended poultry and cows and produced cheese and butter. When farm chores declined in the winter and early spring, they often turned their energies to weaving yarn from local spinning mills or braiding

---

1. Carl F. Kaestle and Maris A. Vinovskis, *Education and Social Change in Nineteenth-Century Massachusetts* (Cambridge: Cambridge University Press, 1980), chap. 2, especially figs. 2.1, 2.3, and 2.5. Recalculating means from data offered by Kaestle and Vinovskis suggests that in Massachusetts in 1840, children who attended school did so for about one hundred days annually.

palm-leaf hats for the local storekeeper. In this manner, young women gained experience at waged work without ever leaving home, and they fit the demands of such work into the rhythms of their daily lives. If caring for younger siblings, cooking meals, preserving food, or nursing the sick took a great deal of time, daughters did little outwork. The flexibility of outwork appealed to members of rural families and eased concerns farmers might otherwise have felt working for others. The fact that the fathers or husbands of female outworkers typically were credited with the proceeds of their labors meant that outwork meshed well with the power dynamics of patriarchal farming families.

There was little overt opposition to women undertaking these new activities because they were well integrated on several levels into the operations of the family farm. Over time, however, women outworkers began to claim the proceeds of their labors, and the first signs of conflict between individual and familial interests became apparent. The spread of outwork into the New England countryside before 1850 shows some of the more general implications of wage labor for women across the nineteenth century. Rural outwork, in the end, proved something of a way station on the path from unwaged labor on the family farm to individual wage work in urban factories. In this manner, outwork simultaneously propped up the traditional family farm economy while preparing the way for the individual wage economy that would eventually displace it.

Curiously enough, we know far more about rural outwork in industrializing Europe than in the United States. European historians, debating the concept of "proto-industrialization," have been extremely interested in the economic and social impact of the growth of rural putting-out systems.[2] In standard accounts of the transformation of the economy of

2. Franklin Mendels, "Proto-Industrialization: The First Phase of the Industrialization Process," *Journal of Economic History* 32 (1972): 241–61; Jean Quataert, "A New View of Industrialization: 'Protoindustry' or the Role of Small-Scale, Labor-Intensive Manufacture in the Capitalist Environment," *International Labor and Working-Class History*, no. 33 (Spring 1988): 3–22; Maxine Berg, Pat Hudson, and Michael Sonenscher, eds., *Manufacture in Town and Country before the Factory* (Cambridge: Cambridge University Press, 1983), especially chap. 1; D. C. Coleman, "Proto-Industrialization: A Concept Too Many," *Economic History Review*, 2d ser., 36 (1983): 435–48; Myron P. Gutmann and René Leboutte, "Rethinking Protoindustrialization and the Family," *Journal of Interdisciplinary History* 14 (Winter 1984): 587–607; and Gay L. Gullickson, "Agriculture and Cottage Industry: Redefining the Causes of Proto-Industrialization," *Journal of Economic History* 43 (December 1983): 831–50.

the United States in the nineteenth century, outwork is generally mentioned only in passing, and few studies of rural outwork in the United States have viewed it as a form of women's wage labor.[3] Our knowledge of the phenomenon comes largely from the work of economic historians on the early growth of the cotton textile industry. Caroline Ware, in *The Early New England Cotton Manufacture*, for instance, treats at some length the rise of outwork weaving in association with the growth of cotton-spinning mills in southern New England. She draws extensively on records of an early firm that installed power looms only in the mid- and late-1820s. Ware offers little, however, on outworkers themselves; her emphasis is on the implications of outwork for the firm. She points out the limits to expanding weaving output, noting that yarn production continually outdistanced the ability of local residents to weave it into cloth. Consequently, firms had to search at greater distances for weavers. Rhode Island firms commonly put yarn out for weaving to storekeepers in Maine and New Hampshire and sold yarn in Philadelphia and Baltimore, where artisan handloom weavers offered additional markets for their output.[4]

We have a reasonable understanding of the attractions and limitations that the organization of weaving on an outwork basis entailed for early cotton textile firms and of the process by which weaving by power loom steadily displaced handloom weaving in the years between 1815 and 1830.

3. George Rogers Taylor, *The Transportation Revolution, 1815–1860* (New York: Rinehart, 1951), pp. 217–20, and Gregory H. Nobles, "Commerce and Community: A Case Study of the Rural Broommaking Business in Antebellum Massachusetts," *Journal of the Early Republic* 4 (Fall 1984): 287–308.

4. Caroline F. Ware, *The Early New England Cotton Manufacture: A Study in Industrial Beginnings* (New York: Russell & Russell, 1966; originally published in 1931), pp. 32, 36, 42–43, 50–53. For more recent accounts of outwork weaving, see Peter J. Coleman, "Rhode Island Cotton Manufacturing: A Study in Economic Conservatism," *Rhode Island History* 23 (July 1964): 65–80; Jonathan Prude, *The Coming of Industrial Order: Town and Factory Life in Rural Massachusetts, 1810–1860* (Cambridge: Cambridge University Press, 1983), pp. 72–77; Cynthia J. Shelton, *The Mills of Manayunk: Industrialization and Social Conflict in the Philadelphia Region, 1787–1837* (Baltimore: Johns Hopkins University Press, 1986), pp. 48–53; Gail Fowler, "Rhode Island Handloom Weavers and the Effects of Technological Change, 1780–1840," Ph.D. diss., University of Pennsylvania, 1984; and Gail Fowler Mohanty, "Putting Up with Putting-Out: Power Loom Diffusion and Outwork for Rhode Island Mills," *Journal of the Early Republic* 9 (Summer 1989): 191–216, and "Handloom Outwork and Outwork Weaving in Rural Rhode Island," *American Studies* 30 (1989): 41–68.

We have a less clear picture, however, of the place of outwork in the lives of farm women who wove yarn for spinning firms in the early decades of the nineteenth century. Furthermore, weaving was only one of a series of processes amenable to organization on an outwork basis. With the decline of handloom weaving after the mid-1820s, rural storekeepers and urban manufacturers continued to supply farm women with raw materials for fabrication. Straw braiding, palm-leaf hat making, shoebinding, and sewing provided considerable employment to members of farming families through 1870. Despite the persistence of rural outwork for sixty years, its social significance and development over time remain largely unexamined by historians.

These issues provide ample reason for a renewed interest in rural outwork in the first half of the nineteenth century. For our purposes, however, outwork takes on still greater significance. Women predominated among those employed on an outwork basis; furthermore, outwork provided the major source of paid employment for New England women before mid-century. Finally, the existence of a massive employable female labor force in the countryside exerted an important influence on early industrialization in New England.

We need to examine outwork on multiple levels and with diverse sources. This chapter explores regional sources that address the impact of this system of production on communities, families, and individuals. Contemporary statistical evidence and literary sources together offer an initial view. With this basis established, a case study of outwork in two adjacent communities in southern New Hampshire—Richmond and Fitzwilliam—permits the reconstruction of weaving and palm hat outwork networks that flourished between the 1820s and the 1850s. Examination of the experiences of individuals and families and an analysis of changing patterns over time illuminate the role of outwork in the transformation that brought wage labor into the lives of nineteenth-century New England women.[5]

5. The analysis offered here represents a revision of Thomas Dublin, "Rural Putting-Out Work in Early Nineteenth-Century New England: Women and the Transition to Capitalism in the Countryside," *New England Quarterly* 64 (December 1991): 531–73, which appears by courtesy of the journal. My earlier explorations of this palm-leaf hat network include "Women and Outwork in a Nineteenth-Century New England Town: Fitzwilliam, New Hampshire, 1830–1850," in Steven Hahn and Jonathan Prude, eds., *The Countryside in the Age of Capitalist*

Outwork grew dramatically in the course of the first half of the nineteenth century, although the production activities organized in this manner shifted over time. A brief boom of handloom weaving provided the first outwork employment. The practice first developed with the cutoff of English imports that accompanied the passage of the Embargo Act in December 1807.[6] Subsequently, the Non-Intercourse Act and war with Great Britain further stimulated American reliance on domestic textiles, giving a tremendous boost to New England's fledgling cotton-spinning industry.[7] The new firms expanded between 1808 and 1815 and developed their market by putting out cotton yarns to rural weavers in the surrounding countryside. Outwork weaving peaked around 1820, employing approximately twelve thousand weavers across New England.[8] With the adoption of the power loom and the consequent decline of outwork weaving after 1820, the rise of straw braiding and palm-leaf hat making more than made up for the loss of weaving employment. By 1837, hat production in Massachusetts had reached $1.9 million in value and employed more than fifty-one thousand women and children.[9] The

Transformation: Essays in the Social History of Rural America (Chapel Hill: University of North Carolina Press, 1985), pp. 51–69, and "Women's Work and the Family Economy: Textiles and Palm Leaf Hatmaking in New England, 1830–1850," *Tocqueville Review* 5 (1983): 297–316.

6. For a good discussion of earlier attempts to employ skilled male handloom weavers in shops adjacent to power-spinning operations, see Gail Fowler Mohanty, "Experimentation in Textile Technology, 1788–1790, and Its Impact on Handloom Weaving and Weavers in Rhode Island," *Technology and Culture* 29 (1988): 1–31. On the shift to outwork and its subsequent decline, see Mohanty, "Putting Up with Putting-Out."

7. Ware, *Early New England Cotton Manufacture*, chap. 3, and Coleman, "Rhode Island Cotton Manufacturing." Mohanty, "Putting Up with Putting-Out," pp. 193–94, takes issue with Coleman's assessment of Rhode Island manufacturers as particularly conservative in their adoption of the power loom, viewing outwork "as the most proper and profitable method of cloth production" at the time.

8. U.S. Department of the Treasury, *Letter from the Secretary of the Treasury . . . on the Subject of American Manufactures* (Washington: Roger C. Weightman, 1810), table D and p. 11; for 1820, see Robert Brooke Zevin, "The Growth of Textile Production after 1815," in Robert Fogel and Stanley Engerman, eds., *The Reinterpretation of American Economic History* (New York: Harper & Row, 1971), pp. 123–24.

9. Mass. Secretary of the Commonwealth, *Statistical Tables Exhibiting the Condition and Products of Certain Branches of Industry in Massachusetts for the Year Ending April 1, 1837* (Boston: Dutton and Wentworth, 1838), p. 181. The employment figures are derived from my study of the palm-leaf hat making network organized by Dexter Whittemore of Fitzwilliam, N.H., discussed below. There I found that the most committed outworkers, single women

hats produced by New England outworkers found their way to the South and the Midwest, where slaves, farmers, and farm laborers wore them for inexpensive protection while working outdoors.[10] Although mechanization undermined outwork weaving by 1830, the Civil War, with its resulting interruption of interregional trade, spelled the end of the outwork manufacture of palm-leaf hats. Straw braiding, on the other hand, survived for several decades after the war, declining as outmigration reduced the rural labor supply and changing fashions reduced the demand for straw bonnets.

Shoes were another consumer good that occupied the energies of rural outworkers in New England in the antebellum decades. Beginning in the 1820s, manufacturers in Lynn and Haverhill, Massachusetts, routinely cut out the thin leather for shoe uppers and shipped the pieces by express team or railroad into the countryside, where farmers' wives and daughters stitched and bound them for three or four cents a pair.[11] As rural outwork increased, shoe manufacturers established central shops, bringing the cutting of the leather and the finishing and inspecting of shoes under their direction. Nonetheless, virtually all the binding and

---

working on their own account, produced on average one hundred hats in a year. Applying that figure to overall Massachusetts output data yielded the employment estimate noted here. By using a mean output figure derived from the most productive workers in one network, I likely understate the total number of outworkers who braided hats at some point in the year. For other states, see Conn. Secretary of State, *Statistics of the Condition and Products of Certain Branches of Industry in Connecticut, for the Year Ending October 1, 1845* (Hartford: J. L. Boswell, 1846), p. 217, and R.I. Secretary of State, *Report upon the Census of Rhode Island, 1865* (Providence: Providence Press, 1867), p. 92. For treatment of one palm hat network in Massachusetts, see Christopher Clark, *The Roots of Rural Capitalism: Western Massachusetts, 1780–1860* (Ithaca: Cornell University Press, 1990), pp. 181–90.

10. One Alabama planter's account book, for instance, reveals the purchase of "12 palm leaf hats—for women" in 1843. These were probably slave women. Henry Watson, Jr., Account Book, 1841–1844, Manuscript Department, William R. Perkins Library, Duke University, Durham, N.C., entry of June 6, 1843. For a similar record of a Noxubee County, Mississippi, storekeeper, see A. H. Jones Invoice Book, 1848–1849, Manuscript Department, William R. Perkins Library, Duke University, Durham, N.C., entry for February 21, 1848. I thank Anne F. Scott for these two references. For invoices of the palm hat purchases of a St. Genevieve, Missouri, storekeeper, see Francis C. Rozier collection, 1841–1857, Historical Society of Pennsylvania, Philadelphia.

11. Mary H. Blewett, "Women Shoeworkers and Domestic Ideology: Rural Outwork in Early Nineteenth-Century Essex County," *New England Quarterly* 60 (1987): 403–28.

much of the shoemaking continued to be done in the countryside. Paul Faler has estimated that in 1855, 60 percent of Lynn shoes were made outside of the city by rural outworkers. The first cracks in this system came with the application of the sewing machine to the stitching of uppers in the 1850s. Then, with the adoption of the McKay stitcher during the Civil War years, New England shoemaking moved irreversibly from rural outwork to urban factory production.[12]

Even with the decline of rural shoebinding and shoemaking, outwork did not disappear. After the Civil War, it persisted in the New England countryside, where Boston garment manufacturers sent work to take advantage of the rural labor market. An 1871 report described the operations of this new outwork network.

A great deal of Boston work, clothing and other, is sent out to different parts of New England, because it can be done more cheaply at country homes than in town. For instance, eight or ten years ago, the country storekeepers, experiencing the difficulty of getting ready cash for their sales, and being overburdened with agricultural products, introduced through the direction of the Boston clothing trade, the making of clothing among their female customers, as a means of earning funds to meet the necessary store purchases.

Sewing for the urban market offered rural women the credits at the local store for purchases needed to supplement farm production that weaving cloth, braiding hats, and binding shoes had provided them before the Civil War. By 1870, this new trade linking Boston wholesale clothiers, country storekeepers, and members of farming families in New Hampshire and Maine was providing $2 million in wage payments annually to a work force that probably consisted of fifty thousand farm women.[13]

12. Paul G. Faler, *Mechanics and Manufacturers in the Early Industrial Revolution: Lynn, Massachusetts, 1780–1860* (Albany: State University of New York Press, 1981), p. 223; and Mary H. Blewett, *Men, Women, and Work: Class, Gender, and Protest in the New England Shoe Industry, 1780–1910* (Urbana: University of Illinois Press, 1988), pp. 142–53.

13. Mass. Bureau of Statistics of Labor, *Annual Report*, 1870–71, pp. 201–2. The estimate of 50,000 women workers is based on the assumption that the average female outworker earned $40 annually with outwork sewing. This figure is high, as outwork hat braiders averaged only $20 each in the antebellum period. If the typical rural garment worker earned less than $40 a year, this estimate may well understate the size of the rural labor force for Boston garment firms. The

Although the focus here will be on the specific forms of outwork common in southwestern New Hampshire between 1820 and 1850—weaving and hat making—it is important to remember that the domestic employment of New England farm women in geographically dispersed outwork networks persisted for more than sixty years.

Two features of rural outwork contrasted sharply with the defining aspects of factory production in the same period. First, production under the outwork system grew by extension over a growing geographical area rather than by the intensification of its demands on individual workers. Despite numerous efforts, textile manufacturers (and hat merchants and shoe and garment manufacturers after them) were largely unsuccessful at increasing the productivity of dispersed rural outworkers or at imposing uniform standards of quality. These difficulties resulted from the second defining characteristic of outwork in rural New England. Under the outwork system, merchants and manufacturers had remarkably little control over their work force. Workers were members of rural property-owning families who engaged in outwork in slack periods when it suited their purposes. They might weave a piece of cloth in a week or keep the yarn for three months before completing their work. Similarly, farm women might braid six palm-leaf hats in a month or forty depending on the demands of other farm work and their economic needs. The limited control that manufacturers exerted over outworkers necessitated a stupendous effort at distribution and introduced significant costs associated with the length of time intermediate goods were out in the hands of otherwise preoccupied workers.

The independence of rural outworkers set their experience apart from that of their urban counterparts in the same period. Christine Stansell has movingly described the contrasting circumstances of outwork seamstresses in New York City's needle trades before 1850. Given the great numbers of recent immigrants struggling to support themselves in the city, the imbalance of women and men in the city's population, and the irregularity and low level of wages for unskilled male laborers, immigrant

---

Whittemore store in Fitzwilliam, N.H., whose outwork weaving and palm hat accounts are analyzed below, also engaged in garment putting-out in the 1850s. Fourteen accounts with garment outworkers between 1853 and 1856 are recorded in the Dexter Whittemore & Son Collection, vol. 91, BL.

women and children were literally compelled to take in sewing at whatever wages tailors and contractors would offer.[14] Outwork earnings were much more crucial to the immigrants' subsistence than to that of rural families and the outwork system far more exploitative in metropolitan centers than in the New England countryside. Urban outworkers had fewer economic options than their rural counterparts and were thus far more vulnerable in their dealings with outwork middlemen. The ability of yeoman farmers to produce a portion of their own subsistence and to sell their farm surplus on broader markets gave members of farmers' families a measure of protection in their dealings with New England textile manufacturers and middlemen. Still, the competition between rural and urban outworkers may well have contributed to levels of urban outwork wages that simply could not provide adequate means of support.

Contemporary writings reveal much about these aspects of early nineteenth-century outwork. The geographical spread of weaving outwork is particularly striking. At first, textile firms often employed artisan weavers in rooms adjacent to their factories; over time, however, such weavers were too expensive or they could not keep up with factory output, and mill managers began giving out yarn to local residents to be woven.[15] One contemporary described the practices of Pawtucket, Rhode Island, manufacturers who "have shops or stores in Providence. On their doors is affixed 'Weaving given out.'" Weavers would come to these shops to pick up yarn and return woven cloth. This same report described the operations of the network: "A considerable portion of weaving is done by women, who have or live in farm-houses. They . . . do not in general follow the occupation regularly; it is done during their leisure hours, and at the dull time of the year."[16] There was a clear division of

14. Christine Stansell, "The Origins of the Sweatshop: Women and Early Industrialization in New York City," in Michael H. Frisch and Daniel J. Walkowitz, eds., *Working-Class America: Essays on Labor, Community, and American Society* (Urbana: University of Illinois Press, 1983), pp. 78–103. For discussion of twentieth-century developments, see Eileen Boris and Cynthia R. Daniels, eds., *Homework: Historical and Contemporary Perspectives on Paid Labor at Home* (Urbana: University of Illinois Press, 1989).

15. Mohanty, "Experimentation in Textile Technology."

16. Henry Bradshaw Fearon, 1818, as quoted in Gertrude S. Kimball, *Pictures of Rhode Island in the Past, 1642–1833* (Providence: Preston and Rounds, 1900), pp. 165–66. For further discussion of the putting-out practices of Providence-area mills, see Rhode Island Society for the Encouragement of Domestic Industry, *Transactions* (1861), pp. 77, 88, 120.

labor in early weaving, as commercial artisan weavers appear always to have been male, and outwork weavers were overwhelmingly female.

Outwork weaving also appeared in the vicinity of rural mills. For instance, in the town of Griswold, Connecticut, "the sound of the loom was heard increasingly, for the cotton spun in the village factory was woven in the homes of the people, and the price paid, from seven to ten cents per yard, wonderfully stimulated production." The picture in New Ipswich, New Hampshire, was similar: "Almost every farmhouse in the country was furnished with a loom, and most of the adult females were skilled weavers. Mr. Batchelder [the mill agent] made contracts with many of them . . . to weave cloth for him, and often had in his employ more than a hundred weavers, some of whom came six or eight miles, to receive the yarn and to return the woven cloth."[17] Rural and urban mills alike depended on outworkers from nearby farming families. Outwork weaving typically engaged a considerably larger number of workers than did the spinning mills themselves and thus broadened the impact of the early factories on the surrounding countryside.

As the growing production of yarn outstripped the ability of outworkers in the immediate vicinity of the mills to weave it into cloth, millowners began to look farther afield. One Fall River, Massachusetts, firm set up a store in Hallowell, Maine, to put its yarn out into farming families. Other companies advertised the availability of their yarn and secured the services of rural storekeepers as middlemen for putting out yarn.[18] Finally, companies employed agents who loaded a wagon with

17. Daniel L. Phillips, *Griswold—A History; Being a History of the Town of Griswold, Connecticut, from the Earliest Times to the Entrance of Our Country into the World War in 1917* (New Haven: Tuttle, Morehouse, & Taylor, 1929), p. 107; and William R. Bagnall, *The Textile Industries of the United States*, vol. 1 (Cambridge, Mass.: Riverside Press, 1893), pp. 476–77. For further references to dispersed outwork weaving, see Federal Manuscript Census of Manufactures, 1820, N.H. returns, microfilm, BL, pp. 85, 92, and Sarah Anne Emery, *Reminiscences of a Newburyport Nonagenarian* (Newburyport, Mass.: William H. Huse, 1879), pp. 72–73.

18. Victor S. Clark, *History of Manufactures in the United States*, vol. 1 (New York: Peter Smith, 1949; originally published in 1916), p. 539; and Walter Palmer, Jewett City, Conn., to Trumbull Dorrance, Dalton, Mass., November 4, 1817, April 9, 1818, Letters, Jewett City Cotton Manufacturing Company Records, Urban Archives, University of Connecticut, Storrs. See also Blackstone Manufacturing Company Records, ser. F, boxes 1 and 2, Rhode Island Historical Society, Providence; Coleman, "Rhode Island Cotton Manufacturing," p. 73; and Mohanty, "Putting Up with Putting-Out," p. 199.

yarn and drove regular routes through the countryside to supply yarn and pick up completed pieces of cloth. Through such means, spinning firms managed to find outlets for their yarn and to meet the ever-growing demand for woven cloth.

Weaving middlemen typically received detailed instructions from agents of the Rhode Island firms with whom they dealt. Surviving letters between mill managers and middlemen in southern New England reveal the second characteristic of outwork as a system of production— the exasperating limitations in the control manufacturers and middlemen exerted over the outworkers they used.

Outwork middlemen typically acted as agents for the textile firms with which they contracted for yarn to put out. They were held responsible for the quality of the woven cloth they returned to the firm and were paid according to the quantity of weaving done under their direction. They, in turn, paid weavers a piece wage for each yard woven, the price varying with the complexity of the fabric. They also enforced a system of fines and deductions intended to ensure uniformity and quality in the woven cloth. One mill manager wrote to a Connecticut middleman and described his firm's provisions in unusual detail.

> If the cloth is wove more than one Inch wider, or two Inches narrower than what is prescribed a deduction of one cent pr yard on that price will be expected & for every mistripe in warping any piece one cent pr yd. on that price is to be deducted, & for mistripes in filling, being wove too sleazy, or with a bad selvedge or otherwise injured, a deduction to be made proportionate to the damage; & if any cloth is so badly wove as not to be worth so much as the yarn would be of which it is made, we are to have the liberty of returning it to you, & charging you the amo[un]t.[19]

This list of possible problems in the weaving is so extensive that one wonders whether any finished cloth ever met these standards without deductions.

19. Stephen Tripp to Frederick A. Avery, Providence, March 11, 1814, Blackstone Manufacturing Company Records, ser. F, box 2, folder 9. See also Barbara Tucker, *Samuel Slater and the Origins of the American Textile Industry* (Ithaca: Cornell University Press, 1984), pp. 104–5; and Mohanty, "Putting Up with Putting-Out," p. 198.

Despite this array of threatened deductions, textile firms and out-work organizers remained unable to control outworkers. Many manu-facturers needed the services of weavers, and farming families had other sources of support, so that they could not be effectively coerced to work at terms that did not suit them. Moreover, storekeepers needed their customers' business and thus could not or would not discipline out-workers as well as textile manufacturers desired. From the perspective of textile managers, this state of affairs led to several difficulties. First, great quantities of yarn were out with members of farming families for extremely long periods of time, thus tying up a great deal of a firm's working capital. In addition to being slow, outworkers were choosy about the work they accepted. One middleman wrote to the agent of the Blackstone Manufacturing Company: "My weaving has all been put out for some days except that intended for Bedticking, which I am fearful will not go readly. . . . I think you had better not send any more Tick-ing untill I have an opportunity of putting out that now on hand."[20] A year later, this middleman again noted the problems posed by out-workers' preferences: "You may think me verry difficult to request par-ticular kinds of weaving but I wish you to reflect that there is a great supply of weaving sent into this part of the world to be wove and weavers will furnish themselves with such as they chose when they can when equally conveniant." This comment raised the hackles of the mill agent, Stephen Tripp, who responded: "I did not expect but that your weavers would take from you such yarn as you had to put out. You will on a little reflection see, that if the weavers are to weave just such kind of goods as they chuse and those only, that we are in but a sorry way, what advantage shall we derive from putting out yarn in large quanti-ties, if it is to be selected by the weavers & that which they do not like is to be returned unwoven."[21] Tripp did not like it, but outworkers ex-ercised considerable independence in relation to middlemen. Because they did not derive a significant amount of their income from weaving,

20. Frederick A. Avery to Stephen Tripp, July 28, 1814, Blackstone Manufacturing Com-pany Records, ser. F, box 2, folder 9. Errors evident in the quote appear in the original. Bedticking is a striped heavy fabric typically used in mattress covers.

21. Avery to Tripp, October 16, 1815, and Tripp to Avery, November 22, 1815, Blackstone Manufacturing Company Records, ser. F, box 2, folder 9.

their resulting economic independence proved a continual thorn in outwork operations.

Correspondence such as Tripp's offers insight into the perspective of
the manufacturer or outwork organizer. To explore outwork from the
point of view of rural residents who chose to weave cloth, braid hats, or
bind shoes, we first need to identify outworkers and to place them within
the economy of the New England countryside. The survival of the weaving account of Silas Jillson of Richmond, New Hampshire, permits the
reconstruction of one such network and the placing of outwork within
the broader rural economy.[22]

Only scant evidence survives to help identify outwork middleman
Silas Jillson. Born in Richmond of parents who had recently migrated
from Rhode Island, Jillson worked first as a farmer, but he and his father also made spinning wheels. He probably had the woodworking
skills to make handlooms as well, although surviving sources are silent
on this point. In any event, a decade after his marriage, not content simply to till a rocky homestead, Jillson began to put out machine-spun
cotton yarn to be woven in families in and around Richmond.[23]

The character of outwork emerges clearly in accounts Jillson kept between September 1822 and June 1829. In all, he recorded 2,041 separate
transactions and credited account holders more than $12,000 for their
output, about half of which was completed in 1823 and 1824.[24] Richmond residents did not become dependent on weaving earnings. Although Jillson put out yarn to be woven for almost seven years, few accounts remained open over the entire period. On average, individual
account holders returned 5.4 pieces of cloth, totaling 579 yards in length,
over a period of seventeen months, work for which they received $31.81.
A typical weaver completed a piece of cloth of about 108 yards in length

22. Silas Jillson Weaving Account, 1822–1829, MATH. See Appendix 1 for a discussion
of the methods employed in coding this account and linking it with other contemporary
records.

23. William Bassett, *The History of the Town of Richmond, Cheshire County, New Hampshire*
(Boston: C. W. Calkins, 1884), pp. 176, 178–79. See also David Jillson, *Genealogy of the Gillson
and Jilson Family* (Central Falls, R.I.: E. L. Freeman, 1876), p. 66.

24. The most common outwork products were denims, plaids, checks, and stripes, fabrics
which required four harnesses or multiple shuttles and which power looms could not handle
in this period.

every three months.[25] Given the time it would take to warp, size, and draw in the yarn and weave the finished cloth, output likely averaged about four yards per day.[26] At this rate, Jillson's outworkers probably put in twenty-seven full days of work every three months, averaging two days of weaving per week.[27] Even given the fact that outwork was concentrated in the winter and spring months, weaving likely occupied no more than three days a week during the busy season.[28]

Outwork weaving was widespread in Richmond in this period. At least 42 percent of families living in Richmond in 1830 had taken yarn from Jillson in the previous decade.[29] Although surviving contemporary sources and reminiscences invariably indicate that women wove the yarn put out into farming families, the majority of Jillson's accounts were held by men. Almost 63 percent of all account holders were males. Of those successfully traced in local sources, 64 percent were male household heads, 8 percent were widows, another 6 percent were wives, and

25. The shift in language here is purposeful. It is impossible to be certain of the output of individual weavers from an account held in the name of a male household head because several family members could have been contributing to the output credited to the account. The output figure noted in this final sentence reflects cloth credited to unmarried daughters with accounts in their own name—the group of account holders most likely to be exchanging with Jillson the product of their own labor.

26. I am grateful to Adrienne Hood, assistant curator of textiles at the Royal Ontario Museum, for the calculations on which this estimate is based.

27. Comparison of the output of Richmond weavers with that of Elizabeth Fuller of Princeton, Massachusetts, is instructive in this regard. Fuller wove steadily for almost two months in the spring of 1792, producing by her own count 140 yards in that period. She wove on occasion as much as eight and a half yards in a day. Taking into account the greater complexity of the fabrics woven by Richmond outworkers, I feel this estimate is reasonable, if conservative. Were I to use a higher figure, of course, it would simply strengthen the point that outworkers were very much part-time weavers. See "Diary Kept by Elizabeth Fuller," in Francis Blake, comp., *History of the Town of Princeton . . . Massachusetts* (Princeton: By the Town, 1915), pp. 313–15.

28. November and December accounted for just over 26 percent of all webs given out; in contrast, in July–October, Jillson gave out less than 21 percent of his webs. Unfortunately, Jillson did not record the dates that woven cloth was returned, so we do not know precisely when the work was completed. Jillson's weavers do not appear to be unrepresentative of outworkers generally. See Prude, *Coming of Industrial Order*, pp. 76–77; Fowler, "Rhode Island Handloom Weavers," pp. 145–47, 168–71; and Coleman, "Rhode Island Cotton Manufacturing," p. 74.

29. This figure is based of the linkage of Jillson account holders with households enumerated in the 1830 federal manuscript census for Richmond, Cheshire County, N.H.

Table 2.1. Earnings of Jillson account holders,
by sex and family status

	Males	Females
Household heads	$33.86 (126)	$44.64 (15)
Spouses	—	14.30 (12)
Children	9.42 (3)	31.34 (41)
Missing data	52	

Sources: Silas Jillson Weaving Account, 1822–1829, MATH, linked to local vital, genealogical, and census sources.

the remaining 22 percent were unmarried children, presumably living with their parents.[30] Unfortunately, nothing in the surviving record indicates who did the weaving as opposed to the name of the account holder. Our analysis, then, must focus on account holders rather than on weavers themselves.

Analysis of individual accounts reveals how weaving fit into the family economy of a farming community. Weaving output varied according to the sex and family status of account holders (see Table 2.1). Virtually all males who held accounts with Jillson were household heads; in contrast, only about a fourth of female account holders headed their own households. Unmarried daughters made up fully 60 percent of women with accounts, and their earnings from weaving were comparable with those of male household heads. Sons, in contrast, averaged only $9 for their weaving, compared with more than $31 for daughters. The data suggest that unmarried daughters did most of the outwork weaving, either within parental accounts or on their own.

30. Information on likely family status in 1825 was found for 197 of 249 account holders. Linkage in local genealogical and vital records, the 1830 federal manuscript census, and a Richmond tax list for 1826 provided the grounds for inferences as to family status. Major sources for genealogical links included: Bassett, *History of the Town of Richmond*; John F. Norton, *History of Fitzwilliam, New Hampshire* (New York: Burr, 1888); Albert Annett and Alice E. E. Lehtinen, *History of Jaffrey (Middle Monadnock) New Hampshire*, 2 vols. (Jaffrey: By the Town, 1937); M. T. Stone, *Historical Sketch of the Town of Troy . . . 1764–1897* (Keene, N.H.: Sentinel Press, 1897); and Benjamin Read, *The History of Swanzey, from 1734 to 1890* (Salem, Mass.: Salem Press, 1892).

For comparable evidence of the predominance of males among outwork weaving account holders of the Blackstone Manufacturing Company in the 1810s, see Mohanty, "Outwork Weaving in Rural Rhode Island," p. 57.

A comparison of female household heads and married women with accounts in their own names is also instructive. Widows had the largest accounts of any group, averaging over $44 in weaving credits. Married women, by contrast, earned only $14 on average for weaving. Widows undoubtedly were credited for weaving done by other family members; married women probably were credited simply for weaving they completed interspersed with their other domestic duties. Unmarried daughters had earnings between those of wives and widows. Daughters had strong motivation to weave diligently, most likely contributing to their marriage portions.[31] Still, the overall picture that emerges from examining Jillson's weaving accounts is one of male household heads being credited with the majority of proceeds of outwork weaving performed by female family members.

How did these outwork families compare with others in their community? Two differences stand out. First, outwork families were significantly larger than families that did not weave for Jillson, with 6.1 versus 5.1 members on average.[32] Half of this difference was due to the number of teenage children residing in these families. Thus outwork appealed to rural residents as an economic strategy at a certain point in the family cycle, when available family labor was greatest and when the labor of teenage daughters could be shifted from agricultural work to weaving.

Second, heads of outwork families were wealthier than their neighbors, with property in 1826 assessed at $392, almost 30 percent more than the average of $305 for heads of nonoutwork families. This difference in wealth is confirmed by an examination of the incidence of outwork across the wealth distribution of the community. Outwork was far more common among wealthier families than among poorer ones. A bit more than 40 percent of families in the bottom 60 percent of taxpayers did outwork weaving for Silas Jillson; in contrast, more than 63 percent of families in the top 40 percent of Richmond taxpayers wove for Jillson.[33]

31. For an autobiographical account of one young Connecticut woman who did outwork weaving to provide for her trousseau, see *Bessie; or, Reminiscences of a Daughter of a New England Clergyman; Simple Facts, Simply Told by a Grandmother* (New Haven, Conn. J. H. Benham, 1861), chap. 18.

32. Figures are based on linkage with the 1830 federal manuscript census of Richmond.

33. Means and proportions based on linkage of Jillson account holders with 1826 Richmond tax inventories and the 1830 federal manuscript census of population.

Figure 2.1. Woman weaving a rug at a handloom, 1894. Notice the size of the frame in which the loom is set. From Alice Morse Earle, *Home Life in Colonial Days* (New York: Macmillan, 1898).

The greater wealth of outwork families may seem anomalous at first glance but can be readily explained. Weaving offered families extra income, yet the opportunities it opened up were not completely free. First, a family had to build or purchase a loom; second, a family had to have space in the house to leave a loom set up more or less permanently. Those families with greater income and more household space were more able than poorer families to weave, hence the disparity in wealth between outwork and nonoutwork families in Richmond.[34]

All in all, older, larger, and wealthier families were most likely among Richmond residents to do outwork weaving. Laurel Thatcher Ulrich has found contemporary evidence for just this sort of relationship between wealth and family cycle for rural families. Drawing on *Northwood*, an 1827 novel written by Sarah Josepha Hale (and set, appropriately enough, in

34. I have not found evidence indicating that manufacturers or middlemen rented looms to outwork families, a strategy that might have permitted members of poorer families to weave.

New Hampshire), Ulrich comments astutely on changing family fortunes related to the family cycle: "Hale caught the Romolees of *Northwood* in a charmed instant when their daughters were old enough to work but too young to marry."[35] Such also describes weaving families in Richmond and may account, in part, for their greater wealth in relation to nonweaving neighbors.

Outwork families were engaged primarily in farming. More than 72 percent owned land for tillage, almost 77 percent owned acreage for mowing, and fully 89 percent owned livestock.[36] These proportions were uniformly greater for Richmond families that did outwork than for those that did not. Nonoutworkers were also predominantly farmers, though typically less well off than those who wove for Jillson. Also included among nonoutworkers were some wealthy families, however. Their presence in this group was reflected by the fact that the property of nonoutworkers exceeded that of outworkers in three categories—money at interest, stock in trade, and carriages. Few Richmond residents had sizable nonfarm assets, but those who had were unlikely to weave for Jillson.

Outworkers employed by Jillson were not limited to Richmond residents. Two storekeepers in the neighboring town of Fitzwilliam accepted cloth for Jillson and probably employed about 25 percent of his outworkers.[37] Just as Silas Jillson operated as a middleman for Rhode Island textile manufacturers, so these two storekeepers facilitated the distribution of yarn and the picking up of woven cloth for outworkers who lived at some distance from Jillson. A ledger for one of these stores, that of John Whittemore & Son, has survived and offers insights into the operation of this system of subcontracting.

From the ledger we learn that outwork weavers paid a price for having the convenience of returning cloth to the Whittemore store and

35. Laurel Thatcher Ulrich, "Housewife and Gadder: Themes of Self-Sufficiency and Community in Eighteenth-Century New England," in Carol Groneman and Mary Beth Norton, eds., *"To Toil the Livelong Day": America's Women at Work, 1780–1980* (Ithaca: Cornell University Press, 1987), p. 28.

36. In all, 56 percent of Jillson account holders (139 of 249) were successfully traced into the 1826 Richmond tax list.

37. These were John Whittemore and Luke Richardson; see Norton, *History of Fitzwilliam*, pp. 396–402. For Jillson's account in the Whittemore account book, see John Whittemore & Son Ledger, 1821–1824, p. 112, private collection of the late Joel Whittemore; photocopy in the possession of the author.

receiving payment in credit toward store purchases. Richmond weavers were commonly paid six to seven cents a yard for their cloth in 1823 and 1824, and Jillson paid the Whittemores similar prices for the cloth he collected. But, the Whittemores credited Jillson's weavers only four cents for each yard they brought him. Typically the Whittemores enjoyed a profit margin of two to three cents per yard on the cloth they accepted on behalf of Jillson. In addition, of course, they made further profits on the goods they sold to customers. Given that they did not have to travel to Rhode Island or otherwise deal with the textile firms that supplied the cotton yarn, the Whittemores must have felt satisfied with this initial exposure to outwork operations.

The Whittemore ledger also provides additional information on the identity of outwork weavers. Fitzwilliam weavers, like those in Richmond, were somewhat wealthier than their farming neighbors. Fitzwilliam residents who brought Jillson cloth to the Whittemore store were taxed on average for property valued at $346, almost 30 percent more than the mean of $265 for taxed nonoutworkers. As were outworkers in adjacent Richmond, these families were primarily farmers. More than 77 percent owned land, and 95 percent owned livestock; both these proportions were larger for outworkers than for nonoutworkers.[38]

The picture of outwork that emerges from the Whittemore account book is consistent with that of the Jillson weave book, but in one respect it is considerably more informative. In analyzing outwork, we invariably find our view clouded by conventions common to early nineteenth-century accounting. The most troublesome practice was that of recording accounts almost exclusively in the names of male household heads, regardless of who actually did the weaving. Thus males made up 63 percent of account holders in the Jillson weave book and 89 percent of those trading at the Whittemore store. There is no way to determine who did the actual weaving recorded in the Jillson accounts, but the Whittemore ledger offers a clearer view.

An example may be helpful in thinking about this issue. Mary Cummings repeatedly came into the Whittemore store in the spring and

38. Fitzwilliam 1819 Tax List, Fitzwilliam (N.H.) Town Hall. For a discussion of the methods employed in record linkage with the John Whittemore & Son and Dexter Whittemore & Son accounts, see Appendix 1.

· 47 ·

summer of 1822. On March 15, April 19, May 29, July 29, and August 22, she brought to the store sizable pieces of woven cloth that Whittemore eventually turned over to Silas Jillson. Her name and her 430 yards of weaving are recorded carefully in Silas Jillson's account in the Whittemore ledger. Mary Cummings, however, had no account of her own in the store's ledgers, but her transactions were duly recorded in the account of her physician husband, Thaddeus Cummings. In that account the entries read, typically, "weaving 89 yd" and "weaving 83½ yds," and one can determine that the Cummingses received $18.74 for her weaving in this six-month period. Still, nothing in the Thaddeus Cummings account gives a clue as to who actually did the work. Only because of the existence of the Jillson account do we know that Mary Cummings (and/or her daughters) wove steadily over this period, earning sizable credits toward her family's store purchases.

The division of labor and accounting evident for the Cummings family was common enough in the Whittemore ledger. In all, Whittemore recorded sixty-nine pieces of cloth in the debit column of Silas Jillson's account; he noted women's names in just over 62 percent of these transactions, a figure that provides a lower limit on women's share of outwork weaving.

Putting out yarn to weave never became a major activity for John Whittemore or his son Dexter, but acting as middlemen for Jillson did familiarize them with outwork as a form of rural production. Outwork weaving, moreover, did not long outlast the period covered by Jillson's weave book. By 1829, when Jillson recorded his last transactions with outworkers, most cotton textile mills in New England had added power looms and had discontinued the putting out of yarn for weaving. As power-loom production increased, handloom-weaving prices declined markedly. Jillson's weavers earned a third less for their weaving in 1829 than in 1822, with average prices falling from 6.9 to 4.6 cents per yard. As Jillson closed up his outwork network, the bottom was falling out of the handloom-weaving market.

Just as Richmond and Fitzwilliam residents were returning their last pieces of handwoven cloth to Silas Jillson, however, Dexter Whittemore was inaugurating a new form of outwork, the braiding of children's and men's palm-leaf hats. Whittemore bought palm leaf from Boston wholesale merchants, who imported it from the Caribbean. He had it split locally and sold the split leaf (on credit) to his customers.[39] They, in turn, braided the hats, following directions he supplied, and sold them back to Whittemore for credits against their store purchases. Typically, customers brought back about fifteen hats at a time, picked up additional split palm leaf, and utilized their credit to buy store items. The frequency of hat transactions suggests that customers came in once every two months, which indicates that they were making perhaps two hats a week.

Palm-leaf hats were summer wear, and braiding hats was a seasonal activity, concentrated between October and April.[40] In the busy spring season, taking in hats and crediting customers' accounts could dominate store business. Dexter Whittemore's son Joel, who had charge of the store in March and April 1841, described business in a letter to his absent father: "We got along well to day; full as well as I expected. We have wrote down over 4 pages in the Daybook & taken about 550 hats." A bit later that same spring, in the week following April 12, some seventy-seven customers brought more than thirty-seven hundred hats to the store.[41] Piles of hats must have cluttered the store's back room. To keep up with his outworkers, Whittemore periodically shipped sacks of hats by express team to Massachusetts firms that bleached, pressed, sorted, and boxed them for shipment to wholesalers in Boston, New York, Philadelphia, and Baltimore.[42] These wholesalers completed the trading chain when they shipped the hats to midwestern

39. Outworkers "bought" the split leaf and "sold" their hats to Whittemore, but they were not really independent producers of palm-leaf hats. Prices for leaf and braided hats reflected a competitive market in which storekeepers competed for rural customers. For convenience, it is likely that outworkers purchased leaf where they sold their hats and bought other store goods; it did not make sense to buy leaf at one store and trade hats at another given the distances involved.

40. Volumes 87 and 88, Dexter Whittemore & Son Collection, provide solid evidence of this seasonality as they include Whittemore's accounts with hat processors in neighboring Worcester County and with the urban wholesalers with whom he dealt.

41. Joel Whittemore to Dexter Whittemore, March 14, 1841, family letters, box 6, store daybook, and vol. 17, Dexter Whittemore & Son Collection.

42. Charles Miles to Dexter Whittemore, February 27, March 18, 1854, and Lee & Stearns to Dexter Whittemore, Baldwinville, Mass., September 7, 1855, box 7, incoming letters, Dexter Whittemore & Son Collection. See also numerous letters in these folders from urban wholesalers in the 1830s.

and southern storekeepers and to southern planters to be worn by farm laborers and slaves.[43]

Hat making became a major element in Whittemore's business and continued to expand throughout the antebellum period. In 1830, Dexter Whittemore employed more than 250 individuals making 23,000 hats a year, and their earnings made up almost half of all credits in his store accounts.[44] This represented a dramatic increase in outwork, for between 1821 and 1824, handwoven cloth had totaled only about $270 a year, accounting for less than 10 percent of the credits of Whittemore's customers. In contrast, hat credits averaged about $5,000 per year in the early 1830s and more than $15,000 annually twenty years later.[45] By the early 1850s Whittemore employed more than 800 hat makers producing 80,000 hats annually. Outwork promoted a tremendous expansion in his store trade and made him one of the richest men in Fitzwilliam.[46] His two-story columned store and adjoining house stood prominently in the center of town, adjacent to the town common and across from the meeting house (see Figure 2.2).

Whittemore's palm hat network extended well beyond the boundaries of Fitzwilliam. His growing reliance on outwork, in fact, steadily brought new customers from greater distances into his store. Only 12 percent of customers recorded in Whittemore's accounts between 1821 and 1824 resided outside Fitzwilliam. In 1830, 21 percent of his customers came from neighboring towns, and by 1850 this proportion had increased still further, to 51 percent. At its height, then, Whittemore's palm hat network drew more workers from surrounding towns than from Fitzwilliam itself.[47]

43. Accounts, 1845–1847, box 2, Fisher, Blashfield & Co., New York Public Library; and Francis C. Rozier Collection, 1841–1857, Historical Society of Pennsylvania, Philadelphia.

44. Whittemore was not unique in his adoption of hat making; in fact, neighboring Worcester County, Massachusetts, was the center for palm-leaf hat making. By 1832, residents of that county were braiding 1.5 million hats annually. See Louis McLane, "Report of the Secretary of the Treasury, 1832," *Documents Relative to the Manufactures of the United States*, vol. 1 (Washington: Duff Green, 1833), pp. 474–577.

45. Dexter Whittemore & Son Collection, vols. 3, 4, 87, 88.

46. New Hampshire, vol. 2, p. 192, R. G. Dun & Co. Collection, BL. For discussion of an even larger palm hat operation in Amherst, Massachusetts, see Clark, *Roots of Rural Capitalism*, pp. 182–84.

47. The Dexter Whittemore & Son Collection contains ninety manuscript volumes and seven wooden cases of accounts and correspondence for the period 1826–1857. The extensiveness of the collection makes possible this analysis but at the same time calls for sampling to

Figure 2.2. Whittemore & Co. Store, Fitzwilliam, N.H. Courtesy of Baker Library, Harvard Graduate School of Business Administration, Boston, Mass.

Although the Whittemores appear to have stayed in their store, requiring that outworkers bring in their completed hats, some palm hat middlemen evidently drove wagons around the countryside, selling split palm leaf and "gathering in the hats" from scattered farm women (see Figure 2.3). In this respect, they resembled an earlier generation of weaving

make such analysis manageable. I have focused primarily on two ledgers, volumes 44 and 55, chosen to permit linkage of account holders in the federal manuscript census of Fitzwilliam and neighboring towns in 1830 and 1850.

Figure 2-3. "Gathering in the Hats." Woman outworker bringing in palm-leaf hats and receiving a bundle of split palm leaves for further work. Notice the man at the front of the wagon recording the transaction in his accounts, c. 1880. Courtesy of Vermont Historical Society.

middlemen who rode on horseback distributing webs of yarn and collecting completed pieces of woven cloth.

The Whittemores had a clear advantage over such itinerant middlemen—the ability to profit on both their outworkers' labor and outworkers' store purchases. And although both putting out split palm leaf and selling store goods were integral to their operations, it is evident that it was outwork hat making, not simply the variety of store goods or low prices, that brought extralocal customers into Whittemore's store. Fitzwilliam residents with accounts at the store in the early 1850s financed 38 percent of their purchases with the proceeds of hat making; for Whittemore's out-of-town customers, the comparable proportion was almost 59 percent. Almost a quarter of Fitzwilliam customers at the Whittemore store in 1850 did not make palm-leaf hats; only 12 percent of out-of-town customers made no hats. These differences indicate that hat making was the primary magnet that attracted customers from neighboring towns to the Whittemore store.

If hat making could attract customers to the Whittemore store, then it might also attract middlemen able to link Whittemore to prospective hat makers. Such subcontracting did develop over time, as some of Whittemore's customers brought in hats made by their neighbors rather than by members of their own families. In 1850, for instance, the largest "hat maker" in Whittemore's ledger was Abel Smith, a 78-year-old farmer who resided in the adjoining town of Rindge. In an account that extended over five and a half years, Smith marketed more than 2,900 hats through the Whittemore store, averaging 525 hats per year. It is unlikely (though not impossible) that Smith's 74-year-old wife and 44-year-old single daughter braided that many hats by themselves. Although the Smiths were only one of thirty-three Rindge families trading at the store, the family accounted for more than 37 percent of Rindge-made hats credited in Whittemore's ledger in the early 1850s.

Outwork grew dramatically between 1820 and 1850, but it grew more by geographical extension than by any intensification of the work and commitment of individuals. More people made palm-leaf hats and more traded with Whittemore, as evidenced by the growing number of accounts, but the hat making of individual account holders remained relatively constant. On average, Whittemore customers earned annual credits of $16.43 for their hat making in the early 1830s, a figure that rose only slightly to $16.96 in the early 1850s. Surprisingly, their annual store purchases actually fell from $23 to $18 over these two decades. For the typical farm family in Fitzwilliam, involvement in outwork and the broader consumer markets it opened up remained modest.[48]

Just as outworkers' hat production for Dexter Whittemore remained relatively stable between 1830 and 1850, so too was there little change in the identity of hat makers. In fact, the makeup of Whittemore's palm hat outworkers was similar to that of outwork weavers employed earlier by Silas Jillson. Male household heads made up about 60 percent of all account holders; unmarried daughters were consistently the second largest group, with over 15 percent of accounts in both 1830 and 1850 (see Table 2.2).

The composition of Whittemore account holders in 1830 speaks to the place of different groups in broader exchange. Among adults there were 145 accounts held in the names of male household heads compared with only 16 widows and 8 wives. These figures suggest that adult men had formal control of much of the exchange economy operating through the store. Moreover, the credit profiles of these accounts varied dramatically along gender lines. Male household heads averaged $12 in agricultural credits in their accounts, widows mustered only $7 of such credits, and wives had still fewer, with a trifling $1.25 in farm products on average. Finally, household heads had more access to cash and notes than did wives. More than 57 percent of the accounts for male household heads and 62 percent for widows had cash credits; none of the wives' accounts did. Similarly, no wives gave Whittemore notes to cover outstanding balances in their accounts, whereas 25 percent of widows and

48. Because the Whittemore accounts maintained running balances that varied from year to year, credits and debits did not necessarily balance within a specific ledger. Thus, it was perfectly reasonable for customers to make slightly more hats as recorded in the 1850 ledger than in 1830, while purchasing fewer store goods.

Although overall purchases remained modest, it is clear that by organizing outwork hat making, the Whittemores increased sales at their store. Hat credits represented almost half of all credits in both 1830 and 1850. Moreover, hat makers in 1830 made purchases of goods other than split palm leaf that averaged $35 per account; other customers purchased only $21 in goods on average.

Table 2.2. Composition of account holders at the
Whittemore store, 1830 and 1850

Family status	1830		1850	
	all	plh[a]	all	plh
Male household heads	63.0%	62.8%	59.7%	59.1%
Female household heads	7.0	6.3	5.0	5.2
Wives	3.5	3.7	4.6	5.6
Unmarried sons	5.7	3.1	4.9	2.3
Unmarried daughters	17.8	20.4	15.6	18.6
Others	3.0	3.6	9.2	9.1
Totals[b]	230	191	737	597
Missing, indeterminate	68		254	

[a] Abbreviations for column headings refer to "all accounts" and to "accounts with palm-leaf hat credits."

[b] Totals include only account holders placed within families in 1830 and 1850 through census or genealogical linkage. The larger share of "others" for 1850 results from the identification of boarders in that census and does not necessarily reflect change over time.

Sources: Dexter Whittemore & Son ledger accounts and linkage with local vital, census, and genealogical sources.

38 percent of male household heads had such notes. The economic disabilities of married women are clearly evident.[49]

The place of hat credits in these accounts reflected the differing work roles and power relations of husbands, wives, and widows in the local farm economy. For husbands, who controlled a diverse family economy, hats accounted for only 41 percent of all credits; for widows, 47 percent; and for wives, more than 77 percent. The hat-making activity of married women in Fitzwilliam was generally subsumed within a family economy governed by their husbands. In the rare cases in which wives traded in their own names, they bought store goods from the limited proceeds of their own and their children's hat making.

These broad patterns become sharper when we look at specific families. Of the eight wives with accounts at the Whittemore store in their own names in the early 1830s, six of their husbands also held accounts. William and Polly Whittemore, Josiah and Betsey Carter, and the other

49. For the broader legal ramifications of these disabilities and women's efforts to provide legislative remedies, see Norma Basch, *In the Eyes of the Law: Women, Marriage, and Property in Nineteenth-Century New York* (Ithaca: Cornell University Press, 1982).

four couples reflected in their own trading habits the broader patterns apparent for the community as a whole. Husbands traded a variety of goods at the store and brought diverse resources to bear in their accounts, and their agricultural credits in these six families averaged $10 apiece compared with only $1.67 for their wives. Husbands used notes and paid cash at the store and had third-party credits that evidenced other trading that men carried on beyond the bounds of the Whittemore store.[50] No wives had notes or spent cash at the store, and only one of six had any third-party credits to her name. Wives had greater credits than their husbands in only one category—their palm hat credits averaged a bit more than $23 each, whereas the hat credits in their husbands' accounts totaled just under $22. For wives, hat credits amounted to 69 percent of the value of their purchases; for husbands, they amounted to less than 34 percent. Once again, we can see in the experiences of these couples the different ways that married men and women operated within the commercial economy of Fitzwilliam.

Not everyone who traded at the Whittemore store necessarily made palm-leaf hats, though for the most part, groups marketed hats in numbers similar to their proportions among account holders. In 1830, for instance, male household heads made up 63 percent of all account holders and the same proportion of those with palm-leaf hat credits. By 1850 these proportions had declined somewhat, but male household heads still constituted more than 59 percent of both all account holders and those marketing hats.

Among unmarried children with accounts in their own names, a different pattern emerged, with girls making more hats than did boys. In 1830, unmarried sons were 5.7 percent of individuals with accounts but only 3.1 percent of those with hat credits, and they were credited with only 1.4 percent of the hats made for Whittemore. Unmarried daughters, in contrast, made up at that date 17.8 percent of Whittemore account holders and 20.4 percent of those with hat credits. They were credited,

50. Third parties who owed money to an account holder could pay off their debt by marketing goods to Whittemore and having their credits recorded to the benefit of that particular account holder. The practice was extremely common in 1830, though it declined somewhat over the next two decades. For discussion of this trend, see Dublin, "Women and Outwork," pp. 55–56.

moreover, for 21.7 percent of the hats sold to Whittemore. Daughters outnumbered sons by three to one among account holders, but their hat output exceeded that for sons by a factor of fifteen. These figures reveal that despite conventions by which most store accounts were kept in the names of males, hat making was primarily a female activity.

Sons did not make nearly as many hats as daughters because they had other sources of income with which to buy goods at the Whittemore store. Earnings from making hats accounted for only 6 percent of store credits for sons, compared with 80 percent for daughters. Because sons could earn cash elsewhere, wages, notes, and third-party payments made up the majority of their credits, whereas daughters relied almost entirely on hat making to finance their purchases. Neither group spent much cash at the store in 1830—$2.31 on average for sons and $0.81 for daughters—but by 1850, a large gap had opened between the two groups: sons spent $27 in cash on average on store purchases compared with $6 for daughters. Sons in the 1850s basically spent at the store money they earned elsewhere, perhaps working on neighbors' farms or in the woodenware shops that were common in Fitzwilliam.[51] For daughters, store accounts continued to represent payrolls recording their hat making and the purchases they made with the proceeds of their labor. Hat making appears to have been the only significant source of female wage labor in Fitzwilliam in this period.

Careful analysis of the Whittemore ledgers makes clear the central place of rural women in the braiding of palm-leaf hats. One other contemporary source confirms this conclusion—the visual record. An engraving in a popular magazine of the 1850s offers a collage consisting of "Scenes and Occupations Characteristic of New England Life" (see Figure 2.4). We see there a variety of men at work—a farmer, drover, and lumberman—but also three workingwomen—a "factory girl," a "palm-leaf hat braider," and a woman picking hops. It seems remarkable to a

---

51. According to the 1850 federal manuscript census of manufactures, six Fitzwilliam shops gave employment to an average of seventy-nine men, producing pails, tubs, boxes, and woodenware. Some of these men may well have been the unmarried brothers of hat braiders and have had accounts of their own at the Whittemore store. Federal manuscript census of manufactures, 1850, Fitzwilliam, vol. 25, *Industry*, pp. 75–76, New Hampshire Division of Records Management and Archives, Concord.

Figure 2.4. "Scenes and Occupations Characteristic of New England Life," from *Ballou's Pictorial*, June 16, 1855.

late twentieth-century viewer that palm-leaf hat making, today an almost totally obscure activity, should occupy the central and most con-
spicuous place in this engraving.[52]

Although contemporaries rarely wrote about hat braiding—rather
taking for granted this commonplace rural activity—they did preserve a
consistent visual record. A second illustration, "The Idyll of the Palm
Leaf Hat," offers a romanticized view of a domestic group busily at
work (see Figure 2.5). With a caged bird hanging from a nearby tree,
two children look on as two older women—one presumably the mother,
the other perhaps an older sister of the children—are splitting a palm
leaf and braiding a hat at the kitchen table. The older of the onlooking
children, a boy, is carrying a bundle of palm leaves to be split for further braiding. Although the winter months were the period of greatest
hat making activity, the open kitchen door and the light streaming
through the doorway and into the adjoining bedroom suggest a spring
or summer setting for this scene. In any event, as in the other illustration, all those associated with the hat making in this view are women
and children—men and older boys had other activities "characteristic"
of their economic and social roles.[53]

Although hat making offered young women in Fitzwilliam their major source of wage income, they rarely worked at it full-time. They remained, after all, farmers' daughters. Hat credits in daughters' accounts
in 1830 averaged only $20.68 a year. Given a mean annual output of
104 hats, unmarried daughters, although the most conscientious hat
makers in town, were only putting in about seventy-eight full days of
work per year, a figure roughly comparable with that for Jillson's outwork weavers earlier.[54] In all, young women braided hats about a day
and a half a week on average, a quarter of all possible workdays.

Though they worked only part-time braiding hats, daughters with
accounts in their own name did market about 25 percent more hats at
the Whittemore store in 1830 than did other account holders. This margin actually understates the extra work performed by single daughters
because other accounts typically represented the combined output of

52. "The Palm-Leaf Hat Braider," *Ballou's Pictorial*, June 16, 1855, p. 384.

53. "The Idyll of the Palm Leaf Hat," *Frank Leslie's Illustrated Newspaper*, July 15, 1871, p. 293.

54. For an estimate that one could braid one hat in three-fourths of a day, see McLane,
Manufactures of the United States, vol. 1, pp. 786–87, 792–93.

Figure 2.5. "The Idyll of the Palm Leaf Hat," from *Frank Leslie's Illustrated Newspaper*, July 15, 1871. This romanticized view has one woman splitting palm leaf while a second braids the rim of a hat on a wooden mold.

several family members. Male household heads, for instance, marketed 75 hats a year on average, compared with 104 for daughters with their own accounts. These 75 hats were probably produced by several family members, though we will never know for certain who did the actual braiding. Whatever the actual output figures per worker, it is evident that single daughters with accounts in their own names were the most productive hat makers in Fitzwilliam.

What did daughters acquire with the store credits they earned for their hat making? Analysis of a sample of accounts reveals that daughters spent more than 67 percent of their credits on sewing supplies. In contrast, only 28 percent of the value of sons' purchases consisted of similar goods. Sons bought many household furnishings and agricultural implements, these two categories accounting for more than 34 percent of sons' purchases (compared with less than 7 percent of daughters' purchases). Sons and daughters were both making purchases at the Whittemore store to enable them to bring goods into their likely marriages, but the patterns of purchasing were highly gendered. Daughters used their hat credits to purchase goods for clothing and linens, whereas sons used other resources to buy goods to furnish and work the farms they planned to establish.[55] These aggregate differences, in turn, reflected the ways sons and daughters used the Whittemore store. Sons rarely did any hat business when they were in the store; daughters, on the other hand, typically either bought split palm leaf, returned braided hats, or did both more than 80 percent of the times they transacted business in the store.

55. Sons' and daughters' purchases differed dramatically from each other's but also from the pattern for all Whittemore accounts sampled. The distribution of purchases (of seventy-eight accounts sampled) evident generally for Whittemore customers in 1830 is serving goods, 44.7 percent; food, 22.8 percent; ready-made clothing, 10.1 percent; household furnishings, 8.8 percent; agricultural implements, 6.3 percent; books and stationery, 1.7 percent; and sundries, 5.5 percent. These figures represent an analysis of debits in a stratified sample with 20 male household heads, 20 daughters, 17 female household heads, 13 sons, and 8 wives among account holders. One cannot know from an analysis of the distribution of goods purchased whether cash, notes, or hat or other credits were used to pay for specific purchases. Hats and other goods sold by customers to Whittemore, however, accounted for more than 75 percent of the value of all goods they purchased at the store between 1829 and 1831. See Dublin, "Women and Outwork," p. 57.

This gendered difference between sons and daughters was mirrored more generally in the ways Whittemore's older customers used his store. The accounts of Ezra Hayden and Luther Damon probably reflected the practices of other male household heads. Palm hats accounted for a relatively small share of the business they transacted with Whittemore, and they either purchased split leaf or brought in braided hats on about one-fourth of the days they did business at the store. Hats made up only one of quite varied goods that men brought into the store for credit against their purchases. Ezra Hayden, for instance, had credits in 1829 for butter, rags, and ashes, as well as for palm-leaf hats. Hat making played a much greater role in the trading activity of women customers at the Whittemore store. Marsylvia Kendall (who headed her own household) and Polly Whittemore (wife of a Fitzwilliam manufacturer) conducted hat business about half the times they came to the store. Kendall had nineteen separate credit entries in her account between November 1829 and September 1830. Seventeen of the nineteen credits were for palm-leaf hats, which amounted to $52 overall. She earned only $1.17 for the ashes and butter she marketed at the store in this period. All of Polly Whittemore's store credits between January 1830 and April 1831 were accounted for by her hat making. These four Fitzwilliam residents all had accounts with Whittemore, but they brought different resources to their trading and used the store in very different ways.

Examining hat making among individuals who traded at the Whittemore store reveals much about the varying places of individuals in the rural economy; such a process makes clear that young women predominated among hat makers in Fitzwilliam in the 1830s and 1840s. Shifting the focus from individual account holders to families that traded with Whittemore reinforces this picture of women's role in rural outwork. For the period 1829–1831, there were 178 individuals from 142 different Fitzwilliam families with accounts at the Whittemore store; 123 of these accounts had palm hat credits. These families made up more than 55 percent of Fitzwilliam families in 1830, a figure that grew to 69 percent by 1850.[56]

---

56. These proportions are based on linkage of Whittemore account holders in the 1830 and 1850 federal manuscript censuses of population for Fitzwilliam.

At least three differences distinguished outwork and nonoutwork families in Fitzwilliam in these decades. Families doing hat outwork for Whittemore were typically somewhat poorer than their neighbors, more likely to be engaged in farming, and larger than average. Fitzwilliam hat-making families owned less property in 1850 than non-hat-making families, with male household heads in families making hats reporting an average of $1,319 in real property compared with $2,180 in those not making hats.[57] Sixty-seven percent of fathers in hat-making families were enumerated as farmers in 1850, compared with only 47 percent among non-hat makers.[58] Even focusing just on farming families, we find that the property differential remains substantial. Non-hat-making farm families owned real property valued at $1,100 more than their hat-making farming neighbors.

Not only were they poorer, but outwork families in Fitzwilliam were also larger than families not engaged in outwork, with 5.9 versus 4.9 members respectively in 1830. In 1850, the same pattern held, as hat-making families averaged 2.6 children, whereas the figure was only 1.7 for non-outwork families.[59] The difference in family size was primarily due to differences in the number of daughters living in these families. In 1830, for instance, families making palm hats had twice as many teenage daughters as did non-hat families.[60] The composition of hat-making families confirms the earlier conclusion that unmarried daughters living at home were the leading participants in Whittemore's outwork network.

57. This comparison is based on linkage of account holders in the 1850 federal manuscript census of population for Fitzwilliam.

58. After farmers and laborers, who accounted for 59 percent of employed males in Fitzwilliam in 1850, carpenters, painters, workers in the woodenware industry, and other artisans made up more than 25 percent of workingmen. Families headed by artisans would have had greater access to cash wages and hence less need for the store credit provided by outwork hat making. Proportions here are based on the 1850 federal manuscript census of population for Fitzwilliam, M432, reel 428.

59. The differential was even greater for Fitzwilliam farm families. In 1850, non-hat-making farming families averaged only 1.17 co-resident children, compared with 3.08 children among farming families making hats for Whittemore.

60. The figures result from linkage of hat-making families in the 1830 federal manuscript census of Fitzwilliam and are based on the number of daughters 10–19 years of age. By 1850, hat-making families had three times as many teenage daughters on average as did non-hat-making families.

A more fine-tuned analysis of family hat making lends further support to this finding. For all Fitzwilliam families in the 1830 ledger, the mean value of hats made in a year came to $18.62, but this figure varied according to the number of daughters between the ages of 10 and 19. Families with no daughters in this age group averaged about $12 of hat credits each year; families with one or two daughters averaged almost $25; and families with three or more teenage daughters averaged more than $33 in hat business. This concentration of hat making in families with teenage daughters became still greater over the next two decades. By 1850, Whittemore families with three or more teenage daughters were making four times as many hats annually as families with no teenage daughters (see Table 2.3).[61]

The concentration of hat making within Fitzwilliam families with teenage daughters is clear. Still, the focus on family aggregates obscures relations between family members. Returning to individual accounts is instructive. There we find that when daughters had accounts in their own names, fathers marketed fewer hats. Two examples make this point clear. Ezra Hayden had an account at the Whittemore store that was typical of those held by male household heads. He alone in his family had a store account, and between 1829 and 1831 he averaged just over $17 a year in hat credits. His family included four sons ranging in ages from 11 to 23 and two daughters, 10 and 19. His older daughter and his wife were the likely hat makers in the family.

Philemon Fairbanks also had a store account. Fairbanks's family in 1830 included his wife, two daughters, aged 22 and 20, and a 12-year-old son. Fairbanks marketed on average $8 of hats annually, a figure undoubtedly influenced by the fact that his younger daughter, Sarah, also had an account at the store. On her own account, Sarah made ninety hats over a sixteen-month period that overlapped with her father's account. Had all Sarah's hats been marketed by her father, his annual output would have exceeded that of Ezra Hayden by a considerable margin. As it was, his hat credits were less than half those of Hayden.

61. The differences evident here between families' production of hats in 1830 and 1850 are significant in statistical terms. For the 1830 breakdown, $F = 7.05$, with a significance of .009; for 1850, $F = 20.29$, with a significance of .0001.

Table 2.3. Annual hat credits for aggregate family accounts, 1830 and 1850, broken down by number of daughters, ages 10–19

	Mean hat credits per year	
Number of daughters	1830	1850
0	$12.01 (75)	$ 7.57 (160)
1–2	24.69 (57)	17.35 (76)
3+	33.58 (10)	30.69 (11)
Overall	$18.62 (142)	$11.61 (247)

Sources: Dexter Whittemore & Son ledger accounts, aggregated and linked to 1830 and 1850 federal manuscript censuses for Fitzwilliam.

The patterns evident for these two families were typical of accounts at the Whittemore store in 1830. Fathers whose daughters did not have accounts in their own names marketed hats worth $16.43 a year on average. Fathers with daughters who had separate accounts averaged only $11.24 in annual hat credits.[62]

We can see the influence of daughters' accounts on hat credits in their fathers' accounts, but what factors had the greatest impact on the hat making of daughters for their own accounts? Two influences stand out: the age of the young woman and the sex of the household head. Table 2.4 summarizes the evidence.

Age was a strong influence on daughters' hat making. Girls under nineteen averaged about $19 per year of hat credits, whereas by their late twenties, daughters were earning more than $27 a year through their efforts. The evidence is clear: the older the daughters, the greater the hat credits in their accounts.

The greatest influence on hat making in daughters' accounts was the sex of the household head. In male-headed households—the predominant form—daughters marketed hats on their own account valued at a bit more than $20 annually. Daughters in female-headed households, by contrast, marketed hats worth more than $43 a year. If we control for age and the presence of parental accounts, daughters in female-headed

62. These figures result from a multiple classification analysis of the value of hats per year by the number of teenage daughters and the presence of daughters' accounts. The influence of the number of teenage daughters was roughly five times greater than the presence of daughters' accounts; the adjusted betas were 0.41 and 0.08 respectively.

Table 2.4. Annual hat credits for daughters in Fitzwilliam
families, 1830, by various factors

Age	By age	By sex of head of household	
9-18	$19.19 (7)		
19-23	22.49 (13)	Male	$20.84 (26)
24-41	27.22 (9)	Female	43.29 (3)

Source: Multiple classification analysis of daughters' hat credits in the Whittemore
1829–1831 ledger, vol. 44, Dexter Whittemore & Son Collection, BL. This method
controls for the influence of the variables noted here and the presence of a father's or
a mother's account.

households braided more than twice as many hats as those in male-
headed households. This evidence reveals the importance of hat making
as a source of income in some households. The death (or absence) of the
male household head dramatically cut into the agricultural labor and
wage income of a farming family. Members of the family responded by
earning wages however they could. Sons found work as farm laborers or
in woodenware shops; daughters braided palm-leaf hats. Their hat-
making activity showed up in the high level of hat credits in their accounts at the Whittemore store. Daughters' wages played a significant
role in the subsistence of female-headed farming families—much more
so than in male-headed ones.

Specific examples help to clarify this argument. There were three
single daughters living at home in female-headed families with their own
accounts recorded in the 1830 Whittemore ledgers. Among them, Ruth
Howe, Mary Whittemore, and Nancy Foster averaged more than $45 a
year in credits from their hat making. Many more young single women
living at home in male-headed households—twenty-nine in all—had accounts in their own names at the Whittemore store. These women,
however, did not braid hats in anywhere near the numbers evident for
Howe, Whittemore, and Foster. On average their hat making netted
them less than $20 a year in store credits. The statistical methods em-
ployed here reveal a substantial difference that is not simply the result
of age differences between these two groups of women or some other
factor. Economic necessity compelled daughters in female-headed families to shoulder a larger share of providing for the family subsistence.

The evidence from the Whittemore ledger indicates that for these families, hat making was a major source of family income, not simply a supplement to farm output.[63]

Although a few families were particularly dependent on hat-making income, it is safe to say that the community as a whole never developed anywhere near the reliance on outwork that was evident in some English straw-plaiting areas. Near Luton, England, for instance, women ran plaiting "schools" attended by area children. Parents paid one pence a day, and their children spent the day plaiting straw; bible reading and the singing of hymns provided the basis for the pretense at education that gave the institution its misleading name. Family financial need lay behind the establishment of the plaiting schools; young children might begin working as early as the age of 3 or 4. Commonly they worked each day until they had plaited a certain amount of straw, known as their stint. This English practice had no equivalent in New England, undoubtedly reflecting the greater degree to which a dependent rural proletariat had emerged in mid-nineteenth-century England.[64]

Braiding palm-leaf hats never took on the same urgency in rural New England as straw plaiting did in parts of England, but it did provide a source of supplementary income well suited to the varying demands on farm women at different points in their lives. And although hat making was concentrated among single daughters in their teens and twenties, farm women made hats at all points in the life cycle—as daughters working for their families, as young women working on their own account, as

63. Blewett, "Women Shoeworkers," pp. 413–20, provides similar evidence of the high level of production of a limited number of shoebinders.

64. Jennie Kitteringham, "Country Work Girls in Nineteenth-Century England," in Raphael Samuel, ed., *Village Life and Labour* (London: Routledge & Kegan Paul, 1975), pp. 119–21. See also Judy Lown, *Women and Industrialization: Gender at Work in Nineteenth-Century England* (Cambridge: Polity Press, 1990), pp. 25–26, 48; and Charles Freeman, *Luton and the Hat Industry* (Luton, Eng.: Luton Museum, 1953). Straw braiding in New England was concentrated in southeastern Massachusetts, but it had a character more similar to palm hat making elsewhere in New England than to its English counterpart. For a useful contemporary account, see Emery, *Reminiscences of a Newburyport Nonagenarian*, pp. 62, 69–72. For a recent analytic treatment, see Caroline Sloat, "'A Great Help to Many Families': Strawbraiding in Massachusetts before 1825," in Peter Benes, ed., *House and Home*, Proceedings of the Dublin Seminar for New England Folklife, Dublin, N. H., 1988, pp. 89–100.

newly married women in accounts under their husbands' names, and as widows, again in accounts under their own names.

A specific example illustrates the influence of life cycle transitions on women's hat making. Martha Alexander had an account with Whittemore from January 1831 until October 1834, the month of her marriage. She was 18 years of age when she opened an account in her own name, and in a forty-five–month period braided 341 hats. Her annual output of 91 hats was comparable with that of other unmarried daughters. In October 1834, Martha Alexander married Edward Allen, two years her senior, also of Fitzwilliam. He had not previously had a store account, but he opened one forthwith, his first transaction being the purchase of split palm leaf. Martha Alexander Allen kept right at her hat making, with 162 hats credited in the next two years. This output represented only a slight decline from the pace just before her marriage.

Martha Alexander's account in the two-year period before her marriage suggests that she was using hat credits to purchase items to bring into her marriage. Her purchases included teacups and saucers, a tea set, plates, platters, and butterboats, as well as yards of muslin, cord, calico, and shirting.

Men's store purchases commonly underwent a shift with their marriages. In the months before marriage, their purchases generally were not focused on items likely to be useful in their new homes. After their marriages, the purchases take on a more utilitarian bent. The month he married Rebecca Whittemore, Edmund Blodgett purchased a rocking chair and six dining chairs. In succeeding months his new bride brought to the store forty palm-leaf hats, the credits for which amounted to slightly more than the cost of the chairs.

Martha Alexander Allen and Rebecca Whittemore Blodgett were typical of other unmarried daughters who had accounts in their own names and married in the course of the 1830s. For twelve of sixteen such women noted in Whittemore's accounts, the exact dates of their marriages are known. On average these women opened accounts in their own names almost five years before their marriages. Thus they would have had ample time to build up credit or make purchases of goods to bring into their marriages. Moreover, twelve husbands subsequently had store accounts. Only five of the men had accounts before their marriages, three of whom had had previous hat credits. All twelve husbands, however, did have hat credits in their postmarriage accounts. The median output for these young wives amounted to 265 hats in the first five years of their marriages. Hat making was a skill well adapted to the family economy in Fitzwilliam. In terms of the store goods these young women brought into marriage and the store credit their hat making provided in the first years of their marriages, it is evident that outwork permitted women to make a significant contribution to their new families.[65]

Outwork hat making had an even greater impact on the incomes of widows in the community. Tracing the experiences over time of married couples and surviving widows makes this point most graphically. In the Whittemore ledger for 1850 there were hat-making accounts for eight widowed women that can be linked back to the accounts of their husbands before they died.[66] Hat credits in widows' accounts were slightly less than had been the case in their husbands' accounts, with the median figure declining from eighty-nine to seventy-eight hats per year after the husbands' deaths. Widows' hat output probably declined as they aged and also as daughters married and left their households. Still, hat making remained a significant source of income for widows, whose hat-making accounts continued for 12.5 years on average after their husbands' deaths.

The experiences of these women reveal how Fitzwilliam families came to rely on the steady, if modest, income that hat making provided. All told, these eight families made more than twenty thousand hats for Whittemore, earning $220 each over periods that averaged eighteen years. Hat making had become a major source of cash income for Fitzwilliam women in these decades. Although hat-making income amounted to a modest $12 a year, the total of $220 per family was quite substantial. It probably would have taken a teenage daughter four or five years of mill employment to have saved this much money to contribute toward her

65. There is a striking similarity here to the pattern described for English outwork knitting regions in David Levine, *Family Formation in an Age of Nascent Capitalism* (New York: Academic Press, 1977), pp. 51, 61–62.

66. Dexter Whittemore & Son Collection, vol. 55. Linkage is based on tracing backward from the widows' accounts in volume 55 to widows' and husband's accounts in earlier volumes. Excluded are cases where no husband's account was found or cases in which the dates of husbands' deaths were unknown.

family's expenses. A son employed as a farm laborer might have had to work three or four seasons to have earned as much.

Much of what emerges from this analysis of palm-leaf hat making is consistent with the picture presented earlier of outwork weaving. There are, however, two important differences. First, hat makers accepted outwork much more steadily, and they continued working for Dexter Whittemore for much longer than had earlier handloom weavers. Although Jillson's outworkers had averaged $31 in weaving over a seventeen-month period, palm hat outworkers continued to braid for Whittemore throughout the 1830s and 1840s. Single women appeared in accounts in their own names and continued to work on their husbands' accounts after marriage. Married women, in turn, continued to braid hats as widows after their husbands' deaths. Hat making became a lifelong activity for women in Fitzwilliam in this generation. Rather than being simply a short-term expedient as weaving had been, outwork hat making was fully integrated within the family economy of this farming region in the antebellum decades.

Outwork weaving was short-lived and episodic in comparison with the braiding of hats. Moreover, there was a distinct shift in the groups performing outwork over time. As noted earlier and in sharp contrast to the pattern for outwork weavers, Fitzwilliam hat-making families were considerably poorer than non-hat-making families, owning on average almost $900 less in real property in 1850.

The difference between property ownership among hat makers in Fitzwilliam and weavers in Richmond reflected an important change in the place of outwork in the countryside. Both forms of outwork provided by-occupations for farmers' wives and daughters during the slack winter season. Weaving, however, required investment in a loom; hat making did not. Furthermore, weaving made sizable permanent demands on space within the home, whereas hat braiding could be taken out or put away at a moment's notice. Members of poorer farming families with small homes could have undertaken hat braiding, although earlier they might not have been able to buy a loom and take in yarn for weaving. Finally, the growing variety of store goods available as the century progressed may well have tempted more families to do outwork to gain access to this growing market. These factors meant that hat braiding at mid-century appealed to a larger proportion of the rural community than had weaving earlier. Although 42 percent of Richmond families wove for Jillson at some point in the 1820s, the proportion of Fitzwilliam families making hats for Whittemore reached 69 percent by 1850.

This increase in the proportion of outworkers meant that growing numbers of rural residents were drawn within the orbit of capitalist wage and market relations. Not only were more rural families drawn into outwork over time, but the economic standing of these families shifted as well. Increasingly, families making palm-leaf hats were drawn from among poorer families in the community, although outwork and the market involvement that it permitted had first appealed to wealthier farming families.

Contemporaries were aware of the place of outwork hat making in rural New England. Charles Carleton Coffin, the local historian of Boscawen, New Hampshire, writing in 1878, recalled the concentration of hat making among poorer farming families of that community.

> The industry [hat making] was not a universal one. The merchants paid cash only in part, making, of course, a large profit on the goods sold. Families in comfortable circumstances would not engage in an employment in which they would be at the mercy of the merchant, who, though he might be scrupulously honest, yet could fix his own profit and their measure of gain. It was a jug with only one handle, and that in the hands of the merchant. Notwithstanding this drawback, the industry gave employment to a large number of women and girls, who otherwise had little chance of earning money.[67]

This New Hampshirite had an understanding of the place of hat making in the rural economy that is confirmed by the Fitzwilliam evidence.

The impact of outwork on rural communities in New England in the first half of the nineteenth century was significant. Outwork income permitted rural families to supplement their agricultural earnings and to support themselves on steadily smaller holdings in the face of increasing competition from more productive midwestern farms. In Fitzwilliam, for instance, the number of households increased from 222 to 297 between 1830 and 1850, numbers that reflect declining farm sizes. In this

67. Charles Carleton Coffin, *The History of Boscawen and Webster, from 1733 to 1878* (Concord, N.H.: Republican Press Association, 1878), p. 641.

way, outwork contributed to the family farm and lessened the flow of outmigration that so troubled New Englanders in the second half of the century.[68] Yet, although outwork lent support to the farm economy, it also reflected forces changing that economy over time. Farmers and members of farming families were far more engaged in markets, both as producers and consumers, at mid-century than had been the case two generations earlier.

Outwork had a contradictory impact on the transition to wage labor for New England women in the nineteenth century. It offered women an alternative to factory employment, permitting them to live at home and continue to participate in the family farm economy while earning wages. Thus it allowed married women both to contribute to their families' purchasing power and to fulfill their domestic responsibilities. In this respect, outwork was an alternative to the emerging system of urban female wage labor.

On the other hand, outwork was an early form of wage labor; members of farming families provided labor for outwork organizers and in return were paid in yarn, cash, or store credit. They were dependent on their suppliers for raw materials—machine-spun yarn, split palm leaf, or leather uppers—and for the marketing of finished products. Outworkers were no longer independent producers of agricultural goods that might be consumed, traded with neighbors, or sold to a variety of purchasers. In this regard outwork did not offer women and their families the kind of independence offered in this period by dairying and butter making.[69]

Still, outwork shielded women workers (and their families) from a number of the consequences generally associated with wage labor. Their labor did not require them to leave their own homes. Moreover, their

68. Between 1820 and 1850, Fitzwilliam's population grew by 27 percent; in contrast, three Merrimack County, New Hampshire, towns with less outwork and more migration to the mill town of Lowell—Boscawen, Canterbury, and Sutton—suffered a population loss of 6 percent in the same period. Obviously, multiple factors were at work here, not outwork alone. The growth of a vigorous woodenware industry in Fitzwilliam, with resulting employment opportunities for young men, may also have played a part in its population growth.

69. Joan M. Jensen, *Loosening the Bonds: Mid-Atlantic Farm Women, 1750–1850* (New Haven: Yale University Press, 1986). On the changing character of farm women's roles in butter making in the second half of the nineteenth century, see Nancy Grey Osterud, *Bonds of Community: The Lives of Farm Women in Nineteenth-Century New York* (Ithaca: Cornell University Press, 1991).

work remained entirely unsupervised. There was no disjuncture between home and workplace and no factory discipline dictating their every action while at work. These facts meant that women could work at a pace dictated by their own (or their families') needs and circumstances. The lack of any sort of industrial work discipline among dispersed outworkers was a source of distress to mill agents and shoe manufacturers, but it must have been a source of satisfaction to rural workers unwilling to accept the new discipline of factory production.

One might argue that poverty and declining agricultural productivity provided a spur to outwork production that factory overseers otherwise supplied, but the evidence is weak for this line of argument. Average outwork income was extremely low; outwork simply could not have provided a major source of income for most farm families. Furthermore, there is no indication that outwork production of individuals or families increased over time. Recall, after all, that average annual hat credits for Whittemore's customers grew only marginally, from $16.43 to $16.96 between the early 1830s and the 1850s. Farm families did not become increasingly dependent on outwork income but used it to supplement agricultural income.

A third transitional element is evident in the way that outwork accommodated the demands of family farming. Outwork was done when it suited farming families, by those family members most free from farm responsibilities. First, family members wove cloth or braided hats in the winter months when the seasonal demands of farming were least. Second, work was concentrated at a point in the family cycle when labor was most available (that is, when the children were teenaged and still unmarried) and the individual or family income provided was most needed. On all three scores—the location of work, the lack of factory discipline, and the compatibility of outwork and farm work—outwork was well suited to rural beliefs and practices.

And yet outwork was not simply a replication of existing work practices on the family farm. Some young women did work for themselves and controlled the store credits they amassed. Equally significant, young women with their own accounts worked considerably harder at hat making than did their sisters who worked on family accounts, which suggests that they exercised some control over how they allocated their labor. For example, such hat making may well have come at the expense of farm chores they had formerly been expected to do. It certainly came at the expense of hat making done on their fathers' accounts. In this regard, the coexistence of factory wage labor in mill towns and outwork in rural communities may have given farm daughters a new leverage within their families. It seems likely that some fathers had to permit daughters to earn more by outwork, lest they follow others they knew who had left for mill towns such as Lowell or Lawrence. In that case, fathers risked losing the domestic labor and home earnings of their daughters altogether.

Even so, the experience of outwork may well have prompted some young women to seek the greater earnings that textile factories offered, often only a few miles from their farm homes.[70] Reminiscences of millworkers often compared mill wages quite favorably with more limited outwork earnings.[71] These differences were undoubtedly common knowledge among rural women. Outwork and factory work were part of the same world for daughters of New England farmers, and by the 1830s and 1840s, young women moved freely between the two.

In this context rural outwork must be viewed as transitional; it shared characteristics of earlier labor practices and at the same time opened the way for new ones. It was integrated within the rural family economy, and the income earned by farm women helped them sustain the family farm in this period. Yet, at the same time, outwork provided prospects for and imperceptibly merged into individual wage labor. As such it in-

70. Evidence of subsequent employment of outworkers at rural mills is mixed. In Dudley and Oxford, Massachusetts, few outworkers apparently found their way into Slater's mills; see Jonathan Prude, *Coming of Industrial Order*, pp. 87–88. At the Jewett City Cotton Manufacturing Company, about 20 percent of families employed inside the mill were simultaneously doing outwork weaving for the firm. See Home Production Book, Labourers' Time Book, and Agreements of Firm for the 1811–1814 period, Urban Archives, University of Connecticut, Storrs. Finally, Fowler argues that many outworkers for the Blackstone Company found their way into factory occupations; see "Rhode Island Handloom Weavers," p. 229.

71. Harriet Farley, editor of the *Lowell Offering*, had worked at straw braiding and shoebinding before she began work in Lowell. See Edward T. James et al., eds., *Notable American Women, 1607–1950: A Biographical Dictionary*, vol. 1 (Cambridge: Belknap Press of Harvard University Press, 1971), p. 596. See also Harriet H. Robinson, *Loom and Spindle; or, Life among the Early Mill Girls* (Kailua, Hawaii: Press Pacifica, 1976; originally published in 1898), p. 87. For a woman who gladly gave up shoebinding for mill employment, see Blewett, *Men, Women, and Work*, p. 44.

conspicuously facilitated the entry of New England women into wage labor as the century progressed. The full implications of this development became apparent only gradually. It was in the early cotton textile mills of New England that rural women in large numbers had their first taste of the social and economic independence that wage labor outside the home made possible, and it is to that experience that we now turn.

3. Lowell Millhands

The growth of industrial outwork in the New England countryside reflected the emergence of manufacturing and broader markets for consumer goods in the region. Such work offered farmers' daughters opportunities to contribute to their families, save for their marriages, and
sample a widening range of purchases available in country stores. For
many young women who enjoyed the economic benefits of outwork employment in the first third of the nineteenth century, still greater opportunities beckoned in New England's cities and mill towns. The rapid
growth of textile manufacturing in the region meant there were commonly shortages of workers in the antebellum mills, and mill agents
periodically hired recruiters to go into the countryside and bring newcomers to the mills.[1] Between 1830 and 1860, tens of thousands of these
"daughters of freemen" answered the call of urban employment and
made the journey from farm to factory.[2]

One of these young women was Mary Paul. At the age of fifteen,
Mary Paul had already left home and was living with a farming family
in Bridgewater, Vermont. The life of a farm servant did not agree with
her, however, and she left to reside with relatives. From there she wrote
home to her father in nearby Barnard: "I want you to consent to let me
go to Lowell if you can. I think it would be much better for me than to
stay about here. I could earn more to begin with than I can any where
about here. I am in need of clothes which I cannot get if I stay about

1. For early correspondence between a Lowell mill agent and a labor recruiter, see John
Clark to Jesse Huse, July 27, 1847, Lowell Historical Society Collection, Center for Lowell
History.

2. The language quoted here is that of Lowell mill operatives during an early labor protest in
February 1834. See Thomas Dublin, *Women at Work: The Transformation of Work and Community
in Lowell, Massachusetts, 1826–1860* (New York: Columbia University Press, 1979), p. 93.

75 Young Women

From 15 to 35 Years of Age,

WANTED TO WORK IN THE

COTTON MILLS!

IN LOWELL AND CHICOPEE, MASS.

I am authorized by the Agents of said Mills to make the following proposition to persons suitable for their work, viz:—They will be paid $1.00 per week, and board, for the first month. It is presumed they will then be able to go to work at job prices. They will be considered as engaged for one year, cases of sickness excepted. I will pay the expenses of those who have not the means to pay for themselves, and the girls will pay it to the Company by their first labor. All that remain in the employ of the Company eighteen months will have the amount of their expenses 'to the Mills refunded to them. They will be properly cared for in sickness. It is hoped that none will go except those whose circumstances will admit of their staying at least one year. None but active and healthy girls will be engaged for this work as it would not be advisable for either the girls or the Company.

I shall be at the Howard Hotel, Burlington, on Monday, July 25th ; at Farnham's, St Albans, Tuesday forenoon, 26th, at Keyse's, Swanton, in the afternoon; at the Massachusetts' House, Rouses Point, on Wednesday, the 27th, to engage girls,---such as would like a place in the Mills would do well to improve the present opportunity, as new hands will not be wanted late in the season. I shall start with my Company, for the Mills, on Friday morning, the 29th inst., from Rouses Point, at 6 o'clock. Such as do not have an opportunity to see me at the above places, can take the cars and go with me the same as though I had engaged them.

I will be responsible for the safety of all baggage that is marked in care of I. M. BOYNTON, and delivered to my charge.

I. M. BOYNTON,

Agent for Procuring Help for the Mills.

Figure 3.1. Broadside advertising for women operatives, 1859. Courtesy of Baker Library, Harvard Graduate School of Business Administration, Boston, Mass.

here and for that reason I want to go to Lowell or some other place."[3] With these lines, one teenage New England daughter began a journey that took her from the farming country of the northern Connecticut River Valley to the burgeoning mill town on the Merrimack River.

3. Mary Paul to Bela Paul, September 13, 1845, Mary Paul Letters, VHS.

Paul's experience was much like that of other female operatives in the antebellum period. She arrived in Lowell in November 1845 and worked in the mills off and on for almost four years. Surviving letters to her father chronicle a series of subsequent moves and jobs until in 1857, at the age of 27, she married Isaac Guild, a marbleworker and son of her former boardinghouse keeper in Lowell. The couple moved to Lynn, Massachusetts, where over the next five years Mary Paul Guild gave birth to two sons. For this Vermonter, the mill experience marked a permanent shift from a rural childhood to an adult life within the expanding urban industrial world of Massachusetts. After Lowell, she lived briefly with her widowed father, but once married and settled in Lynn, she left her rural past behind. The cultural distance she traveled was reflected in an 1855 letter in which she described meeting acquaintances from her Vermont hometown whom she found "rather countryfied in their ideas."[4]

Mary Paul's years in Lowell are more fully documented than those of the tens of thousands of other New England daughters who took similar stagecoach trips from their farming homes to work brief stints in the cotton textile mills of Massachusetts and southern New Hampshire and Maine. Still, we are not limited to surviving letters, diaries, and reminiscences in our efforts to reconstruct the mill experience of women in the antebellum decades. The early textile mills pioneered in the keeping of corporate records, and the register books of the Hamilton Manufacturing Company in Lowell, Massachusetts, permit a fuller and more representative view of women millworkers than do surviving writings.

When a newcomer appeared at the gates of the mill yard of the Hamilton Manufacturing Company in the mid-1830s, she was ushered first into the ground-floor counting room of the corporation. There the mill agent, clerk, and paymaster had their desks and saw to the smooth running of the record keeping associated with a large manufacturing establishment. The agent was in touch with overseers in the various mill departments and if he knew of an opening would see that the newcomer was properly placed. The clerk, in turn, would record in leather-bound

4. Mary Paul to Bela Paul, June 11, 1855, Mary Paul Letters, VHS. For the full text of this correspondence and an introduction to the letters, see Thomas Dublin, ed., *Farm to Factory: Women's Letters, 1830–1860*, 2d ed. (New York: Columbia University Press, 1993), pp. 121–53.

Figure 3.2. Hamilton Manufacturing Company, Lowell, Mass., c. 1850. Courtesy of Lowell Historical Society.

register books, in a neat, slanted hand, information summarizing the assignment. He noted in ruled rows and columns the name of each operative and her nativity, room assignment, residence in Lowell, and date of entry into the mill work force. A narrow blank column permitted the clerk to note the operative's subsequent date of departure and a wider column remained for lengthier comments. There the clerk might record information about the operative's previous work experience, such as "new," "never in Lowell," "old," "on Lawrence last," or "worked in Nashua." Conversely, on signing an operative out of the mill, the clerk might add a comment for future reference: "regular notice," "short notice," "willful," "does not answer the purpose," or "at liberty to work elsewhere."[5] Finally, if the millhand transferred from one room in the mill to another or moved from one boardinghouse to another, the clerk would record that change as well. Theoretically at least, at any given time, the clerk had a record of the room assignment and local address of all operatives in the company's employ.

The Hamilton Company register books provide unique evidence on female workers in a firm typical of a large number of textile mills across northern New England in the antebellum years.[6] They contain information that permits one to explore labor discipline and turnover. Because they record nativity, they also permit exploration of the changing ethnic makeup of the mill work force.[7]

Entries in the register books provide the actual hometowns of New England operatives, allowing analysis of the geographical origins of the company's female work force. Over the antebellum decades, as the proportion of immigrant Irish working in the mills increased, the number of New England women entering the company's employment declined. Still, in the mid-1830s, the native-born made up more than 95 percent of the mill work force, and in the first six months of 1836, almost 600 women left 249 hometowns in Massachusetts, Maine, New Hampshire,

5. Hamilton Manufacturing Company Records, vols. 481–505, BL.. For an analysis of discipline problems evident in the register volumes, see Carl Gersuny, "'A Devil in Petticoats' and Just Cause: Patterns of Punishment in Two New England Factories," *Business History Review* 50 (Summer 1976): 131–52.

6. On the representativeness of the Hamilton Manufacturing Company, see Dublin, *Women at Work*, app. 5.

7. See Dublin, *Women at Work*, pp. 26, 139.

and Vermont to work at the Hamilton Company. Over a similar six-month period in 1855, only 170 New England women from 111 different hometowns entered employment at the company.

Northern New England was a major supplier of new recruits to the female work force at the company. Initially, New Hampshire towns predominated among those communities sending young women to the Hamilton Company. That state accounted for 44 percent of hometowns represented and almost 55 percent of the women who entered the company's mills in the first half of 1836. By 1855, Maine had become the leading state, accounting for 37 percent of hometowns and 44 percent of women workers starting employment at the company.[8]

Mapping the hometowns of women workers recruited to the Hamilton Company in the first half of 1836 (see Figure 3.3) reveals them to have been widely dispersed across northern New England, with concentrations found in Massachusetts towns close to Lowell and New Hampshire towns in the Merrimack River Valley stretching north of Lowell. These were the areas first joined to Lowell by stagecoach, and once the first recruitment channels were established in the early years, additional newcomers followed a pattern of chain migration. Over time, though, as immigrants came to displace Yankee women in the mill work force, Yankee recruits came from a declining number of hometowns, which were increasingly located in more remote areas in New England. Thus, between the mid-1830s and the mid-1850s, the number of women millhands from Maine increased relative to those from Merrimack River Valley towns in New Hampshire.

Mapping the hometowns of women operatives at the Hamilton Company reveals much about changing recruitment patterns over time but is valuable for other reasons as well. Knowing the hometowns of Yankee women operatives permits one to examine changes in the countryside that contributed to the growth of mill employment among rural young women. Moreover, pinpointing workers from specific New England hometowns allows one to trace women millworkers back to their families of origin, follow their careers in mill employment, and examine

8. For parallel evidence on the shifting geographic origins of New England women workers at the Hamilton Company between 1830 and 1860, see Robert G. Layer, "Wages, Earnings, and Output of Four Cotton Textile Companies in New England, 1825–1860," Ph.D. diss., Harvard University, 1952, pp. 184–89.

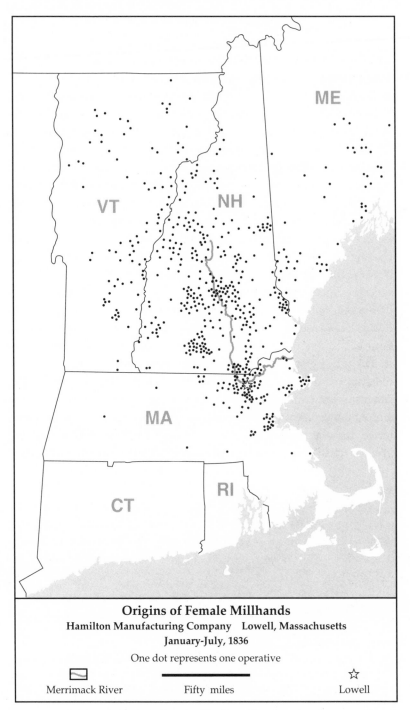

Origins of Female Millhands
Hamilton Manufacturing Company   Lowell, Massachusetts
January–July, 1836

One dot represents one operative

Merrimack River   Fifty miles   Lowell

Figure 3.3. Origins of female millhands, Hamilton Manufacturing Company, Lowell, Mass., January–July 1836. Outline map courtesy of the National Survey, Chester, Vt.

their lives after they left the mills. A population of 410 millhands who entered employment at the Hamilton Company between 1830 and 1850 and who came from six New Hampshire towns—Boscawen, Canterbury, Lyndeborough, Northfield, Sanbornton, and Sutton—provides the focus for the following analysis of women operatives (see Figure 1.1 in Chapter 1 for the locations of these communities).[9] Tracing the lives of these women mill operatives offers a broad view of the impact of mill employment on this first generation of factory workers.

At the outset it should be noted that there was considerable variety in terms of the kinds of towns from which women millworkers came. Boscawen, Canterbury, Northfield, and Sanbornton, for instance, were river valley towns with level bottomlands periodically enriched by soil deposited by the flooding of the Merrimack River. Sutton and Lyndeborough, in contrast, were hill-country towns where sheep grazing predominated and less farm produce was shipped to markets beyond the towns' boundaries (see Figure 3.4). Still, population pressure on limited farm acreage led sons and daughters in both valley and hill-country towns to look for opportunities in New England's expanding urban centers in the decades before the Civil War. These six towns had a combined population in 1830 of 10,362, a figure that fell by 3 percent over the course of the next two decades.[10] Excellent stagecoach and then railroad service linked these rural communities to Lowell and other mill towns and made it relatively easy for young women, even from hill-country towns

9. I began mapping the hometowns of mill operatives by drawing populations of 587 women workers who entered the Hamilton Company between January and June 1836, another 297 for six months in 1845, and another 171 for 1855. The final selection of hometowns was a two-step process, as I first selected for tracing the towns of Boscawen, Canterbury, and Sutton with 175 millhands. I reported findings for that population in *Women at Work*, chap. 3 and app. 2. Subsequently, I selected another three towns—Lyndeborough, Northfield, and Sanbornton—to raise the size of the millhand population to 410, a number I felt would provide more reliable results. I continued to trace millhands from the first three towns, so the findings reported here reflect new evidence on that group as well. For a discussion of the drawing of the mill population, see Appendix 2 below. For information on the methods employed in record linkage, see Appendix 3.

10. "Aggregate Amount of Each Description of Persons," *Fifth Census; or, Enumeration of the Inhabitants of the United States, as Corrected at the Department of State, 1830* (Washington: Duff Green, 1832), p. 11; and J. D. B. DeBow, *Statistical View of the United States . . . Being a Compendium of the Seventh Census* (Washington: Beverly Tucker, 1854), pp. 338–93.

Figure 3.4. Keyser Lake and the hill farms of Sutton, N.H., hometown for forty-eight women operatives employed at the Hamilton Company in Lowell between 1830 and 1850. Courtesy of Robert Bristol.

such as Sutton, to travel between their farm homes and urban locations (see Figure 3.5).

To anticipate how these broader pressures were felt in the lives of rural women who became millworkers, we can outline the experiences of four New Hampshire sisters who worked at the Hamilton Company in the 1830s and 1840s. No single biographical sketch—not even a composite based on four sisters—can entirely capture broader social patterns, but the family of Samuel and Eunice Fowler of Boscawen, New Hampshire, will serve us well, and the survival of extensive evidence on numerous family members makes the resulting portrait far richer than is possible for most families of millhands in the antebellum decades.

In 1830 we find the family of Samuel and Eunice Fowler residing on Corser Hill overlooking the Blackwater River in the western part of Boscawen, just north of Concord.[11] As spring turned to summer, Samuel

11. The following sketch is based on a variety of sources: Hamilton Manufacturing Company Records, vols. 481–505; Charles Carleton Coffin, *The History of Boscawen and Webster, from 1733 to 1878* (Concord, N.H.: Republican Press Association, 1878), p. 531; Federal Manuscript Census of Population, Boscawen, M19, roll 76, 1850 M432, roll 436, families 13 and 47 and 1860, M653, roll 676, families 759 and 917; Federal Manuscript Census of Agriculture, 1850, Boscawen, New Hampshire Division of Records Management and Archives, Concord;

Figure 3.5. North Sutton store and stagecoach, before 1910. Regular stagecoach service made it relatively simple for young women from New Hampshire to go to and from Lowell and other mill towns. Courtesy of Robert Bristol.

and Eunice, both 49, found themselves directing the three children still living at home in the tasks that were needed to make their farm productive.[12] One son, Stanton, 19 years old that summer, undoubtedly helped his father with the work in the fields. A younger son, Nathaniel, had died in 1825 at age 6. Two older sons, Rufus and Cephas, lived elsewhere,

Lowell, Mass., city directories; *Vital Records of Lowell, Massachusetts, to the End of the Year 1849,* 4 vols. (Salem, Mass.: Essex Institute, 1930); N.H. Dept. of Vital Statistics, indexes of births, marriages, and deaths; Boscawen and Webster, N.H., town vital records; "Deaths in Boscawen," NHHS; Merrimack County Registry of Probate, Concord; and Boscawen tax inventories, 1830. I especially thank Dorothy Sanborn and David Ruell for assistance with this sketch.

12. A fourth youngster, a boy between 5 and 9 years of age, also resided in the household according to census enumerators, but his age does not agree with surviving genealogical evidence, so he cannot be identified with any of the known Fowler children. The uncertainty of the language here stems from the fact that the 1830 census records only the names of heads of households. All other household members are recorded by sex within age categories, which then requires inferences to specify which family members lived at home at this date.

although Rufus later returned to work the family homestead. Of the five Fowler daughters, only two, probably Harriet, 13, and Elizabeth, 6, were enumerated as living at home in the census. Three other daughters, probably Mary, Eunice, and Sarah, ranging in age from 24 to 16, were not living with their parents at this date. Several may have been working in Lowell, although surviving mill records only confirm their employment at slightly later dates. We see as early as 1830 that the Fowler family was already beginning to disperse from the family homestead, even before any of the children married.

The Fowlers worked a farm that was typical for Boscawen in this period. Their tax placed them at the sixty-eighth percentile among taxpayers in 1830, paying more taxes than about two-thirds of Boscawen's residents at this date. The farm included an acre of orchard, an acre of tillage, five acres of mowing, and another twelve of pasture. Unimproved land and buildings were valued at $150, but we do not know precisely how many additional acres were available to expand the improved portions of the farm. A horse, two asses, and six cows constituted their livestock. It was actually a rather small operation. Although six people lived there in June 1830, the Fowlers probably would have been hard-pressed to house and support ten family members had all been living at home that summer. Moreover, it would have been a tight fit to squeeze the entire family into the farmhouse, a two-story Georgian colonial that still stands today.[13]

Crowding at home and the need to save something in the way of marriage portions probably motivated the daughters' decisions to work in the cotton mills of the Hamilton Company. Sarah worked off and on for four years beginning in 1831, and her sister Harriet worked for six years. She was joined at the mill in 1836 by her older sister Mary. Finally, the youngest of the Fowler sisters, Elizabeth, left home in February 1841 at 16 and spent just over a year as a weaver in the Hamilton mills.

Four of the five Fowler daughters worked in Lowell in their teens and through their midtwenties. The work enabled them to see more of the world, to earn something in anticipation of marriage, and to ease crowding within the Fowler home. All five of the daughters married,

13. See Webster History Committee, *Webster, New Hampshire, 1933–1983: History* (Webster: Webster Publishing Committee, 1984), pp. 206–7.

two settling in Boscawen, two in or adjacent to Lowell, and the other marrying a man from Boston. Only one of the five appears to have become a farmer's wife like her mother.

We know less about the sons, though two did settle in Boscawen and become farmers. Stanton married and operated a farm in 1850 with seventy-five improved and ten unimproved acres. His older brother Rufus remained unmarried in 1850, living with his parents on the family homestead. Together, son and father (now 72 and probably no longer the chief worker on the farm) cultivated one hundred acres, harvesting 80 bushels of Indian corn, 35 bushels of oats, 14 bushels of rye, 30 tons of hay, and 250 pounds of potatoes. The women in the household kept busy as well, producing 100 pounds of butter and 200 pounds of cheese.

Samuel Fowler probably counted himself a lucky man. In 1860, though widowed at the death of his wife, Eunice, three years earlier, Fowler was a ripe 82, residing with his son Rufus, with another son and two married daughters living nearby. From the smallish farm of seventeen improved acres that he had cultivated in 1830, Fowler had lived to see four of his nine children settled in Boscawen. And the mill employment of his daughters had contributed to the social reproduction of his family over time. In a world marked by dramatic economic change and significant migration out of rural New England in these decades, Samuel Fowler had seen his children well off into their lives as adults. He and his oldest son, Rufus, died within six months of each other in the first half of 1867.

The Fowler story contains virtually all the elements that emerge in an analysis of the 410 women operatives who came from six New Hampshire towns to work at the Hamilton Company between 1830 and 1850. The four daughters came from a large farming family of above average wealth. They worked in Lowell for brief stretches and then married. Two returned to their hometown upon marriage; two settled in Massachusetts. Within a single family they encompass the range of experiences shared by mill women in these decades. Let us turn now to that broader story.

The New Hampshire millhands were representative of native-born women employed at the Hamilton Company before 1850. About 73 percent began work before 1840. About half worked in the weaving department, with spinning and carding accounting for the next largest groups of women. Like most workers in this period, the millhands had short careers at Hamilton. Almost half worked less than a year at the company, a quarter worked one to three years, and the final quarter worked three or more years in the factory. If we take into account previous and subsequent work stints (as best one can determine from Hamilton and census records), the women averaged 2.7 years of mill employment, a figure that undoubtedly understates reality.

Judging from this population, we find that mill employment attracted young single women who came to Lowell on their own. Almost half of the millhands were between 15 and 19 years of age at entrance, with the mean age being just under 20. On average, the women were only 22 when they left the company. Altogether, only 5 percent of millhands were employed at Hamilton while married or widowed. Furthermore, less than 7 percent of the women lived at home with family in Lowell while employed at the company.[14] More than two-thirds lived in company boardinghouses, the remainder residing with private families or in boardinghouses in the city. All the evidence for the population confirms the contemporary generalization that the mills attracted young single women from rural families for a brief period of years before marriage.[15]

The process of tracing women back to their hometowns and to their families of origin, however, permits us to go beyond contemporary remarks and analyze the backgrounds of this group of mill operatives in greater depth. We know, for instance, the occupations in 1850 of the fathers of somewhat more than a fourth of the millhands. Farmers accounted for more than 76 percent of this group; professionals, in contrast, made up less than 3 percent of fathers with known occupations. The distribution of occupations among fathers of millhands was comparable with that for all male household heads of similar ages in their hometowns (see Table 3.1). Fathers of millhands were slightly more likely to be farmers than were all male household heads of roughly the same age. The property holdings of millhand fathers and of other male household heads were roughly comparable, with medians for real property in 1850

---

14. Altogether, twenty-eight millhands were recorded in Hamilton register volumes as living with family, but only eleven of these women resided with parents. Millhands who lived "off the corporation" were about as likely to reside with married sisters, aunts, and uncles as with parents.

15. Henry A. Miles, *Lowell as It Was and as It Is* (Lowell, Mass.: Powers and Bagley, 1845), pp. 162–94.

Table 3.1. Occupations of fathers of New Hampshire millhands,
1850, compared with male household heads,
ages 60–69, N.H. towns

Occupational group	Millhand fathers	Household heads
Farmers	76.4%	69.2%
Skilled	13.2	13.2
Laborers, semiskilled	7.5	11.2
Professionals, proprietors	2.8	6.4
Totals	106	250

Sources: 1850 Federal manuscript census of population; and linkage of fathers of Hamilton millhands in hometown censuses.

Note: Columns may not add up to 100.0% because of rounding.

being $1,000 for each group. The mean for all household heads was slightly higher than for millhand fathers—$1,410 compared with $1,266— but the difference can be explained primarily by the absence of the very wealthy or the very poor among millhand fathers. On the whole, one can conclude that millhand daughters came from families fairly representative of their rural communities.

Local tax records in 1830 confirm the census findings: millhand fathers were slightly less wealthy than their neighbors. On average, such fathers linked in local tax inventories owned $736 worth of property compared with a mean of $791 for all male household heads in the six towns. Millhand fathers were concentrated in the middle ranges of property owners. Among male household heads unrelated to Hamilton millhands, fully 5.8 percent were recorded in tax inventories as propertyless. Among fathers of millhands, the comparable proportion was only 2.5 percent. Similarly, millhand fathers were considerably underrepresented among the very richest members of these communities. Only 5.6 percent of millhand fathers had real and personal property totaling $2,000 or more, compared with 9.7 percent among other male household heads in the six towns.[16]

16. There were 2,174 taxpayers recorded in inventories for the six towns, 123 of whom were fathers of Hamilton millhands.

Analysis of the tax inventories was aided considerably by linkage in the Federal Manuscript Census of Population, 1830, which permitted identification of taxed individuals as household

A closer examination of the kinds of property owned by millhand fathers and other household heads is revealing. In Lyndeborough, for instance, millhand fathers owned improved acreage valued at $255 on average, compared with only $176 for other male household heads in 1830. Similarly, millhand fathers in Northfield were taxed for 15.3 improved acres, whereas all other male household heads owned only 12.7 acres on average. Unfortunately, such detailed breakdowns on land ownership were not recorded for the other four towns. The evidence here suggests that millhand fathers operated farms that were slightly larger than those of their neighbors. Livestock was an important element in New Hampshire farming in this period, and millhand fathers were taxed for livestock valued at $151 on average, almost identical to the $153 figure for all other male household heads. The families of millhands were not so much poorer than their farming neighbors as they were more likely to be solely engaged in farming than were their neighbors. Census and tax records confirm this pattern.

We may breathe life into these averages by examining two fathers of Sutton millhands, Jonathan and John Harvey. The Harveys were brothers, sons of Matthew Harvey, a town founder and a leading citizen of Sutton, who served in the state legislature and died in 1799, "the wealthiest man in town."[17] Sons Jonathan and John took very different economic paths after their father's death. Jonathan, the eldest son, inherited the family homestead of five hundred acres, located on a level hill above the village of North Sutton, and became a prosperous farmer and the leading politician of the town, serving three terms in Congress. In 1840, his house, barn, and acreage were valued at $2,500, and he had

---

heads. To facilitate such record linkage, I recorded the 1830 tax inventory for each town. In the case of Sanbornton, however, the closest surviving inventory covered 1836, so I used that record. Although the difference in dates for census and tax records for Sanbornton reduced the rate of linkage between the two documents, it did not materially affect the overall analysis.

Tax records for Boscawen, Canterbury, Lyndeborough, and Sutton are found in town offices and were provided through the assistance of town officials. Northfield and Sanbornton inventories survive in the collections of the New Hampshire State Archives, Concord.

17. Augusta Harvey Worthen, comp., *The History of Sutton, New Hampshire*, vol. 1 (Concord, N.H.: Republican Press Association, 1890), p. 41. Biographical sketches of the four sons of Matthew Harvey are offered in vol. 1, pp. 42–46, with genealogical information on the families given in vol. 2, pp. 748–56.

Figure 3.6. Jonathan Harvey homestead, Sutton, N.H., where Caroline Harvey grew up before beginning work at the Hamilton Company in Lowell in 1849. Courtesy of Robert Bristol.

seventeen head of livestock and thirty-one sheep, valued altogether at another $492. A decade later the value of his real estate had reached $4,000. He lived in a substantial farmhouse built by his father, which consisted of two stories and an attic with a center chimney. A one-story ell connected the house to his good-sized barn (see Figure 3.6). After Jonathan Harvey's death in 1859, his widow, Ruth, shared this homestead with the families of two of their married children.

Jonathan and Ruth Harvey had a small family by contemporary standards, four daughters and a single son, who died before reaching his second birthday. Of the four daughters, at least two—Hannah and Caroline—lived in Lowell for stretches in the late 1840s. Caroline lived with her married older sister in Lowell while working as a weaver at the Hamilton Company in 1849.

John Harvey "was not fond of farming" according to his daughter, the compiler of Sutton's local history.[18] He learned a mechanical trade

18. Worthen, *History of Sutton*, p. 45.

Figure 3.7. John Harvey homestead, Sutton, N.H., where Theresa and Sophia Harvey grew up before entering the Hamilton mills in Lowell in 1838 and 1848, respectively. Courtesy of Robert Bristol.

but did not fare nearly as well as his older brother. In 1840 he was taxed for only one hundred dollars of real estate and apparently owned no live-stock whatsoever. A decade later, he owned three hundred dollars worth of real estate and a single cow. No wonder that he reported his occupa-tion on the census as that of laborer; there was no way that he could have supported his wife, son, and five daughters on a holding of this scale. The family home, though good-sized, was much simpler and less well situated than that of his older brother (see Figure 3.7).

Two of John Harvey's daughters, Theresa and Sophia, worked at the Hamilton Company between 1838 and 1850, and a third married a Lowell man and lived there for at least four years. Sophia worked only a few months in Lowell in 1848 and married in June 1849. She bore three children in Sutton between 1851 and 1856, but her husband and father both died in that decade, leaving her a 38-year-old widow who worked as a tailoress to support her young children. She reported a paltry thirty dollars in personal property and no real property to the census enumerator who visited her household in 1860.

Neither Jonathan nor John Harvey was typical of the fathers of millhands generally, but their circumstances give a sense of the upper and lower bounds as far as the economic fortunes of the families of millhands are concerned. Overall, absolute economic need does not appear to have been the primary determinant that led rural women to Lowell and mill employment. Had that been common, one would expect a larger proportion of women to have come from the poorest of rural families, which was not the case. Neither did large numbers of rural families move to Lowell with their children to send daughters into the mills. Still, we may reasonably ask: Did these daughters feel an obligation to contribute to their families back home? Did their parents demand that they contribute toward family support? In other words, did the family economy perspective argued by Tilly and Scott in the European context hold for early millhands in New England?[19]

On an ideological level, the belief that single daughters "should" contribute to help support their families was widespread in New England in this period. In stories appearing in the *Lowell Offering*, for instance, millhand authors invariably noted the selfless motives that led women to enter mill employment. Several stories showed that mill wages permitted orphaned daughters to contribute to the support of younger siblings; in another, two sisters contributed to pay off the mortgage on the family farm; and in yet another tale, a widow worked in the mills to support her children.[20] Still, we should be skeptical of these stories as representative of actual behavior. Writers in the *Lowell Offering* marshaled evidence against contemporary critics who complained about the new freedoms and independence that mill employment allowed women. Whether always self-consciously or not, these millhand authors were making their best case that mill employment, after all, was compatible with traditional values, such as the subordination of daughters within the patriarchal family economy.[21]

---

19. Louise A. Tilly and Joan W. Scott, *Women, Work, and Family* (New York: Holt, Rinehart, and Winston, 1978), p. 109, as discussed above in Chapter 1.

20. *Lowell Offering*, vol. 1, pp. 161–71, 263–66, and vol. 2, pp. 145–55, 246–50.

21. For an exchange along these lines where the contemporary debate is explicit, see *Lowell Offering*, February 1841, p. 45.

For a more believable and more complex view of women's motivations and women's place in the rural family economy, the surviving correspondence of millhands for these years is particularly useful. There the picture that emerges is a more mixed one than is evident in the pages of the *Lowell Offering*.

Some women did send money back to their families in the countryside. Jane Tolford Stevens, a 42-year-old widow, left her 14-year-old daughter with an aunt when she first entered employment in Lowell. After working for a period, she encouraged her aunt to send her daughter Sophie to Lowell and mailed five dollars to help pay for stage fare and cloth for a new dress. She added, however, that if Sophie already had the dress, her aunt should keep the extra money for her own use.[22]

Where mill operatives sent money home, one can almost always find specific family difficulties that made such aid necessary. Between 1850 and 1855, Anna Mason worked in the mills of the Amoskeag Corporation in Manchester, New Hampshire. Her Vermont family had recently suffered economic misfortune, and she expressed satisfaction in her newfound independence: "I am not living upon my friends or doing housework for my board but am a factory girl."[23] Her parents had evidently been forced to give up the family homestead, and Anna Mason sent store goods and money to help them improve their situation. She sent ten dollars in September 1851 and another thirty dollars in March 1853. She may well have sent money on other occasions, because in two other letters she asked her parents if she should send them something.[24]

The letters are also interesting because of the relationship they reveal between Anna Mason and her parents. Anna did not have to work in the mills; she had attended the Thetford Academy and had experience as a teacher.[25] Several times in her correspondence she mentioned opportunities to teach, but it does not appear that she accepted the

22. Jane Stevens to Jane Patten, Lowell, March 22, 1835, Tolford-Patten Collection, box 6, New Hampshire State Library, Concord.

23. Anna Mason to her parents, Manchester, N.H., n.d., Anna Mason Letters, Bronson Collection, Huntington Library, San Marino, Calif.

24. Anna Mason to her father, Manchester, September 25, 1851, March 28, 1853, and Anna Mason to her mother, Manchester, October 14, 1853, Jan. 13, [1856], Bronson Collection.

25. In the period before high schools were common in rural communities and before normal schools developed a monopoly on teacher training, it was common for young women to attend a private academy for a number of years to prepare themselves for teaching. There was

offers.[26] Furthermore, she repeatedly indicated her love for her parents and her desire to spend more time with them. Still, she noted frequently the good wages she was earning in the mills and her need to remain in Manchester. In a typical comment she wrote, "I want to see you all very much but I am making good wages now and if I go home I see no way of earning anything through the spring."[27] Her parents occasionally asked her to return home, but Anna Mason exercised her own judgment in deciding how long to remain in Manchester. As she wrote her mother: "I did not mind you when you wished me to leave the mill. We were making such good pay that I wanted to work a little longer." Two months later, Anna reported her earnings at more than four dollars per week, an excellent wage for a workingwoman at this date.[28] Although Anna Mason felt responsible to assist her parents, she evidently had a major voice in determining how she provided that assistance, when she returned home, and how long she continued to work in the mills.

The Larcom sisters in Lowell in the early 1840s helped support their widowed mother back in Beverly, Massachusetts. Theirs is an unusual case, for the family moved to Lowell from Beverly in 1835 after the death of their father. Lois Larcom took charge of a company boarding-house, and her daughters worked at the Lawrence Manufacturing Company.[29] At least two, and sometimes four, daughters worked at any one time, earning a total of almost eleven hundred dollars in the years between 1836 and 1839.[30] Their combined mill income was undoubtedly

---

such a school in Thetford, Vermont, which Anna Mason attended before working in the Manchester mills.

26. Anna Mason to her parents, Manchester, February 12, 1853, and March 18, 1853, Bronson Collection.

27. Anna Mason to parents, Manchester, February 12, 1853, Bronson Collection.

28. Anna Mason to her mother, Boscawen, March 18, 1853, and Anna Mason to her mother, Manchester, May 16, 1853, Bronson Collection. Typical women's mill wages at this date were around $3.50 a week; see Dublin, *Women at Work*, pp. 66, 159, 197.

29. Lucy Larcom, *A New England Girlhood: Outlined from Memory* (Boston: Northeastern University Press, 1986; originally published in 1889), chap. 7; and Shirley Marchalonis, *The Worlds of Lucy Larcom, 1824–1893* (Athens: University of Georgia Press, 1989), especially chap. 2.

30. The earnings of the Larcom sisters at the Lawrence Manufacturing Company have been determined by tracing their employment in the mills of that company between 1835 and 1846. Volumes in ser. GA, GB, GD, GE, and GF, Lawrence Manufacturing Company Records, BL.

greater than that of their mother in these years. The next year, their mother returned to Beverly, but the sisters continued to work in the mills until at least 1845.[31] Emeline, the oldest of the Larcom sisters in Lowell, took charge of the others and kept up a regular correspondence with her mother. On ten occasions between May 1841 and May 1842, Emeline sent her mother small sums, which together totaled more than fifty dollars. She typically wrote once a month, just after payday, and commonly enclosed five or six dollars with each letter. This total is probably an underestimate of the daughters' contributions, as there are gaps in the correspondence, months when Emeline (or another daughter) may have sent money home but for which letters have not survived. Moreover, the daughters visited Beverly regularly, occasions when they also may have brought money home.

Emeline Larcom's letters are revealing about the circumstances that influenced the amount she and her sisters were able to send their mother. In August 1841, Emeline noted that she would have sent more, "but as Lucy is coming to B[everly] we have not quite so much as usual." In February 1842, she explained why the sum she was sending was a dollar short: "Lucy found it necessary to spend more for herself than usual this month." In January 1841, Emeline expressed her disappointment at not being able to send as much as she would have liked. Future prospects, however, were good: "After this month Octavia will be in the mill, and then I shall not have her board to pay and she will be earning, then we shall be able to send more." The letters indicate that the Larcom sisters met their own immediate needs first and then cooperatively sent money through Emeline to support their mother.[32]

Whether or not daughters actually contributed directly to their families back home, their departures from the rural home relieved their parents

31. Lowell city directories show Lois Larcom residing in the city between 1835 and 1839 and then again in 1844. The Lawrence Company payrolls are the only way to trace the whereabouts of her daughters.

32. Emeline Larcom to Lois Larcom, August 18, 1841, Larcom Collection, Marion B. Gebbie Archives and Special Collections, Wheaton College, Norton, Mass.; Emeline Larcom to Lois Larcom, February 5, 1842, January [15], 1841, Larcom Family Collection, Emeline Larcom Letters, EI. For a fuller discussion of these letters and transcriptions of the set, see Thomas Dublin, "The Mill Letters of Emeline Larcom, 1840–1842," *Essex Institute Historical Collections* 127 (July 1991): 211–39. The letters are also reprinted in Dublin, *Farm to Factory*, 2d ed., 1993, pp. 97–119.

Figure 3.8. Middlesex Manufacturing Company, Lowell, Mass., c. 1840, where Susan Brown worked. Courtesy of the Museum of American Textile History.

of the necessity of supporting them. Eben Jennison of Charleston, Maine, wrote to his daughter in Lowell in 1849 in words that reflect this aspect of the difficulties facing rural families: "The season with us has been verry Dry and the Drough[t] verry severe. The crops are very light indeed and business verry Dull. If you should be blessed with your health and are contented I think you will do better where you are than you could do here." By 1858, two of Jennison's daughters were working in Lowell, apparently sending money occasionally to help him out. In one of his letters, Jennison acknowledged receipt of five dollars and expressed the hope that "some day or other" he would be able to repay them with interest. It is clear that Jennison supported his daughters' decisions to go to Lowell, but not because he expected them to contribute to his subsistence as a matter of course. Their contributions were freely offered.[33]

Not all millhands, of course, were able to save from their earnings to help out their parents back home. Mary Paul, for one, felt bad that she was unable to help her aged father: "I hope sometime to be able to do something for you and sometimes feel ashamed that I have not before this." She noted, in a letter in 1853, the obstacles that prevented her: "I am not one of the *smart* kind, and never had a passion for laying up money, probably never shall have, can find enough ways to spend it though. . . . Putting all these things together I think explains the reason that I do not 'lay up' anything."[34]

Susan Brown of Epsom, New Hampshire, worked for eight months as a weaver at the Middlesex Company in Lowell in 1843 (see Figure 3.8). While working she kept a diary that indicates the range of purchases that might have kept a mill operative from saving very much out of her earnings. During the eight-month period, Susan Brown earned just over $86, which probably left her about $42 after paying for room and board. In her diary, she recorded purchases that totaled almost $19 plus a number of additional items without prices noted. Add to these expenditures the costs of at least fifteen plays, concerts, and lectures she attended and a two-day excursion to Boston, and it is unlikely that Susan

33. Eben Jennison to Elizabeth Jennison, Charleston, Maine, September 2, 1849, and Eben Jennison to Elizabeth and Amelia Jennison, July 13, 1858, Jennison Letters, in possession of Mary A. Dinmore, Cheshire, Conn.

34. Mary Paul to Bela Paul, November 27, 1853, and December 18, 1853, Mary Paul Letters, VHS.

Brown had much money jingling in her pockets after paying the stage-coach fare that brought her back home in late September. Susan Brown's diary does not explicitly indicate why she worked in Lowell, but the extent of her evening activities, purchases, and social life suggests distinctly personal motivations.[35]

Susan Brown's motivations remained unstated, but others went to the mills quite consciously to meet purely personal goals. At times, millhands viewed their personal desires as clearly at odds with parental or family needs. Sally Rice left her home in Somerset, Vermont, in 1838. Her work and travels took her first to a farm in Union Village, New York, and then to a textile mill in Thompson, Connecticut. That she rejected life back on the family farm is clear from an 1839 letter: "I never can be happy there in among so many mountains. I feel as tho I have worn out shoes and strenth enough riding and walking over the mountains. I think it would be more consistent to save my strength to raise my boys. . . . I shall need all I have got and as for marrying and settling in that wilderness I wont. And if a person ever expects to take comfort it is while they are young I feel so."[36] Sally Rice was only eighteen and single when she penned these lines. Still, she had a sense of what her future would bring and how she would shape that future. Working a hard-scrabble farm in northern Vermont was evidently not in her plans.[37]

Another millhand who had personal goals was one Lucy Ann working in Clinton, Massachusetts, in 1851. She had her sights set on

35. Susan E. P. Brown Forbes Diary, January–September 1843, AAS. See also Mary H. Blewett, ed., *Caught between Two Worlds: The Diary of a Lowell Mill Girl, Susan Brown of Epson, New Hampshire* (Lowell, Mass.: Lowell Museum, 1984). My thanks to Mary Blewett for bringing this material to my attention.

36. Sally Rice to her father and mother, Union Village, New York, 1839 (date unknown), Hazelton Rice Papers, VHS. My thanks to Michael Folsom for making photocopies of the original letters available to me. For published versions of the letters, see Gary Kulik, Roger Parks, and Theodore Z. Penn, eds., *The New England Mill Village, 1790–1860* (Cambridge: MIT Press, 1982), pp. 385–92; and Nell Kull, ed., "'I Can Never Be Happy There in among So Many Mountains'—The Letters of Sally Rice," *Vermont History* 38 (1970): 52.

37. Lest the reader feel that only young workingwomen could resist the pressures of the rural family economy, similar expressions of independence are evident in the writings of young men as well. James Metcalf left Lowell during one period of unemployment and took a tour of

attending Oberlin College and wrote a bit defensively in a letter to a cousin, "I have earned enough to school me awhile, & have not I a right to do so, or must I go home, like a dutiful girl, place the money in father's hands, & then there goes all my hard earnings." Lucy Ann summed up her thinking: "I merely wish to go [to Oberlin] because I think it the best way of spending the money I have worked so hard to earn." Clearly, some mill women felt their earnings were their own, to dispose of as they wished.[38] As did Sally Rice, Lucy Ann evidently felt some pressure to be a "dutiful girl" and contribute her earnings to the family till. Still, she resisted this pressure and followed her own inclinations.

Although some millhands may have been able to express these independent sentiments only beyond the bounds of their families, in other cases family members obviously supported daughters' decisions as to how to spend their hard-won earnings. In 1840, Elizabeth Hodgdon of Rochester, New Hampshire, wrote to her sister, Sarah, who worked in the nearby mills of Great Falls: "You say you want to come home when we all think you have staid long enough, but we do not know better than you or so well either when you have earned as much as you will want to spend. Yet it is Mothers opinion & mine that you have already as much as you will probably want to spend if you lay it out to good advantage which we doubt not but you will."[39] One does not sense from this letter (or from others in the series) that the Hodgdon parents were counting on using their children's earnings for some familial purpose. Nor does one sense that Sarah Hodgdon was saving for any particular purpose; her marriage, for instance, was more than five years in the

---

a number of industrial towns in New England. His purpose, however, was not to find work. As he wrote to his mother, "I have but one life to live and while I live I has as good enjoy my money so hardly earned, in innocent pleasures, you may say it is foolish, it may be." James Metcalf to Chloe Adams Metcalf, Lowell, July 19, 1846, Adams-Metcalf Letters, MATH.

38. Loriman Brigham, ed., "An Independent Voice: A Mill Girl from Vermont Speaks Her Mind," *Vermont History* 41 (1973): 142–46, quotation, p. 144.

39. Elizabeth H. Hodgdon to Sarah D. Hodgdon, Rochester, N.H., March 29, 1840, Hodgdon Letters, NHHS. These letters are also reprinted in Dublin, *Farm to Factory*, 2d ed., pp. 39–57.

future at this time. Mill earnings (or earnings from teaching, for that matter) appear most commonly to have belonged to the young women who earned them to spend or save as they chose.[40]

Women also generally decided when they would return home and when they would continue working. Sarah Metcalf worked in Lowell in the mid-1840s and had two brothers and two sisters also employed in that city. Writing home to her mother in Winthrop, Maine, she expressed the way millhands took responsibility for their wage work.

> Mary [a sister] gets along well also. I do not think it is best for her to go home this fall on any account unless you need her as she has just got to earning something, if her health remains good as I think it will.

She was no more reticent in expressing her own plans.

> And now Mother I am going to propose a plan that we Lowell folks have formed, which is, that I stay here all winter, and go home in the spring, and then I shall not feel obliged to come back again for a year, if ever, whereas if I go home this fall I shall have to come back in the spring. My reasons for this are, first, I am here *now* and *very pleasantly situated* which is a good deal for factory girls to say, and I think if I am going to work in Lowell any more, I had better stay now, for it is ten chances to one if I can get so good a chance to board, if I do to work. Secondly, I am making three dollars, and three and a half, a week, and Clough [the overseer] says he will do as well by me all winter if I will stay.

As if to buttress her proposal, Sarah did not take sole responsibility for the plan she proposed, but wrote that "we Lowell folks" had reached this conclusion jointly. She continued with several more good reasons for her plan and concluded by noting what led her to want to spend the winter and spring in Lowell: "I can probably lay up fifty dollars besides having my teeth fixed, and getting my next summers clothes." She was

---

40. The economic independence of the Hodgdon sisters may have been a function in part of their lengthy periods of employment. Sarah worked at least ten years as an operative and married at 32; Elizabeth taught for at least eleven years, marrying at 28. Dublin, *Farm to Factory*, 2d ed., p. 41.

nothing if not practical, and she evidently was confident that these reasons would sit well with her mother.[41] The tone of the letter suggests the degree of independence young people could enjoy while working in the mills.

Evidently millhands were found along a broad continuum representing the degree to which they were enmeshed within a rural family economy while employed in the early mills. At one extreme, we find Anna Mason sending clothing, store goods, and money to her family; at the other, we find Lucy Ann saving her earnings to attend Oberlin College. In between were many women who made small contributions or none at all, depending on their own needs and those of their families, but who in any event appear to have had considerable latitude in deciding how to spend their earnings. The early millhands remained tied, emotionally and economically, to their rural families, but they made choices about where and when to work and how and how much to contribute to their families that set them apart from rural women in earlier generations.[42]

Personal economic gain certainly played a part in motivating young women to leave their rural homes to work in the Lowell mills. Yet not all young women flocked to the mills. On what grounds can we distinguish the women who worked in the mills in the antebellum decades from those who did not? Were there any systematic differences that account for the willingness of some daughters to leave the comfortable and familiar and strike out for Lowell and the mills? A closer examination of the families of Hamilton millhands offers answers to these questions.

The families of millhands were large. On average, they included 7.5 children, with 4.3 daughters.[43] Typically, a Hamilton millhand was a second child but a first daughter in a very large family. Almost a third of first daughters in these families were millhands, a proportion considerably higher than for younger daughters. In fact, as Table 3.2 reveals,

41. Sarah Metcalf to Chloe Adams Metcalf, Lowell, September 29, year unknown, September 25, 1846, Adams-Metcalf Letters.

42. This work also set women apart from other New England daughters engaged in industrial outwork within rural communities in this period. The contrast between mill women discussed here and outwork weavers and hat braiders described in Chapter 2 is particularly striking.

43. These figures exclude children who died before the age of 2 but may include children who did not live to adulthood. In all, the number of children in the family of birth is known for 255 millhands.

Table 3.2. Rank birth order of New Hampshire women employed
at the Hamilton Company, 1830–1850

Rank order among daughters	Number of daughters in rank	Number of daughters at Hamilton	Percentage
First	234	72	30.8
Second	234	68	29.1
Third	199	48	24.1
Fourth	156	32	20.5
Fifth and higher	198	14	7.1
Overall	1,021	234	22.9

Sources: Reconstitution of the families of Hamilton millhands is based on published local genealogies and unpublished local and state vital records.

Note: Includes only daughters drawn from families with two or more daughters for whom rank birth order is known.

the likelihood that a daughter would be employed at the Hamilton Company decreased dramatically moving from first to second and down to fifth daughters. The youngest daughters in these families appeared on Hamilton payrolls in only 7 percent of the cases, a proportion less than a fourth of that for eldest daughters.

Given the large size of these New Hampshire families, pressure on living space in the home would have been greatest as the oldest children entered their teenage years. The domestic labor of first daughters may also have been superfluous by the time they reached twenty, thus making it that much easier for families to permit them to go to Lowell. By the time the younger children reached their late teens, however, the family would have been smaller and the children's contributions to the family farm economy probably more crucial, which offers an explanation for the recruitment pattern evident among millhands at the Hamilton Company.

As a whole, mill women tended to be first and second daughters, but we find an interesting shift over time. A comparison of millhands who first entered the Hamilton mills in the 1830s with those who began work in the 1840s is instructive. Looking at the families of early millhands, we find that almost 32 percent of first daughters were employed at Hamilton. As with the population of millhands as a whole, the proportion declined steadily with second and later daughters. Among the families of later millhands, however, fourth daughters entered mill employment in the highest proportion, 36 percent. First and second daughters were also common, but they did not predominate to the same extent as among the families of early millhands. A good share of millhands in the 1840s were evidently younger sisters of operatives—fully eleven of fourteen millhands who were fourth or fifth daughters in their families of origin and began working at Hamilton in that decade worked with or were preceded by older sisters.

If birth order influenced whether a particular daughter entered mill employment, early parental deaths also played a role. In a fair share of millhand families, the father died before or during the daughter's stint in the mills. Such was the case for fully 17.6 percent of the families of millhands where evidence survives. Examination of censuses of the six New Hampshire towns in 1850 confirms this finding. Among families of millhands found living in their hometowns in 1850, more than 21 percent were headed by females; for all households in these towns headed by men or women of similar ages, the comparable proportion at that date was less than 16 percent. The difference here is not dramatic but does indicate the slightly greater proportion of daughters who entered mill employment from female-headed households.

At this point we can summarize factors that did or did not influence the entrance of young women into the mill work force. Poverty itself did not drive rural daughters to enter the mills, as millhands came from middling farm families. These were large families, however, and a lack of future prospects in static or even declining farming communities undoubtedly played a role in women's choices. Initially, millhands were drawn disproportionately from first daughters in large farming families. Later, however, both younger daughters and first daughters came in large numbers. Finally, the death of one or both parents sometimes contributed to daughters' decisions to seek work. Ultimately, young women and their families made very individual decisions, and there are limits to our ability to reconstruct their motivations. Another way to get at the issue is to examine factors that influenced not the decision to enter the mills but the length of time a millhand remained in employment. Indirectly, at least, this approach addresses the question of motivation.

As contemporaries noted, the careers of women millworkers were brief. New Hampshire women at the Hamilton Manufacturing Company remained in the employ of the firm for an average of only 2.3 years and worked in mills for at least 2.7 years overall.[44] Clearly, the fact that millhands came from propertied farming families and could return to the family homestead influenced this pattern. We might expect that rural families who migrated to Lowell were more dependent on the earnings of their daughters and that their daughters, in turn, would work longer periods in the mills. Surprisingly, however, those millhands who lived with family in Lowell while working at the company did not work longer than did those who came on their own and boarded in the city. Mill hands who lived at home with parents or relatives in Lowell worked for 2.2 years on average at the Hamilton Company, a figure identical to that for those who resided in company boardinghouses.

Furthermore, the early death of a parent was not associated with longer careers at the Hamilton Company. Millhands whose fathers died before or during their stints in the mill worked 3.0 years at Hamilton on average; women whose fathers died later worked 2.6 years on average. Similarly, the difference in the lengths of careers of millhands according to the dates of death of their mothers is a slight 0.3 years. In this instance, millhands whose mothers died early actually had slightly shorter stints at Hamilton than did others. As millhands were often oldest daughters, perhaps they were called home to take over the domestic work previously done by their mothers. In neither case, however, is the difference large enough to provide assurance that it represents a significant trend.

One final factor that did not influence the length of women's employment was family wealth. In all, it was possible to ascertain the local property tax paid in 1830 by the fathers of 180 millhands.[45] Millhands whose

44. This transiency of Lowell millhands contrasts with the experience of female operatives in English silk mills. Judy Lown found that a majority of women workers employed in the Courtauld Mill in Halstead in 1861 worked ten or more years for the firm. They continued to work after marriage, taking off only brief periods for the birth of children. Lown, *Women and Industrialization: Gender at Work in Nineteenth-Century England* (Cambridge: Polity Press, 1990), p. 49.

45. This number is greater than the figure of 123 fathers given in n. 12 above because of the large number of sisters working at Hamilton. In all, 123 fathers of 180 millhands were successfully traced in local tax inventories.

fathers paid taxes below the median for the whole group worked 2.5 years on average at the Hamilton Company. Those whose fathers were in the richer half of the population worked 2.9 years on average. Ruling out these possible familial influences on the length of women's employment in Lowell reinforces the argument that emerged from women's letters: it was a woman's personal situation and preferences rather than family need that most influenced what she did after arriving in Lowell.

Two factors were associated with longer stints of work at the Hamilton Company: having other relatives employed in the firm and remaining single. Family information has been uncovered for 255 of the 410 women from the six New Hampshire towns and clearly reveals that women did not come to the mills as solitary individuals. Overall, more than 63 percent of millhands of known families had siblings also working at Hamilton in the period; including cousins raises this figure to 67 percent. And fully 82 percent of millhands had relatives living in Lowell in these decades.[46]

Millhands with other family members at Hamilton remained in the work force longer than those who worked entirely on their own. Those with siblings at Hamilton, for instance, worked 3.3 years at the firm on average; for those working alone, the comparable figure was only 2.2 years. Shifting our focus from employment at the Hamilton Company to residence in the city of Lowell yields similar results. Millhands with siblings in the Hamilton work force remained in Lowell for 7.3 years on average, compared with only 5.4 years for the others.

Family members eased the shock of adjusting to an urban setting for newcomers to Lowell. They also assisted siblings and cousins in finding jobs. Julia A. Dutton, of Clintonville, Massachusetts, described the arrangements she made in an 1847 letter to her mother in Vermont: "I have engaged a place for Martha Coffren the first of Nov[ember]. The overseer sayed she might come at that [date] and if she is large enough for a weaver he will take her if not she can go into some other room. There is no doubt but she will work a plenty. She will have [$]1.25 [a week above board] while she is learning to weave."[47] Similarly,

46. As in the earlier discussion of residence patterns, it should be emphasized that these relatives living in Lowell rarely included either parent.

47. Julia A. Dutton to Lucretia Dutton, Clintonville, Mass., September 26, 1847, Lucretia Wilson Dutton Papers, Special Collections, University of Vermont Library, Burlington.

Elizabeth Jennison undoubtedly provided support for her 19-year-old sister, Emily, who joined her in Lowell in 1849. Their father, Eben Jennison, wrote to his daughter in Lowell to fill her in on her sister's plans: "A few words in relation to Emily. She has got about ready to come to Lowel. Martha A. Marshall expects to return to Lowel in the course of some two or three weeks and if Emily comes she will come with hir. I should not consent to hir coming at any rate if you was not there. She is young and needs a mothers care and a mothers advise. You must se to hir and give hir such council as you thinks she needs. She may be Homesick for a spell but if you comfort hir up she will soon get the better of it."[48]

Another mill operative in Lowell took just this kind of maternal interest in her younger sisters. Emeline Larcom wrote to her mother in Beverly, Massachusetts, about her youngest sister, Octavia: "She is doing pretty well, though you know she needs much cultivation. I do not forget that you have given her to me with a charge. I hope I shall always be to her what you wish me to be." We do not know how Octavia responded to her sister's oversight, but another sister, Lucy, described Emeline's efforts in very positive terms: "She watched over us, gave us needed reproof and commendation, rarely cosseted us, but rather made us laugh at what many would have considered the hardships of our lot."[49]

Emotional support was only a small part of what an experienced millhand might offer a younger sibling interested in working in Lowell. She could lend money to permit a sister or brother to come down to Lowell by stagecoach in the first place; she could make arrangements with her boardinghouse keeper for housing or with an overseer for a job and generally provide information and personal support crucial to finding one's way in the mills. Charles Metcalf, at work as a doffer in the Massachusetts mills in 1844, did all these things to help his sister Mary make the transition to Lowell.[50]

48. Eben Jennison to Elizabeth Jennison, September 2, 1849, Jennison Letters. The next summer found Emily and Elizabeth Jennison residing together in a Lowell boardinghouse. Federal Manuscript Census of Population, 1850, Lowell, M432, roll 328, family 1176.

49. Emeline Larcom to Lois Larcom, Lowell, January [15], 1841, Emiline Larcom Letters; and Larcom, p. 167.

50. Charles Metcalf to Joseph and Chloe Metcalf, Lowell, April 27, 1844, Adams-Metcalf Letters. Rebecca Ford offered the same help to her sister Caroline; see David A. Zonderman,

Kin support proved helpful to newcomers in adjusting to the demands of mill employment in Lowell, but it made life easier for them in yet another way. A word from an older sibling to an overseer could smooth the way for a better job assignment for a newcomer. Among New Hampshire millhands at the Hamilton Manufacturing Company, for instance, women with siblings employed at the company were more likely to begin in better-paying jobs than women without such support. Although 51 percent of millhands with siblings at the company began work in the weaving department, only 44 percent without siblings did so. One reason women with relatives at Hamilton remained longer at the company must have been the better job placement and higher pay they enjoyed because of this kin support.

In taking advantage of kin networks in securing work, finding housing, and persisting in Lowell, Yankee millhands established practices that remained common in New England mill towns even after immigrants had displaced native-born operatives. Tamara Hareven found similar patterns among French Canadians in Manchester, New Hampshire in the early twentieth century.[51] What distinguished Yankee patterns in the 1830s and 1840s from later developments was the almost exclusive reliance on siblings and cousins for assistance and the relative absence of parents from these early kinship networks in Lowell. More than 230 millhands from the six New Hampshire towns had relatives in Lowell while they were working at the Hamilton Company, but only two of their fathers and nine of their mothers ever definitely resided in the city.[52]

Although kin connections led millhands to work longer in the mills, marriage—the formation of new family ties—generally marked the end

---

"From Mill Village to Industrial City: Letters from Vermont Factory Operatives," *Labor History* 27 (Spring 1986): 265–85, especially pp. 274, 276.

51. Tamara K. Hareven, *Family Time and Industrial Time: The Relationship between the Family and Work in a New England Industrial Community* (Cambridge: Cambridge University Press, 1982), chap. 5.

52. The disparity in numbers for mothers and fathers reflects the opportunity that Lowell offered to widowed women to keep a boardinghouse and send some of their children into the mills. At least three mothers of New Hampshire millhands kept boardinghouses for the Appleton or Hamilton Company. For contemporary reminiscences by members of the families of Lowell boardinghouse keepers, see Larcom, *New England Girlhood*, and Harriet H. Robinson, *Loom and Spindle; or, Life among the Early Mill Girls* (Kailua, Hawaii: Press Pacifica, 1976; originally published in 1898).

of women's mill employment. Single women made up virtually the entire female work force.[53] It is not surprising, then, that women who
never married had longer careers at the Hamilton Company, remaining
an average of 3.9 years. Those who definitely did marry averaged only
2.4 years. Clearly, neither group made mill employment a lifelong undertaking. Still, the difference between the two groups is striking. The
evidence reinforces the generalization that emerges from examining the
property ownership of the parents of millhands. Family economic need
was not a crucial determinant of the length of time women workers remained at the Hamilton Company. Individual need more than family
need influenced the lengths of women's careers in the mills. The evidence demonstrates that mill employment offered single women economic support that permitted them a degree of independence unusual
in New England in the first half of the nineteenth century. Still, single
women did not remain in Lowell very long, and when they reached
their thirties, they made other living and working arrangements. Even
for this group, mill employment was simply a brief encounter.

The evidence on the careers of women mill operatives corroborates
contemporary accounts that emphasized the impermanence of the textile
mill work force in the antebellum decades. Contemporary observers,
however, were not united in their accounts of the effect of mill employment on the marriageability of female millhands. Orestes Brownson, for
instance, complained:

> But the great mass [of operatives] wear out their health, spirits, and
> morals, without becoming one whit better off than when they com-
> menced labor. . . . The average . . . working life . . . of the girls that
> come to Lowell . . . is only about three years. What becomes of them
> then? Few of them ever marry; fewer still return to their native places
> with reputations unimpaired. "She has worked in a Factory," is al-
> most enough to damn to infamy the most worthy and virtuous girl.[54]

53. Again, the contrast with the British experience is striking here. At the Courtauld Mill
in Halstead, more than a third of women operatives were married and over 20 in 1861. See
Lown, *Women and Industrialization*, p. 58.

54. Orestes Brownson, "The Laboring Classes," *Boston Quarterly Review* 3 (July 1840):
369–70.

Writers in the mill operatives' magazine, the *Lowell Offering*, did not take kindly to Brownson's remarks and strongly defended their choice to work in the mills.[55] Other writers, even without sharing Brownson's critique of early wage labor, had concerns about changing tastes among rural women which reflected the growing influence of urban practices. In 1824 a Vermont writer complained about "a propensity among those in ordinary circumstances, to ape the rich, and also a false taste, by which some of our country misses attempt to heighten the charms of their persons by excessive ornament in dress."[56] Critics of this variety may have felt that mill employment made farmers' daughters less fit for marriage—not because they had been exploited and worn down by their work in the mill but because they had become citified and uppity.

With the opinions of contemporaries so divided, we had best turn to the direct evidence concerning the 410 New Hampshire millhands working at the Hamilton Manufacturing Company between 1830 and 1850. What do their life experiences offer to the debate?

The first thing we can say is that mill employment did not disqualify women for marriage. Evidence is available for almost 72 percent of the women, or 295 in all. Fully 85 percent of these women did marry, generally soon after their stints of mill employment. The proportion of mill women who never married, or 14.6 percent, is strikingly similar to statistics calculated by demographers for all New England women in this period. Peter Uhlenberg has estimated that 14.6 percent of Massachusetts women born in 1830 never married. The demographic data confirm the finding that mill employment did not disqualify New England women for subsequent marriage.[57]

55. *Lowell Offering*, December 1840, pp. 17–18.

56. Zadock Thompson, *A Gazetteer of the State of Vermont* (Montpelier: E. P. Walton, 1824), p. 39.

57. Peter R. Uhlenberg, "A Study of Cohort Life Cycles: Cohorts of Native Born Massachusetts Women, 1830–1920," *Population Studies* 23 (November 1969): 411, 420. Moreover, if one excludes those women who died before reaching the age of 20, Uhlenberg's proportion of never-marrying women increases to 20.0 percent. See also Yasukichi Yasuba, *Birth Rates of the White Population of the United States, 1800–1860: An Economic Study* (Baltimore: Johns Hopkins University Press, 1962), p. 109. Yasuba offers higher estimates than Uhlenberg for the proportions of married women, but differences in the methods employed may account for this discrepancy.

Millhands, however, do appear to have married later—at 25.3 years of age on average—than was common for New England women generally in this period. Comparable New England studies have generally yielded lower ages at first marriage for women in the antebellum period. Massachusetts vital records reveal a mean age at first marriage of 23.6 for women in 1850, 1855, and 1860. Vermont figures for 1858 show women marrying at 21.4 years of age. For Hingham and Concord, Massachusetts, local studies demonstrate ages for women at first marriage of 23.3 and 23.4, respectively. In only one of five studies, that for Sturbridge, Massachusetts, between 1820 and 1849, did the mean of 25.5 for women's age at first marriage equal that for Lowell millhands.[58] Overall, it would appear that mill employment led rural women to postpone marriage relative to the practices of their peers who did not enter the mills. Perhaps this was the phenomenon that contemporary critics noted when they argued that mill employment unfit young women for marriage.

Millhands tended to marry husbands who were also older than most grooms in this period, averaging 27.4 years of age. Limiting the calculation to cases in which both the husband's and the wife's ages are known reveals an average difference of 2.4 years between the ages at first marriage of millhands and their husbands, a figure comparable with the patterns reported for other studies of marriage in New England in this period.[59]

Although they generally married later than did other New England women in the antebellum decades, millhands were not an entirely homogeneous group. Differences in the timing of marriage are evident based

58. Thomas Monahan, *The Pattern of Age at First Marriage in the United States* (Philadelphia: By the Author, 1951), pp. 161, 173–74, 316–18; Daniel Scott Smith, "Parental Power and Marriage Patterns: An Analysis of Historical Trends in Hingham, Massachusetts," *Journal of Marriage and the Family* 35 (1973): 419–28; Marc Harris, "A Demographic Study of Concord, Massachusetts, 1750–1850," Undergraduate honors thesis, Brandeis University, 1973, p. 42; and Nancy Osterud and John Fulton, "Family Limitation and Age at Marriage: Fertility Decline in Sturbridge, Massachusetts, 1730–1850," *Population Studies* 30 (1976): 481–94.

59. The numbers of cases with known ages at first marriage are 191 for millhands, 117 for husbands, and 114 for millhand and husband together. The conclusion here contrasts with an earlier finding for Lowell millhands based on a smaller number of marriages. See Dublin, *Women at Work*, p. 52. The larger number of cases makes the finding reported here more reliable than was the earlier figure.

Table 3.3. Work and marriage patterns for millhands,
by place of residence for married women, 1850

	New Hampshire	Massachusetts
Age beginning work	20.2 (74)	17.8 (25)
Age ending work	22.0 (74)	20.2 (25)
Age at first marriage	30.5 (74)	23.2 (25)
Husband's age at marriage	34.8 (70)	26.2 (17)
Years between leaving Hamilton and marriage	8.5 (74)	3.0 (25)

Sources: Hamilton millhands and linkage in the 1850 federal manuscript census of population, state and local vital records, and genealogical records.

Note: Numbers in parentheses indicate the number of nonmissing cases.

on the subsequent residence of millhands. Those who married and settled in Massachusetts towns tended to follow the dominant New England pattern, marrying at about 23 years of age men three years older. Those millhands who returned home, however, and married and settled in their hometowns or in neighboring towns waited on average until they were over 30 to marry men who were almost 35 years of age. Table 3.3 summarizes the evidence on the work and marriage patterns of these two groups of millhands. Millhands who married and settled in Lowell or other Massachusetts towns were younger than most millhands when they began work at the Hamilton Company, averaging slightly less than 18 years of age. They typically worked at the company 2.4 years but then married three years after their stint at the company. Those who married and settled in their hometowns or elsewhere in New Hampshire began work somewhat later and worked a slightly shorter length of time at Hamilton—only 1.8 years on average—but the main factor that distinguished them from the Massachusetts residents was the period of 8.5 years between their departures from the Hamilton work force and their marriages.

The older age at marriage of millhands who settled in the countryside undoubtedly reflected rural couples' desire to settle on land of their own before getting married. Husbands in Massachusetts couples resided in cities, followed urban occupations, and had no such need to buy or inherit land before marriage. A steady wage and prospects for advancement came at an earlier age in the growing urban centers of

Massachusetts than did land for homesteads in New Hampshire and surely influenced the marriage pattern evident for Hamilton millhands.[60]

Although female millhands who settled in New Hampshire delayed their marriages until they were 30 years of age on average, we should not assume that they simply lived with their families in the years between working in Lowell and their marriages. The experiences of Rebecca and Caroline Ford of Granville, Vermont, are instructive in this regard. The Ford sisters each worked at the Lawrence Manufacturing Company in Lowell for about a year in the early 1840s. From their correspondence with their family, however, it is clear that they continued to work in a woolen mill in Middlebury, Vermont, for six or seven years after their departures from Lowell. These two working-women appear never to have married, but undoubtedly some of the Hamilton millhands who eventually married back in their hometowns had similar additional work stints closer to home in smaller mills in New Hampshire or Vermont. By no means did Lowell offer the only opportunities for mill employment for Yankee women in these decades.[61]

The evidence on women's age at marriage and the relationship of the timing of marriage to mill employment raise larger questions as to the broader impact of early industrialization on the family lives of millhands. Several authors have explored these issues within a European setting and provide useful comparisons with the Lowell evidence. David Levine, writing about the introduction of framework knitting in the village of Shepshed, in Leicestershire, England, found a decline in the age

60. The seven-year difference in age at first marriage for millhands depending on where they eventually settled may in part be the result of bias introduced in the linkage process. Evidence on marriage comes primarily from two sources: state local records and genealogies. The genealogies, in particular, were compiled well after the dates of millhands' marriages, and those who continued to live in their hometowns for considerable lengths of time were more likely to be recorded subsequently in genealogies. Those millhands who married in their hometowns at a relatively young age may have found no opportunities to own land and set themselves up on a homestead of their own. They would thus have had to move to another town, and the likelihood of their being recorded years later by a local genealogist would have been less than had they married later. Later-marrying millhands would have been more likely to inherit land from fathers or fathers-in-law and thus remain in town and eventually have their marriages recorded in local genealogies. Unfortunately, there is no way to "correct" the data for possible linkage bias on this score.

61. Zonderman, "From Mill Village to Industrial City." See also the letters of Sarah and Elizabeth Hodgdon in Dublin, *Farm to Factory*, 2d ed., pp. 39–57.

at first marriage with industrialization. He argued that the growth of employment opportunities led couples to marry earlier and begin having children immediately. No longer did couples have to wait until they inherited land; they could support themselves in large part on their wages. Furthermore, children were viewed as an economic asset, and framework knitters sought to benefit from their contributions to the family economy as soon as possible.[62]

Framework knitting was an outwork industry that permitted families to remain in the countryside, combining industrial employment and agricultural work. In contrast, employment in the Lowell mills required at least a temporary migration. Millwork was not so readily integrated into the fabric of rural life; it offered rural women an alternative to the family farm, either for a period of years or for good. Its impact as such was not uniform. Some women left their rural homes and married and settled in Lowell. These women married at 23 years of age on average, a figure comparable with that for rural women throughout New England. Curiously, the marriage patterns of millhands who returned to their rural hometowns were most affected by the years in the mills. These women postponed their marriages until they were 30 on average, and a fair proportion—as will become clear shortly—returned home but never married. In either event, mill employment was a major interruption in the life cycle of rural women in the antebellum decades.

Whether they married and settled in the city of Lowell or married later in their hometowns, millhands were clearly influenced by their factory years. The impact of mill employment on women operatives was evident not only in the timing of marriage but also in the occupations of the men they married (see Table 3.4). Although three-fourths of the fathers of millhands had been farmers, only half as many of their husbands were farmers. The low proportion of farmers among the husbands of millhands resulted primarily from the fact that many of the couples settled in cities or mill towns after their marriages. Focusing on

62. David Levine, *Family Formation in an Age of Nascent Capitalism* (New York: Academic Press, 1977), pp. 51, 60–62; and Hans Medick, "The Proto-Industrial Family Economy: The Structural Function of Household and Family during the Transition from Peasant Society to Industrial Capitalism," *Social History* 3 (1976): 291–315. For a useful recent discussion of this literature, see Elinor Accampo, *Industrialization, Family Life, and Class Relations: Saint Chamond, 1815–1914* (Berkeley: University of California Press, 1989).

Table 3.4. Occupations of husbands
of New Hampshire millhands

Occupation	Percentage
Farmers, farm laborers	37.4
Artisans, skilled	36.0
Semiskilled	9.4
Unskilled	9.4
White-collar, professional	7.9
Total cases	139

Sources: Linkage for Hamilton millhands in genealogical and vital records and of their husbands in Lowell city directories and federal manuscript census of population, 1850 and 1860.

Note: Percentages may not add up to 100.0 because of rounding.

husbands who resided after marriage in the six New Hampshire home-towns of millhands produces a different picture. More than 65 percent of these husbands were farmers, a proportion slightly greater than that for other young men in their age cohort in their hometowns.[63] Another way to view this development is to note that rural daughters who had been exposed to urban employment in Lowell but had returned to their hometowns were more committed to farm life than were other young women who had remained at home all along.

Still, for millhands as a group, the proportion of husbands employed as farmers was only about half that for fathers. This was a development, moreover, of which contemporaries were keenly aware. One writer noted the phenomenon in an 1858 article, "Farming Life in New England": "The most intelligent and enterprising of the farmer's daughters become school-teachers, or tenders of shops, or factory-girls. They contemn the calling of their father, and will, nine times in ten, marry a mechanic in preference to a farmer. They know that marrying a farmer is a very serious business. They remember their worn-out mothers."[64] Needless to say, contemporary writers were not pleased to see farmers' daughters apparently rejecting young farmers and demonstrating a preference for urban artisans or white-collar workers. In a declining rural

63. The findings here are based on linkage of husbands in the 1850 federal manuscript census and comparison with other male household heads between the ages of 29 and 40.

64. "Farming Life in New England," *Atlantic Monthly*, August 1858, p. 341.

Table 3.5. Residence at death of New Hampshire millhands,
by marital status

Residence	Did marry	Never married
Hometowns	24.3%	46.2%
Other New Hampshire	37.4	34.6
Massachusetts	33.0	19.2
Outside New England	5.2	0.0
Total cases	115	26

Sources: Linkage of Hamilton millhands in published genealogies, local vital records, and New Hampshire and Massachusetts vital records.

region, the departure of grown sons and daughters simply contributed to further decline. Young people voted with their feet, and their elders did not approve.

Marriage was the means by which millhands who wanted to do so were able to make a break from their families of origin and from the rural communities in which they grew up. Over time there was a steady increase in the proportion of former millhands living away from their hometowns. Just over 19 percent of millhands, for instance, appear to have married in Lowell; by 1850, however, more than 29 percent resided in Massachusetts, most in Lowell. At their deaths, 31 percent resided in Massachusetts towns. That marriage enabled women to move away from their hometowns is evident if we examine millhands' places of residence at death (see Table 3.5). Among former millhands who married, a larger share (33 compared with 24 percent) resided in Massachusetts at their deaths than lived in their hometowns. For former millhands who remained single, the proportion living in their hometowns was more than double that residing in Massachusetts. Single women, although able to support themselves through mill employment, eventually returned to their hometowns to live in the households of parents or married siblings.[65]

All in all, the evidence on marriage and residence patterns points to the influence of mill employment on rural women's lives. For a substantial share of millhands—roughly a third—Lowell represented the

65. For a fuller discussion of the lives of single women in this period, see Lee Virginia Chambers-Schiller, *Liberty, a Better Husband: Single Women in America: The Generations of 1780–1840* (New Haven: Yale University Press, 1984).

first stage in a journey that took women from the rural New Hampshire homes of their childhood into urban adult lives in neighboring Massachusetts. Their first steps through the factory gates began this process, and their choice of husbands often finalized it. The mills offered these rural women a way out and a good proportion took it, thereby declining to follow in the footsteps of their "worn-out mothers."

Several conclusions emerge after following these four hundred New Hampshire women from their rural homes to their entry into mill employment in Lowell and to their lives after the mills. Although economic motives undoubtedly loomed large for these women workers, family economic need was not the principal motivation that led them to enter the mills. Mill employment offered young single women economic and social independence unknown to previous generations of New England women. After brief periods of wage labor, mill women did marry, but a significant proportion, on the order of one-third, did not return to New Hampshire but spent the remainder of their adult lives in Massachusetts cities. The mill experience signaled a decisive step away from their rural pasts. Paid employment in the mills offered young rural women a route to independence from their families of origin. Such a development would not be repeated in the lives of New England workingwomen in succeeding generations.

4. *Lynn Shoeworkers*

Although women textile workers in the antebellum years garnered the lion's share of contemporary notice, they were by no means the only women working for wages. For Massachusetts as a whole, more than sixty-nine thousand women were employed in manufacturing jobs in 1850, with cotton and woolen textiles employing nearly four of ten. After textile operatives, the leading female occupational group in manufacturing consisted of shoeworkers. Totaling more than twenty-two thousand, shoeworkers accounted for almost a third of women employed in manufacturing in Massachusetts at this date.[1]

Their numbers offer one reason for a focus here on women shoeworkers, but there are more compelling reasons to explore the experiences of this group of workingwomen. In contrast to women mill operatives in Lowell, women shoeworkers in Lynn typically lived with their families. Single migrants boarding in the city made up a much smaller share of women workers in Lynn than was the case in Lowell. This difference had important implications for an understanding of the impact of increased wage work for Lynn women in the Civil War period.

Mechanization after mid-century contributed to the growth of Lynn's shoe industry, but shoemaking had employed ever-increasing numbers of women since the last decades of the eighteenth century. Initially, at least, women worked at stitching and lining the upper halves of boots and shoes in their own kitchens. They worked for their shoemaker husbands, who took from them the bound shoe uppers and turned out completed shoes in their artisan workshops. Between 1810 and 1850, the work of shoebinding was steadily dissociated from the family economy,

1. U.S. Census Office, *Abstract of the Statistics of Manufactures According to the Returns of the Seventh Census* (Washington, 1859), pp. 15, 43, 129, 143.

and increasing numbers of women bound shoes for piece wages, working in the employ of unrelated shoe manufacturers. A sexual division of
labor with roots in the division of work roles within artisan families persisted into this later period and relegated women to the lower-paying
work of shoebinding. Male workers, by contrast, enjoyed artisan status
and considerably higher wages as journeymen cordwainers.[2]

At mid-century, women shoebinders typically worked in their own
kitchens, whereas male shoemakers worked in small workshops known
as "ten-footers." Neither group, in 1850 at least, relied on machinery.[3]
During the 1850s, however, the adaptation of the sewing machine for
use in the stitching of leather uppers led to a dramatic transformation of
women's involvement in shoemaking. As binding shoes by hand gave
way to the machine stitching of shoes in home or factory, the number
of women employed in the shoe industry declined significantly. Mary
Blewett has estimated that one full-time machine stitcher could do the
work of eleven hand shoebinders.[4] Consequently, between 1855 and 1865,
the proportion that women made up of the shoemaking labor force of
Lynn declined from 59 to 45 percent, with the total number of women
slipping by almost fifteen hundred over the decade.[5]

2. Mary H. Blewett, "Work, Gender, and the Artisan Tradition in New England Shoemaking, 1780–1860," *Journal of Social History* 17 (Winter 1983): 221–48.

3. Blanche Evans Hazard, *The Organization of the Boot and Shoe Industry in Massachusetts
before 1875* (Cambridge: Harvard University Press, 1921), especially chaps. 4 and 5; Paul G.
Faler, *Mechanics and Manufacturers in the Early Industrial Revolution: Lynn, Massachusetts,
1780–1860* (Albany: State University of New York Press, 1981); and Ross Thomson, *The Path
to Mechanized Shoe Production in the United States* (Chapel Hill: University of North Carolina
Press, 1989), chaps. 3 and 4.

4. Mary H. Blewett, *Men, Women, and Work: Class, Gender, and Protest in the New England
Shoe Industry, 1780–1910* (Urbana: University of Illinois Press, 1988), p. 112.

5. Alan Dawley, *Class and Community: The Industrial Revolution in Lynn* (Cambridge: Harvard University Press, 1976), table 8, p. 246. For a fuller treatment of technological change
in the adoption of the factory system, see Thomson, *Path to Mechanized Shoe Production*,
chaps. 5, 9–11, and *Scientific American*, October 6, 1860, p. 230, and July 4, 1863, p. 4. See
also Helen Sumner, *History of Women in Industry in the United States*, vol. 9 of *Report on
the Condition of Woman and Child Wage Earners in the United States* (Washington: 1910),
pp. 167–74. The richest analysis of the impact of these developments on women shoeworkers
is found in Blewett, *Men, Women, and Work*, chap. 3; see also Mary H. Blewett, "Women
Shoeworkers and Domestic Ideology: Rural Outwork in Early Nineteenth-Century Essex
County," *New England Quarterly* 60 (1987): 403–28.

Although the absolute number of women employed by Lynn shoe firms declined with mechanization, the city itself became a factory town, as central shops and stitching firms recruited full-time, native-born workers for their increasingly centralized operations. The attraction of Lowell for Yankee women declined at the same time, as growing numbers of Irish immigrants found employment there. By contrast, the Lynn shoe industry continued to rely almost entirely on native-born Yankee workers, giving shoe work an appeal that textile factory employment had lost by the 1850s. Finally, shoe stitching customarily paid women $5–6 a week, considerably above the weekly wage of $3.00–$3.50 common in the Lowell mills in 1860. This wage differential and the entry of immigrants into textiles made Lynn an attractive alternative for members of farming families from Maine and New Hampshire eager to earn wages. Lynn therefore attracted a sizable population of recent rural migrants on the eve of the outbreak of the Civil War.[6]

This shift in the relative attractiveness of Lowell and Lynn should not obscure the similarities that mark the histories of these two communities. Lowell between 1830 and 1850 and Lynn during and after the Civil War had much in common. Both were expanding factory towns geared to the production of a single commodity. They were of comparable size, with Lowell growing from about 18,000 in 1836 to 33,000 in 1850, whereas Lynn increased from 19,000 to 38,000 in the twenty years after 1860. Finally, employers in both communities relied on a largely native-born labor force, although the Irish came to play an increasingly important role in each city toward the end of the periods under consideration.[7]

Even with these similarities, however, striking differences distinguished the two employment centers. Textile manufacturing emerged in Lowell after 1823 as a fully mechanized and tightly organized industry. A few textile firms (with interlocking ownership and management) controlled most of the city and operated their businesses to minimize competition. In contrast, shoe production in Lynn evolved more slowly

---

6. Thomas Dublin, "Rural-Urban Migrants in Industrial New England: The Case of Lynn, Massachusetts, in the Mid-Nineteenth Century," *Journal of American History* 73 (1986): 623–44.

7. Dawley, *Class and Community*, p. 245; and Arthur L. Eno, ed., *Cotton Was King: A History of Lowell, Massachusetts* (N.p.: New Hampshire Publishing, 1976), p. 255.

VIEW OF LYNN, MASS.

Figure 4.1. View of Lynn, Mass., by Edwin Whitefield, 1869, Acc. 131,968. Courtesy of Essex Institute, Salem, Mass.

and steadily over three generations after the American Revolution. This resulted in three major differences in the structures of industry in Lowell and Lynn. First, corporations owned by Boston investors dominated Lowell textiles, whereas individual proprietorships and partnerships predominated in Lynn. Second, only gradually did the factory production of shoes emerge out of an earlier system that combined artisan labor within Lynn and outwork labor in surrounding farming communities. Outwork persisted even within Lynn after the Civil War, and considerable work continued to be put out to shoemakers in adjoining communities such as Marblehead.[8] The uneven development of shoe manufacturing led to a greater diversity in working and living arrangements for Lynn shoeworkers in the 1860s than for millhands in antebellum Lowell. Third, shoemaking employed far greater numbers of male workers than did textiles. In 1836, Lowell's work force was 85 percent female; for Lynn in 1860, the comparable figure was only 40 percent. These differences held important implications for the family lives of workingwomen in the two factory towns.

The Civil War period was a boom time for Lynn shoemaking, as firms mechanized and shoe output skyrocketed. The wartime inflation raised shoe prices, and the resulting profits underwrote extensive new investment that contributed to the growth of the city and the emergence of a downtown shoe factory district (see Figure 4.1). Federal manuscript censuses of manufacturing taken in 1860 and 1870 provide vivid evidence of this expansion (see Table 4.1).[9]

In the ten-year period, capital invested in shoemaking increased by 50 percent (in real terms), and the value of boots and shoes produced by

8. See the Marblehead listings in Federal Manuscript Census of Manufactures, 1870, in which more than five hundred shoemakers were recorded as employed for manufacturing firms outside the town. Microfilm from the National Archives, T1204, roll 21.

9. Dawley, *Class and Community*, p. 95; and Federal Manuscript Census of Manufactures, 1860, T1204, roll 15, and 1870, T1204, roll 21. I also examined the 1880 manufacturing census for Lynn, T1204, roll 31, but found serious discrepancies in comparison with previous years, which indicated that major portions of the industry in Lynn were not properly enumerated in the latter year. For fuller comments on the adequacy of Lynn manufacturing censuses, see Appendix 6. Inflation of the overall cost of living between 1860 and 1870 amounted to 45.6 percent, a figure based on averaging the three major series, E135, E183, and E184, found in U.S. Bureau of the Census, *Historical Statistics of the United States: Colonial Times to 1970* (Washington: GPO, 1975), pp. 211–12.

Table 4.1. Aggregate statistics for Lynn shoe manufactures,
1860 and 1870

	1860	1870
Capital invested	$1.04M	$1.56M
Value, raw materials	$2.29M	$4.25M
Value, products	$4.91M	$7.64M
Number of workers	9,568	6,849
Number of firms	132	102

Sources: 1860 and 1870 federal manuscript censuses of manufactures, for Lynn, Mass. M = millions. In constant 1860 dollars.

Lynn firms grew by almost 56 percent. Particularly striking about these increases is the fact that they occurred simultaneously with a 28 percent decline in the total number of shoeworkers. Two processes account for this remarkable growth in worker productivity: first, more investment in sewing machines operated by women and McKay machines operated by men greatly increased the productivity of both male and female shoeworkers; and second, with their growing investment in shoe machinery, manufacturers steadily brought more workers into stitching shops and shoe factories powered by steam. Given the new levels of capital investment and the greater productivity thus achieved, manufacturers increasingly relied on full-time workers rather than the part-timers who had characterized the earlier outwork system.

Mechanization in the shoe industry initially affected women's work more than it did that of men. At least 57 percent of women shoeworkers in Lynn in 1870 were employed as machine stitchers in shops and factories.[10] Skilled male shoeworkers were also drawn into factories in the Civil War period, but the displacement of handicraft work by machine production was considerably slower for men than for women. Artisanal

10. The 102 firms enumerated in Lynn in Federal Manuscript Census of Manufactures, 1870, owned 1,525 sewing machines and employed 2,649 women shoeworkers. Of the more than 1,100 women shoeworkers in Lynn not necessarily operating sewing machines in a factory setting, a large proportion likely worked on sewing machines at home. Dawley reports a strong private market for sewing machines in Lynn in the 1860s, and even as late as 1875 about a fifth of females employed in shoemaking in Lynn continued to work in their own homes. Dawley, *Class and Community*, pp. 76–77, 276. See also "The Bay State Strike," *New York Times*, February 29, 1860, p. 3, cited in Eileen Boris and Nelson Lichtenstein, eds., *Major Problems in the History of American Workers* (Lexington, Mass.: D. C. Heath, 1991), pp. 89–90.

work continued within the new factories because it took five or six skilled shoemakers to prepare the shoe uppers and soles for joining by the McKay stitcher or to finish the shoes once the halves were joined.[11] Moreover, the McKay machine so increased productivity that several teams of skilled handicraft workers were needed to supply each McKay machine and operative. Therefore, in the 1860s and early 1870s, only a small share of male factory shoemakers actually tended shoe machinery. Lynn firms in 1870 employed more than four thousand male shoemakers but owned fewer than two hundred McKay machines operated by men. Estimating that perhaps twenty-five hundred of these shoemakers actually worked in factory settings, we find that there were likely ten or eleven male artisan shoemakers employed in Lynn factories for each man operating a McKay stitcher or some other shoe machine.[12]

All in all, a larger proportion of women shoeworkers in postbellum Lynn worked in factory settings than did men, and more of them operated newly developed shoe machinery (see Figure 4.2). The entrance of women into Lynn's emerging stitching shops dramatically changed the nature of women's employment in the shoe industry and coincided with the first systematic recording of women's occupations in the contemporary censuses of population. The richest of these sources, the Massachusetts state census in 1865, noted women's occupations and also recorded specific hometowns of birth for residents of Lynn's three central working-class wards.[13]

11. Dawley, *Class and Community*, p. 93, describes the increased division of labor that accompanied installation of the McKay stitcher in Lynn factories.

12. Federal Manuscript Census of Manufactures, 1870, Lynn. For a slightly smaller estimate, see Mass. Bureau of Statistics of Labor (hereafter cited as Mass. BSL), *Annual Report*, 1871, p. 248. Dawley, utilizing the 1870 population census for Lynn, estimates the number of male factory shoemakers at 2,435. See *Class and Community*, p. 135. On Lynn use of the McKay machines, see Thomson, *Path to Mechanized Shoe Production*, p. 164.

13. Mass. State Census of Population, 1865, Massachusetts State Archives, Boston, wards 3, 4, and 5. The main limitation in drawing a sample of female shoeworkers from this source results from the timing of the census, taken as it was during a slack period in shoe production. Mary Blewett's estimates suggest an average female employment in Lynn of fifteen to eighteen hundred in the mid-1850s and twenty-five hundred in the 1860s, which indicates that only 40–50 percent may have been enumerated in the 1865 state census. In this case, census figures may considerably understate the proportion of single boarders among women shoeworkers, as this group would have been most likely to leave the city in slack periods. Blewett, *Men, Women, and Work*, pp. 105, 329–31.

Figure 4.2. Interior view of I. C. Pray's stitching shop, Salem, Mass., c. 1863. Notice fifteen women working around the outside of the room at sewing machines while two or three others perform handwork at the central table. Courtesy of Lynn Historical Society, Lynn, Mass.

The zealous enumeration by census takers in Lynn in 1865 provides an unusually rich source for exploring the work and family lives of women shoeworkers in that city. Women shoeworkers born in specified hometowns in Massachusetts, New Hampshire, and Maine provide the basis for a random sample for further analysis. Tracing these women in earlier and later censuses and vital records reveals family origins and work patterns among Lynn shoeworkers in the 1860s that contrast sharply with those of Lowell mill operatives a generation earlier.[14]

I had originally intended to draw a sample from the 1860 federal manuscript census, but the relatively low number of female shoeworkers enumerated led me to examine the 1865 census. In all, there were only 486 female shoeworkers enumerated in Lynn in 1860, less than a fifth of the likely number of residents employed by Lynn shoe firms. Underenumeration, and hence bias in sampling, would have been much greater had I relied on the 1860 census for the sample. For counts of women shoeworkers in Lynn in 1860, see Blewett, *Men, Women, and Work*, pp. 330–31. For methods employed in the sampling, see Appendix 2.

14. Given the wider range of hometowns of shoeworkers and the later date of the sample, record linkage for this sample differed markedly from that for Lowell millhands between 1830 and 1850. For a fuller discussion of methods, see Appendix 4.

We may preview the broader differences between women workers in Lowell and Lynn in the experiences of Harriet Jarvis, a member of the 1865 Lynn sample. We cannot be sure precisely when Harriet began working, but in 1865, at the age of 17, she was recorded as a shoe fitter by the enumerator for Lynn's third ward.[15] As such she would have handstitched linings into bound shoe or boot uppers (see Figure 4.3). Her stepfather, George Hale, was a shoemaker, as had been her father, Charles Jarvis, before his death in December 1855. Her mother, Martha, headed the household between her first husband's death and her second marriage in December 1861.

At the age of 18, Harriet married Charles Huse, a McKay operator in a Lynn shoe factory, in September 1866. The young couple continued to live with Harriet's mother and stepfather until at least 1880. Even though the couple's first child, George H. (after his step-grandfather perhaps), was born in September 1869, Harriet Huse was still working as a shoe stitcher when the census enumerator passed through the following June. Given the availability of sewing machines, Harriet may well have been working on shoes at home. Even if she did work in one of Lynn's stitching shops, her mother would have been available to care for the infant. Her husband and stepfather were also employed at shoemaking, so the extended family would have had three wage earners at this date. Young George Huse died in July 1870; a decade later Harriet Huse, now 32, was said to be "at home," where she joined her 55-year-old mother "keeping house." Once again, husband and stepfather were regularly employed in shoe factories.

Harriet Jarvis Huse's story anticipates a number of themes that emerge in the analysis of the 1865 sample of shoeworkers. She was born in Lynn into a shoemaking family. In addition, she worked at least five years in shoemaking, living at home with her parents throughout her employment. Finally, she married a shoemaker and even continued to work as a shoe stitcher for a period after the birth of her first child. On each of these points her career profile diverged from patterns evident earlier for Lowell textile workers.

15. This paragraph and the next are based on tracing Harriet Jarvis and her family, first found in dwelling 157 in ward 3 of Lynn in the 1865 Massachusetts state manuscript census of population. Sources employed in that work included the 1855 state census, federal censuses in 1860, 1870, and 1880, and Massachusetts vital records.

Figure 4.3. "Shoe Fitting," shoe fitters handstitching the linings of women's shoes, *Harper's Bazar*, detail from *Women and Their Work in the Metropolis*, 1868. Courtesy of Smithsonian Institution, Washington.

Shifting our focus from a single individual to women shoeworkers generally reinforces the distinctions apparent thus far. Female shoe-workers in Lynn in 1865 were not drawn from the same population of unmarried young rural migrants who had filled the Lowell mills a gen-eration earlier. Shoe stitchers in Lynn were considerably older than millworkers in the 1830s. They were also more likely to be living with family in Lynn and to be married or widowed than had been true of Lowell operatives. On average, Lynn female shoeworkers were 26 years of age when they began work, whereas their Lowell counterparts were less than 20 (see Table 4.2). The contrast between the two groups is most evident at the extremes of the age spectrum. Almost 14 percent of millhands began work before the age of 15; only 5 percent of female

Table 4.2. Ages of female millhands and shoeworkers
on beginning work

Ages	Millhands	Shoeworkers
Less than 15	13.7%	5.0%
15–19	47.8	35.1
20–24	25.4	25.1
25–29	8.2	12.7
30 and above	4.8	22.2
Total cases	291	402
Missing cases	119	0

Note: Columns may not add up to 100.0% because of rounding.

Sources: Linkage of Hamilton millhands and the 1865 sample of
Lynn native-born shoeworkers.

shoeworkers did so. Conversely, almost 35 percent of shoeworkers began
at 25 or older, whereas only 13 percent of millhands waited that long.[16]

The age difference between millhands and shoeworkers is real and
persists even with a more focused comparison. Migrant shoeworkers who
had been born in Maine and New Hampshire, for instance, had a mean
age at beginning work of 24.9. Migrant shoeworkers were thus about
five years older, on average, than were similar rural migrants to the
Lowell mills a generation earlier.

Lynn female shoeworkers also differed from their Lowell counterparts in terms of marital status. Women shoeworkers were older than
female millhands in large measure because many married and widowed
women found employment with Lynn shoe manufacturers. Fully 19 percent of female shoeworkers in Lynn in 1865 were married; another 10 percent were widowed. In contrast, the proportion of female millhands working after marriage in Lowell in the mid-1830s was only 5 percent. Lynn

16. For both groups, limitations to the available data give the age figures a definite upward
bias. We know when millhands began work at the Hamilton Manufacturing Company, but undoubtedly some of the women worked elsewhere earlier. Similarly, we only have recorded employment for shoeworkers in census years and only beginning in 1860. On both counts we will
understate the number of years a woman worked. Many may well have done some shoebinding in their homes before the advent of machine stitching in Lynn. Still, the contrast between
the ages of millhands and shoeworkers as they began work is too great to be entirely an arti-
fact of census enumeration practices.

shoeworkers were evidently a more diverse group than had been Lowell operatives a generation earlier.[17]

Age and marital status were two dimensions in which shoeworkers differed from millhands; residence was yet another. At the Hamilton Company in Lowell in 1836, more than 88 percent of female millhands boarded in company or private housing. Only 11.5 percent lived with their families in Lowell. In contrast, among Lynn female shoeworkers in 1865, almost 69 percent resided with their families and only 31 percent boarded or lived alone. Although most antebellum Lowell women left their families in the countryside to enter the mills, most Lynn workers were part of an urban family group.[18]

Women shoeworkers in Lynn in 1865 were very much part of a family wage economy. The 272 families living with members of the sample included 615 shoeworkers, an average of 2.3 per family. Shoemaking employed parents and children alike in these households. Almost 58 percent of the fathers of working daughters in the sample were employed in shoe trades. Almost 70 percent of the husbands of married shoeworkers were similarly employed. Unlike the pattern that developed among immigrants in textile towns, the family economy in Lynn involved parents and children, males as well as females.[19]

17. For further evidence from a variety of Lynn censuses that confirms these findings on marital status, see Blewett, *Men, Women, and Work*, app. B. Interestingly, the proportion of married and widowed women among immigrant textile workers in Lowell in 1860 was less than that for native-born shoeworkers in 1865 Lynn. Altogether, 18 percent of immigrant female textile workers in an 1860 Lowell sample were spouses or headed their own households. See Thomas Dublin, *Women at Work: The Transformation of Work and Community in Lowell, Massachusetts, 1826–1860* (New York: Columbia University Press, 1979), p. 168. For a discussion of patterns among French Canadians in Lowell a decade later, see Frances H. Early, "Mobility Potential and the Quality of Life in Working-Class Lowell, Massachusetts: The French-Canadians, ca. 1870," *Labour/Le Travailleur* 2 (Fall 1977): 214–28.

18. The low Hamilton figures are not an aberration, for an 1841 survey of the Boott Manufacturing Company found that only 9 percent of the women had families in Lowell. Mass. House Document no. 50, 1845, app. A, p. 19. Even as late as 1860, only 23 percent of native-born female millworkers in Lowell lived with their families. Dublin, *Women at Work*, pp. 27, 166.

19. The Lowell immigrant work force, by contrast, consisted primarily of teenage daughters; few sons, fathers, or married women worked in the mills in 1860. For a fuller discussion of the immigrant family economy in Lowell, see Dublin, *Women at Work*, chap. 10.

From census enumerations one can see the reliance of Lynn families on the employment of several family members; other studies permit us to quantify earnings of women shoeworkers and determine their significance for family income. Shoeworkers typically earned piece wages, which in Lynn in 1871 averaged a bit more than $10 weekly. Shoe production was seasonal, however, with two slack periods annually, whose lengths varied from year to year. Altogether, shoe stitchers probably averaged eight or nine months of employment a year. Contemporary studies set women's annual earnings at figures that ranged from about $270 to $345, figures influenced no doubt by the overall health of the nation's economy.[20]

Although women shoeworkers earned significantly greater wages than did their textile counterparts, their earnings averaged only 61 percent of those of male shoeworkers. The fact is, however, that male and female shoeworkers were employed in distinctly different occupations. Only six of twenty-four shoe occupations surveyed by the Massachusetts Bureau of Statistics of Labor employed both males and females. Furthermore, 89 percent of male shoeworkers were employed in occupations that were 80 percent or more male; among women, 81 percent were employed in occupations so dominated by females. In other words, the significant male-female wage differential among shoeworkers resulted largely from gender segregation in the shoe industry. In this respect, the shoe factory of the post–Civil War decades continued practices established by the antebellum cotton textile mills.[21]

Most studies of shoe wages focus on individual workers. An 1875 report, however, noted the earnings and expenditures of 397 male-headed, working-class families across the state. Of this survey group, the heads of thirty-five families were employed in boots or shoes. Analysis of the income and expenses of these families reinforces the picture evident from the 1865 census of Lynn.[22]

20. Mass. BSL, *Annual Report*, 1872, pp. 103–7, and 1876, pp. 123–24. For additional contemporary references to this seasonality, see John Taylor Cumbler, ed., *A Moral Response to Industrialism: The Lectures of Reverend Cook in Lynn, Massachusetts* (Albany: State University of New York Press, 1982), pp. 9, 49, 76–77; and Mary H. Blewett, *We Will Rise in Our Might: Workingwomen's Voices in Nineteenth-Century New England* (Ithaca: Cornell University Press, 1991), pp. 113–18.

21. Mass. BSL, *Annual Report*, 1876, pp. 123–24; and Dublin, *Women at Work*, p. 66.

22. Mass. BSL, *Annual Report*, 1875, pp. 191–450.

In only fourteen of the thirty-five families (40 percent) did male household heads account for all family wage income. In the other families, in addition to the male breadwinners, two wives and twenty-seven children brought in earnings over the course of the year. Sons and daughters had almost identical annual earnings, about $230 on average; however, 17 sons and only 10 daughters in these families were employed. In all, children accounted for almost 24 percent of family wage income, with wives earning under 2 percent. The impact of multiple incomes on living standards is evident if we compare the situations of families with and without secondary wage earners. In the fourteen families where the father alone was employed, family income averaged $610. By contrast, for the twenty-one families with two or more wage earners, mean family income totaled almost $845, a figure fully 38 percent higher.[23]

The 1875 survey actually understates the dependence of shoemaking families on the earnings of women and children because it was limited to families headed by male workers. Children's earnings played an even greater role in families headed by widowed women, none of which were included among families interviewed in the 1875 survey.[24] In more than half of female-headed shoeworker families in the 1865 Lynn sample, children were the only wage earners. In 101 female-headed families, working children far outnumbered working mothers, 85 to 48. Even when

23. Mass. BSL, *Annual Report*, 1875, pp. 240–53, 359–79. Families with two or more wage earners were larger than those in which the male household head was the sole source of income. The difference, 1.15 family members on average, was not so great, however, as the income differential between these two groups of families. The data from this study, prepared by John Modell, are available in machine-readable form from the Interuniversity Consortium for Political and Social Research, Ann Arbor, Mich. See John Modell, "Patterns of Consumption, Acculturation, and Family Income Strategies in Late Nineteenth-Century America," in Tamara K. Hareven and Maris A. Vinovskis, eds., *Family and Population in Nineteenth-Century America* (Princeton: Princeton University Press, 1978), pp. 226–40.

24. Despite the usefulness of the study by the Massachusetts Bureau of Statistics of Labor, it has real limitations, which subsequent scholars have noted. Nonwage income and the rental value of home ownership both are unreported, market exchanges are emphasized to the exclusion of other kinds of cooperation or exchange, and throughout the report not very thinly veiled moral judgments intrude into the presentation. See Daniel Horowitz, *The Morality of Spending: Attitudes toward the Consumer Society in America, 1875–1940* (Baltimore: Johns Hopkins University Press, 1985), pp. 17–27; and Jeffrey G. Williamson, "Consumer Behavior in the Nineteenth Century: Carroll D. Wright's Massachusetts Workers in 1875," *Explorations in Entrepreneurial History*, 2d ser., 4 (1967): 98–135.

widows did work—primarily as shoe stitchers—they earned annual wages that were less than half those of male household heads working as shoe-makers.[25] Thus, whereas children of shoemakers in the 1875 survey ac-counted for 24 percent of reported family income, children in Lynn shoeworker families contributed more than 41 percent of family earnings.

In addition, wives of male shoeworkers in Lynn in 1865 found paid employment far more frequently than was reported in the 1875 survey. The survey recorded the employment of only two wives of the thirty-five shoemakers—less than 6 percent. Based on the 1865 Lynn evi-dence, a more reasonable estimate would have 15–18 percent of wives earning about 6 percent of family income, figures about three times the proportions reported for shoemakers' families in the 1875 survey. Based on shoeworker families in Lynn in 1865, it is likely that male household heads accounted for only slightly more than half of family income, with wives and children together accounting for 47 percent of family income. Clearly, a family wage economy was in operation.[26]

Age and marital and family status were characteristics that distin-guished Lowell mill operatives in the 1830s from Lynn shoeworkers in 1865. The two groups also differed in terms of birthplaces. The vast ma-jority of women in early Lowell had been migrants from surrounding rural communities in northern New England. Few had been immigrants, and few lived with their families while working in the mills. Of female operatives employed at the Hamilton Company in Lowell in July 1836, less than 4 percent were foreign-born; of some seven hundred entrants into the firm's work force between January and July of that year, only 7 percent gave Lowell as their hometown.[27]

25. In the 1875 survey, for instance, twelve working wives averaged annual earnings of $223 compared with $559 for thirty-five male shoeworker household heads.

26. The proportions reported here are based on the occupations of members of the 272 shoeworker families included in the 1865 Lynn sample. Using annual income figures drawn from the 1875 survey of the Bureau of Statistics of Labor, I have estimated annual income for family members working in the proportions evident among Lynn families in 1865. Such a cal-culation provides the following estimates: fathers earned 47.7% of family income; wives, 6.0%; female heads of households, 4.8%; and children, 41.5%. These proportions undoubtedly reflect the large number of female shoeworkers in sampled families. Their bias may compensate for that in the Mass. BLS study; the truth probably lies midway between the figures each offers.

27. Dublin, *Women at Work*, p. 26; and Hamilton Manufacturing Company Records, vol. 483, BL.

Table 4.3. Birthplaces of Lynn female shoeworkers,
1865

Place of birth	Percentage
Lynn	48.8
Other Massachusetts	29.6
New Hampshire, Maine	21.6
Total cases	402

Source: 1865 Massachusetts state census of Lynn, wards 3, 4, and 5, native-born sample.

Although Lynn in 1865 also had a predominantly native-born population (over 85 percent), it had far fewer northern New England migrants than had been common earlier in Lowell.[28] Among women shoeworkers residing in Lynn in 1865 and born in Massachusetts, Maine, or New Hampshire, almost half had been born in the shoe town (see Table 4.3). This difference proved important because it also meant that women shoeworkers in Lynn resided with their families and contributed to a family wage economy. Their Lowell counterparts a generation earlier lived alone in that city and did not necessarily contribute their earnings to help support their distant rural families.

Other differences distinguished Lynn-born shoeworkers from those who migrated from New Hampshire and Maine. First, they began work at an earlier age than did rural migrants. Almost 47 percent of the Lynn-born began shoe employment before the age of 20 compared with only 31 percent among northern New England migrants. Furthermore, the Lynn-born worked longer on average than did migrants—4.1 compared with 2.2 years. Finally, as Table 4.4 reveals, the Lynn-born typically lived at home with their parents, whereas migrant female shoeworkers most frequently boarded by themselves in Lynn. Although more than two-thirds of the Lynn-born female shoeworkers in 1865 lived at

28. Mass. Secretary of the Commonwealth, *Abstract of the Census of Massachusetts, 1865* (Boston: Wright & Potter, 1867), pp. 64–65. In fact, 81 percent of the native-born in Lynn in 1865 were Massachusetts-born. In the mid-1830s, among operatives employed by the Hamilton Manufacturing Company in Lowell, only 43 percent of the native-born had been born in Massachusetts. Robert G. Layer, "Wages, Earnings, and Output of Four Cotton Textile Companies in New England, 1825–1860," Ph.D. diss., Harvard University, 1952, table 20, pp. 184–85.

Table 4.4. Family status of female shoeworkers in Lynn, 1865, by birthplace

Family Status	Born in Lynn	Born in New Hampshire or Maine
Household head	6.1%	4.6%
Spouse	9.2	13.8
Child	67.3	16.1
Other relative	5.6	10.3
Boarder	11.7	55.2
Total cases	196	87

Note: For the sake of clarity, the table excludes shoeworkers born in Massachusetts outside of Lynn. Columns may not add up to 100.0% because of rounding.

Source: 1865 Massachusetts census of Lynn, wards 3, 4 and 5.

home with their parents, less than a sixth of migrant shoeworkers did so. Conversely, less than an eighth of the Lynn-born resided as boarders in others' households, whereas the majority of northern New England migrants did so.

Clearly, two distinct groups of women shoeworkers coexisted in Lynn in 1865—Lynn-born family residents and migrants from the surrounding countryside. Occupying a place intermediate between these two groups were migrants from nearby Essex County towns. They included fewer boarders than among Maine and New Hampshire migrants but also fewer family residents than among the Lynn-born. Given their intermediate status, the Lynn-born and migrants from northern New England will be our focus, for between them these groups encompassed the range of experiences encountered by female shoeworkers in Lynn in these decades.

A number of differences distinguished the urban and rural families of Lynn shoeworkers. The typical urban shoeworker family consisted of two parents and three children. The mean age of the father in 1850 was 39.6, and the average value of his real property $578. Just over 65 percent of urban fathers of shoeworking daughters were employed in the shoe or leather trades themselves at this date.

Maine and New Hampshire families of shoeworkers in 1850 had a distinctly different cast. More than 60 percent of the rural fathers were employed as farmers at this date, with another 17 percent employed in shoemaking occupations.[29] In addition, rural families were larger and parents were older than urban ones, with a median of four children, and the fathers' mean age of 43.5. Fathers owned $1,107 in real property on average, almost twice that of their urban counterparts. Although rural families appear to have been wealthier than urban ones, two factors should promote caution in any comparison. First, rural families were larger than urban ones; second, census enumerators in 1850 did not record personal property, and one would expect that unrecorded personal property represented a larger share of the wealth of urban than of rural families. In sum, typical fathers of Lynn female shoeworkers were thus Lynn shoemakers and Maine or New Hampshire farmers. Rural fathers were older and wealthier and had somewhat larger families than their Lynn counterparts.

For both urban and rural families, the proportion of fathers employed in shoe or leather trades is striking, and the occupational continuity across generations is significant. Before 1855 much of shoemaking was carried out on a domestic basis, so it is very likely that many urban and rural daughters began binding shoes in their homes. From that work it was but a short step for young women to enter Lynn's stitching shops as they went into operation in the 1850s and 1860s. Lynn families, for that matter, could purchase a sewing machine, and a daughter could stitch shoes at home.

Although it is understandable to emphasize the division between shoeworkers born in Lynn and those born in the countryside, such an emphasis should not lead us to view migrants among female shoeworkers as an entirely homogeneous group. Some of the women migrated alone and boarded while working in Lynn; others migrated with their families and resided with their parents in Lynn. Examining residence patterns of rural migrants in their hometowns in 1850 and in Lynn in 1860 and 1865 reveals differences between families that migrated and

29. Fathers of shoeworkers born in Massachusetts but not in Lynn had much more in common with Lynn fathers of shoeworkers than with New Hampshire or Maine fathers. Typically they came from Essex County, quite close to Lynn, and two-thirds of those traced in the 1850 census were shoeworkers or skilled workers, whereas less than one-ninth were farmers at that date.

those that remained in the countryside. In all, there were 206 migrants in the shoeworker sample; in 1865 the families of origin of at least forty-nine of these migrants were also residing in Lynn.[30] Families that remained in the countryside were considerably wealthier than those that later migrated to Lynn. Fathers in nonmigrant families owned an average of $1,156 in real property in 1850 compared with only $860 for migrant fathers. Migrant fathers were already more likely to have shifted away from farming as well. Almost 43 percent of rural fathers who migrated to Lynn after 1850 were employed in shoe occupations in 1850 compared with only 14 percent who were farmers. Among nonmigrant fathers the proportions were almost exactly reversed. Only 22 percent of nonmigrants were shoeworkers, whereas almost 49 percent were farmers in 1850. Family migration was a strategy employed chiefly by the less prosperous rural families in Lynn's hinterland.[31] Families with adequate land and resources to make a living at farming evidently remained in the countryside, even if one or two sons or daughters chose to work in Lynn.

The family backgrounds of women shoeworkers take on particular significance because they influenced women's subsequent employment. Overall, women's length of employment in shoe work averaged 3.8 years. Women born in Lynn, however, worked 4.1 years on average, whereas those born in Maine or New Hampshire were employed only 3.1 years. Similarly, daughters of farmers averaged only 2.8 years in shoemaking compared with 4.3 years for daughters of nonfarmers.

Birthplace and father's occupation appear on first glance to be the most influential factors affecting the length of a woman's career in shoemaking. On closer analysis, however, other factors come to the fore. Whether a

30. This number should be viewed as a minimum because it includes only families of those migrant shoeworkers recorded in the 1865 census as children living at home. It is possible that some of the families of migrants who were boarding in Lynn lived elsewhere in the city.

31. Linkage was not complete, but the numbers are large enough to sustain the argument here—for occupations, forty-five fathers of nonmigrants and fourteen migrant fathers linked in the 1850 federal manuscript census of their rural hometowns. For property, I have limited the comparison to families that lived in Maine and New Hampshire in 1850—twenty-five nonmigrant families and five migrant families in all. For a fuller development of this argument, see Dublin, "Rural-Urban Migrants."

Table 4.5. Influences on women's length of employment in shoemaking, 1865 Lynn shoeworker sample

Factor	Subgroup	Years shoemaking	Difference
Birthplace[a]			0.62
	Lynn	3.82 (118)	
	Maine, New Hampshire	3.20 (26)	
Father's occupation			0.61
	Farmer	3.21 (17)	
	Nonfarmer	3.82 (163)	
Marital status			2.57
	Did marry	3.20 (141)	
	Never married	5.77 (39)	
Work and marriage			2.92
	Only worked single	2.88 (126)	
	Worked after marriage	5.80 (54)	
Total cases[b]			180

Source: Linkage of 1865 Lynn shoeworker sample.

[a] For the sake of clarity, shoeworkers born in Massachusetts outside of Lynn have been excluded from birthplace subgroups.

[b] Includes only cases with nonmissing data on all variables in the analysis. Findings are based on multiple classification analysis, which simultaneously controls for the influence of other independent variables in calculating means for subgroups on a particular variable.

woman married and whether she worked while married ultimately had greater impact on the length of time she worked in shoemaking than did her family background. Table 4.5 summarizes the respective influences of these factors. Two groups of women shoeworkers had particularly lengthy periods of employment: women who never married and women who worked in shoemaking after their marriages. Women in each of these groups were employed for periods that averaged more than 5.75 years, over 2.5 years longer than the average for those who married or worked only while single.

Textile workers who never married also had relatively long periods of employment, so there is nothing very surprising about the employment patterns of single shoeworkers. The group that stands out in this discussion consists of women who worked in Lynn's stitching shops while married or widowed. They had, in fact, no significant counterpart in the early Lowell mills. Yet married or widowed women made up more than 29 percent of female shoeworkers in Lynn in 1865. Tracing sample members over time indicates that 44 percent of the women did shoe work for wages at some point after marriage. Among women who definitely did marry, almost 54 percent were employed as shoeworkers at some point after their marriages, a remarkably high proportion for the mid-nineteenth century.[32] Given these figures, it will be worthwhile to consider these women in some detail.

Two married shoe stitchers enumerated in the 1865 census of Lynn dramatize this group of workingwomen. Hannah Pierce, a 39-year-old stitcher, lived in ward 3 with her husband George, a shoemaker, and their 22-year-old son, Lewis, a fish trader. A fourth person, a shoe cutter, boarded in their household. Five years earlier the Pierces had also lived in Lynn, and George was enumerated as a shoemaker, but Hannah appears to have been at home with a daughter at that date. Melissa Stackpole is a second married shoeworker of interest. She was much younger than Hannah Pierce, being only 25 in 1865, and she and her husband, Samuel, boarded in the ward 4 household of Laura Smith. Like all other boarding married stitchers in 1865, Melissa Stackpole had no co-resident children. By 1870 the Stackpoles' economic situation may have improved, as the couple lived with a daughter in their own household, and Melissa was no longer recorded as employed.[33] The intermittent employment evident for Hannah Pierce and Melissa Stackpole was typical of the work patterns of married women shoe stitchers in Lynn in the post–Civil War years.

32. This figure must be taken as a low estimate of the actual proportion of female shoeworkers who worked while married or widowed because marital status is not given in the 1855, 1860, and 1870 censuses. I felt able to infer married or widowed status for linked shoeworkers in those censuses only when they lived with plausible husbands or children. The proportions designated married or widowed are undoubtedly on the low side for these years, which makes the share of widowed or married shoe stitchers all the more striking. For similar evidence on employed wives among Irish women in New York, see Carol Groneman, "'She Earns as a Child; She Pays as a Man': Women Workers in a Mid-Nineteenth-Century New York City Community," in Milton Cantor and Bruce Laurie, eds., *Class, Sex, and the Woman Worker* (Westport, Conn.: Greenwood Press, 1977), p. 89.

33. The curious feature of the successive portraits of the Stackpole family is the fact that their daughter was recorded as 9 years old in 1870. If her age is correct, then she must have been living elsewhere (perhaps with other relatives) in 1865 when her parents were enumerated as boarding shoeworkers in Lynn. The evidence would suggest that at some point after 1865,

Married women shoeworkers in Lynn in 1865 were a relatively young group. They averaged 32 years of age, with husbands about 5 years older. Somewhat more than 57 percent resided with husbands in their own households, almost 19 percent of the couples boarded in others' homes, 13 percent resided with families of origin, and the remainder lived with other relatives. Fully 65 percent of their husbands also worked in shoe trades. Given stereotypes about women's domestic lives, one would generally assume that these women worked only before or after the years in which they were raising their children. This was not the case, however. Three-fourths of married stitchers who resided in their own households, for instance, had children living with them. On average, the oldest child was 12 years old. These workingwomen were able to combine childrearing and domestic responsibilities with paid employment. The fact that one could purchase or lease a sewing machine and work at home must have contributed to the large proportion of married women among Lynn shoe stitchers. Unfortunately, the census does not indicate the location of employment, but it seems probable that many of these women earned their wages working at home. One account reported five thousand sewing machines employed in boot- and shoemaking in Essex County in 1860: "These machines are usually owned by the operatives themselves, who are mostly women, and who do the work at their homes." Over the course of the 1860s, the expansion of factory operations in Lynn cut into domestic production, but as late as 1875, more than 18 percent of female shoeworkers in Lynn labored in their own homes.[34] Given the persistence of homework for shoe stitchers, there was evidently a steady demand for the labor of married women in Lynn in these decades.

No surviving diaries or letters permit the reconstruction of the work experiences of married Lynn shoe stitchers in this period. But a diary kept by Irena Knowlton, a married shoe stitcher in rural Hamilton, about fifteen miles northeast of Lynn, is revealing about the integration of work and family life for married women workers after the Civil War.[35]

---

the Stackpoles moved into an apartment or home of their own, their daughter returned to their household, and Melissa Stackpole resumed the role of housekeeper.

34. *Scientific American*, October 6, 1860, p. 230; and Carroll D. Wright, *The Census of Massachusetts: 1875*, vol. 2 (Boston: Albert J. Wright, 1876), pp. 825–28.

35. Irena M. Knowlton Diaries, Hamilton, Mass., 1879–1888, EI. A telling excerpt from the diary is reprinted in Blewett, *We Will Rise in Our Might*, pp. 152–54.

Irena Knowlton was a hard worker. "Done some shoes" is a typical part of a daily entry for this 41-year-old mother of four children and wife of George Knowlton, a shoe manufacturer.[36] Over a two-year period beginning in January 1879, Irena Knowlton recorded shoemaking activity on 224 different days. Other than Sabbath days, when Knowlton did not record any work, she did some shoe stitching about every third day, which was integrated into the flow of an extremely busy schedule. She sometimes had boarders during this period, and cooking, washing, and ironing occupied much of her time. She baked pies and also sold eggs and chickens in large quantities, apparently to a local hotel.[37] She cut out and made clothes for her children and also for paying customers. And during the summer months, berry picking took much of her time. Knowlton was clearly earning money for herself and her family, and the range of her income-producing activities was quite remarkable.[38]

Knowlton's diary was written in brief snippets run together in a stream-of-consciousness fashion. She dwelled little on the nature of her work routines. Occasionally, however, there are passages that are more revealing than most. "Lua and I done 60 pr of shoes feel tiered" was an entry for March 17, 1879, that summarized the work that she and her 16-year-old daughter had recently completed. Whether her daughters worked regularly with her or only sometimes is unclear. Whether Irena Knowlton worked for her husband or for another shoe manufacturer is also uncertain. Moreover, it is likely that Knowlton used a sewing machine, as she noted once that she ran a needle through her finger. Finally, Knowlton's own feelings about her work emerge on occasion, and they are generally negative. "Tiered" appears frequently

36. Federal Manuscript Census of Population, 1880, Hamilton, Mass., T9, reel 326, family 20.

37. Six families away in the Hamilton census for 1880 was the household of Samuel Whipple, enumerated as a hotelkeeper.

38. Irena M. Knowlton Diaries, January 1, 2, February 8, 21, March 12, 14, May 23, June 20, July 21, December 12, 13, 1879. The range of economic activities that Knowlton undertook is reminiscent of the breadth of the female economy described in Laurel Thatcher Ulrich, "Martha Ballard and Her Girls: Women's Work in Eighteenth-Century Maine," in Stephen Innes, ed., *Work and Labor in Early America* (Chapel Hill: University of North Carolina Press, 1988), pp. 70–105.

in connection with the work; "done shoes all I was able" and "done shoes same old story" are typical of the understated complaints that surface periodically.[39]

From Knowlton's diary one senses that shoe stitching was simply one of many activities married women might turn to in order to earn a bit of extra family income. Urban women may have had somewhat fewer opportunities than did their rural counterparts, as raising chickens and berry picking probably were not options; thus married women's shoe earnings may have represented a greater share of supplementary family income for Lynn residents. Family economic need combined with the availability of home sewing machines meant that homework played an important role in the lives of Lynn families in the post–Civil War decades.

The high proportion of married women among Lynn female shoeworkers in 1865 was not an aberration, resulting perhaps from the unemployment of returning Civil War veterans. Other censuses confirm the pattern evident in 1865. Mary Blewett found that 17 percent of female shoeworkers in 1880 were married. These married shoeworkers were 32 years old on average, more than half their husbands were also shoeworkers, and half had minor children living with them. Another 6 percent of female shoeworkers were widowed or divorced. The overall figure of 23 percent indicates that married, widowed, or divorced women continued to constitute a significant proportion of the female work force in Lynn shoemaking in 1880.[40]

Widowed shoeworkers were probably carrying on work that they had done within marriage. They were older and more likely to be living with older children than were their married counterparts. Still, they were not an entirely homogeneous group. According to the 1865 census sample,

39. Irena M. Knowlton Diaries, February 27, March 1, 17, April 23, November 14, 1879. One cannot be entirely certain that Irena Knowlton injured herself while stitching shoes by machine because the accident occurred on a day when she recorded sewing clothing. See entry for February 27, 1879.

40. Blewett, *Men, Women, and Work*, pp. 335, 338–43. Blewett analyzed a one-in-ten sample of female shoeworkers in Lynn, which amounted to 262 out of an overall enumerated work force of about 2,620. The proportion for widows noted here has been calculated from Blewett's separate figures for boarders and residents in female-headed families. Blewett found that wives increased as a proportion of female shoeworkers after 1880 (p. 351).

more than half of these women headed their own households, whereas 26 percent resided in their parents' homes and another 16 percent boarded out. They were considerably older than married shoeworkers, averaging 41 years of age. Almost 63 percent of widows had co-resident children, and the mean age of the oldest child was 17.6.

Married and widowed women shoeworkers in 1865 were part of a family wage economy. Married women and their husbands were the primary wage earners in their families, and one might have thought that their combined earnings would have been adequate for family support; still, 24 percent of their children were also employed. In female-headed households, widows relied more heavily on the earnings of their children, fully 42 percent of whom worked. The presence of so many married and widowed women employed in the boot and shoe industry in Lynn, often working as adjuncts to wage-earning children, reveals how crucial the wages of adult women could be in working-class families during industrialization.

Although the 1865 census offers no evidence on property ownership or income, extreme financial need must have been the motivating factor for both widows and married women who went against public sentiment to take on paid employment while raising children. Although such practices were not unusual for Irish immigrants in Boston or Lowell in the Civil War period, such behavior set Yankee women apart from their neighbors in Lynn at this date.[41]

Self-supporting widows, especially in the years immediately following the Civil War, were perfectly understandable to contemporary observers, but the prevalence of working wives in Lynn did cause something of a stir. Such wage earning called into question the dominant ideology of domesticity that viewed home, hearth, and family as "woman's place." It should come as no surprise, then, that there arose in the 1870s in Lynn newspapers a lively debate as to the propriety of the employment of married women in the boot and shoe industry of the city.

41. In what was undoubtedly a response to contemporary concerns that shoe employment threatened female character, Lynn workingwomen in the Daughters of St. Crispin described themselves as "lady stitchers" and sought to defend themselves from charges of immorality. See below and Blewett, *Men, Women, and Work*, chap. 8.

One writer, in an article entitled "Married Women in Shoe Shops," attributed the low wages of women shoeworkers to the presence of married women and daughters who were working, although they had no real economic need: "The shops are thronged with married women, the greater portion of whom . . . have good comfortable homes, and girls whose fathers are amply able to provide them with all the necessaries and comforts of life, but their inordinate love of dress, and a desire to vie in personal adornments with their more wealthy sisters, takes them into the workrooms that they may earn a little money with which to buy gewgaws and finery."[42] "Unnecessary" consumption is the villain in the morality play outlined by this commentator.

The argument here is reminiscent of complaints that arose on both sides of the Atlantic a generation or two earlier concerning the spending habits of women workers in the first textile mills. An English writer criticized the extravagant dress of mill operatives, noting that "on Sunday those who formerly moved in the most humble social sphere . . . have lately been so disguised as to be mistaken for persons of distinction." Sarah J. Hale, editor of *Godey's Ladies Book*, commented similarly on the pretensions of New England mill operatives. "Many," she wrote, "wear gold watches, and an imitation at least, of all the ornaments which grace the daughters of our most opulent citizens." What were these gold watches, other than an 1840 version of the "gewgaws and finery" that upset the Lynn writer almost forty years later? One mill operative, writing in the *Lowell Offering*, made short shrift of Hale's complaint. In a sarcastic response she decried: "O the times! O the manners! Alas! how sadly the world has changed. The time was when the *lady* could be distinguished from the *no-lady* by her dress . . . but now . . . you cannot tell 'which was which.' "[43]

As did her mill operative counterpart, a former shoe stitcher, writing under the pen name "Americus," took strong exception to the complaints about married workingwomen in Lynn. She answered back, "There are not many women inside our shoe shops to-day who are not

42. "Married Women in Shoe Shops," *Lynn Record*, February 1, 1879.

43. *Chelmsford Gazette*, September 12, 1823, quoted in Judy Lown, *Women and Industrialization: Gender at Work in Nineteenth-Century England* (Cambridge: Polity Press, 1990), pp. 30–31; and *Lowell Offering*, February 1841, p. 45, emphasis in original.

obliged to work." She noted the impact of the depression of the mid-1870s in putting male shoemakers out of work and viewed the employment of wives as an example of self-sacrifice actuated by family concerns: "There are more [wives] who leave their homes each morning with an aching heart, and who wend their weary way to the shop, not from motives of selfishness, but with every thought and feeling devoted to the interest and welfare of those they love." A "Married Stitcher" joined the debate and drew upon personal experience in supporting "Americus": "I for one, and I know many more situated in the same way, work to get bread for my children; my husband has been cut down so that in the short time he has work he cannot support us. I wonder what many of the men would have done in the lockout last winter if their wives had not worked in the shops." The debate grew more acrimonious; the original author accused working wives of making their husbands henpecked, and her opponent, "Married Stitcher," accused single women of preferring to work in mixed settings rather than in the all-female stitching rooms where they belonged. The large number of working wives struck many contemporaries as unprecedented and led to a debate as to the reasons for the development and its broader significance.[44]

As was true of the writers associated with the *Lowell Offering* earlier, there is no doubt that shoeworkers participating in the Lynn debate were out to defend their behavior in terms they felt others would find acceptable. They emphasized, once again, selfless and familial motivations to the exclusion of more individualistic ones. This time, however, the evidence on the family backgrounds of Lynn workers and the family budget data lend support to their arguments in ways that simply were not true for Yankee textile operatives earlier. The presence of shoeworker families in Lynn, the prevalence of multiple wage earners within these families, and the frequency with which married and widowed

---

44. *Lynn Record*, February 8, 15, March 1, 1879. My thanks to Mary Blewett for sharing the "Americus" letters. In this argument, "Married Stitcher" recalled the earlier debate occasioned by the lectures of Reverend Joseph Cook, who argued against the "promiscuous" mingling of men and women in shoe factory workrooms. See Cumbler, ed., *Moral Response to Industrialism*, pp. 48–55. For additional excerpts from this debate, see Blewett, *We Will Rise in Our Might*, chap. 10.

women worked for wages all suggest the greater significance of family economic strategies in Lynn in the 1860s and 1870s than in Lowell in the 1830s and 1840s. Wage work for women in Lowell had offered opportunities that commonly drew Yankee women away from their families of origin; work in Lynn a generation later reinforced the economic ties of women shoeworkers to their families.

Marriage was no obstacle to female employment in the shoe industry, and the evidence suggests that women shoeworkers married at younger ages than was common for native-born women in New England in this period. As had been the case in antebellum Lowell, most female shoeworkers married. Overall, 81.8 percent of those who could be traced did marry. The mean age at first marriage for Lynn shoeworkers was 22.2 and for their husbands, 25.3. Lynn-born shoeworkers married somewhat earlier than did migrants to the city—at an average age of 21.4 years old. All female shoeworkers, however, whether Lynn-born or migrant, married considerably earlier than had New Hampshire millhands in Lowell a generation earlier, for whom the mean age at first marriage was 25.3.[45]

The urban world of Lynn was the focus of the lives of women shoeworkers, and they generally found their prospective husbands within the city's borders. This was understandable for the Lynn-born, but it held true for migrants to the city as well. Almost 84 percent of Maine and New Hampshire migrants, for example, married in Lynn. Where these migrants can be traced in subsequent censuses, the vast majority remained in the city. In 1870, for example, almost 86 percent of linked migrants resided in Lynn; by 1880, that proportion had climbed to 96 percent; at death, fully 87.5 percent remained in the city. This persistence is all the more remarkable given the fact that more than half of all migrants came alone and boarded on first arriving in Lynn.

---

45. In a comparable cohort of native-born Massachusetts women born in 1850, 79.3 percent did marry, a figure remarkably close to that for Lynn native-born shoeworkers. See Peter R. Uhlenberg, "A Study of Cohort Life Cycles: Cohorts of Native Born Massachusetts Women, 1830–1920," *Population Studies*, 23 (1969): 23:410–11. For ages at first marriage, see Thomas Monahan, *The Pattern of Age at First Marriage in the United States* (Philadelphia: By the author, 1951), p. 161; and Daniel Scott Smith, "Parental Power and Marriage Patterns: An Analysis of Historical Trends in Hingham, Massachusetts," *Journal of Marriage and the Family* 35 (1973): 419–28.

Table 4.6. Occupations of husbands of Lynn shoeworkers,
by birthplace

Occupational group	Born in Lynn	Born in New Hampshire or Maine
Shoe trades	56.0%	47.7%
Manufacturer, proprietor	10.0	15.9
Skilled	19.0	27.3
Semi- or unskilled	6.0	2.3
Farmer	0.0	0.0
White-collar, professional	9.0	6.8
Total cases	100	44

Source: Linkage of 1865 Lynn shoeworker sample.

Whether Lynn-born or migrant, women shoeworkers tended to marry men who were either shoemakers or skilled workers (see Table 4.6). None of the Lynn-born or northern New England migrants among shoeworkers married a farmer, in stark contrast to the situation for migrant millhands in Lowell a generation earlier, when more than 37 percent did so. Two Massachusetts-born women in the shoeworker sample (not shown in Table 4.6) did marry farmers, but even counting their numbers, less than 1 percent of women shoemakers wedded farmers. The specific backgrounds of individual women did not make much difference, as so few of Lynn's migrant shoeworkers ever returned to their rural homes.[46]

The marriage patterns of Lowell millhands showed evidence of a division between those women who married and settled in their hometowns and those who remained in Lowell or other Massachusetts towns after marriage. The latter group had married at a relatively early age, whereas rural returnees held off until they were slightly older than 30.

46. The lifetime persistence of such a large proportion of Lynn female shoeworkers stands apart from the body of historical scholarship that has examined geographic mobility in the United States in the nineteenth century. For a useful recent contrast, see Peter R. Knights, *Yankee Destinies: The Lives of Ordinary Nineteenth-Century Bostonians* (Chapel Hill: University of North Carolina Press, 1991). Studying a sample of 2,808 native-born male Bostonians drawn from the 1850 and 1860 censuses, Knights found that only 57 percent of immigrants and 71 percent of the Boston-born died in that city (see chap. 5, "Leaving Boston").

There was no similar division among Lynn shoeworkers, principally because virtually none returned to their rural homes. More than 80 percent married in Lynn, and an even larger proportion died in Lynn.

In their relatively early age of marriage, Lynn shoeworkers resembled
the English framework knitters studied by David Levine.[47] Urban wage
workers in Lynn in 1865, unlike their counterparts in Lowell a generation earlier, were no longer concerned about inheriting land and married
without regard to the availability of a suitable farmstead. Moreover, because it was not unusual for married women to continue working at shoe
stitching, young married families could count on two incomes. Taken
together, the lack of concern for the inheritance of land and the availability of good wages in shoemaking permitted the early age at marriage
evident for female shoeworkers in Lynn.

Female shoeworkers, whether Lynn-born or migrant, spent their adult
lives in the city of Lynn for the most part. Their family lives were in-
tegrally tied up with the shoe industry that dominated Lynn's economy.
More than half of women shoeworkers married men who worked in the
shoe trades. Moreover, a large share of their children took up shoe employment when they came of age. In 1865, for instance, a total of 184
children resided with married or widowed shoeworkers in the Lynn
sample. Most were relatively young and were not employed, but thirty-
five of the forty-three children listed with occupations—more than 81 percent—worked in the shoe trades. Fifteen years later, census enumerators in Lynn recorded forty-six working children in the families of
former shoeworkers; slightly more than half of them were employed in
shoe occupations. Clearly the shoe industry dominated these women's
lives, even if their own periods of paid employment were relatively brief.

The experiences of women shoeworkers in Lynn provide evidence of
important developments in the nature of wage work for women in New
England in comparison with rural outwork and textile employment in
the antebellum years. The growth of putting-out industries brought the
first wage work for women into the countryside and permitted the integration of that work into the flow of women's farming lives. There was

---

47. David Levine, *Family Formation in an Age of Nascent Capitalism* (New York: Academic
Press, 1977), chap. 4; see also Elinor Accampo, *Industrialization, Family Life, and Class Relations: Saint Chamond, 1815–1914* (Berkeley: University of California Press, 1989).

minimal conflict for rural women between their domestic responsibilities and the new opportunities for earning cash or store credit that outwork weaving or hat making provided. They remained living at home, shifting the balance between paid and unpaid work as family needs and personal inclinations dictated.

With the emergence of factory employment in the early cotton textile mills, rural women had to leave their homes and take up residence in the new mill towns to take advantage of the wage work offered by factories. They could no longer balance domestic responsibilities and wage work at the same time, but by working short, repeated stints in the mills and returning periodically to their rural homes, early mill women could live in both worlds. They remained farmers' daughters, integrated within the family farm economy and yet earning the higher wages that urban mill employment offered. They could take advantage of what industrial capitalism had to offer without permanently renouncing their status as "daughters of freemen."

Such a transitional development had advantages for New England's first industrial capitalists as well. Millowners in early Lowell prided themselves on the fact that they recruited daughters of independent yeoman farmers and did not reproduce the kind of permanent urban proletariat that Americans associated with the dark, satanic mills of Manchester, England. They noted in their defense of American manufacturing that mill women were free to return to the countryside and cited proof that they rarely worked in the mills more than three to five years. These writings were certainly self-serving—part of a response to critics of the factory system—but the evidence presented in Chapter 3 indicates that their arguments were basically correct.[48] Few native-born women workers resided permanently in Lowell or had families living in the city, though the proportion living at home while employed did increase from 11 to 23 percent between the mid-1830s and 1860. Only about 20 percent of mill operatives married in Lowell, and perhaps a third continued to reside in the city after their marriages. A somewhat larger share, more than 37 percent, married farmers and settled in their

48. Nathan Appleton, *Introduction of the Power Loom, and the Origin of Lowell* (Lowell, Mass.: B. H. Penhallow, 1858), pp. 15–16; and Henry A. Miles, *Lowell as It Was, and as It Is* (Lowell, Mass.: Powers and Bagley, 1845), pp. 75–76.

New Hampshire hometowns. By no means did Lowell dominate the entire lives of its antebellum female operatives.

The evidence on Lynn shoeworkers suggests that a quiet but dramatic shift had occurred over a thirty-year period. Almost half of Lynn female shoeworkers in 1865 were born in the city. They themselves worked only brief stints at shoe stitching, but their familial experiences suggest a very different set of social relations than those seen earlier in Lowell. Recall that 65 percent of their fathers had worked in the shoe or leather trades, as did 56 percent of their husbands and more than half of their employed children.

Lynn-born shoeworkers were part of a stable, increasingly permanent urban working class. In the career and residence patterns of Maine- and New Hampshire–born shoeworkers, we see evidence of the recruitment of the rural-born into that expanding class. More than 80 percent of migrants married in Lynn, and 87 percent died in the city. The husbands of 75 percent of these women worked in shoemaking or skilled trades and few returned to farming after marriage. No such stable working class evolved in antebellum Lowell, and it took three decades of Irish and French-Canadian immigration to produce the kind of intergenerational occupational continuity apparent among Yankee women in Lynn.[49]

This change derived in part from the ongoing transformation of the New England countryside. Increasingly after 1820, farmers in Maine and New Hampshire saw reduced prospects for settling grown sons and daughters on nearby farmsteads. Although this was true to a certain extent for the farmer fathers of Lowell millhands in the 1830s and 1840s, it held with more force for the rural fathers of female shoeworkers a generation later. Whereas 63 percent of these fathers continued to work farms in 1850, almost 17 percent had taken up shoemaking themselves, even before their daughters left for Lynn. As the more fertile lands of the Midwest came into cultivation and improved transportation permitted midwestern crops to undersell northeastern farm products in mid-Atlantic and New England markets, migration from northern New England's farming towns picked up apace. Lowell millhands constituted

49. Frances H. Early, "The French-Canadian Family Economy and Standard-of-Living in Lowell, Massachusetts, 1870," *Journal of Family History* 7 (Summer 1982): 180–99; and Peter John Richards, "The French Canadians of Lowell: 1880–1900," M.A. thesis, Northeastern University, 1986.

the first telltale signs of this migration and Lynn shoeworkers and their families, the crest of its strongest waves.

Factory work in Lowell in the 1830s and 1840s represented a first step away from the integration of family work and wage work that rural out-work permitted. Lynn shoemaking offered rural women similar oppor-tunities for seasonal employment in the city's stitching shops in the 1850s and 1860s, but for the majority of women shoeworkers, migration to Lynn became a permanent entry into a growing urban working class in the Civil War years. Changing conditions in the New England country-side cut women shoeworkers from their rural roots with a new finality.

Still, for all the newness and growth of Lowell and Lynn in these years, they were only middle-sized, single-industry towns. Both re-mained largely Yankee preserves in the years considered here. In Bos-ton, workingwomen entered a still larger world. There, Yankee and immigrant rubbed shoulders, and the growing commercial metropolis offered an occupational diversity unknown in smaller factory towns. In the experience of workingwomen in the city of Boston, the full implica-tions of wage labor for women in the second half of the nineteenth cen-tury become apparent.

5. *Boston Servants and Garment Workers*

Lowell millhands and Lynn shoeworkers represent two poles on a spectrum that we might envision to conceptualize the relationship between women's paid employment and the family wage economy. The vast majority of millhands left home and sought employment on their own in the expanding mill town on the Merrimack River. Mill employment required a separation from families of origin and for many women proved to be a first step in a journey away from their rural roots. In Lowell, as women's correspondence revealed, millhands generally decided how long to remain in the mills and how to spend their earnings. Female shoeworkers, by contrast, were very much enmeshed within a family wage economy in Lynn after the Civil War. First, about half were born in Lynn (most commonly into shoeworking families) and lived at home while working. Furthermore, a good share of migrants also lived in Lynn with their families. These shoemaking families were dependent for their subsistence on the earnings of wives and daughters. In addition, a large proportion of single women shoeworkers married men who worked in shoe trades and subsequently bore children who followed them into shoe employment. Shoemaking thus proved a lifelong involvement for many Lynn workingwomen. Young single women who came to the city to work for brief periods and returned to their rural homes played a much smaller role in Lynn than had been the case in Lowell earlier.

Lynn and Lowell had two characteristics in common, however, that make their female work forces not entirely representative of broader nineteenth-century practice. Both were single-industry towns in which virtually all employed women worked in a single occupation or related group of occupations. Certainly there were some servants, seamstresses, and teachers in the female labor force of each of these communities.

Still, few women would have moved to Lowell or Lynn with any intention of working outside the single industry for which each was well known. In addition, there was a basic homogeneity in the racial and ethnic composition of the work forces in the two communities. There were few African Americans or immigrants in Lowell before the mid-1840s or in Lynn before 1880, and the experiences of Yankee millhands and shoeworkers are only part of the story of wage-earning women in New England more generally. For an understanding of the occupational and ethnic diversity of workingwomen during the industrial revolution, we do well to shift our focus to a sprawling commercial city such as Boston.

Three findings emerge particularly sharply in examining the work and family lives of wage-earning women in mid-nineteenth-century Boston. First, we become keenly aware that the vast majority of female employment during the early industrial revolution was nonindustrial in character. Employment in domestic service rather than factory work predominated for women in Boston throughout the nineteenth century. In addition, as will become more evident, much of the city's manufacturing work was carried out in private homes, as outwork sewing far outweighed shop or factory work in Boston's garment industry. Second, a focus on Boston reveals the emergence of a clear hierarchy among wage-earning women along lines of race and ethnicity. As women move into an increasing variety of occupations, the jobs they fill are in large measure a function of these factors. Yankee women find relatively greater opportunities in clerical and sales positions, teaching, and self-employment. Daughters of immigrants concentrate in semiskilled factory occupations. Immigrants and African Americans, in turn, find themselves limited for the most part to employment in domestic and personal service. The appearance of this occupational hierarchy among Boston's workingwomen will be a major theme of the discussion that follows. Finally, over the course of the nineteenth century, there is a shift among Boston's workingwomen from boarding out or living with their employers to living at home in family settings. There is a distinct decline in the social and economic independence of Boston women workers as their employment becomes more fully integrated within a family wage economy. This shift coincided with the emergence of daughters of immigrants as the leading group among Boston workingwomen and the decline in the numbers of recent migrants from northern New England within the female labor force of the city. These three developments—the predominance of domestic service, the appearance of an ethnic occupational hierarchy among workingwomen, and the integration of women's wage work over time within the family wage economy—are key elements in an understanding of women's wage labor in the industrial revolution and central themes in the story of workingwomen in nineteenth-century Boston that follows.

These developments occur within a specific historical context, that of the bustling seaport city of Boston in the middle decades of the nineteenth century. The city grew at a breakneck pace, with its population rising from 61,000 in 1830 to 137,000 in 1850 and then to 363,000 by 1880.[1] Migration from the surrounding countryside and foreign immigration both contributed to this growth. The city expanded physically as well, with the filling in of the Back Bay and the annexation of adjoining areas.[2] Commerce, banking and insurance, construction, and diverse manufacturing all expanded as the city grew.[3] Boston "was the manufacturing capital of New England," yet no single industry dominated its economy. The value of manufactured goods produced in the city increased eightfold between 1837 and 1865, reaching an annual figure of $90 million, making the city the fourth largest industrial center in the nation at that date. Boston displayed a diversity of occupations that was unique in New England at mid-century but common enough for the large commercial cities of the Atlantic seaboard.[4]

Although Boston offered a variety of occupational opportunities at mid-century, wage-earning women were concentrated principally in two occupations—domestic service and the needle trades. An 1845 city census

1. Peter R. Knights, *Plain People of Boston, 1830–1860: A Study in City Growth* (New York: Oxford University Press, 1971), p. 20; and Stephan Thernstrom, *The Other Bostonians: Poverty and Progress in the American Metropolis, 1880–1970* (Cambridge: Harvard University Press, 1973), p. 11.

2. Walter Muir Whitehill, *Boston: A Topographical History* (Cambridge: Harvard University Press, 1959), chaps. 6 and 7; and Lawrence W. Kennedy, *Planning the City upon a Hill: Boston since 1630* (Amherst: University of Massachusetts Press, 1992), chap. 3.

3. Oscar Handlin, *Boston's Immigrants: A Study in Acculturation*, rev. ed. (New York: Atheneum, 1968; originally published in 1941); and Francis X. Blouin, Jr., *The Boston Region, 1810–1850: A Study of Urbanization* (Ann Arbor, Mich.: UMI Research Press, 1980).

4. Henry Marcus Schreiber, "The Working People of Boston in the Middle of the Nineteenth Century," Ph.D. diss., Boston University, 1950, p. 13.

and the 1860 federal manuscript census provide unusually rich evidence on female occupations in this period (see Table 5.1).[5]

Early industrialization created considerable wage work for women. In 1845, 23 percent of all adult women in Boston were recorded as wage earners; by 1860, the proportion stood at 25 percent. The vast majority of that employment, however, was not in industrial occupations. Louise Tilly and Joan Scott have pointed out much the same employment patterns in England and France at a similar stage in economic development, noting that "women tended to be concentrated in unmechanized, 'traditional' sectors of the economy."[6] In Boston, domestic servants made up roughly 60 percent of workingwomen at mid-century, and about another 30 percent toiled in the needle trades. Servants worked in the homes of their employers for the most part, though a seventh did work in hotels, boardinghouses, or restaurants, and the majority of garment workers probably plied their needles in their own homes.[7] The tremendous growth in the numbers of females employed in Boston between 1845 and 1860 did not entail a shift in the kinds of work that women performed for wages.

5. Lemuel Shattuck, *Report to the Committee of the City Council Appointed to Obtain the Census of Boston for the Year 1845* (Boston: John H. Eastburn, 1846), pp. 82–85, and app. Y, pp. 39–43; and Federal Manuscript Census of Population, 1860, Boston, M653, rolls 520–26. The 1845 Boston census appears to have been the first taken in the United States that enumerated each resident individually rather than within family or household groups. Unfortunately, the census manuscripts for that year have not survived, and we are limited to working with aggregate statistics published in Shattuck's *Report*. For more on the history of census taking, see Commonwealth of Massachusetts, *Report of a General Plan for the Promotion of Public and Personal Health, Devised, Prepared, and Recommended by the Commissioners Appointed under a Resolve of the Legislature of Massachusetts, Relating to a Sanitary Survey of the State* (Boston: Dutton & Wentworth, 1850), p. 131.

Shattuck reported only 841 female employees in clothing-related trades in 1845, a figure out of line with other data for Boston in this period. In *Report*, app. Z (p. A-45), he cites a figure of 2,402 female workers in the needle trades in 1837. In 1860 almost 4,400 such workers were enumerated in the city in the federal manuscript census. In Table 5.1, I have estimated the number of female garment workers in Boston in 1845 as a linear interpolation between the figures for 1837 and 1860 rather than rely on the obvious undercount by Shattuck. For confirmation of the judgment here, see Jane H. Pease and William H. Pease, *Ladies, Women, and Wenches: Choice and Constraint in Antebellum Charleston and Boston* (Chapel Hill: University of North Carolina Press, 1990), p. 45.

6. Louise A. Tilly and Joan W. Scott, *Women, Work, and Family* (New York: Holt, Rinehart, and Winston, 1978), p. 68.

7. Shattuck, *Report*, p. 84.

Table 5.1. Women's occupations in Boston, 1845 and 1860

	1845	1860
Domestic service	54.8%	62.3%
Clothing trades	33.9	26.0
Teaching	2.7	3.2
Clerical, sales	[a]	2.5
Other occupations	8.6	6.0
Total employed	9,118	16,852

[a] Clerical and sales work is grouped among other occupations.

Sources: Shattuck, *Report to the Committee . . . to Obtain the Census of Boston . . . 1845*, pp. 82–85, and app. Y, pp. 39–43; and 1860 federal manuscript census of Boston. For a discussion of estimating women employed in the clothing trades in 1845, see note 5.

The concentration of workingwomen in mid-nineteenth-century Boston in domestic service and the needle trades meant that wage work followed closely the lines of unpaid domestic labor that young women performed in their families of origin. Caring for younger siblings, keeping house, and sewing were common work for teenage daughters assisting their mothers in urban and rural homes alike,[8] thus it was a relatively simple step for a Yankee daughter to perform the same work for pay in her own or someone else's home. And although domestic service and the needle trades predominated in aggregate statistics, many young women interspersed these jobs with stretches of other kinds of employment.[9] At the entry level at least, neither domestic service nor sewing entailed skills or specializations beyond those acquired within the home.

The employment patterns of Boston's workingwomen reflect broader patterns evident elsewhere in the nation in this period. Domestic service dominated the female labor market throughout the urban Northeast. In 1870, for instance, Boston had one servant for every three and one-half families in the city; for New York City and Philadelphia, the comparable proportions were one servant for every four and five families,

8. For a rich primary account of just such domestic work for two young Vermont women in the 1830s, see Blanche Brown Bryant and Gertrude Elaine Baker, eds., *The Diaries of Sally and Pamela Brown* (Springfield, Vt.: William L. Bryant Foundation, 1970).

9. Louisa Chapman, of Danvers, Massachusetts, worked primarily as a dressmaker, for instance, in 1848 and 1849. Nonetheless, she also taught school and bound shoes in this period. Louisa Chapman Diary, EI.

respectively.[10] Looking at the urban labor force more generally confirms Boston's representativeness. In New York City in 1855, the needle trades were roughly 17 percent of the overall urban labor force; domestic service accounted for about a third of all gainfully employed.[11] Were we to compute the proportions these two occupations made up of New York City's female labor force, the numbers would probably be quite comparable with those evident for Boston. In Philadelphia in 1860, about 40 percent of all females employed in manufacturing were found in the clothing trades, a figure roughly analogous to those for Boston and New York City.[12]

Although domestic service and the needle trades dominated female employment in mid-nineteenth-century Boston, there were significant differences in occupational patterns along ethnic lines. It must be noted that immigrants predominated in Boston's female work force, accounting for almost 64 percent of all workingwomen. Native-born whites contributed another 35 percent, whereas native-born blacks made up just over 1 percent of the female work force. As Table 5.2 indicates, immigrants and blacks were much more concentrated in domestic service than were native-born whites.

Native-born white women in Boston in 1860 worked in a broader range of occupations than did either blacks or immigrants. The proportion of servants among native-born whites was less than half those among immigrants or blacks, whereas the proportion in white-collar occupations—professionals, proprietors, and clerical and sales workers— was more than four times as great. Clearly, the employment opportunities available to Yankee workingwomen were considerably greater than those for black or immigrant women in the city.

10. Daniel E. Sutherland, *Americans and Their Servants: Domestic Service in the United States from 1800 to 1920* (Baton Rouge: Louisiana State University Press, 1981), p. 46.

11. Christine Stansell, *City of Women: Sex and Class in New York, 1789–1860* (New York: Alfred A. Knopf, 1986), p. 108; and Robert Ernst, *Immigrant Life in New York City, 1825–1863* (Port Washington, N.Y.: Ira J. Freeman, 1965; originally published in 1949), pp. 214–17.

12. Bruce Laurie and Mark Schmitz, "Manufacture and Productivity: The Making of an Industrial Base, Philadelphia, 1850–1880," in Theodore Hershberg, ed., *Philadelphia: Work, Space, Family, and Group Experience in Philadelphia in the Nineteenth Century* (New York: Oxford University Press, 1981), p. 47.

Table 5.2. Occupations of Boston workingwomen, 1860,
by race and nativity

	Native-born white	Native-born black	Foreign-born
Domestic service	32.6%	86.9%	78.1%
Needle trades	43.4	9.5	16.8
Professional, proprietor	9.1	1.8	1.7
Clerical, sales	5.3	0.5	1.0
Other occupations	9.7	1.4	2.4
Total cases	5,895	221	10,734

Source: 1860 federal manuscript census of Boston.
Note: Percentages may not add to 100.0 because of rounding.

In terms of job opportunities, black women in Boston were more similar to immigrants than to native-born whites.[13] In fact, judging from 1860 occupations, we find that black women had even fewer opportunities than did immigrants. They were more highly concentrated in domestic service than were immigrants, with almost 87 percent found in these occupations. In addition, fewer black than immigrant women found employment in white-collar work, 2.3 versus 2.7 percent. To the extent that occupational variety implies occupational choice, black women fared poorly in Boston in 1860.[14]

Black women were concentrated in domestic service, and within that category, they were crowded still further into specific occupations. Thirty black women, for instance, were employed as laundresses and washerwomen—more than 15 percent of blacks in domestic service. Although blacks numbered only 1.8 percent of Boston servants, they constituted 5.5 percent of washerwomen in the city. Twelve blacks accounted for more than one in seven female cooks in Boston in 1860. Finally, blacks

13. This generalization stands in contrast to the view expressed by Oscar Handlin, who has argued that Boston blacks were closer to native-born whites than to the immigrant Irish in terms of their occupations. He based his argument entirely on evidence of male employment patterns. See *Boston's Immigrants*, pp. 69–70, 250–51.

14. This situation worsened still further after the Civil War. See Elizabeth Hafkin Pleck, *Black Migration and Poverty: Boston, 1865–1900* (New York: Academic Press, 1979), especially chap. 5.

made up 3.6 percent of chambermaids in the city's hotels, a figure twice their proportion among servants generally. Occupational clustering was the fate of working African-American women in Boston, clear evidence of the segregation by race and sex in the city's labor markets.

Black women did wrest one advantage from the particular occupations they filled within domestic service. A larger proportion of black women in domestic service than of native-born white women were able to live by themselves or with their own families. More than 25 percent of black female domestic servants lived outside the households of their employers, whereas just under 11 percent of native-born white women in domestic service did so. Their reliance on day domestic service for employment gave these black women a measure of autonomy in their lives.[15]

Black workingwomen stood out from white native-born and foreign-born women in another important respect. Black women were considerably older and more likely to be married or widowed than either of the other groups of workingwomen in Boston in 1860. On average, black women workers were 32 years old, compared with 27 and 28 for white native-born and immigrant women, respectively. Almost 30 percent of black workingwomen were 40 years of age or older, about double the proportions for the other two groups. This wide age spread among black workingwomen was reflected in figures for their marital status. Almost 16 percent of black workingwomen were married or widowed, in contrast to less than 9 percent for each of the other groups. Paid employment extended over a considerably longer period of time for black women in Boston at mid-century than for other women in the city. Even at this relatively early date, in a city with a reputation for abolitionism, blacks clearly constituted a class apart. An apparent contradiction existed between the improving legal status of Boston blacks—as evidenced by the end of school segregation in 1855—and the harsh economic realities of black lives.[16]

15. That such autonomy remained important for black women is a theme developed by Elizabeth Clark-Lewis with regard to southern migrants employed as domestic servants in Washington, D.C., in the twentieth century. See Clark-Lewis, "'This Work Had a End': African-American Domestic Workers in Washington, D.C., 1910–1940," in Carol Groneman and Mary Beth Norton, eds., *"To Toil the Livelong Day": America's Working Women, 1780–1980* (Ithaca: Cornell University Press, 1987), pp. 196–212.

16. John Daniels, *In Freedom's Birthplace: A Study of the Boston Negroes* (Boston: Houghton Mifflin, 1914), p. 84; and James Oliver Horton and Lois E. Horton, *Black Bostonians: Family*

Black women stood out among workingwomen in Boston, but they made up only about 1 percent of the female labor force in 1860. Immigrants, however, made up about 64 percent of all workingwomen in the city. As with black women, immigrant women were concentrated heavily in certain occupational groups. Young single immigrants predominated among the more than ten thousand domestic servants in Boston in 1860. Just over 80 percent of all female servants were foreign-born at that date. In addition, more than 54 percent of all female servants were under 25, and more than 94 percent were single.[17]

At mid-century, between 80 and 85 percent of Boston servants worked in private households. The 1845 census recorded 14.6 percent of servants working in hotels and boardinghouses.[18] In 1860 only 7 percent of female servants resided in large institutions—primarily hotels and boardinghouses—but it is very likely that the proportion working in these locations was considerably higher. Another 10.5 percent of servants in 1860 lived alone or with their families and went out to work. A good share of these women probably worked in hotels and restaurants. Finally, just under 83 percent of servants boarded in private households in the city, a share strikingly similar to that recorded for servants in 1845.

Life and Community Struggle in the Antebellum North (New York: Holmes & Meier, 1979), pp. 70–75. Still, discrimination remained rampant. For the implications of these developments for the life of one black woman, see Harriet E. Wilson, *Our Nig; or, Sketches from the Life of a Free Black*, ed. Henry Louis Gates, Jr. (New York: Random House, 1983; originally published in 1859). Although the events described in *Our Nig* take place in New Hampshire or in rural Massachusetts, it appears that Harriet E. Wilson moved to Boston, where she was enumerated in the 1860 federal manuscript census (see pp. xiv, xxvi–xxvii).

17. Marital status was not explicitly recorded in the federal manuscript census until 1880. I have inferred marital status from the listings of household members in the census. Needless to say, some of the apparently single servants employed in Boston households may have been married (with husbands living elsewhere) or widowed. This same difficulty would hold for other occupational groups at this date, so comparisons among groups may be more reliable than actual proportions.

Unfortunately, comparable distributions are not available for servants in other cities. See Ernst, *Immigrant Life*, p. 215, for New York City data. The incomparability of Ernst's tabulations and published census data makes it impossible to determine the proportions of immigrants and native-born among New York City servants. Stansell, *City of Women*, pp. 156–57, suggests that no more than 4 percent of servants in New York were native-born whites. She uses Ernst's figures, however, without acknowledging the limits of the sources that he explicitly pointed out.

18. Shattuck, *Report*, p. 84.

Two occupational groups among servants stood out in terms of their patterns of residence. More than 76 percent of laundresses and washerwomen lived at home, as did a similar proportion of chambermaids. Some laundresses went out to work in the households of their employers; others took laundry in and worked in their own homes.[19] Chambermaids probably were employed almost exclusively in Boston's downtown hotels.[20] Domestic workers in hotels earned more than those in private homes, but they did not typically receive room and board, so their living expenses would have been correspondingly greater.[21] Laundresses and domestics in hotels grew in numbers in the second half of the nineteenth century, part of a pattern of increasing day domestic service.

Contemporary descriptions of domestic service in this period reveal a major contradiction. On the one hand, servants' earnings were among the highest for workingwomen in Boston. On the other hand, women who had any options avoided domestic service. One study summarized the material conditions of servants in 1871: "This class of [women] workers live, as a rule, in greater comfort than any other; that is, their food is better, lodgings more comfortable, and their wages enable them to dress neatly and comfortably and to save something." Yet, despite the material comforts of domestic service, "many who try this kind of labor become discouraged. . . . Especially is this true of the American girl, whose inherited love of freedom leads her to suffer much before placing herself in a position where she readily perceives tyranny to be possible." One Yankee servant expressed precisely this complaint when she wrote in her diary of feeling like "a slave to others wants."[22] Fundamentally, domestic service seemed like domestic tyranny to many potential servants and created a degree of dependence on the employing family that many young women felt to be degrading.

19. "Needle and Garden: The Story of a Seamstress Who Laid Down Her Needle and Became a Strawberry-Girl," *Atlantic Monthly*, March 1865, pp. 325–26, offers an account of one such laundress who worked out in the household of her employer.

20. The residence patterns of the two groups confirm these generalizations. Laundresses were distributed among eleven of twelve wards of the city, with no single ward including more than 30 percent of the group. In contrast, more than 93 percent of chambermaids resided in a single ward.

21. Massachusetts Bureau of Statistics of Labor (hereinafter cited as Mass. BSL), *Annual Report* 1871, pp. 199–201. See also Mass. BSL, *Annual Report*, 1872, p. 67.

22. Mass. BSL, *Annual Report*, 1871, pp. 198–99; and Lizzie A. Wilson Goodenough Diary, July 16, 1865, AAS.

On the whole, servants were slightly younger and considerably less propertied than workingwomen generally (see Figure 5.1). The average age of servants in 1860 was 27.0 (compared with 27.8 for all other workingwomen). Only 3.5 percent of servants reported owning any real or personal property compared with 11.6 percent of all other workingwomen. The median property holding for those servants who owned property was only $50 in contrast to $200 for all other women workers with property. Moreover, the low property ownership was not simply a function of the age and household status of servants. Live-in servants, for instance, were distinctly less propertied than other workingwomen who boarded. Among those who owned some personal property, both groups had median holdings valued at $300. Less than 1 percent of the servants owned any personal property, however, whereas more than 4 percent of other workingwomen owned some. Clearly, domestic service represented the lowest rung on the female occupational ladder in Boston at this date.

Women employed in the needle trades differed not only from domestic servants but also from all Boston workingwomen in a number of important respects. A relatively large share of these women lived at home while working—49.5 percent compared with only 26.4 percent for all Boston workingwomen. In addition, women in the needle trades were more concentrated in their teens and early twenties than were all workingwomen. The high proportion of needleworkers who were children living at home was principally responsible for both these differences. Among female garment workers in 1860, 33.5 percent lived at home with their parent(s); among all workingwomen, the comparable proportion was only 14.1 percent.

Needleworkers were not an entirely homogeneous group, consisting as they did of some thirty separate occupations. Tailoresses, dressmakers, seamstresses, and milliners were the four largest occupational groups within the needle trades in 1860. Together, they constituted about 84 percent of all Boston women recorded in the 1860 census as employed in garment work.[23]

23. The other leading occupations within Boston's needle trades in 1860, in order of descending numbers, were cap maker, vest maker, sewing, upholstress, and cloak maker. No other occupations employed as many as 1 percent of female needle trades workers in Boston in 1860.

Figure 5.1. Domestic servants posing for photographer. Courtesy of Smithsonian Institution, Washington.

Although the census did not record the actual place of employment, we can draw reasonable inferences. Milliners were the most likely of the major groups of needleworkers to have been employed in shops or factories outside their own homes. They were the youngest of the occupational groups, averaging 23.4 years of age; consequently, they were much more likely to be free of family responsibilities that might keep them at home than were other needleworkers. Just over 94 percent of milliners were single, and almost 90 percent were either boarders or children living at home. Seamstresses, by contrast, were 28.8 years old on average; moreover, a smaller share, 78 percent, were children (i.e., living at home) or boarders, whereas 16 percent were married or widowed.[24] Seamstresses were most likely among needleworkers to have worked at home, combining sewing outwork with their domestic responsibilities (see Figures 5.2 and 5.3).[25]

Differences in property ownership among these occupational groups are revealing as well. Dressmakers owned more property than any other group of women needleworkers, though the mean of $54 was by no means impressive. Still, compared with $10.60 on average for tailoresses or $25.47 for seamstresses, this figure does stand out.[26] Overall, 9.5 percent of dressmakers owned some property, compared with only 5.4 and 6.0 percent, respectively, of tailoresses and milliners.

Two factors probably account for the greater property ownership of dressmakers. First, dressmaking, when carried out in custom shops, was the most skilled of the needle trades occupations, often entailing an apprenticeship of several years.[27] Second, dressmakers were older than

24. Milliners remained among the youngest of Boston's needle trades workers throughout the final decades of the nineteenth century. In 1880, milliners in a sample of Boston working-women averaged 24.73 years of age, considerably younger than dressmakers or seamstresses. See Carroll D. Wright, *The Working Girls of Boston* (Boston: Wright and Potter, 1889; originally published in 1884), p. 39. For a fuller, more recent exploration of many of these issues, see Wendy Gamber, "The Female Economy: The Millinery and Dressmaking Trades, 1860–1930," Ph.D. diss., Brandeis University, 1990, especially chap. 2.

25. The two illustrations here come from a composite lithograph, "Women and Their Work in the Metropolis," *Harper's Bazar*, April 18, 1868, p. 394. My thanks to Helena Wright of the Smithsonian Institution for help identifying this illustration.

26. The means reported here are for all women in these occupational groups, both those who owned property and those who did not.

27. Gamber, "Female Economy," pp. 2, 6. For telling accounts of the experiences of would-be dressmakers in New Hampshire in the 1830s, see Jo Anne Preston, "'To Learn Me

Figure 5.2. "Milliners," from *Harper's Bazar*, detail from *Women and Their Work in the Metropolis*, 1868. Courtesy of Smithsonian Institution, Washington.

most other groups of needleworkers, though their mean age of 27.5 years did not quite match the figure for seamstresses. Dressmakers included a number of women who ran their own shops—about a tenth of dressmakers in the 1860 sample were listed as proprietors in the *Boston Business Directory*. For these women, dressmaking offered a measure of economic independence. Perhaps their female employees perceived the prospect of a degree of economic independence for themselves as well.[28]

---

the Whole of the Trade': Conflict between a Female Apprentice and a Merchant Tailor in Antebellum New England," *Labor History* 24 (1983): 259–73, and "Learning a Trade in Industrializing New England: The Expedition of Hannah and Mary Adams to Nashua, New Hampshire, 1833–1834," *Historical New Hampshire* 30 (Spring/Summer 1984): 24–44.

28. See Wendy Gamber, "A Precarious Independence: Milliners and Dressmakers in Boston, 1860–1890," *Journal of Women's History* 4 (1992): 65–66, and "Female Economy," table 1.1, p. 35. Although proprietors undoubtedly owned more real and personal property than typical needleworkers, Gamber found that only 31 percent of proprietors from an 1860 Boston sample of milliners and dressmakers were recorded as owning property ("Female Economy," p. 56).

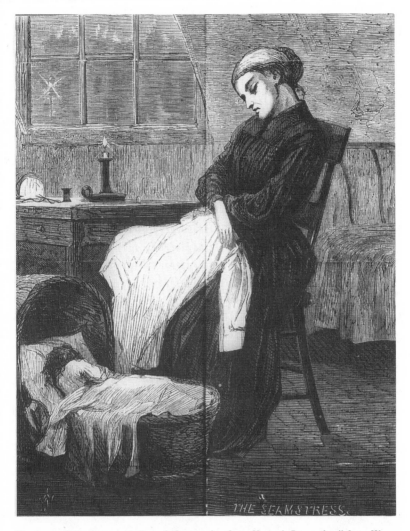

Figure 5.3. "The Seamstress," an 1868 engraving from *Harper's Bazar*, detail from *Women and Their Work in the Metropolis*. Courtesy of Smithsonian Institution, Washington.

Curiously, property ownership was actually most widespread among seamstresses—over 10 percent owned some property—though their actual mean figure of $25 was low. Skill did not play much of a part here, for seamstresses were the least skilled and most poorly paid of all needle trades workers. The large number of widowed household heads among seamstresses accounts for the relatively wide dispersal of property ownership among them. The low mean property figure suggests, however, that few seamstresses had the measure of independence that a self-employed dressmaker might enjoy.

Garment work in Boston in 1860 was divided into outside and inside work.[29] The vast majority of needleworkers probably worked in their own homes, that is, in the outside system, periodically picking up bundles of precut work at a downtown shop. Having completed the work, they would carry it downtown once more, where they would return it to the contractor's shop and be paid a piece wage according to their output.[30]

The outside system in the Boston garment industry was a highly developed, but largely unmechanized, system of outwork production. Manufacturers and wholesalers depended on members of underemployed farming families in the countryside and recent immigrants in the city. The cheap wages for needlework that resulted from competition between these two groups undercut any incentives that mechanization might have offered to employers. One historian has described what came to be known in the period as the "Boston system."

> Here the tailoring process in the middle of the century had been evolved into an efficient and carefully divided system of manufacture. Several cutters and trimmers laid out the cloth into the necessary pieces which would compose the garment and then these pieces were sent to thousands of women living in Boston or scattered throughout New England to be sewn into a whole garment. These latter seamstresses, the wives and daughters of farmers, would sew these pieces in their spare time and especially during the long winter's evenings. . . . After the sewing machine was introduced, more of this work was done in the city, either in homes or factories.[31]

---

29. Ava Baron and Susan E. Klepp, "'If I Didn't Have My Sewing Machine . . .': Women and Sewing Machine Technology," in Joan M. Jensen and Sue Davidson, eds., *A Needle, a Bobbin, a Strike: Women Needleworkers in America* (Philadelphia: Temple University Press, 1982), pp. 20–59; and Christine Stansell, "The Origins of the Sweatshop: Women and Early Industrialization in New York City," in Michael H. Frisch and Daniel J. Walkowitz, eds., *Working-Class America: Essays on Labor, Community, and American Society* (Urbana: University of Illinois Press, 1983), pp. 78–103.

30. Baron and Klepp, "'If I Didn't Have My Sewing Machine,'" p. 22.

31. Schreiber, "Working People of Boston," pp. 204–5.

The fact that manufacturers could play urban and rural workers off against each other kept wages low. As was the case for rural outworkers fifty years earlier—such as the handloom weavers and braiders of palm-leaf hats discussed in Chapter 2—outworkers in New Hampshire and Maine in the 1860s and 1870s did not depend on sewing as their main source of income. Urban seamstresses also needed to combine their earnings with the wage income of other family members to make ends meet. The Boston garment industry expanded at the expense of poorly paid rural and urban outworkers.[32]

One result of this expansion of urban outwork in the Boston garment industry was extremely low wages for semiskilled seamstresses. Reports in the mid-1860s placed the wages of sewing women between $3.00 and $3.50 per week, wages no higher than those of Lowell millworkers thirty years earlier. Testimony before a Massachusetts state legislative committee in 1869 indicated that there were more than 18,000 needlewomen in the city and estimated their weekly wage at $3.00.[33]

Inside workers were said not to fare much better than homebound seamstresses. Aurora Phelps reported in May 1869: "Girls are employed on Federal, Washington, and other streets, in the numbers of 40, 50, and 60 in a shop, at less than $3.50 a week. Sewing-machine operators average $2.50 a week in those shops. You can see them in those shops seated in long rows, crowded together in a hot, close atmosphere, working at piecework."[34] Still, there were variations among the earnings of different classes of women workers in the needle trades. The wages of garment workers varied drastically from ill-paid shirtmakers, who probably worked in their own homes, to relatively skilled coat makers, who were employed in custom shops. A survey of shopwork in Boston in 1870 found all groups earning more than homeworkers, with wages ranging from $4.60 per week on average for shirtmakers to $10.72 a week for

32. For contemporary descriptions of the rural side of the "Boston system," see Mass. BSL, *Annual Report*, 1871, pp. 201–2, and 1872, pp. 72–73.

33. Helen Sumner, *History of Women in Industry in the United States*, vol. 9 of *Report on the Condition of Woman and Child Wage Earners in the United States* (Washington: GPO, 1910), pp. 145–46, 149. Note how much greater is the contemporary estimate than the census count of less than 4,400 just nine years earlier, further evidence of census underenumeration of women's paid employment.

34. *American Workman*, May 1, 1869, as quoted in Sumner, *History of Women in Industry*, p. 149.

coat makers. Earnings of other needle trades workers fell between these two extremes (see Table 5.3).

Judging from this report, we find that the typical Boston garment shopworker in 1870 probably earned about $8 a week and $200 over the course of a year. With annual earnings at this level, she was paid only about three-fourths what a Lowell textile operative or Lynn shoeworker might earn at the same date.[35] A garment worker could be self-supporting while she was employed but would be hard-pressed to support herself through the entire year. Most, in fact, probably lived at home and contributed their earnings when working to the family till; single boarders in the city may well have returned to live with their families in the countryside during the slack seasons.

The evidence highlights the difficulty needleworkers faced because of the seasonality of their employment. Such problems were not unique, however, to needleworkers. An 1884 study offers insights into the ways that women workers in Boston coped with slack time. In a sample of 1,032 women employed outside of domestic service, about three-fourths had been out of employment for three months in the previous year on average. Of the 758 women who lost some time from work during the year, only 61 reported any additional paid employment, about 8 percent of those who faced periods of enforced unemployment.[36] There were limitations to a needleworker's ability to patch together year-round work. One contemporary noted the source of this difficulty: "But from all the dress-making, cap-making, cloak and paper-collar establishments in the city, a large portion of the employes are turned away, unable, for nearly or quite half the year, to obtain any employment, and the circumstances specially distressing, that the dull season occurs in nearly all these trades *at about the same time*, destroying all chance of obtaining employment at any price at some other occupation."[37] Since the "dull season" affected so many of the needle trades at the same time, many

35. One study put the annual average earnings of women operatives in the state's cotton textile mills at $265 and in boots and shoes at $283 at about this date. Mass. BSL, *Annual Report*, 1873, table 3, pp. 76, 78; see also Mass. BSL, *Annual Report*, 1876, pp. 123–24.

36. Wright, *Working Girls of Boston*, pp. 56–57, 88.

37. Mass. BSL, *Annual Report*, 1871, p. 206, emphasis in original. These difficulties persisted at least into the World War I era in Boston; see Gamber, "Female Economy," pp. 147–52.

Table 5.3. Earnings of Boston garment workers
employed in shops and manufactories, 1870

Occupation	Mean weekly wage	Weeks in year	Yearly earnings	Number
Shirtmakers	$ 4.60	40	$184	952
Dressmakers	7.01	16	112	281
Cloak makers	7.86	22	173	1,313
Vest makers	8.99	24	216	179
Pants makers	9.07	24	218	214
Coat makers	10.72	24	257	315

Source: Mass. Bureau of Statistics of Labor, *Annual Report*, 1871, pp. 209–19. Mean wages are calculated from grouped data provided in the report.

workingwomen simply had to accept a period of unemployment. Those with families outside the city might take advantage of the break to return to their family homes until employment picked up.

Although seasonality affected all needleworkers, significant wage differentials persisted. The range of women's earnings reflected the varied wage prospects in the outside and inside sectors of the city's garment industry. Shirtmakers probably worked in their own homes on goods put out by wholesale clothiers; coat makers, on the other hand, plied their skilled trades in small shops across the city. Low-paid outwork did not entirely displace employment in shops and factories, because there were still garment trades that required skilled workers. Small dressmaking and tailoring establishments continued to cater to the custom trade. In addition, the appearance of foot-powered sewing machines at mid-century stimulated the growth of factory stitching operations. Younger women, probably most often boarders or daughters living at home, made up the largest share of inside workers in the garment trades. They worked in small tailoring, dressmaking, and millinery shops and in factory workshops associated with the larger clothing wholesalers and department stores.

Inside workers in 1860 did not necessarily work at sewing machines, although where mechanization had occurred, by this date it was concentrated in the inside shops. Only twenty-nine Boston women were recorded in the 1860 census as operating sewing machines—the actual number must have been much higher. But we may draw some conclusions about these inside workers to the extent that they were representative of machine stitchers generally. All twenty-nine women were single, more than 75 percent were boarders, and they were considerably younger than female needle trades workers generally, with a mean age of 23 compared with over 26 for all sewing women. Moreover, 73 percent (eleven of fifteen) of the native-born among these machine stitchers had been born in Maine and New Hampshire. In other words, the native-born among them were typically single migrants living in the city and supporting themselves. By contrast, fewer than half of all native-born needleworkers in Boston in 1860 had been born outside of Massachusetts. The census evidence shows, then, that homework included young women and old, widows, and children. Inside work drew disproportionately from younger boarding women who had migrated to the city expressly to take up this employment.

Contemporary sources permit an estimate of the proportions of women who worked in the inside and outside sectors of the industry. In 1875 more than nine thousand women statewide worked at home in the needle trades. Fully two-thirds of these women resided in Boston, where a majority of all female garment workers were employed in their own homes.[38] Given the greater reliance on the sewing machine in 1875 than fifteen years earlier, a somewhat larger proportion of needleworkers were probably employed in their own homes in 1860. To this proportion we might add the number of women who boarded in households headed by tailors or dressmakers—9 percent of boarding needle trades workers—who may very well have worked in the homes of their landlord-employers. Altogether, it is unlikely that more than a third of garment workers in Boston in 1860 actually went out to workshops or factories to ply their trades.

One additional set of sources permits a closer view of women's work in the Boston garment trades in this period—the federal manuscript censuses of manufactures. Every ten years between 1850 and 1880, census enumerators recorded information concerning all Boston establishments—whether proprietorships, partnerships, or incorporated businesses—that manufactured goods valued at five hundred dollars or more.

38. Carroll D. Wright, *The Census of Massachusetts: 1875*, vol. 2 (Boston: Albert J. Wright, 1876), pp. 196–98, 437–41.

The manufacturing census schedules complement the population censuses and are particularly useful in analyzing the work settings of women garment workers.[39]

Viewing the Boston needle trades in terms of garment firms underscores the diversity of the industry. At one end of the spectrum were numerous small tailoring shops with a tailor and his assistant or a dressmaker and several seamstresses. Typical of these firms was the bonnet shop of Mimi Hutchinson. With a capital investment of $100, Hutchinson employed two other milliners. Together in 1850 they produced an annual output of bonnets valued at only $650. On an entirely different scale were the wholesale clothiers and department stores with vast outwork networks employing hundreds of needlewomen who worked in their own homes on goods distributed by the firms. W. R. Lovejoy & Sons was one of the largest of these establishments, employing seventy-five men and seven hundred women stitching ready-made clothing worth $250,000 a year.[40]

The years between 1850 and 1880 saw a substantial increase in the number of garment firms in Boston, the capital invested, and the value of goods produced (see Table 5.4).[41] The evidence suggests a decline in the reliance on outwork in the Boston garment industry between 1850 and 1880. Despite growth in terms of capital invested and the value of goods produced, the average number of workers per firm declined by more than a third, from sixty-one to thirty-nine. Even with this 36 percent reduction in the average size of the labor force in individual firms, average annual wages paid by each firm declined by only 9 percent,

39. The manuscript manufacturing schedules are an underutilized source and deserve more attention than labor historians or women's historians have typically given them. Useful exceptions to this pattern include Laurie and Schmitz, "Manufacture and Productivity," and Bruce Laurie, Theodore Hershberg, and George Alter, "Immigrants and Industry: The Philadelphia Experience, 1850–1880," both in Hershberg, *Philadelphia*.

40. Federal Manuscript Census of Manufactures, 1850, Boston, T1204, roll 6.

41. Initially I intended to use the 1860 census of manufacturing as a starting point to permit direct comparison with the detailed information on needle trades occupations in the population census. On coding and analyzing that data, however, I discovered that enumerators in 1860 had undoubtedly failed to canvass the city fully. Whereas 198 garment firms were noted in 1850 and 348 in 1870, enumerators recorded only 82 in 1860. Rather than be uncertain as to the representativeness of the 1860 census, it made sense to use 1850 as a starting date.

Table 5.4. Garment firms in Boston, 1850 and 1880:
mean values for representative variables

Variable	1850	1880[a]
Capital invested	$7,239	$13,988
Value, raw materials	$21,904	$32,667
Annual wages paid	$12,595	$11,442
Value, products	$39,376	$52,829
Males employed	16.1	8.9
Females employed	45.2	30.2
Monthly male wage	$32.20	n.a.
Monthly female wage	$11.75	n.a.
Number of firms[a]	197	322

Sources: 1850 and 1880 federal manuscript censuses of manufactures for Boston.

[a] In constant 1850 dollars.

[b] The number of firms varies slightly among variables depending on the completeness of the responses that proprietors provided census enumerators.

which indicates a gain in the average annual earnings of workers.[42] These greater annual earnings reflected a declining reliance on part-time outside workers over the period. In this respect, Boston clothing firms experienced a development similar to that in the Lynn shoe industry. Firms in both sectors displayed a steady shift from decentralized outwork to centralized factory production in the Civil War period. Even though we do not know for certain the proportion of Boston clothing workers laboring in shops or factories, it is clear that firms were concentrating their operations in centralized locations. The increasing capital investments and earnings per worker and the declining number of workers certainly point to that conclusion.

A closer examination of the sizes of work forces in Boston garment firms in 1850 and 1880 reinforces this conclusion (see Table 5.5). Between 1850 and 1880 the proportion of small garment firms—those employing ten or fewer workers—increased from 34 to 52 percent. The proportion of workers employed in such settings more than doubled,

42. Inflation of the overall cost of living between 1850 and 1880 amounted to 19.2 percent, a figure based on averaging three major series, E135, E174, and E184, found in U.S. Bureau of the Census, *Historical Statistics of the United States: Colonial Times to 1970* (Washington: GPO, 1975), pp. 211–12.

Table 5.5. Distribution of garment firms and workers,
Boston, 1850 and 1880, by firm size

Firm size (workers)	1850		1880	
	Firms	Workers	Firms	Workers
1-10	34.0%	3.1%	51.6%	7.2%
11-20	20.8	5.5	17.2	6.7
21-50	21.8	11.1	16.2	13.2
51-99	10.2	10.8	7.2	12.0
100+	13.2	69.5	7.8	60.9
Total cases	197	12,065	320	12,750

Sources: 1850 and 1880 federal manuscript censuses of manufactures for Boston.

from 3 to 7 percent. The shares of intermediate-sized firms remained basically stationary over the period, whereas the proportion of firms with greater than fifty employees declined sharply. In 1850, more than 23 percent of all garment firms reported over fifty employees. By 1880, only 15 percent of all firms had operations on that scale. These shifts did not occur in a declining market for ready-made clothing, for the overall number of garment workers increased by 6 percent. The data reveal a shift away from vast outwork operations in which women sewed at home on a part-time basis under minimal supervision and an increase in the share of needleworkers employed in workshop and factory settings. This shift was only partial, however, as more than 60 percent of needleworkers continued to be employed in 1880 by firms with work forces of one hundred or more. Put-out work persisted as the most typical form of employment in the needle trades, and a majority of Boston sewing women probably continued to work in their own homes throughout the nineteenth century.

Female proprietors directed a number of Boston's garment operations. About 7 percent of firms in 1850 where owners could be identified were owned by women; for 1880, the comparable proportion was less than 4 percent. The tiny numbers of female-headed firms recorded in the manufacturing censuses—twelve in 1850 and ten in 1880—represented only a small share of such businesses throughout the city and indicate that enumerators failed to record a great many small firms headed by women.[43] Still, the differences between male- and female-headed garment firms as enumerated in 1850 are of some interest. Male-headed firms were considerably larger operations than female-headed businesses: capital invested by men averaged $8,000 compared with only $600 for women. Males employed 68 workers on average in contrast to 7.5 for females. In addition, the value of products for male-headed firms was more than ten times greater than for female-headed ones at mid-century. The evidence indicates that female milliners and dressmakers typically ran small shops, whereas male entrepreneurs ran both shops and outwork operations.[44]

Urban outwork remained the dominant form of employment in the needle trades between 1850 and 1880 because of demographic and technological factors. The tremendous growth of Boston in these decades and the continuing high numbers of immigrants entering the city created an abundant labor force for unskilled and semiskilled sewing work. Moreover, the availability of relatively cheap sewing machines for the home permitted immigrant families to rent or purchase these machines, thus enabling manufacturers to shift an important overhead expense onto the shoulders of their employees. Ladd & Webster, a Boston firm, advertised its sewing machines in 1861 at prices ranging from fifty to one hundred dollars. Between 1860 and 1870, sales of the two leading sewing machine manufacturers in the nation increased from 38,000 to 211,000 annually, and prices dropped accordingly. Boston clothing firms simultaneously broadened their labor pool and increased their profits by renting machines to outworkers for a dollar a week, thus recouping 80 percent of the cost of the machine over the course of a year.[45] Clearly,

43. In 1880, for instance, the *Boston Business Directory* (Boston: Sampson, Davenport, and Company, microfilm ed. from Research Publications) recorded the names of more than six hundred milliners and dressmakers compared with the total of ten female proprietors who were actually enumerated in the manufacturing census for that year. See Gamber, "Precarious Independence," p. 83.

44. Gamber, "Precarious Independence," p. 70. Gamber offers strikingly parallel evidence for 1860. A third type of firm eludes our attention here, largely because it is obscured in surviving sources, that of a husband and wife together operating a dressmaking or millinery shop. For a good discussion by Gamber of marriage and female entrepreneurship, see pp. 76–80.

45. *Boston Business Directory*, 1860–1861, p. 495; Baron and Klepp, "'If I Didn't Have My Sewing Machine,'" pp. 32, 34; and Mass. BSL, *Annual Report*, 1871, p. 221. Since outworkers' employment was seasonal, firms probably did not rent machines out for a full fifty-two

the needle trades in Boston were immensely profitable for the leading outwork organizers and department stores in the 1860s and 1870s.

The federal manuscript censuses of population and manufactures offer telling views of Boston workingwomen, but they are limited to snapshots of female employment at particular moments in time. There is much to be said for drawing samples of wage-earning women and tracing them over the course of their lives. Servants and garment workers made up more than 78 percent of native-born workingwomen in Boston in 1860, thus providing justification for a focus on these two groups. Two random samples of about four hundred native-born servants and garment workers drawn from the 1860 federal manuscript census of Boston provide a basis for further analysis and permit comparison with findings for Lynn shoeworkers and Lowell millhands.[46] The samples exclude the foreign-born but include both white and black workingwomen, permitting analysis of the impact of race on women's work and family lives. Moreover, the prevalence of daughters of immigrants in the Boston female labor force adds another dimension to the analysis. Finally, parallel samples from the 1880 federal manuscript census of Boston offer views of the changing structure and composition of the female labor force in these occupations over time.[47]

---

weeks a year; still, a rental of thirty weeks' duration would result in a return of 46 percent of the purchase price of a sewing machine. See also Priscilla J. Brewer, *The Queen of Inventions: Sewing Machines in American Homes and Factories, 1850–1920* (Pawtucket, R.I.: Slater Mill Historic Site, 1986).

46. For analysis of a sample of six hundred Boston domestic servants in 1860, see Carol S. Lasser, "Mistress, Maid, and Market: The Transformation of Domestic Service in New England," Ph.D. diss., Harvard University, 1983, chap. 7. Although not based on linkage with additional records, Lasser's sample has the distinct advantage of encompassing both native-born and immigrant servants.

47. The use of samples of servants and garment workers complements an analysis of the entire population of Boston workingwomen. By focusing on 800 women rather than on more than sixteen thousand, we know a great deal more about each worker and can explore her situation in 1860 in considerable detail. More important, it is possible to trace these workingwomen over time through census, marriage, and death records. We gain a sense of their employment and marriage patterns that eludes our grasp when dealing with a vast population of workingwomen at one particular date. We can also examine their family origins whether in Boston or beyond the city's boundaries. Finally, for domestic servants, one can trace their employers over time and gain a sense of employment patterns in private households. Reliance on reasonable-sized samples facilitates record linkage beyond our original sources and opens up a

We may preview the findings that emerge from analysis of these samples and gain a sense of the rich possibilities of tracing working-women over time by focusing briefly on three Boston women. Following their work and family lives between 1850 and 1880 speaks to the range of wage opportunities in Boston in these decades and to the ways workingwomen accommodated multiple demands in their lives.

Elizabeth Day grew up in Damariscotta, on the coast of Maine, the daughter of Hartley and Mary Day. In 1850, when Elizabeth was 11 years old, her father worked as a carpenter in a shipyard and owned real property valued at $1,000. At some point in the next decade Elizabeth moved on her own to Boston, and the 1860 census found her working as a servant in the household of Levi Fitts, a teamster.[48] Less than three years later, in April 1863, Elizabeth Day married in Boston. Her husband, Herbert Winsor, also from Maine, was employed as a postal clerk. Elizabeth Winsor gave birth to a son, Joseph, in 1864, and her younger sister, Jennie, came to Boston and lived with the young family, perhaps helping to care for the infant. The child died of pneumonia in 1868, and the next census found the couple boarding together in a Boston household.

Mary Curran was a second native-born workingwoman in Boston in 1860. Curran was employed as a milliner at that date, but unlike Elizabeth Day, she lived at home with her Irish-born parents. Her father, James Curran, was 52 years old and worked as a laborer. The family had resided in Boston at least five years, as the 1855 state census had recorded 14-year-old Mary and her family in the city at that date. She continued to live at home and earn wages as a milliner until at least 1865. The census in 1870, however, found her boarding in the household of Patrick Fox, another Irish-born laborer. She continued to work as a milliner but no longer lived at home. She married Dennis

world of analytic possibilities. For a fuller discussion of the methods employed in the sampling and study of these groups, see Appendixes 2, 5, and 6 below.

48. Elizabeth Day was enumerated both as a servant in Boston and with her family in her hometown of Damariscotta. Federal Manuscript Census of Population, 1860, Boston, ward 1, M653, roll 520, dwelling 1169, and Damariscotta, Lincoln County, Maine, M653, roll 442, family 697. Such multiple listings of single women who worked away from home are quite common in 1850 and 1860. Parents gave enumerators the names of children who were not necessarily living at home at the time of the census.

McLaughlin in May 1875 and kept house for this Massachusetts-born stevedore, though the couple had no children as of 1880.[49] She may also have taken in some sewing, as the census often failed to record wives' employment.

Our third workingwoman in Boston in 1860 is Mary Sandling, an 18-year-old mulatto servant in the household of Thomas Steanbury, a 37-year-old, English-born mulatto barber. Mary's father was a North Carolina–born black; her mother was Irish. The family had resided in Boston for some time, as the 1850 census recorded John Sandling, a 35-year-old laborer, his wife, and five children, including 9-year-old Mary. Mary may have gone out to work at a very young age, as the 1855 census noted a 14-year-old Mary Sandlin residing in the household of the 70-year-old invalid Thomas Chase.[50]

Mary Sandling escaped domestic service when she married a black man, Benjamin Washington, in May 1865. The newlyweds moved into the household of the groom's parents, and father and son supported this extended family by working as waiters. By 1870 the couple had moved into their own household. Benjamin Washington had become a clothing dealer, and his wife kept house for a growing family, which included son Benjamin, 3, and daughter Rachel, a year old at this date.

These three examples express the range of occupational and family experiences of native-born workingwomen in Boston in the years between 1860 and 1880. Elizabeth Day left home seeking work in Boston and supported herself as a servant in the years before her marriage. Mary Curran lived at home while employed as a milliner for at least five years before moving into her own residence and supporting herself. And Mary Sandling's work experience was typical of black women in Boston in these decades. She worked as a domestic servant and married a black man also employed in a service occupation. Work provided wages for

49. Record linkage for Mary Curran, as for many of the American-born children of Irish parents in the Boston samples, was more uncertain than for individuals with less common names. The 1855 and 1865 census links were unambiguous because Mary Curran continued to live with her parents and names and ages could be checked for consistency. Her 1870 residence and 1875 marriage are plausible links but less certain because only her name, age, and birthplace are available for verifying the consistency of the linkage.

50. What makes this linkage somewhat uncertain is the lack of racial identification. In both 1850 and 1860, census enumerators recorded Mary Sandling as mulatto, but the appropriate column is blank for the 1855 census.

black women in this period but, as we shall see, precious little opportunity for advancement.

All three women first entered the Boston work force as single women. In this respect they were typical of Boston workingwomen generally. Native-born women employed in domestic service and in the needle trades in 1860 were overwhelmingly young, single boarders in the city. More than 48 percent of female servants and 40 percent of garment workers were 22 or younger. Roughly 90 percent of both groups were single, though a difference did emerge in terms of marital status. Although 8 percent of domestic servants were married or widowed, the comparable proportion was 13 percent for women in the needle trades. A major difference also existed in the residence patterns for women in the two groups. More than 94 percent of domestic servants resided in the households of their employers, whereas almost half of needle trades workers, or 45 percent, lived at home while working.

These young workingwomen came from families that were distinctly poorer than most Boston families. Evidence for needle trades workers living at home makes this fact clear. About a third were children living in the homes of their parents. More than a fourth of these homes, or 27 percent, were female-headed households, a proportion almost double that for all households in Boston.[51] Slightly more than 80 percent of employed fathers worked in manual occupations, with unskilled laborers accounting for the largest single share.[52]

The parents of needle trades daughters living at home were divided equally between immigrants and the native-born. A family wage economy is evident in households headed by both groups of parents. Immigrant parents had 4.0 children living at home on average, about 60 percent of whom were earning wages. There were no major differences based on parental nativity as far as the number of working children was concerned. Native-born parents averaged only 3.4 children each, but more than 65 percent of them were working.

51. Knights, *Plain People of Boston*, p. 83, indicates that females made up 15 percent of all household heads in four samples he drew from the federal manuscript censuses of 1830–1860.

52. By contrast, in an 1860 sample of Boston native-born male household heads, only about 60 percent were employed in manual occupations. See Peter R. Knights, *Yankee Destinies: The Lives of Ordinary Nineteenth-Century Bostonians* (Chapel Hill: University of North Carolina Press, 1991), p. 74.

Children in the families of immigrants probably made a greater contribution to their families' economic well-being since their fathers owned less property than did native-born fathers and were typically employed in less well-paying occupations. Native-born fathers owned on average $1,252 of real and personal property, compared with a mean of only $586 for immigrant fathers. These differences in levels of wealth reflected, in turn, the very different occupational worlds open to the native-born and immigrants. Almost 78 percent—thirty-five of forty-five—of the Yankee fathers were employed in skilled occupations or as proprietors. In contrast, more than 71 percent—thirty-five of forty-nine—of immigrant fathers were unskilled workers. Clearly, children's wages contributed relatively more to family income for households headed by immigrants than for those headed by the native-born.

Despite these differences in family circumstances, much the same motivation must have prompted children of immigrants or children of Yankees to seek employment: a desire to contribute to their own support and not to depend on their families. One anonymous writer, who grew up in a Philadelphia neighborhood and had assisted her mother at sewing from an early age, captured this feeling well in an 1865 article that appeared in the *Atlantic Monthly*: "As I was animated by the common ambition of all properly educated girls in my position, to pay my own way, so I worked with my needle with the utmost assiduity. I worked constantly on such garments as my mother could obtain from the shops, going with her to secure them, as well as to deliver such as we made up, each of us very frequently carrying a heavy bundle to and fro."[53] Many others shared this feeling, according to the author. "A girl in my station in life feels an honorable ambition to clothe herself and pay for her board, as soon as she reaches eighteen years of age," she wrote. "They pay their parents from their weekly wages as punctually as if boarding with a stranger."[54] The statements of this young seamstress are self-serving (as those of writers in the *Lowell Offering* had been a generation earlier), but they probably do reflect the motivations of a fair share of working daughters who lived at home in Boston in the 1860s.

53. "Needle and Garden," *Atlantic Monthly*, February 1865, p. 169. This account, published serially, appeared in the magazine between January and October 1865.

54. "Needle and Garden," pp. 165–66.

These lines indicate one young woman's sense of responsibility toward her family, but they also reveal the growing feeling of independence among employed daughters living at home. Greater economic independence may also have nurtured social independence. Daughters who earned their own way may well have felt more able to come and go as they chose, to go out with friends in the evening, or generally to determine important elements of their lives than was common for otherwise dependent children. As historian Kathy Peiss expressed this element in the family lives of young workingwomen in New York City at the turn of the twentieth century, "As wage-earners and contributors to the family, they sought to parlay their new-found status toward greater autonomy in their personal lives."[55]

Unfortunately, it is not possible to determine the proportions of daughters in different groups who lived at home while working. The 1860 census does not permit the calculation of separate figures for daughters of native-born or immigrant parents who lived at home and contributed to family support. The ethnic backgrounds of daughters who lived in boardinghouses or with their employers are elusive because the nativity of their parents is not recorded. Still, counting both the native-born and immigrants, only about 26 percent of workingwomen resided with their families in Boston in 1860 while working.[56] This figure sets an upper limit on the proportion of Boston workingwomen operating entirely within a family wage economy at that date.

Analysis of the families of women workers in 1860 is limited to those employed in the needle trades because of the residence patterns of servants. We can enlarge on 1860 evidence, however, by tracing servants and garment workers back to their families in 1850. In all, it was possible to find 120 sample members in 1850 living with their parents—thirty-five future servants and eighty-five future garment workers. Somewhat more than half resided in Boston; the remainder lived in towns in surrounding Massachusetts or northern New England. Analysis of the parents of women in the two groups is useful in exploring the connections between

55. Kathy Peiss, *Cheap Amusements: Working Women and Leisure in Turn-of-the-Century New York* (Philadelphia: Temple University Press, 1986), p. 69.

56. This proportion is based on all workingwomen enumerated in the 1860 federal manuscript census of Boston and is not limited to the two samples of native-born workingwomen in domestic service and the needle trades.

Table 5.6. 1850 property ownership of parents of
Boston women workers, by occupation and residence

Occupation of daughter	Percentage owning some real property	
	Boston	Rural towns
Domestic service	0.0 (14)	76.2 (21)
Needle trades	9.8 (51)	55.9 (34)

Sources: Linkage of 1860 native-born samples in the 1850 federal manuscript census.

women's work and family in this period (see Table 5.6). Native-born
women workers in Boston in 1860 came from either propertyless urban
families or propertied rural families. Only five of sixty-five urban families reported owning real property in 1850 compared with thirty-five of
fifty-five rural families. Moreover, the urban families of women who entered the needle trades appear to have been better off than the urban
families of women who became servants.

Occupational data are also revealing. More than 75 percent of the urban
fathers of domestic servants were employed in 1850 as unskilled laborers
compared with only 39 percent of the Boston fathers of garment workers.
Interestingly enough, the higher status of urban fathers of garment workers did not carry over into the countryside. There, almost 58 percent of
the fathers of servants were farmers, whereas only 28 percent of the fathers
of garment workers farmed. On average, rural fathers of servants owned
real property valued at twice that for the rural fathers of garment workers.

The evidence on property ownership suggests a difference in the way
families may have viewed domestic service. Among urban families, only
daughters from the poorest families (and large immigrant families at
that) entered domestic service. Daughters from propertied urban families were more likely to go out to work in garment shops or take work
into their homes. Among rural families, by contrast, daughters of
propertied families did migrate to Boston and take domestic work in
private households. For them, the prospect of free housing and steady
employment (and for their parents, perhaps, the prospect of supervision
and guidance) may well have made the move to the city appear less
risky. Because room and board were assured, wages represented
"clear" income, and savings were possible. The apparent difference in the

economic backgrounds of rural and urban recruits into domestic service can then be understood as a reflection of different familial needs and expectations.

Subsequent reminiscences confirm the existence of this group of rural farmers' daughters among Boston servants at mid-century. Bostonian Louisa Crowninshield Bacon, recalling her childhood in Pemberton Square, noted: "In those days we always had American servants, though already some country girls were beginning to work in the mills. If one of the maids left to be married, or for some other reason, a sister or cousin usually turned up to take her place. These maids came from Vermont, New Hampshire and Maine, and had often strange names."[57] Upper-class reminiscences are not useful in reconstructing the perspectives of Yankee servants in Boston, but they do reveal their presence in upper-class households.

Three groups are evident among the families of Boston workingwomen, reflecting both rural-urban and ethnic differences in women's backgrounds. The first of these groups—accounting for 57 percent of the women's families that were successfully linked—consists of rural, native-born propertied families that did not migrate to Boston. Yankee servants came predominantly from this group. More than 95 percent of the rural fathers of servants were native born—twenty of twenty-one— and on average they owned $1,550 in real property in 1850.[58] Daughters from these families probably migrated to Boston to support themselves and save for their future marriages. Their earnings were likely not needed for everyday family support, but they could prove helpful to families that otherwise might have had difficulty placing children on farms of their own in increasingly crowded rural communities.

The second major grouping—accounting for 29 percent of the linked families of Boston workingwomen—was recruited from propertyless urban immigrant families residing in Boston. Linkage in the 1850 census

---

57. Louisa Crowninshield Bacon, *Reminiscences* (Salem, Mass.: Privately Printed, 1922), p. 34.

58. The economic standing of the families of Yankee servants in Boston may well have given them a degree of independence that bothered their employers. Contemporaries commented on the "impertinence" of Yankee servants. See Carol Lasser, "The Domestic Balance of Power: Relations between Mistress and Maid in Nineteenth-Century New England," *Labor History* 28 (Winter 1987): 5–22.

succeeded in tracing thirty-nine immigrant fathers of sample members, fathers of ten servants and twenty-nine garment workers. In only one instance did a father in this group report any real property. For these urban immigrant families, a daughter's earnings as a seamstress or domestic servant were probably crucial to family subsistence. Two-thirds of the fathers were unskilled laborers whose employment was seasonal and whose earnings probably did not exceed $250 a year on average.[59] We do not have to probe very deeply to understand the motivation of these daughters of immigrants in taking up paid employment.

The third significant group among Boston workingwomen consisted of women from rural or urban native-born families who were employed in the needle trades. Unlike the families of Yankee domestic servants, most of these families (59 percent) lived in Boston. Their real property holdings averaged $691 in 1850, a figure midway between the holdings of rural Yankee families of servants and urban immigrant families. Whether they remained in the countryside or moved to Boston, these families were likely considerably more dependent on the earnings of their working children than would have been the case with the more propertied rural families of servants. Still, fathers in these families were concentrated in skilled occupations and family need would have been less than in the case of the families of unskilled recent immigrants. A combination of contributing to the family standard of living and providing savings for future marriages likely motivated Yankee women employed in Boston's needle trades in 1860.

A finer-tuned analysis of the rural families of Boston workingwomen offers further insights into the migration process. For instance, in 1850 the rural fathers of migrant daughters owned real property valued on average at $1,100. Rural fathers who themselves migrated to Boston in the next decade averaged only $724 in real property. Migrant fathers were not simply poorer than those who remained in the countryside but were also less likely to be farmers. Only 17 percent— two of twelve— of migrant fathers had been recorded as farmers in their hometowns

59. Clarence D. Long, *Wages and Earnings in the United States, 1860–1890* (Princeton: Princeton University Press, 1960), p. 99; Stanley Lebergott, *Manpower in Economic Growth: The American Record since 1800* (New York: McGraw-Hill, 1964); and Mass. BSL, *Annual Report, 1873*, p. 94, also cited in Stephan Thernstrom, *Poverty and Progress: Social Mobility in a Nineteenth-Century City* (Cambridge: Harvard University Press, 1964), pp. 20, 244n.

compared with more than 45 percent—sixteen of thirty-five—of fathers who remained in the countryside. Rural families that migrated to Boston had already moved away from a total reliance on farming even before they left the countryside. The pattern here for the rural families of Boston workingwomen is strikingly similar to that for the rural families of Lynn shoeworkers at this time.

Migrating families were less wealthy than families that remained in the countryside while a daughter worked on her own in Boston, but they should not be viewed as a displaced rural proletariat helplessly buffeted by economic forces beyond their control. Evidence exists that migrating families may well have improved their fortunes once in the city of Boston. The fathers, once settled in Boston, were concentrated in skilled and white-collar occupations. More than 83 percent—ten of twelve—found work in skilled or artisanal trades or as merchants or proprietors. In addition, the property they owned increased over the decade of the 1850s. They averaged almost $1,500 in real and personal property according to census enumerators in Boston in 1860, a figure that set them well above the ranks of unskilled or semiskilled workers in the city.[60]

The property holdings of these migrant families in Boston, though greater than those of many urban neighbors, were less than those of families that remained in the countryside. Tracing in censuses of rural communities in 1860 located eighteen families whose daughters worked as domestic servants and garment workers in Boston. On average, those families owned $1,960 of property, compared with $1,500 for migrant families in Boston. The numbers of families are admittedly small, but they suggest that the Yankee families of Boston workingwomen— whether these families persisted in the countryside or migrated to Boston—were property owners. They were not drawn from the bottom ranks of either rural or urban society.

60. Unfortunately, the 1850 census did not record personal property, so the comparison presented here cannot be as precise as one would like. Looking at real property alone, migrating fathers increased their average holdings from $724 to $892 as they moved from the countryside to the city over the decade 1850–1860. The increase in the value of the real property of fathers was 23 percent over the decade, considerably greater than inflation for these years, which was a bit more than 9 percent. U.S. Bureau of the Census, *Historical Statistics*, pp. 211–12, ser. E135, E174, E183, and E184. For comparable evidence that confirms the relative well-being of these migrant families, see Knights, *Plain People of Boston*, pp. 92–93.

Linkage back to the families of Boston workingwomen extends our knowledge in useful ways. The total number of linked families of women workers is only 120 out of the two samples totaling 808 women, but the patterns indicate a revealing difference between garment workers and servants. Recent solitary rural migrants to the city made up a much larger share of servants than of garment workers, who most frequently came from urban families. For both servants and garment workers, the daughters of immigrants were more likely to have family in Boston than were Yankee daughters, and among those employed in the needle trades, the daughters of immigrants were more likely to live at home with their parents. Moreover, rural families of migrant workingwomen in Boston were considerably better off than rural families that migrated to the city, who, in turn, enjoyed clear advantages in comparison with immigrant families recently arrived in the city.

Confirming evidence concerning differences in the backgrounds of domestic servants and garment workers appears in a study of residents of the Boston Home for Aged Women. Carol Lasser found that only 18 percent of former domestics who entered the home between 1850 and 1886 were born in Boston compared with 40 percent of those who had been employed in the needle trades.[61] The pattern here parallels that evident for members of the 1860 Boston census samples. Neither the residents of the Boston Home for Aged Women nor linked sample members are entirely representative of all native-born workingwomen in the city, but the similarity of these independent findings lends added support to the point that relatively few domestic servants were recruited from among Boston-born young women.

Single migrants to Boston predominated among native-born domestic servants and accounted for a large share of women employed in the needle trades as well. Although they resided on their own, there is evidence that they remained close to their families in the countryside and made periodic economic contributions. Surviving correspondence and diaries are much fewer in number for migrants in Boston than for Lowell millhands in the antebellum period. Still, sources do permit a glimpse of strong family relations maintained over a distance.

61. Lasser, "Mistress, Maid, and Market," table V-3, p. 185.

The surviving diaries of a Maine-born domestic servant working in Boston provide a perspective on this issue. Lorenza Stevens Berbineau worked as a housekeeper for the family of Francis Cabot Lowell II in Boston for almost forty years. Lowell, son of a leading textile entrepreneur, was one of the richest men in Boston and a leading millowner and merchant in his own right.[62]

Lorenza Stevens Berbineau was unusual among servants on a number of counts. Most striking was the longevity of her work in the Lowell household. She began work with the Lowells in 1830 and married in 1842, but the desertion of her French husband (apparently with the good-sized savings that Stevens had brought into marriage) led her to return to the Lowell family, for whom she continued to work for twenty-eight more years.[63] Furthermore, the household had a large servant staff, in part because the Lowells also maintained a summer residence in Waltham, a short train ride from the city. Lorenza Stevens Berbineau, in turn, had a relatively privileged position within the household, acting as something of the head of the staff, often hiring and paying other servants on behalf of her employers.

Clearly, then, the diaries of Lorenza Stevens Berbineau reveal a life that could not have been typical of native-born domestic servants in Boston in the years between 1840 and 1870.[64] Still, they reveal values and behavior that may well have been common among servants regardless of their age, length of service, or household position. Despite living

62. Lorenza Stevens Berbineau was not recorded in the Lowell household in 1860, but one of her fellow servants, Laura Brackett, was included in the 1860 servant sample. From her diaries it is evident that Berbineau also worked at times in the households of the Lowells' married children. For commentary by a contemporary on servants in the Boston household of John Amory Lowell, see Bacon, *Reminiscences*, p. 37. See also P. A. M. Taylor, "A New England Gentleman: Theodore Lyman III, 1833–1897," *Journal of American Studies* 17 (1983): 371; and Robert F. Dalzell, Jr., *Enterprising Elite: The Boston Associates and the World They Made* (Cambridge: Harvard University Press, 1987), especially chaps. 1, 2.

63. Berbineau died in 1870, leaving behind a will designating her employer, Francis Cabot Lowell II, as her executor. The probate inventory noted $800 worth of cash and possessions. P. A. M. Taylor, "A Beacon Hill Domestic: The Diary of Lorenza Stevens Berbineau," *Proceedings of the Massachusetts Historical Society* 98 (1986): 90–115; on the probate, see pp. 95–96, n. 20.

64. Lorenza Stevens Berbineau diaries, 1851–1854, 1858, 1866–1869, Francis Cabot Lowell II Papers, MHS. Volumes 76–89 of the latter collection include diaries and travel journals of Berbineau's mistress, Mary Gardner Lowell, covering (with gaps) the period 1830–1853.

apart from her family, Berbineau accepted considerable responsibility for her sister and mother in Maine and made frequent trips home and numerous financial contributions toward the support of her family.

Like most servants, Berbineau was paid irregularly, with the entry "Settled with Mrs Lowell" appearing occasionally throughout her diaries. Her wages were substantial and provided the means to assist her family quite frequently. Her earnings in 1866 totaled $98; in 1867, $140; and in 1868, $224, the only years in which Berbineau noted the actual payments made at each settlement. In addition, Berbineau received two payments totaling $260 in this period from George Lowell that appear to have been dividends.[65] As the Lowell family owned extensive shares in textile firms, Berbineau may have invested her savings in mill stocks or may have inherited a share at the death of her mistress, Mary Gardner Lowell. Even without the dividends, Berbineau's wage income of $462 above room and board in a three-year period permitted her to save a portion of her earnings.

Berbineau may not have saved very much while her mother was alive, however, because she noted numerous bank withdrawals in her earlier diaries. In May 1851 she wrote, "I went in town took out some money for my mother from the Bank took for her 30 dollars." She recorded similar transactions in January and September 1853 and in May 1854. The references to withdrawals ceased with her mother's death in November of that year.[66]

She also made contributions to a brother William and a sister Lydia. Her sister apparently had a chronic illness, and for a period, Lorenza paid for her stay in a Lynn hospital. She also loaned money to her brother, for she noted his repayment of fifty dollars in November 1853.[67] Altogether, the frequent trips to Maine to visit family, the bank

65. Berbineau Diaries, March 3, October 19, November 30, 1866, January 1, April 26, June 17, October 17, November 23, 1867, and January 1, July 11, and December 28, 1868.

66. Berbineau Diaries, May 24, 1851, January 29, September 16, 1853, and April 27, 1854. For her mother's death, see November 14, 1854. There is a chance that the withdrawals may have been from her mother's savings rather than her own. In an entry for November 23, 1854, Berbineau recorded, "I took Mother's money out of the Bank 31 doll for Mary." It is possible that Berbineau had helped her mother by placing her savings in a Boston bank. Whether the earlier payments to her mother came from her savings or her mother's cannot be readily determined.

67. Berbineau Diaries, May 28, October 8, November 11, 1853, and December 13, 1854.

withdrawals, and the numerous expressions of concern for her sister's health all indicate a woman who was very much tied, emotionally and economically, to her family of origin. Separation from her family and residence in the Lowell household for almost forty years did not negate these familial bonds. Although similar evidence for other servants and seamstresses in Boston is lacking, it is likely that others shared the values and attitudes revealed here.[68]

Few servants in Boston worked and lived in one family for anything like the period evident for Lorenza Stevens Berbineau, and in any event we do not have other surviving diaries to permit the reconstruction of their employment. Still, the 1860 census sample does speak to the nature of the careers of servants and garment workers. Tracing working-women in manuscript censuses and city directories before and after 1860 allows the re-creation of their employment patterns over time.

Boston workingwomen worked longer than did Lowell millhands and Lynn shoe stitchers. Servants averaged 4.8 years of employment and women in the needle trades, 5.9 years. These figures represent substantial increases over the mean lengths of employment for millhands and shoe stitchers, 2.7 and 3.8 years, respectively.[69]

Significant proportions of both servants and garment workers linked in successive censuses were employed at the later dates, with relatively more garment workers than servants continuing to work (see Table 5.7). Two patterns emerge from this evidence. First, for those women actually found in successive censuses, relatively large proportions continued to be employed—roughly 50 percent, for instance, in 1870, a decade after their initial enumeration in 1860. Second, garment workers continued to work for considerably longer periods than did servants. After twenty

68. Taylor, "Beacon Hill Domestic," pp. 98–99, notes the continuing connection with family back in Maine: "Lorenza sent money and parcels to Portland and Gardiner, just as if she had been a European immigrant sending home remittances." For similar practices among Irish servants in a slightly later period, see Hasia R. Diner, *Erin's Daughters in America: Irish Immigrant Women in the Nineteenth Century* (Baltimore: Johns Hopkins University Press, 1983), pp. 71, 90.

69. Because of difficulties in linking Boston sample members in additional censuses, I have excluded from the calculation of these figures those women—43 percent of the original samples—who were not found in any census other than the 1860 federal manuscript census of Boston. See Table A.2 in Appendix 5 below.

Table 5.7. Proportions of Boston 1860 workingwomen
still employed at later dates, by occupation in 1860

	1865		1870		1880	
Servants	57.0%	(86)[a]	47.0%	(83)	15.2%	(46)
Garment workers	65.4	(130)	52.6	(95)	37.8	(90)

Sources: Linkage in 1865, 1870, and 1880 censuses of 1860 Boston samples.

[a]Numbers in parentheses represent the number of women in each occupational group successfully linked in each census.

years, more than a third of garment workers successfully traced in censuses were still employed, compared with only 15 percent of servants.

At each census after 1860, a greater proportion of sewing women continued to be employed than was the case for servants. For both groups, however, there was little movement out of the occupations in which they first worked. Of servants found working in a subsequent census, more than 66 percent were still employed as servants. Among women in the needle trades, 71 percent continued in the same occupational grouping. For each group there was only slight movement into higher-ranking occupations. Roughly one in seven in each group subsequently found work in a skilled or white-collar occupation. The proportion held steady for domestic servants across the next three censuses. For needle trades workers, the proportion increased consistently from one census to the next.

One reason for the lengthier employment experience of women in the needle trades and their movement into more skilled occupations may have been the opportunities for running a small dressmaking or millinery business. Among the more than 400 women in the needle trades sample, nineteen were listed as proprietors in the *Boston Business Directory* at some point between 1850 and 1880. These women averaged careers that lasted more than fourteen years in contrast with less than four years for all other needleworkers. On average, they were older than 33 years of age in 1860, whereas others in the needle trades were younger than 27. The existence of opportunities for self-employment and entrepreneurship for women in the garment industry set that sector apart from most other areas of female employment in these years.

Finally, we should acknowledge that the needle trades afforded women more opportunities for upward occupational mobility than are revealed in the number of women who became proprietors. In the millinery trade, for instance, women workers could move up over time from apprentices to makers to trimmers, yet census enumerators probably recorded all of these positions simply as "milliner." There was undoubtedly more movement up the occupational ladder for long-term workers than is revealed in record linkage in censuses, city directories, and business directories.

The longer employment of women in the needle trades was reflected in the different marriage patterns for the two groups. Although servants and garment workers were equally likely to marry—with proportions that hovered around 84 percent for each group—women in the needle trades did marry two years later on average than did servants, at 27.8 compared with 25.6 years of age. This difference may well account for the somewhat greater degree of occupational mobility evident for garment workers.

In any event, marriage most commonly led workingwomen to give up paid employment. At least, it led census enumerators to record wives as "keeping house," for it is very likely that part-time wage work of married women went unrecorded in censuses. Lacking other comparably inclusive sources for evidence on women's wage work, we must rely on subsequent censuses, in which 66 percent of sample members recorded as single were said to be employed and only 5 percent of married women living with their husbands—seven of one hundred and thirty-four—were reported as employed.[70] Widowed women fell halfway between the two extremes; about 34 percent of sample members who were widowed—twenty-four of seventy-one—were employed according to subsequent censuses.

---

70. The annual *Boston Business Directory* and the credit reports of R. G. Dun & Company offer evidence on female entrepreneurs that slightly extends coverage of women's employment. Linkage in the business directory did permit a more accurate reconstruction of the careers of those needle trades workers who went into business for themselves. The most significant example of census limitations emerges in the case of one sample member, Margaret Costello Grace, who ran a substantial millinery business jointly with her husband for more than fifteen years. The census did not record her employment as a married woman, though her business activities were duly noted by the credit reporter for R. G. Dun & Company. See Gamber, "Precarious Independence," pp. 78–79. My thanks to Wendy Gamber for sharing evidence from these credit reports.

The differences in the employment patterns of single, married, and widowed women combined to produce life-cycle differences for women. Comparing the employment of women who married with that of women who remained single all their lives is instructive. Boston workingwomen who married—and were linked in at least one source in addition to the 1860 census—were employed on average for 3.1 years; women who did not marry worked for a mean of 10.5 years. Marriage did not necessarily reduce women's work, but it did cut off paid employment outside the home. The data on Boston women workers underline this fact of nineteenth-century life.

Focusing on individuals offers useful evidence on the employment patterns of workingwomen in Boston in 1860. For domestic servants, the census is also informative about places of employment because the vast majority of servants lived and worked in the households of their employers. Shifting the focus to these households offers insights into domestic service from another vantage point.

Boston servants worked almost exclusively in private households. Overall, 83 percent of servants enumerated in the 1860 sample resided with private families other than their own, presumably their employers.[71] On average, 1.85 servants lived in each household, and native-born women held the vast majority of such positions.[72] Only 5 percent of all servants in these households were males; only 28 percent were foreign-born. Given that 80 percent of all female servants in Boston in 1860 were foreign-born, it is evident that ethnic segregation was common in household domestic staffs. The native-born made up only 20 percent of

71. This proportion is based on excluding servants who lived alone or with their families and servants who resided in hotels or boardinghouses. Obviously there is no hard-and-fast distinction between a private household and a boardinghouse. For purposes of the discussion here, all households with more than twenty boarders have been excluded. Using a somewhat different set of definitions, Lasser, "Mistress, Maid, and Market," p. 312, found that 24 percent of servants in her Boston 1860 sample resided in institutions. Her sample included immigrant and native-born servants and is thus not strictly comparable with the native-born sample discussed here.

72. The households discussed here were not representative of all households employing servants, because each household in the current sample included at least one native-born female servant. Recall that 80 percent of all female servants in 1860 were foreign-born. Probably the typical household with servants employed a single Irish servant and thus would be excluded from the sample under consideration here.

female domestic servants in Boston but more than 71 percent of female servants in private households where they were employed. This pattern could only have developed where there were also large numbers of hotels, boardinghouses, and private households in which immigrants were overwhelmingly predominant.

This last fact is not easily deducible from a sample consisting entirely of native-born female servants. Still, by focusing on sample members employed in hotels or other institutions, we see the disparities in the scale and ethnic composition of the servant work force in these different settings. Sample members who lived in large institutions found themselves working on average with more than thirty-six other servants. Almost 73 percent of servants residing in these workplaces in 1860 were foreign-born.[73] The relative shares of immigrants and native-born among servants in hotels and private households employing sample members were almost exactly reversed. Finally, a very large number of households employed only a single immigrant domestic servant. Lasser found that 85 percent of Boston households employing one servant in 1860 hired an immigrant. For a family of middling income, only the lower wages paid to a recent immigrant made it possible to hire a domestic servant.[74]

Even among households employing native-born servants in 1860 there was quite a range in terms of the backgrounds and circumstances of household heads. Although 86 percent of these heads were native-born, the range of property owned was enormous. At the bottom, 18 percent of household heads reported no property. Several household heads, on the other hand, owned property valued at greater than $500,000. The median value of property, however, was a more modest $2,100. Accordingly, the number of servants employed was one or two in more than

73. Lasser, "Mistress, Maid, and Market," table VII-7, p. 288, offers comparable data from her 1860 Boston sample. Of 162 servants in institutions, the native-born made up 20 percent, compared with 27 percent in the sample discussed here.

74. Lasser, "Mistress, Maid, and Market," table VII-5, p. 284. Lasser finds for her sample that the native-born constituted only 15 percent of sample members working as sole servants in their households in Boston in 1860 compared with 19 percent of servants in households with two or more servants. See also table VII-1, p. 263, which shows that the proportion of native-born in the female household staff increased with the personal property owned by the household head.

78 percent of these households. Only 9 percent of households employed four or more servants.[75]

As one would expect from the earlier consideration of the lengths of women's employment, turnover of servants in these households was high. About a quarter of the 1860 households could be found in the 1850 census of Boston; sample members were present in only 13 percent of these. Similarly, roughly 30 percent of these families could be traced into the 1870 Boston census; in these households, less than 16 percent of sample members remained after the passage of a decade. In fact, a larger proportion—almost 28 percent—of the linked households employed no servants whatsoever at this later date. The evident high turnover among servants may have resulted in part from the financial uncertainties of employers. A fair share—more than a quarter in the 1860–1870 period—simply could not afford or chose not to employ servants steadily for a decade.[76] Servants' marriages would also have contributed to the high turnover. Finally, departure on the servant's part or dismissal on the mistress's part would have been viewed as solutions for the inevitable friction that was an integral part of the relationship between servant and mistress.

Because the census reports only the makeup of households every ten years, it may actually understate turnover among Boston servants. Roughly 13–16 percent remained in the employ of the same family over each decade, but we cannot determine the actual degree of turnover in the families where this was not the case. Diaries of the employers of servants, however, speak graphically to this issue.

Two surviving diaries tell of the difficult social relations that entwined mistress and servant in Boston in the middle decades of the

75. The key assumption I am making here is that the number of servants residing in a household is equal to the number working in that household. To the extent that some servants lived on their own and worked days in private households, these figures will understate the actual numbers. As only 10.5 percent of Boston female servants in 1860 lived alone or with their families, the figures presented here are likely to be quite accurate.

76. This turnover may also have resulted from a heightened ability on the part of servants to maneuver within an increasingly market-oriented set of social relations between servants and their employers. For an argument that develops this point, see Lasser, "Domestic Balance of Power," p. 20. Given the commonality of servants' names, I cannot be certain that servants unlinked in subsequent censuses had all married, died, or left Boston.

nineteenth century. Caroline Barrett White had a veritable trial by fire, which she recorded in her diary. She hired her first servant in December 1855, after having been married four years: "Today has been my first experience in housekeeping with a servant. Had an Irish girl come this morning—think from appearances that she will suit very well."[77] White and her servant seem to have worked together well, but six months later an acquaintance told White of "a good girl who would be glad of a place." White was thinking about whether or not to dismiss her servant, but when the new one arrived, her old one "left without saying goodbye." The new servant apparently got along well enough with White, but after nine months, she gave notice and departed.[78]

From this point on, it was rough going for Caroline Barrett White. Between March 1857 and May 1858, servants were constantly coming and going in her household. The Whites moved during this period to their own home—a substantial mansion outside of the city in Brookline—and they employed two servants and a cook at their new residence. Still, they repeatedly found servants unsatisfactory; their servants, likewise, also found the Whites wanting. In September 1857, White gave a "walking ticket" to one servant. By February 1858, she employed two servants, both of whom departed on the same day. She soon hired replacements, but when the family moved out to Brookline, Caroline Barrett White noted in her diary, "Our girls do not suit us very well, and we have told them they may go—one will go tomorrow, the other next week." They went through three cooks and as many servants in the first two months in Brookline. In all, the Whites employed no less than eighteen servants over two and a half years, with only one remaining as long as nine months.[79]

77. Caroline Barrett White Diaries, December 20, 1855, AAS. For an interesting perspective on the White diary, see Faye E. Dudden, *Serving Women: Household Service in Nineteenth-Century America* (Middletown, Conn.: Wesleyan University Press, 1983), pp. 55–60.

78. White Diaries, June 19, 26, 1856, and March 21, 1857.

79. White Diaries, February 19, April 9, 10, 12, 17, 18, 26, May 6, 10, 28, 1858. The comings and goings are almost daily in April. The Brookline location may have seemed out of the way for some servants, but clearly the Whites must have been contributing to this turnover. Another Brookline mistress had this to say about her experience: "When living in Brookline I passed most of my time frequenting intelligence offices in search of servants." Bacon, *Reminiscences*, p. 63.

The experience of Caroline Barrett White must have been extreme, but it was not unique. Mary Bradlee lived with her mother and brother in Boston in the early 1870s. The family was not nearly as wealthy as the Whites, and Mary worked briefly as a store clerk and a dressmaker. Still, the family employed a series of servants during this period. Their first, Nellie, left to get married in May 1872, and the Bradlees hired six different servants over the course of the next year in an effort to fill the position. One Boston upper-class mistress noted in her diary, and she would probably have been seconded by Caroline Barrett White and Mary Bradlee, that servants could be "a dreadful torment." Historians Jane Pease and William Pease, commenting with somewhat more distance on the high turnover among Boston servants, captured its essence: "All the quittings and firings were tests of will across class lines."[80]

Louisa May Alcott described such "tests of will" from the point of view of the servant, for she had gone out to service at a young age as a companion to a chronically ill older woman. She soon learned, however, what it meant to be a servant. She particularly resented her employer, one Josephus R., who had misrepresented the nature of her work at the outset. "I was to serve his needs, soothe his sufferings, and sympathize with all his sorrows—be a galley slave, in fact," she wrote in a newspaper article recounting her experience. She was strong, however, and did not put up with his impositions for long: "I bore it as long as I could, and then freed my mind in a declaration of independence, delivered in the kitchen, where he found me scrubbing the hearth." In all, Alcott lasted a month in this household and soon returned to her family home, accepting irregular and often minuscule payments for her early literary efforts rather than continue putting up with the trials of service.[81]

Even when a servant did not have particularly vexatious relations with her employers, domestic service could begin to grate on her sensibilities.

80. Mary E. Bradlee Diary, December 2, 6, 10, 1871, May 17, June 12, July 21, September 14, 1872, and January 31, February 12, 25, 26, May–June, 1873, MHS; Elizabeth Rogers Mason Cabot, as quoted in P. A. M. Taylor, ed., *More Than Common Powers of Perception: The Diary of Elizabeth Rogers Mason Cabot* (Boston: Beacon Press, 1991), p. 26; and Pease and Pease, *Ladies, Women, and Wenches*, p. 48.

81. Louisa May Alcott, "How I Went Out to Service," *Independent*, June 4, 1874.

Lizzie Wilson, who worked as a servant in Brattleboro, Vermont, in the mid-1860s, expressed well a feeling of discontent that must have been shared by many other servants: "Still another lonesome dreaded week of tiresome housework and drudgery is begun for me. nothing better was my lot it seems than to be a slave to others wants. oh would that I knew when I might be free to call my time my own and think once if I had a will of my own or not."[82] Domestic servants, like Louisa May Alcott and Lizzie Wilson, had a sense of pride and independence that made waiting on others difficult even in the best of circumstances. Add to these feelings the idiosyncrasies of often difficult employers and the class and ethnic differences that divided servants and employers in urban areas, and one can easily understand the high level of turnover evident among Boston servants.

Given the frequent tensions between mistress and servant, native-born women increasingly avoided the occupation. Over time, immigrants with fewer options replaced the native-born. This was also true in the Boston households employing members of the 1860 servant sample. Although more than 70 percent of servants in these households in 1860 were native-born, the ethnicity of servants in these households changed dramatically over the next decade. Of the 142 servants working in linked households in 1870, two-thirds were foreign-born. There had evidently been a substantial exodus of native-born servants over the decade and their replacement with immigrant newcomers.

Only a small proportion (13 to 16 percent) of servants in the 1860 sample remained in the same Boston household for at least a decade. They were a small fraction of servants, and they did not work in typical households employing servants. Families with a servant sample member remaining over a ten-year period were roughly twice as wealthy as other families employing servants. Families in 1860 with a servant who had worked for at least ten years reported more than $47,500 worth of property on average; for other families, the comparable figure was $23,100. In 1870, families with servants who had worked for them for at least ten years averaged $80,575 in total property and other families, $38,367. Families with long-term servants also had larger household staffs, though

---

82. Lizzie A. Wilson Goodenough Diaries, July 16, 1865, AAS.

here the difference was not as dramatic as with property holdings. Families in 1860 with long-term servants employed on average 2.5 compared with 1.8 servants in other households.

Families who managed to keep a long-term servant were able to stave off to a degree the inevitable shift from a native-born to an immigrant household staff. In 1860, fifteen families had a servant sample member who would remain in the household over the next decade. At that date these families employed thirty-seven servants, 40.5 percent of whom were foreign-born. Ten years later these families employed thirty-one servants, 48.4 percent of whom were foreign-born. Among the less well-off families without a long-term servant, the change in the ethnic makeup of the household staff over the decade was more dramatic. In this group, only 29 percent of servants in 1860 were foreign-born; a decade later, more than 72 percent were foreign-born. For the typical employer of servants, then, there was a steady shift away from native-born to foreign-born servants. The very wealthiest families were probably willing to pay particularly high wages and may have kept servants on in good times and bad. For the more typical family, however, native-born servants were hard to find by 1870. Most Bostonians shared the servant situation described by Louisa Crowninshield Bacon: "When no more American servants could be found, like everyone else we had Irish, in fact, they were the only ones available."[83]

Tracing the careers of workingwomen in these Boston samples provides insights into the place of paid employment in women's lives. Still, there are limitations as to what can be learned from these sources. Several factors make it difficult to use the 1860 samples to discuss changes in the employment and family patterns of native-born women in Boston over time. Workingwomen had extremely brief periods in paid employment. Thus the 1860 sample permits exploration of employment patterns in 1860, but it has little to say about developments ten or twenty years later. Even when sample members did work in 1880, they no longer constitute a representative sample as they had in 1860. To overcome these difficulties, we had best return to aggregate evidence on all Boston workingwomen in 1880 and explore changes in the nature of

83. Bacon, *Reminiscences*, p. 37.

Boston's female work force in the two decades between 1860 and 1880. With the overall picture in place, analysis of 1880 samples of servants and garment workers offers a more focused view of changes in women's wage labor over the period.[84]

Between 1860 and 1880 there was a sharp increase in the number of workingwomen in Boston and a shift in their nativity. The number of women workers rose from just under seventeen thousand in 1860 to almost thirty-nine thousand two decades later. The proportion that immigrants made up of workingwomen, in turn, declined from 63.7 to 45.3 percent over the period. Increasingly, the daughters of immigrants found places for themselves as servants in Boston's homes and as workers in the city's shops and factories. Native-born workingwomen in Boston in 1880 were probably divided fairly evenly, with daughters of immigrants and daughters of the native-born each accounting for about 27 percent of the city's female work force. In other words, only about a fourth of Boston workingwomen in 1880 were of American parentage.[85]

The main occupational change for workingwomen was in the relative decline in domestic service over these decades. A comparison of the occupations of workingwomen in 1860 and 1880 shows this shift clearly (see Table 5.8).[86] Over the twenty-year period, the proportion

84. See Appendix 6 for a discussion of the methods employed in drawing these two samples from the 1880 federal manuscript census of Boston.

85. Although census enumerators in 1880 did ask Boston residents the birthplaces of their parents, published census aggregates did not determine the parentage of workingwomen in the city. This estimate is based on the proportions of women of native-born parentage among servants and garment workers in the 1880 samples analyzed here—45 and 54 percent, respectively. For an even higher figure for the proportion of daughters of immigrants, see evidence in Wright, *Working Girls of Boston*, pp. 33–34. Only about a third of 749 native-born women in Wright's sample of Boston women workers had native-born parents.

86. I have reworked the placement of some occupational categories in presenting the 1880 data so that the subgroups employed in Table 5.8 for the two years are consistent with each other. Domestic service occupations include janitors, laundresses, nurses, and stewardesses otherwise included in the 1880 statistics under "personal service." In addition, I have included hotel and restaurant employees in domestic service, whereas the published 1880 census statistics enumerated them in the "boarding and lodging category." Similarly I shifted a number of clerks and copyists from the professional category and hotel and restaurant clerks from "boarding and lodging" into the sales and clerical category. Finally, I excluded from the needle trades category artificial flower makers and lacemakers, two groups not included in the 1860 needle trades aggregates.

Table 5.8. Occupations of Boston workingwomen, 1860–1880

Occupation	1860	1880
Domestic service	62.3%	49.8%
Clothing trades	26.0	25.0
Teaching	3.2	3.4
Clerical, sales	2.5	6.9
Other occupations	6.0	15.0
Total employed	16,852	38,881

Sources: 1860 federal manuscript census for Boston; Wright, *The Working Girls of Boston*, pp. 6–11.

of workingwomen employed in domestic service declined from 62 to 50 percent. Clerical and sales jobs more than doubled, rising to just under 7 percent, and opportunities for women as proprietors and professionals and in other manufacturing employment increased substantially as well.

With these occupational shifts came contrasting changes in the ages of native-born domestic servants and garment workers. Servants were slightly younger in 1880 than had been the case twenty years earlier, with mean age declining from 27.9 to 26.7. Women in the needle trades, by contrast, were almost two years older in 1880 than in 1860—28.9 on average compared with 27.1 earlier.

Among servants, two very distinct groups developed that speak to the changing demographics of workingwomen over the period. Native-born daughters of immigrants comprised a majority of native-born female servants in 1880, and on average they were slightly above the age of 22. Native-born daughters of native-born parents, by contrast, averaged more than 32 years of age.[87] An ethnic divide within native-born servants is evident in 1880.

Generally speaking, the number of daughters of immigrants among Boston wage-earning women grew in these decades, and the number of Yankees declined. Consider the backgrounds of garment workers who lived at home with their parents. In 1860 the co-resident parents of daughters employed in the garment trades were almost evenly divided

87. Interestingly, there was no significant difference of age within this latter group along racial lines. Native-born whites averaged 32.2 years of age; native-born blacks, 32.6.

between native- and foreign-born; by 1880, fully 85 percent of such parents were foreign-born.

This pattern is reinforced by evidence in the samples of the decline in the relative proportions of Yankee migrants from northern New England. In 1860, more than 35 percent of members of the samples of native-born servants and needleworkers had been born in Maine, New Hampshire, and Vermont; in 1880, the comparable proportion was only 20 percent. Rural-urban migration to Boston was declining, and the places of these Yankee women from the countryside were being taken by the Boston-born daughters of immigrants.

Yankee women servants were also being replaced by growing numbers of black women working in Boston households. Between 1860 and 1880 the proportion of black women among native-born servants increased from 3.6 to 9.1 percent. Increasingly, black servants were recent migrants to the city; in 1880, for instance, greater than 80 percent had been born outside New England.[88]

Black servants typically worked in families that were not as wealthy as those employing native-born white servants. In 1860 the mean wealth of household heads employing live-in black servants was about $15,000; for white servants, the comparable figure was $26,000. In 1880, 54 percent of the private employers of native-born white servants were professionals, proprietors, or merchants; for employers of black servants, the comparable share was only 41 percent.

In addition, the employment of increasing numbers of blacks and daughters of immigrants as domestic servants was associated with a distinct increase in day domestic service at the expense of live-in service. This pattern is particularly striking for the 1880 servant sample. Only 9 percent of white servants of native-born parentage lived at home with their families in 1880; among the daughters of immigrants, almost 25 percent lived at home; and among black servants, more than 37 percent lived at home and went out to work as day domestic servants.[89]

88. Pleck, *Black Migration and Poverty*, table V-1, p. 125, found that two-thirds of black employed women in Boston in 1880 had been born in southern states.

89. Although there are no comparable statistics for 1900, it is very likely that the proportions of workingwomen employed in day domestic service in hotels or boardinghouses increased after 1880. For a discussion of hotel work, see "Schools for Domestics," *Boston Sunday Herald*, November 23, 1890.

Table 5.9. Family status of servants and needle trades workers,
Boston, 1860 and 1880

Servants		Relation to	Needle trades	
1860	1880	household head	1860	1880
1.5%	4.3%	Head, spouse	8.8%	8.2%
2.0	11.5	Child	32.8	46.4
2.0	3.3	Other relative	3.6	11.2
94.2	80.1	Boarder or live-in	53.0	31.2
0.3	1.0	Alone	1.7	3.0
397	397	Totals	411	401

Sources: Samples of native-born female domestic servants and needle trades workers drawn from the 1860 and 1880 federal manuscript censuses of Boston.

Note: Percentages may not add to 100.0 because of rounding.

This increase in the proportion of workingwomen living with their families was not limited to domestic servants but held for Boston workingwomen generally. This changing pattern of residence is evident in a significant increase in the proportions of both servants and garment workers residing at home with their parents (see Table 5.9). Among servants, the proportion residing at home with family increased from 6 to 19 percent over the two decades, whereas for garment workers, the comparable gain was from 45 to 66 percent. For both groups, the importance of boarding and living in declined accordingly.

The decline in boarders among Boston workingwomen and the increase in the number living with their families resulted primarily from the displacement of earlier migrants from northern New England by the daughters of European immigrants. The different residence patterns of these two groups emerge most clearly in the experience of needleworkers in 1880. Although more than 77 percent of daughters of immigrants among 1880 needleworkers lived at home with their parents, almost 57 percent of daughters of the native-born boarded on their own. Differences among servants were less sharp, but even for that group, 19 percent of daughters of immigrants lived at home with parents, whereas only 2 percent of daughters of the native-born did so.

The decline in boarding (or, for servants, living in the household of the employer) reflected in part an increase in the employment of married and widowed women. In 1860, only 2.4 percent of native-born

women in the garment trades were married; by 1880, that proportion
had more than tripled to 8.2 percent. The relative share of widows had
increased by almost a half as well. All told, the proportion of widows
and married women among native-born female needleworkers increased
from 13.1 to 23.4 percent. Among servants, the share of married and
widowed workers was lower, but the change was equally dramatic: the
proportion increased from 8.0 to 16.4 percent over the period.

Taken together, these cumulative changes in Boston's female labor
force between 1860 and 1880 anticipate developments that would shape
the city's female labor force into the early twentieth century. First, the
share of domestic servants declined significantly as the range of occupational opportunities in the city's economy expanded. Second, the shares
of immigrants and rural-urban migrants in the female labor force declined as that for daughters of immigrants increased. Third, the average
age of Boston workingwomen increased, as did the shares of married
and widowed women. Finally, the proportions of employed women who
resided with their families while working rose substantially. The proportions of young women boarding on their own or living with their
employers declined, whereas working daughters, wives, and widows became a growing share of the city's female work force. These shifts constituted the first steps in a transformation that would be largely completed by the first decade of the twentieth century. Wage labor, which
had initially offered workingwomen prospects for self-support, became
increasingly integrated within an urban family economy. As daughters
of immigrants steadily replaced Yankee rural-urban migrants of an earlier generation in Boston's labor force, families laid greater claims on
female earnings. Before 1900 this phenomenon remained largely an urban
one, however, as our foray into the working world of New Hampshire
teachers in the next chapter will confirm.

6. New Hampshire Teachers

Throughout the nineteenth century, urban centers offered far more employment opportunities for women than did rural communities. This central truth was reflected in the large numbers of rural migrants living and working in such New England cities as Boston, Lowell, and Lynn. Domestic service and textile employment depended, respectively, on an urban elite and large-scale factories, both of which drew women workers into cities. Shoe and garment manufacture, because both relied on extensive outwork networks, offered greater rural employment opportunities. Still, both these sectors employed primarily urban family labor and drew large numbers of rural-urban migrants and immigrants into their economic orbit.

Yet in the middle decades of the nineteenth century, the New England population remained predominantly rural in character. In 1860, for instance, only 36 percent of New Englanders resided in cities with ten thousand or more in population.[1] And though women's wage labor was concentrated in New England's urban centers, employment opportunities existed for young women who remained in the countryside. Chief among these was teaching in the numerous district schools that dotted the rural landscape (see Figures 6.1 and 6.2). For women who preferred to remain close to home and keep at a safe distance from the demands of machine production in textiles or shoemaking, the common schools offered expanding employment and increasing wages as the century progressed. Teaching was an option that appealed to a good many women; according to one study, as many as 25 percent of all native-born

1. Percy Bidwell, "The Agricultural Revolution in New England," in L. B. Schmidt and E. A. Ross, eds., *Readings in the Economic History of American Agriculture* (New York: Macmillan, 1925), p. 237.

Figure 6.1. Teacher and her class outside district 8 schoolhouse, Fitzwilliam, N.H., 1885. Courtesy of New Hampshire Historical Society, neg. #G416.

Figure 6.2. Interior of Old South School, Sutton, N.H., 1896—Eva Gertrude Davis, teacher, with her students. Notice the substantial age spread between the youngest children at the front of the classroom and the oldest at the rear. Courtesy of Robert Bristol.

Massachusetts women in the pre–Civil War generation may have taught at some point in their lives.[2]

Across New England in 1870, more than twenty thousand women taught school. Altogether, almost 75 percent of teachers in the region were female.[3] Teachers constituted roughly 7 percent of wage-earning women in New England at this date, but the proportion varied considerably

2. Richard M. Bernard and Maris Vinovskis, "The Female School Teacher in Antebellum Massachusetts," *Journal of Social History* 10 (Spring 1977): 333.

3. U.S. Census Office, *The Statistics of the Population of the United States . . . from the Original Returns of the Ninth Census* (Washington: 1872), pp. 461–70.

from state to state.[4] In those states with the least industry, Vermont and Maine, teachers accounted for the largest proportions of the female labor force, almost 13 percent of all workingwomen in each state; in Massachusetts and Rhode Island, on the other hand, teachers were only 5 and 3 percent, respectively, of the female wage labor force.

Moreover, the share that teachers made up of the female work force declined as the relative importance of manufacturing increased over time. Although the number of women teachers in New England increased to more than thirty-four thousand by 1900, teachers were less than 6 percent of all workingwomen in New England at that date.[5] Still, the teaching profession offered significant opportunity to New England women throughout the course of the nineteenth century and remained the leading professional occupation for women in 1900.

To explore in greater depth the experiences of women teachers in this period and to compare teachers with other female occupational groups, we will focus on a specific group of women and follow their experiences over time. Beginning in 1859, the state of New Hampshire required local communities to publish annual school reports, and the existence of long runs of these records provides unusually rich evidence on women teachers.[6] Like the register books of the Hamilton Manufacturing Company utilized in the earlier analysis of millhands, annual school reports are far more useful than decennial censuses for tracing employment over time. In addition, they frequently provide wage data and insightful remarks on the functioning of schools and the performance of individual teachers. Finally, because all New Hampshire towns were required to produce these reports, they offer virtually complete coverage of the teaching labor force in the state.

From the vast body of surviving school reports, I drew a population of 449 female teachers who were employed by the towns of Boscawen,

4. There are discrepancies in contemporary sources on this point. The number of female teachers in New England reported by the U.S. Census Office, *Ninth Census*, varied from 20,140 ("Statistics of Schools," pp. 461–70) to only 16,332 in the detailed occupational statistics reported for each state (pp. 724–60). Underreporting in the manuscript census of population, from which occupational statistics were compiled, was undoubtedly a problem, hence my use of the higher estimate here.

5. U.S. Bureau of the Census, *Occupations at the Twelfth Census* (Washington: GPO, 1904), pp. 92–93, 114–53.

6. Town Reports, NHHS.

Canterbury, and Lyndeborough in the years between 1860 and 1880.[7] These prove a particularly appropriate population for detailed study because teachers in this period taught overwhelmingly in rural areas. In 1860, fully 83 percent of teachers in the nation came from rural areas; in 1880, that proportion had declined only slightly to 76 percent.[8] Tracing the work and family lives of these women speaks to the broader experience of women teachers in these years and provides evidence directly comparable with that presented earlier for Lowell millhands and Lynn shoeworkers.[9]

Before exploring the collective experience of these New Hampshire teachers, let us consider two of their number whose teaching careers were representative. Lucelia Butters and Julia Dodge shared much in common with other women teachers in the three towns. As did most teachers in this period, Lucelia Butters had a brief career. She began by teaching two terms in district 9 of Lyndeborough in the 1861–1862 school year, and her efforts were well-received. "It was her first attempt," noted a member of the Superintending School Committee, "and she came to her task well prepared for a teacher." Butters was 16 years old and earned fifty dollars for nineteen weeks of teaching, probably returning to her parents' farm in Wilmington, Massachusetts, at the end of her teaching. She taught again in Lyndeborough in the

7. These particular communities were chosen, in part, because they were three of the towns from which large numbers of women entered the Lowell mills in the 1830s, and also because they had rich surviving school reports for the years between 1860 and 1880. The prospect of drawing new samples of teachers and of comparing occupational patterns and family backgrounds of rural workingwomen over a seventy-year period suggested the utility of relying on towns examined earlier in studying textile millhands. See Appendix 7 for a discussion of the methods employed in the study of this population of teachers.

8. Joel Perlmann and Robert A. Margo, "Towards a Social and Economic History of American Teachers: Some Preliminary Findings, 1860–1910," paper presented at the annual meeting of the Social Science History Association, Washington, D.C., November 1989, p. 11. My thanks to Joel Perlmann for permitting me to read this unpublished paper and to both authors for permission to cite these preliminary findings, which are based on a national random sample of teachers listed in the 1860 and 1880 federal manuscript censuses of population. On the sampling methods employed, see Perlmann and Margo, "Who Were America's Teachers? Toward a Social History and a Data Archive," *Historical Methods* 22 (1989): 68–73.

9. For a useful overview of the changing social origins of teachers in the United States over time, see John L. Rury, "Who Became Teachers? The Social Characteristics of Teachers in American History," in Donald Warren, ed., *American Teachers: Histories of a Profession at Work* (New York: Macmillan, 1989), pp. 9–48.

summer of 1865, but that appears to have been her last teaching in the town. Whether she taught closer to home is uncertain, but in October 1871 she married Lemuel Pope, and the young couple settled in Hingham, Massachusetts. By 1880 the Pope family included a 7-year-old son and a 6-year-old daughter. Lucelia Butters Pope kept house, and her husband worked as a storekeeper. For Butters, schoolteaching, much like factory work a generation earlier, offered short-term work in the years before marriage.[10]

Two years after Butters's final stint of teaching, Julia Dodge taught a ten-week summer school in district 10 of Lyndeborough. Dodge was 17 that summer and was probably teaching for the first time, judging from her pay of eight dollars a month. She was the daughter of Adoniram and Lucinda Dodge in neighboring Francestown. Her father was a substantial farmer, with $2,500 in real property and another $700 in personal property according to the 1860 census. Hers was actually a "union" school, bringing together students from adjoining districts in Lyndeborough and Francestown.[11]

Julia Dodge was an immediate success as a teacher. E. B. Claggett, in an annual school report, found that she had an "admirable effect in the government of the school" and expressed the hope that "she will continue in the good work of teaching youthful minds." His wish was fulfilled, for Dodge taught in Lyndeborough and the neighboring towns of Mont Vernon, Francestown, and New Boston for at least thirty-one school terms spread over fifteen years. Over that period, she typically earned fifty dollars a year for twelve weeks of teaching. It is likely that she had earned between $750 and $800 when she gave up teaching in 1884 at the age of 34 to marry John Carson.[12] Julia Dodge taught for longer than did most New Hampshire teachers in these decades, but a significant minority had similarly lengthy careers in area schools.

10. Lyndeborough, N.H., *Annual Report*, 1862, p. 3, and 1866, pp. 5, 10. The personal information on Lucelia Butters is based on record linkage in local and state vital records and federal manuscript censuses of population.

11. Lyndeborough, N.H., *Annual Report*, 1868, p. 11. Personal information on Julia Dodge and her family noted in this paragraph and the next is based on linkage in local genealogies, vital records, and federal manuscript censuses of population.

12. Lyndeborough, N.H., *Annual Report*, 1870, p. 11. Dodge earned $360 in seven years of teaching in Lyndeborough schools; the estimate noted here is based on extrapolating from this figure to the fifteen years she taught overall in area schools.

Table 6.1. Ages of New Hampshire teachers at the beginning
and end of teaching careers

	Beginning	End
19 and under	62.3%	21.6%
20–24	26.9	39.9
25–29	7.3	19.6
30 and over	3.5	18.8
Total cases		398
Missing cases		51

Sources: Linkage of New Hampshire teachers in census, vital, and genealogical records and tracing in annual New Hampshire town school reports, 1860–1880.

Note: Percentages may not add to 100.0 because of rounding.

Women teachers in these three communities had much in common with Lucelia Butters and Julia Dodge. They usually began teaching in their teenage years and rarely continued after their marriages. More than 61 percent of women teachers in Boscawen, Canterbury, and Lyndeborough completed their careers in teaching before the age of 25 (see Table 6.1). Altogether, they averaged 5.6 years in teaching.[13] Finally, women rarely continued teaching after marriage, with only 8 percent of those who did marry ever teaching as married women or widows.

As millhands did a generation earlier, women teachers came overwhelmingly from farming families. More than three-fourths of fathers who could be linked in censuses were farmers (see Table 6.2). Only 17 percent of fathers were enumerated in other manual occupations. The proportion of farmers among fathers of teachers was considerably higher than that for all male household heads in rural New Hampshire in this period. In Boscawen, Canterbury, and Lyndeborough, for instance, just under 60 percent of male household heads were recorded as

13. To be precise, these women taught 3.3 years on average over a period of 5.6 years. The common schools remained in session only from ten to twenty weeks over the year, so the actual teaching time was still less than the years taught. The figures for length of employment for other occupational groups also contain periods when women were not employed—recall the trips Lowell operatives made back to their New Hampshire homes and the slack seasons in the garment and shoe industries. For this reason, it is appropriate to use the total elapsed time in teaching rather than actual weeks taught for purposes of comparison with other occupational groups.

Table 6.2. Occupations of fathers of
New Hampshire teachers

Occupational Group	Percentage
Farmers	76.0%
Skilled workers	12.9
Proprietors	5.4
White-collar, professional	3.2
Semi- or unskilled	2.6
Total cases	279
Missing cases	170

Sources: Linkage of fathers of New Hampshire teachers in 1850–
1880 federal manuscript censuses of population.

Note: Percentages may not add to 100.0 because of rounding.

farmers in the 1860 census, whereas 80 percent of the fathers of teachers who resided in these three towns farmed.

The occupational background of the fathers of New Hampshire
teachers is consistent with similar evidence for Massachusetts teachers
in this period. Data on prospective teachers who attended a normal
school in Massachusetts in 1859 reveal that more than 43 percent came
from farming families. As only about a third of Massachusetts families
were engaged in farming at this date, in Massachusetts as well as in New
Hampshire teachers came disproportionately from farming families.[14]

Fathers of teachers were also generally wealthier than their neighbors. The mean property recorded for fathers of teachers who resided
in Boscawen, Canterbury, and Lyndeborough in 1860 was mòre than
$4,300 compared with a figure of less than $2,400 for all male household
heads in these towns. Age and occupation cannot account for this difference. Fathers of teachers were slightly younger than all male household heads in the three communities, 46.7 years on average versus 48.0.
Thus, the greater wealth of fathers of teachers cannot be accounted for
in terms of their age. Moreover, limiting the comparison to farmers

14. Bernard and Vinovskis, "Female School Teacher," pp. 335–36. The disproportionate
recruitment of teachers from farming families continued into the early twentieth century. As
late as 1911, a study found that almost 45 percent of 3,367 fathers of women teachers were
farmers. Lotus Delta Coffman, *The Social Composition of the Teaching Population* (New York:
Teachers College, 1911), p. 73.

indicates that farmer fathers of teachers remained significantly wealthier than their farming neighbors.

Although the families of teachers were wealthier than typical families in these three communities, such was not the case for other rural workingwomen. In 1860, twenty-eight workingwomen other than teachers were enumerated in the households of their fathers in Boscawen, Canterbury, and Lyndeborough. The mean value of property in these families was just under $1,800, a figure substantially below the mean for all male household heads in the three towns at this date.

It is clear from census evidence that teachers came from far more privileged backgrounds than did rural workingwomen generally. Occupations noted for the fathers of women workers in the 1880 and 1900 censuses confirm the findings for property holdings in 1860. Whereas 75 percent of the fathers of teachers who resided in Boscawen, Canterbury, and Lyndeborough in 1880 were farmers, only 19 percent of fathers of other wage-earning daughters in those towns were so recorded in the census. More than twice that proportion of fathers, almost 41 percent, in fact, were unskilled laborers. The proportions remained basically unchanged between 1880 and 1900, when 40 percent of fathers of other workingwomen who lived at home were laborers and only 12 percent were farmers. Teachers constituted a distinct elite among rural workingwomen in the last forty years of the nineteenth century, with workingwomen from poorer backgrounds finding employment chiefly as domestic servants and textile workers.

Boscawen, Canterbury, and Lyndeborough attracted teachers primarily from within their boundaries and adjoining towns. Just over 38 percent of teachers found in censuses between 1860 and 1880 resided in the three towns. Another 42 percent came from adjoining towns, which suggests that less than a fifth of female teachers in the three towns were attracted from beyond the range of neighboring communities.[15] School reports themselves noted the hometowns of about half the teachers. Where the reports neglected to note the hometown, it is likely that the teacher came from the town in which she was teaching. Still, almost

---

15. In all, 65 percent of the 449 teachers were successfully linked in the 1860 census, so the proportions noted here are based on a sizable share of the group.

72 percent of the teachers with a recorded hometown came from within the three towns and adjoining ones.

Although women did not tend to come from very far away to teach in Boscawen, Canterbury, and Lyndeborough, they did have incentives to teach outside their own hometowns. One teacher noted in her journal that she had hoped to get a school in her hometown of Concord so that she could live with her mother, but noted "there is a rule that no young lady shall teach in the city until she has taught elsewhere."[16] At each census year between 1860 and 1880, more than twenty Boscawen and Canterbury teachers lived in Concord, a fact undoubtedly reflecting that city's practice of requiring its native daughters to teach elsewhere before working closer to home.

There was, in fact, considerable circulation of teachers among nearby towns. Almost 48 percent of the women taught in some town other than Boscawen, Canterbury, or Lyndeborough. Sixty women, fully 13 percent of the entire group, taught in Concord at some point in their careers. Lyndeborough teachers had almost one hundred additional stints in schools in neighboring towns. In all, the 449 women teachers had at least 332 different stints in town schools or private academies other than those from which they were originally drawn.

It should also be added that a good share of these women had more than simply a common-school education in their rural hometowns. They came from relatively prosperous families—the analysis of property holdings indicated that clearly—and at least 45 percent of the women attended a private academy before, during, or after their teaching careers.[17] Given the limited size of these schools (and often their brief existence), this is a surprisingly large proportion. Evidently some of the families of teachers had the resources to send them to local academies that provided the training necessary to enter teaching; in other cases, teachers probably

16. Helen A. Stewart Journal, April 12, 1880, NHHS.

17. Linkage was determined by tracing teachers in an assortment of annual catalogues and reunion publications of private academies (all at NHHS) in or near the three towns in which the women taught. They include Appleton Academy, Boscawen Academy (Elmwood Institute), Francestown Academy, Gilmanton Academy, McCollum Academy, Pennacook Academy, Sanbornton Academy, and Tilton Academy. Given the limited range of available sources, we must view the proportion of 45 percent as a minimum estimate.

used their earnings from teaching to finance additional education at local academies. In other words, academy attendance might be either a contributing cause to or a consequence of women's choice of a teaching career.

Teacher training was upgraded in the second half of the nineteenth century with the growth of state normal schools, private academies, and teachers' institutes, but teaching was only a fledgling profession in this period.[18] Teaching, in fact, was very much a "service" occupation in a variety of ways, with teachers serving the parents of their charges. Their initial examinations by members of local school committees, the common practice of boarding around among the families of students, the frequent classroom visits of parents and school committee members, the final public examinations of the scholars at the end of the term—all continuously subjected rural school teachers to public scrutiny.[19]

Parents and school committee members made periodic visits throughout the term into classrooms in their district schools. Martha Osborne Barrett, who taught in East Woburn, Massachusetts, survived one such visit admirably. She recorded in her diary: "The committee made their first visit to my school this morning. All three of the members of the board were in. Drs. Youngman & Rickard & Mr. Converse. The scholars did well, very well, and the com[mittee] seemed perfectly satisfied. They are quite gentlemanly and I enjoyed their visit very much."[20] More than members of the school committee found their way into the district schools. One school report from Sanbornton, New Hampshire, commented favorably about a teacher, noting that "she has served . . . twenty months, under the watchful eye of the parents, who often visit the school room, and have the ability to judge correctly."[21]

18. In describing the experience of one of the sample teachers, the Andover school committee noted that Martha J. Foster had attended one such institute. Andover, N.H., *Annual Report*, 1870, p. 24.

19. Margaret K. Nelson, "Vermont Female Schoolteachers in the Nineteenth Century," *Vermont History* 49 (1981): 5–30, makes a similar argument concerning Vermont teachers in much the same period. She contends that in its subordination to the dictates of male school committee members and the fathers of students, teaching was very much an extension of women's role in the domestic sphere. Women teachers in this perspective were in a role rather like that of a governess or nurserymaid.

20. Martha Osborne Barrett Diary, May 1, 1849, EI.

21. Sanbornton, N.H., *Annual Report*, 1865, p. 15.

Not all teachers could have felt so good, however, about the level of surveillance common in district schools. Mary Metcalf disciplined one "saucy" student by expelling him from the classroom, only to find his father trooping into school to argue that his son had been no worse than the other boys in the class. When the term drew to a close, Mary Metcalf looked forward to working on straw bonnets, where she would not "be accountable to every body for my movements."[22]

The quality of one's teaching was typically a public matter. Near the end of each term it was common to hold a public examination of scholars; but such events were, of course, also examinations of the teachers. Examinations were usually attended by members of the Prudential School Committee but also by parents and others. At these public events, the school committee and other visitors "would hear students recite, read out loud, sing, or do arithmetic problems."[23] For others less involved in daily school events, printed annual reports summarized the main developments in each district school each term and communicated the judgment of school committee members about individual teachers. A member of the school committee in Warner, New Hampshire, offered praise for one of his town's teachers: "This school has been two years under the direction of Miss Lizzie H. Piper. She manifested a deep interest in her work, and spared no labor for the welfare of her scholars." Occasionally, however, reports turned more critical. In Francestown, New Hampshire, one teacher came in for harsh words: "The appearance of school and school room indicated rather a loose state of affairs. Like teacher, like school. Life and energy in teacher and pupils seem well nigh extinct. Scholars were neither punctual, interested, nor thorough, and our opinion is, that the teacher was wanted in her adaptedness to her vocation, and the school next to worthless."[24] Letitia Adams

22. Mary Metcalf to her mother, [no place], January 30, 1853, Adams-Metcalf Letters, MATH.

23. Sari Knopp Biklen, "Confiding Woman: A Nineteenth-Century Teacher's Diary," *History of Education Review* 19, no. 2 (1990): 30. Knopp Biklen relies on the 1854 diary of a Lynn, Massachusetts, teacher, Mary Mudge, and shows that in an urban school district, teachers formed a support group and were well informed about the affairs of one another.

24. Warner, N.H., *Annual Report*, 1868, p. 27; and Francestown, N.H., *Annual Report*, 1868, p. 15. These examples could be multiplied; for similar examples, see remarks on Laura E. Shepard, Gilmanton, N.H., *Annual Report*, 1868, and remarks on Mary E. Marston, Andover, N.H., *Annual Report*, 1872, p. 26.

continued to teach for another five years, but one can only hope her efforts thereafter met with greater success and recognition.

Parents' interest in their children's teachers extended beyond their work in the classroom. In the antebellum years it was common for teachers to "board around," that is, to board for a week or two in different households in the community.[25] A part of local school money was contributed "in kind" by parents who provided room and board to the teacher. Teachers' wages were generally quoted as a given dollar figure per month plus board. Where teachers lived at home, they probably received a somewhat higher wage to take into account the town's savings on room and board. The practice of boarding around, however, was definitely on the decline in the post–Civil War years, and in 1864 the Vermont legislature outlawed the practice by requiring that all school funds be raised by property taxes.[26]

Obviously, to the extent that teachers boarded in the households of the parents of their students, they were subject to considerable scrutiny of their lives outside the classroom. Mary Metcalf, teaching in Hadley, Massachusetts, found false rumors circulating about her conduct which she sought to clear up in a letter to her mother: "You say you hope to hear a favorable report of my school through the term. I hope to be able to give it but do not say it is certain that I can. There has been but little fault found with my school but a lady reported that I attended a ball at Whately with George Marton and got home at five in the morning."[27] Mary Metcalf then described what really happened, admitting she did get in at five o'clock but noting that she did not attend the ball that evening. All in all, teaching in a small town placed one in a goldfish bowl, and a woman had to live with the attention if she wanted the job.

Most rural teachers worked for a limited number of years and then married and left the wage labor force. In this regard, they had much in common with their earlier counterparts who migrated to Lowell to work for brief periods before marriage. Teachers, however, stand out among

25. For contemporary descriptions, see Mary Giddings Coult Diary, January–February, 1851, and Lizzie Piper Diary, November–December, 1867, both in NHHS.

26. Nelson, "Vermont Female Schoolteachers," p. 24.

27. Mary Metcalf to her mother, Hadley, Massachusetts, June 4, 1851, Adams-Metcalf Letters.

nineteenth-century workingwomen in that a sizable fraction had rather lengthy teaching careers. As a group, these New Hampshire women taught on average for 5.6 years, a figure considerably higher than those for the domestic servants, textile operatives, and shoeworkers examined previously. Only Boston garment workers, with an average period of working of 5.9 years, exceeded the figure for rural teachers, and the garment worker data included periods of employment in other occupations. If we include such work for teachers, their overall careers spanned 6.7 years on average, which made them the longest-employed group of New England wage-earning women. The greater length of teachers' careers stemmed from the existence of a significant minority of teachers who never married and who made a long-term commitment to teaching.

Fully 30 percent of teachers for whom solid data survive remained single all their lives.[28] Never-marrying teachers had career profiles dramatically different from the majority who married. Women who married continued to teach on average 4.5 years, typically ending their careers before turning 24. In contrast, women who never married taught for an average of 11.6 years, leaving the profession (or simply disappearing from censuses) at 32 years of age.[29]

Marriage was the most important factor influencing the length of time these New Hampshire women worked as teachers. Comparing the relative influence of marriage and other factors reveals this pattern clearly (see Table 6.3).

Unmarried women worked as teachers for almost six years longer than did women who married. None of the other factors came even close to being this influential. Varying levels of father's wealth, for instance, affected the length of women's teaching by less than a year; age

28. This proportion is considerably above any other estimates for never-marrying women in this period. Peter Uhlenberg, "A Study of Cohort Life Cycles: Cohorts of Native Born Massachusetts Women, 1830–1920," *Population Studies* 23 (November 1969): 411, offers an estimate of 14.6 percent for a native-born cohort of women born in Massachusetts in 1850. For a comparable estimate based on national census data, see Thomas Monahan, *The Pattern of Age at Marriage in the United States*, vol. 1 (Philadelphia: By the Author, 1951), p. 116.

29. There is uncertainty as to the later lives of long-term teachers, but the designation "never-marrying" was limited to those with concrete evidence of dying single. The most likely bias in this discussion is that the mean of 11.6 years may significantly understate the length of the careers of single teachers. That bias, however, only reinforces the point I am making here that marriage dramatically shaped women's teaching careers.

Table 6.3. Influences on women's length of employment in teaching, 1860–1880, New Hampshire sample

Factor	Subgroup	Years teaching	Difference
Marriage			5.94
	Did marry	4.87 (166)	
	Did not marry	10.81 (65)	
Father's wealth			0.95
	0–$1,300	6.07 (45)	
	$1,301–3,650	7.02 (94)	
	$3,651 +	6.28 (92)	
Age at beginning teaching			1.44
	Under 18	7.46 (65)	
	18–19.9	6.02 (87)	
	20 +	6.35 (79)	
Other employment			2.00
	None	6.80 (201)	
	Some	4.80 (30)	
Total cases [a]			231

Source: Linkage of 1860–1880 New Hampshire teacher sample.

[a] Includes only those cases with nonmissing data on all variables in the analysis. Findings are based on multiple classification analysis, which simultaneously controls for the influence of other independent variables in calculating means for subgroups on a particular variable.

at beginning teaching had an effect of less than a year and a half; and whether or not a teacher had any other employment made a difference of only two years in the lengths of women's careers as teachers. As in the case of Lynn shoeworkers discussed earlier, marriage had the greatest influence on women's paid employment as teachers. Unlike shoeworkers, however, married women teachers rarely returned to their careers; rather, those New Hampshire women who had lengthy careers as teachers either married late or remained single all their lives.

For some of these New Hampshire women, teaching provided a close approximation of a career. Almost 16 percent taught for ten or more years. Furthermore, many women combined teaching with additional employment in other occupations. More than 10 percent of women in the sample had other occupations either before, during, or after their years of teaching.[30] A clear pattern emerges in examining these women.

30. This figure, 10.9 percent, is undoubtedly a tremendous understatement of the actual proportion of teachers who held other wage-earning jobs at some point in their lives. Even

Of the seventeen women definitely employed before teaching, thirteen worked as domestic servants. On the other hand, of the thirty-nine women who continued to work after teaching, more than 40 percent held white-collar occupations, and another 23 percent worked in the needle trades. Something of a collective career trajectory is evident in these experiences, as women moved over their working lifetimes from domestic service to teaching to white-collar work. For the minority of women who combined teaching with other kinds of employment, teaching served as a bridge between low-status rural domestic service and better-paid and more desirable white-collar employment.

For those women who had additional work, employment outside teaching actually dwarfed their years in the classroom. Such women who did marry averaged 3.4 years of teaching and 7 years of other employment. For women in this group who did not marry, their teaching averaged 7.8 years and their other employment another 15.1 years. This last subgroup had an average overall employment of almost 23 years, a remarkably long period for workingwomen in the nineteenth century and one that had no equivalent in the careers of millhands, shoeworkers, domestic servants, or needle trades workers in the same period.

It is striking that among all the native-born New England women traced in this study, it is the teachers, drawn from the relatively most propertied backgrounds, who had the lengthiest periods of wage work. The financial circumstances of the families of women teachers suggest that familial need could not have been the dominant influence in women's decisions to seek employment. Their families, after all, were considerably wealthier than was typical for the communities in which they lived.

Although familial need was not the crucial factor, the desire for self-support was no doubt very real.[31] As young women entered their late teens, they did not relish their continuing economic and social depen-

---

though all members of the sample were teachers at some point between 1860 and 1880, only 31.3 percent of the teachers were found so recorded in at least one federal manuscript census over those years. Applying the same proportion to evidence on occupations other than teaching suggests a minimum proportion of 34 percent.

31. Evidence on the wealth of the fathers of women teachers suggests that women who never married came from slightly wealthier families than those who did marry (with means of $4,116 and $3,821, respectively, according to the 1860 federal manuscript census). In turn, those who had other employment were from wealthier families than those who only taught

dence on their parents. That fully 30 percent of teachers from these three New Hampshire communities never married gives added meaning to the women's concern about self-support. Such women undoubtedly desired to earn something of their own and not rely solely on their families or become entirely enmeshed within the family farm economy. Teaching provided a decent wage, though the work was typically limited to two eight- to twelve-week sessions throughout the year. Equally important, teaching was relatively high-status work; it was particularly suited to daughters from the wealthier families in these rural communities.

Teaching permitted women to save from their earnings because the vast majority continued to live at home while teaching. Despite the earlier practice of "boarding around" among families of schoolchildren, women teachers in Boscawen, Canterbury, and Lyndeborough between 1860 and 1880 overwhelmingly lived with their parents. Census enumerations for those years indicate that more than 89 percent of women teachers resided at home with their parents. Only 8 percent of teachers noted in the census were boarding. Given the fact that women teachers were employed only ten to twelve weeks out of the year, the proportion who boarded away from home while teaching was undoubtedly considerably higher. An estimate of 25–33 percent seems reasonable, though we will never know for certain.[32]

Although teachers could save from their monthly earnings, their total savings could not have been great, because schools were in operation for only limited periods of time. Lyndeborough teachers commonly worked an average of eleven or twelve weeks a year. It was an unusual teacher—typically less than one out of ten for a given year—who found employment for as long as twenty weeks over the year. Given this limited teaching time, the average Lyndeborough teacher earned $47 a year for her labors. Over teaching careers in Lyndeborough of somewhat more than eighteen weeks in length, women teachers earned on average a bit

---

(with means of $4,380 and $3,833, respectively). All in all, the data suggest that family wealth had little influence on whether women married or on how long they were employed.

32. Perlmann and Margo, "Towards a Social and Economic History of American Teachers," table 3, indicate that 23 percent of rural female teachers were boarding in 1860 and 25 percent in 1880, though their figures would be subject to the same degree of understatement as the evidence presented here for New Hampshire teachers.

more than $84. This figure represents women's earnings only in Lynde-
borough schools and thus definitely underestimates their overall earnings. After all, almost 44 percent of Lyndeborough teachers were also
employed in some other New Hampshire community between 1860 and
1880. Adjusting their earnings to reflect other periods of teaching leads
to an estimate of $133 for their overall career earnings as teachers.[33]

We may place this figure in context by comparing the earnings of
New Hampshire teachers between 1860 and 1880 with those of other
New England workingwomen. In the mid-1830s, for instance, female
mill operatives in Lowell earned on average just under sixty cents a day.
They did not typically work twelve months in the year, however. If we
assume 240 workdays a year—forty weeks of employment—we find that
millhands earned more than $140 a year. Thus, Lowell millhands in the
mid-1830s commonly earned more in a single nine-month stint in the
mills than did New Hampshire schoolteachers over their entire teaching
careers a generation later. Earnings in Lowell had declined somewhat by
1860, but even at that date, annual earnings of women millhands were
on the order of $136, still greater than the likely career earnings of
Lyndeborough women teachers.[34]

33. Surviving accounts for individual teachers are rare, but two for an earlier period in time
confirm the estimate made here. Sally Brown of Plymouth, Vermont, taught 44 weeks of
school in the period 1836–1837; her weekly wage of $1.25 would have brought her total earn-
ings to $55. Elizabeth Hodgdon of Rochester, New Hampshire, taught a total of 111 weeks in
the period 1832–1841, for which she was paid $184. In the post–Civil War period, weekly
wages were considerably higher—on the order of $4–5—but the intermittent operations of
rural common schools kept total earnings down. Blanche Brown Bryant and Gertrude Elaine
Baker, eds., *The Diaries of Sally and Pamela Brown* (Springfield, Vt.: William L. Bryant Foundation, 1970); and Elizabeth Hodgdon Account, Sanborn Family Papers, MHS. See also
Thomas Dublin, ed., *Farm to Factory: Women's Letters, 1830–1860*, 2d ed. (New York: Columbia University Press, 1993), p. 55.

34. Thomas Dublin, *Women at Work: The Transformation of Work and Community in Lowell,
Massachusetts, 1826–1860* (New York: Columbia University Press, 1979), p. 161. The comparison is somewhat problematic because a certain share of teachers—we don't really know
how large—may also have received free room and board while teaching. Given that Lyndeborough teachers probably averaged 28.5 weeks of teaching overall (and generously assuming
that 50 percent received room and board during those periods of teaching) and valuing room
and board at $1.50 a week lead to a revised estimate of teachers' career earnings of $154.
The change is marginal enough to allow the comparisons made here to stand without serious
modification.

Shoe stitchers in Lynn in the post–Civil War years also enjoyed earnings far greater than those of rural schoolteachers. With mean weekly wages in 1871 of just over ten dollars, shoeworkers earned roughly double that brought home by teachers; moreover, they commonly averaged over thirty weeks of work a year, so that the differential in terms of annual earnings was greater still.[35]

Even urban garment workers could expect to earn more than rural teachers, in terms of both weekly wages and likely annual earnings. Boston figures for 1870 suggest an average weekly wage of eight dollars, with work available for about twenty-five weeks in the year. This figure of two hundred dollars for the annual earnings of a Boston garment worker was about four times what a New Hampshire teacher might expect to earn in a year.[36] Certainly these earnings were dearly won, with overtime work common during the busy season. Still, the point is evident: women who enjoyed the high status and superior working conditions of teaching paid a price in terms of reduced earnings.

One result of the low annual earnings of teachers was the necessity to combine eight- and ten-week stints of teaching with other paid employment over the course of the year. Recall that Mary Metcalf, quoted earlier, had been looking forward to working on straw bonnets when her teaching trials were over.[37] It is impossible to quantify other paid employment that was interspersed with teaching because census enumerators were instructed to record the principal employment of individuals and did not record combinations such as "domestic service and teaching" or "sewing and teaching."[38] Still, census enumerations, when coupled with evidence from annual town school reports, do provide glimpses of teachers combining different kinds of wage work. In eleven instances that occurred during or within a year of women's periods of employment as teachers, the census recorded women teachers in other occupations. In six of eleven cases, the women were employed in

---

35. Mass. Bureau of Statistics of Labor, *Annual Report*, 1872, pp. 103–7.

36. Mass. Bureau of Statistics of Labor, *Annual Report*, 1871, pp. 209–19.

37. Mary Metcalf to her mother, [no place], January 30, 1853, Adams-Metcalf Letters.

38. For a useful discussion of census difficulties in recording women's wage labor, see Marjorie Abel and Nancy Folbre, "A Methodology for Revising Estimates: Female Market Participation in the U.S. before 1940," *Historical Methods* 23 (Fall 1990): 167–76.

domestic service; sewing and white-collar occupations were each noted twice. These jobs were probably undertaken in the periods of time that rural schools were not in session. And for every instance that found its way into the census, there were probably half a dozen that went unrecorded. Undoubtedly, surviving sources provide documentation for only a fraction of the supplementary wage earning of rural teachers in these years.

Intermittent employment and low annual earnings meant that even experienced teachers rarely headed their own households. Tracing the residence patterns of long-term teachers and former teachers who remained single demonstrates this fact. More than three-fourths of twenty-two single women teachers found in censuses in their thirties remained daughters in their parents' households. The other four were boarders. Of the ten single women found in censuses in their forties, five were daughters in their parents' households, two lived with brothers, one boarded, and only two headed their own households. Finally, fifteen single women teachers or former teachers were found in censuses at age 50 or older. Seven lived with siblings, five headed their own households, two boarded out, and one continued to live at home with parents. Altogether, only seven of forty-seven single women teachers or former teachers over the age of 30 were enumerated in a census as heads of households. Women teachers were rarely able to parlay their modest wages into economic and social independence.

A second characteristic of teachers' residence patterns is striking: how relatively close to home they remained throughout their lives. The earlier discussion noted that 70–80 percent came from the towns in which they taught or from neighboring towns. Although teachers did move around and take jobs in nearby towns, few appear to have migrated permanently. In 1880 almost 62 percent of the teachers who came from Boscawen, Canterbury, or Lyndeborough continued to reside in those communities. Finally, almost 60 percent resided in the two counties that include their hometowns at the time of their deaths. Only 22 percent of teachers from the three towns appear to have died in Massachusetts, a distinctly lower proportion than the figure of 31 percent evident for New Hampshire women who had worked in Lowell a generation earlier. Teaching was an occupation compatible with continued rural residence in the post–Civil War period.

Neither the level of annual earnings nor contemporary expectations encouraged rural women to view teaching as a lifetime occupation. Within this context it is really quite remarkable that fully 30 percent of teachers for whom good evidence survives never married, a proportion roughly twice that for the other female occupational groups studied earlier. Given the distinctiveness of women teachers in terms of the numbers who married, we might well expect that in their marriages they also differed from other workingwomen in New England. What can we learn about their marriages by tracing women teachers after their years in schoolteaching? And how do these findings compare with those for other workingwomen?

First, it is evident that women teachers postponed their marriages relative to other women in their age cohort. On average, they married at 26.3 years of age men who were two and a half years their seniors.[39] This age of marriage is higher, in fact, than any of the other ages at first marriage calculated for the other female occupational groups examined in this book. One consequence of the greater length of careers for these New Hampshire teachers relative to other working-class groups was this postponement of marriage.

Additional comparisons confirm the uniqueness of the marriage patterns for teachers. Between 1860 and 1880, Massachusetts women married on average at an age of 23.8 men who were 2.7 years older than themselves.[40] One might argue that this comparison is problematic as the Massachusetts data include urban workingwomen who may have married at relatively early ages because inheritance of a farm was not an issue. In keeping with the rural residence of this group of teachers, we may compare them with a population of married women residing in Boscawen, Canterbury, and Lyndeborough in 1880.[41] Judging from the ages of their oldest children, we find that nonteachers of similar ages had married on average at 21, fully five years earlier than did former teachers.

39. These means are based on 214 women teachers who married and 141 husbands for whom age at marriage is known.

40. Monahan, *Pattern of Age at Marriage*, vol. 1, p. 161. I chose these years because more than 75 percent of New Hampshire teachers for whom date of marriage is known married within this period.

41. See Appendix 7 for a discussion of the methods employed in generating this comparative population of married couples in the teachers' hometowns.

A second development is evident in tracing the marriages of former teachers: their husbands were not so overwhelmingly employed in agriculture as their fathers had been. Just under 46 percent of teachers' husbands were farmers or farm laborers, another 30 percent were white-collar or professional workers or proprietors, and 20 percent were skilled workers. These figures represent a substantial decline in the proportion of farmers—from 76 to 46 percent—and corresponding increases in all other occupational groups. In their choice of husbands, however, teachers did not differ particularly from other young women in their hometowns. Looking at married women of similar ages in Boscawen, Canterbury, and Lyndeborough in 1880 reveals that only 49 percent of husbands were employed as farmers or farm laborers.[42]

A third significant development distinguished former teachers from other married women in these three communities. Former teachers postponed childbearing and had fewer children than did their neighbors. Former teachers linked in the 1880 census had been married an average of almost nine years. Living with them (again, on average) were 1.57 children. In contrast, married nonteachers of comparable ages lived with 2.22 co-resident children, a figure about 40 percent higher. How much of the relatively low fertility of former teachers is due to the greater wealth of these families, the greater education of former teachers, or their relatively late marriages is uncertain; still, the resulting pattern of low fertility stands out sharply.

The fertility of former teachers also stands out in comparison with the experience of former New Hampshire millhands thirty years earlier. Former Lowell millhands enumerated with their husbands in New Hampshire towns in the 1850 census had been married for ten years on average, slightly longer than were former teachers in 1880; they were living with 2.50 children, a figure almost 60 percent higher than that for former teachers in 1880. Clearly, former teachers in the 1870s were spacing their children at wider intervals than had been common among former millhands a generation earlier.

Lengthier careers, fewer and later marriages, and fewer children at greater intervals—these were the principal ways in which women teach-

---

42. Inferred age at marriage is available for 133 of the women in these rural couples and the occupations of husbands for 159 cases.

ers in New England differed from other nineteenth-century working-women. Still, as was true for mill operatives a generation earlier, women teachers were rarely able to provide homes for themselves. Even when they remained single, teachers continued to live with parents or married siblings for the most part. For teachers, as for most other working-women in nineteenth-century New England, wage labor continued to be the domain primarily of single women, and such employment typically afforded a precarious living. Although mill operatives in the 1830s and 1840s had enjoyed a measure of economic and social independence while residing in Lowell and other mill towns, theirs was a transient independence that did not offer young women a viable alternative to marriage. But even that slim measure of independence was eroded in the post–Civil War years. In fact, workingwomen at the turn of the twentieth century commonly found themselves more deeply enmeshed in a family economy than had been the case two generations earlier. The construction of the renewed familial dependence of workingwomen in urban industrial America at the turn of the century signaled the deepening economic subordination of women that has marked women's place in the nation's economy throughout much of the twentieth century. It is to an examination of that development as evidenced by women's occupations in New England in 1900 that we now turn our attention.

7. *Workingwomen in New England, 1900*

In exploring the impact of industrialization on women's wage work in nineteenth-century New England, it has been critical to break down the aggregate picture of women's employment and examine distinct occupational groups of women in particular locations at particular points in time. The reliance on specific case studies has sharpened the analytic focus and illuminated a variety of important differences among groups of workingwomen.

It is now time to bring together these separate stories and to focus on the broader picture of women's wage work in industrializing New England. To do so requires that we move beyond the time frames of the individual case studies and consider how the occupational experiences of New England women changed as the century progressed. How, for instance, did the identities and experiences of textile operatives change between 1850, the closing date for the study of New Hampshire women employed in the Lowell mills, and 1900? What differences distinguished women shoeworkers in Lynn in 1900 from their counterparts enumerated in the 1865 census, the focus of analysis earlier? Similarly, how did workingwomen in Boston at the turn of the twentieth century differ from the domestic servants and garment workers in Boston between 1860 and 1880 who were examined in Chapter 5? How, also, did women's employment in rural areas change in the last decades of the nineteenth century? And how did teaching change as an occupation for women in these years? Each of the case studies had, by necessity, a somewhat different chronological focus, and it will be helpful for comparative purposes to follow each of the female occupational groups until 1900. It should then be possible to synthesize the disparate findings for these occupational groups and consider the overall picture of women's wage work in New England in 1900.

The New England textile industry expanded dramatically between 1850 and 1900. Moreover, after the Civil War its center of gravity shifted from northern to southern New England. In 1850, cotton and woolen textile mills in New England employed about eighty-five thousand workers producing goods valued at just over $68 million. Lowell was the leading mill town in the nation, employing just over twelve thousand operatives and producing more than two million yards of cloth weekly.[1]

Over the second half of the nineteenth century, employment in New England textiles doubled and cloth production quintupled in value. By 1900, mills in the region employed more than 162,000 workers, and the value of cloth production reached $332 million annually.[2] Fall River had displaced Lowell as the leading textile center in the region and the nation, employing at the turn of the century more than 24,000 textile operatives, compared with 18,500 in Lowell. The value of Fall River textiles outpaced those produced in Lowell, reaching $29 million as opposed to $25 million.[3]

As the textile work force grew in the second half of the nineteenth century, its ethnic composition shifted dramatically. In 1850 a substantial majority of textile operatives had been native-born migrants recruited from the surrounding New England countryside. By 1900, only 11 percent of women textile operatives in New England were of native birth and parentage. More than a third were native-born women of immigrant parentage, and more than half were foreign-born. Among the immigrants, French Canadians, Irish, Poles, Greeks, Portuguese, and Italians were found in sizable numbers (see Figure 7.1).[4]

1. J. D. B. DeBow, *Statistical View of the United States . . . Being a Compendium of the Seventh Census* (Washington: Beverly Tucker, 1854), p. 180; and *Statistics of Lowell Manufactures*, 1850, broadsides on microfilm, BL.

2. Mass. Bureau of Statistics of Labor, *Annual Report*, 1905, p. 86; and U.S. Bureau of the Census, *Twelfth Census of the United States*, vol. 7, *Manufactures*, pt. 1, pp. 177, 461, 465.

3. U.S. Bureau of the Census, *Occupations at the Twelfth Census* (Washington: GPO, 1904), pp. 441, 443, 452, 454; and U.S. Bureau of the Census, *Twelfth Census*, vol. 8, *Manufactures*, pt. 2, pp. 383, 391.

4. Thomas Dublin, *Women at Work: The Transformation of Work and Community in Lowell, Massachusetts*, 1826–1860 (New York: Columbia University Press, 1979) p. 139; U.S. Bureau of the Census, *Statistics of Women at Work* (Washington: GPO, 1907), p. 83; George F. Kenngott, *The Record of a City: A Social Survey of Lowell, Massachusetts* (New York: Macmillan, 1912), pp. 32, 35; and Daniel Creamer and Charles W. Coulter, *Labor and the Shut-Down of the Amoskeag Textile Mills* (Philadelphia: Works Projects Administration, 1939), pp. 161–62.

Figure 7.1. French Canadian weavers, Boott Cotton Mills, 1905. Courtesy of the Lowell Museum and the Center for Lowell History.

As immigrants and daughters of immigrants became the vast majority of women mill operatives, the proportion of young single women boarding in New England mill towns declined sharply. At their peak in the mid-1830s, boarding daughters of Yankee farmers had accounted for about three-fourths of the mill work force in Lowell. On the eve of the

Table 7.1. Family status of female millhands in Lowell,
1860 and 1900

Family status	1860	1900
Household head	3.5%	7.6%
Spouse	2.4	11.3[a]
Child	26.9	29.6
Other relative	2.1	9.6
Boarder	65.0	41.9
Total cases	761	4,725

Sources: Dublin, *Women at Work*, pp. 167–68; and U.S. Bureau of the Census, *Statistics of Women at Work*, p. 254.

[a] The spouse category for 1900 may include some married other relatives. The two groups were not differentiated in published census figures.

Civil War, the immigrant Irish had become the leading ethnic group in Lowell's mills, but boarders still constituted 65 percent of the female work force in the mills.[5] By 1900, however, boarders had declined to 42 percent of female mill workers in Lowell (see Table 7.1).

As the proportion of boarders among female millhands declined, the shares of household heads, wives, and other relatives increased substantially, and the proportion of children advanced modestly. Taken together, these changes reflect a significant aging of the female mill work force and the growing importance of a family economy in the mills. In 1836 only a ninth of female millhands in Lowell lived at home while employed in the mills; in 1860 that share stood at 35 percent, and by 1900 it had reached 58 percent.[6] These shifts in the ethnicity, residence patterns, and family status of women millworkers led to a marked decline in the economic and social independence that textile factory workers had enjoyed in the antebellum decades. The French Canadian or Greek mill operative in 1900 was, in fact, "an arm of the family economy," to use Louise Tilly and Joan Scott's phrase, in ways that simply had not been the case for Yankee women workers fifty or sixty years earlier.[7]

Compared with the dramatic transformation of textile employment in New England between 1850 and 1900, change in the shoe industry was

5. Dublin, *Women at Work*, pp. 27, 167.

6. For 1836, see Dublin, *Women at Work*, p. 27. For 1860 and 1900, see Table 7.1 above.

7. Louise A. Tilly and Joan W. Scott, *Women, Work, and Family* (New York: Holt, Rinehart, and Winston, 1978), p. 109.

more restrained. Despite ongoing mechanization and increased reliance
on steam power, shoe factories continued to rely on a predominantly
native-born work force. In Massachusetts as a whole in 1880, for instance, immigrants made up less than 22 percent of employed shoeworkers. By 1900, this proportion had increased but remained only
slightly more than 26 percent.[8]

Lynn shoemaking conformed closely to the statewide pattern. In
1900, the foreign-born were 26 percent of a sample of Lynn female
shoeworkers. A study of three factories in Lynn in 1911 revealed that
almost 29 percent of women shoeworkers were foreign-born. In both
years, native-born women of native-born parentage remained a majority
of women shoeworkers in Lynn. Among women factory workers in the
United States at the turn of the century, Lynn shoeworkers were
unique in the continued predominance of workers of native-born background (see Figure 7.2).[9]

There were other continuities for women shoeworkers in Lynn in the
decades after 1865. Married women remained a large proportion of
women shoeworkers, accounting for almost 24 percent in a 1900 sample
and fully a third of women shoeworkers in three Lynn factories in 1911.
Both figures represented increases over the proportion of 19 percent
that married women made up of women shoeworkers in Lynn in 1865.
The growing share of immigrants in the shoe factory work force contributed to the increasing proportion of married workingwomen, as fully
47 percent of immigrant women in the Lynn factories in 1911 were
married. Shoe manufacturing continued to offer employment to relatively older women, another characteristic that distinguished shoemaking from other factory occupations in this period.[10]

Residence patterns of female shoeworkers in Lynn shifted only modestly in the years between 1865 and 1900. The magnitude of this shift

8. U.S. Immigration Commission, *Reports of the Immigration Commission*, vol. 12, *Immigrants in Industries*, pt. 9, "Boot and Shoe Manufacturing" (Washington: GPO, 1911), pp. 225, 227.

9. Mary H. Blewett, *Men, Women, and Work: Class, Gender, and Protest in the New England Shoe Industry, 1780–1910* (Urbana: University of Illinois Press, 1988), p. 352; and U.S. Bureau of Statistics of Labor, "The Boot and Shoe Industry in Massachusetts as a Vocation for Women," Bulletin no. 180, October 1915, p. 18.

10. Blewett, *Men, Women, and Work*, pp. 344–45; U.S. Bureau of Statistics of Labor, "The Boot and Shoe Industry in Massachusetts," pp. 20–21.

Figure 7.2. Lynn shoeworker, 1895. Photograph by Frances Benjamin Johnston. Courtesy of Library of Congress.

Table 7.2. Family status of female shoeworkers, Lynn, 1865 and 1900

Family status	1865	1900
Household head	7.0%	8.4%
Spouse	10.7	16.3
Child	45.0	46.3
Other relative	7.2	5.2
Boarder	30.1	23.9
246		
Total cases	402	289

Sources: 1865 shoeworker sample; and 1900 Lynn census sample, in Blewett,

was less than for textile workers, but its direction was the same for both groups. An increasing proportion of shoeworkers lived at home with their families as the share of wives rose and that for boarders declined (see Table 7.2).[11] Among both textile operatives and shoeworkers, a family wage economy had come to prevail by the turn of the twentieth century. Fully 58 percent of Lowell female millhands and 76 percent of women shoeworkers in Lynn lived with family in 1900, as one difference that had distinguished the two work settings earlier became muted by the turn of the century.

Moreover, differences that had distinguished Boston workingwomen from women in smaller single-industry towns had also declined. Three basic developments affected the female labor force in late nineteenth-century Boston. First, there was a steady increase in the proportion of adult women earning wages. Second, the proportion of workingwomen employed in domestic service declined sharply. Finally, and in part a consequence of this decline in service, there was a steady increase in the proportion of women who lived at home with their families while working.

As Boston grew after 1850, the number of workingwomen increased at a considerably faster rate. By 1860 fully 25 percent of all females

11. Categories employed in Table 7.2 differ slightly from those implicit in the related discussion in Chapter 4. The 1900 published census figures do not provide evidence on the proportion of shoeworkers residing alone in single-person households, so that group has been combined here with other heads of households. This group made up only 1.2 percent of the 1865 shoeworker sample, which limits the impact of its placement in Table 7.2.

between the ages of 15 and 59 were employed, almost 17,000 in all.[12] In 1880 the proportion had reached 28 percent, and by 1900 it had passed 33 percent. This final figure was considerably greater than the proportion of adult women who were employed in the nation as a whole, a tad over 20 percent in 1900.[13] As the numbers of workingwomen in Boston shot up dramatically after mid-century, there was a decided shift in the kinds of work women did. Declines in the proportions of workingwomen found in domestic service and the needle trades were accompanied by substantial increases in the shares of women employed in sales, clerical, and other occupations (see Table 7.3).

At mid-century, domestic service and the needle trades clearly dominated the female occupational structure in Boston, accounting for more than 88 percent of all women's jobs in 1860. This proportion declined sharply after the Civil War, and by 1900 these two groupings accounted for only 52 percent of all employed women in Boston. Clerical, sales, and other occupations expanded accordingly. In 1860 these three groups made up only 8.5 percent of all women's jobs; in 1900 their combined proportion exceeded 44 percent. The range of occupational opportunities open to Boston women grew considerably in these decades.

One group of Bostonians did not benefit from the overall shift away from domestic service—black women in the city. They stood out on a number of counts. First, a far higher proportion of black women worked

12. For New York City at this same date, Carl N. Degler has estimated that 27 percent of the industrial labor force consisted of workingwomen. See Degler, "Labor in the Economy and Politics of New York City, 1850–1860: A Study of the Impact of Early Industrialism," Ph.D. diss., Columbia University, 1952, pp. 96–97. For Philadelphia in 1850, the comparable proportion was 26.2 percent. See Bruce Laurie and Mark Schmitz, "Manufacture and Productivity: The Making of an Industrial Base, Philadelphia, 1850–1880," in Theodore Hershberg, ed., *Philadelphia: Work, Space, Family, and Group Experience in Philadelphia in the Nineteenth Century* (New York: Oxford University Press, 1981), p. 47.

13. Valerie Kincaid Oppenheimer, *The Female Labor Force in the United States: Demographic and Economic Factors Governing Its Growth and Changing Composition* (Westport, Conn.: Greenwood Press, 1976; originally published in 1970), p. 3; U.S. Bureau of the Census, *Population of the United States in 1860* (Washington: GPO, 1864), pp. 218–19; U.S. Census Office, *Report of the Mortality and Vital Statistics of the United States as Returned at the Tenth Census* (Washington: GPO, 1886), p. 778; U.S. Census Office, *Statistics of the Population of the United States at the Tenth Census* (Washington: GPO, 1883), p. 864; U.S. Census Office, *Twelfth Census of the United States*, vol. 2, *Population*, pt. 2 (Washington: GPO, 1902), p. 124; and U.S. Bureau of the Census, *Statistics of Women at Work*, pp. 222–27.

Table 7.3. Occupations of Boston workingwomen, 1860–1900

Occupation	1860	1880	1900
Domestic service	62.3%	49.8%	35.4%
Clothing trades	26.0	25.0	16.9
Teaching	3.2	3.4	3.6
Clerical, sales	2.5	6.9	18.7
Other occupations	6.0	15.0	25.4
Total employed[a]	16,852	38,881	68,799

Sources: 1860 Federal manuscript census for Boston; U.S. Census Office, *Statistics of the Population of the United States at the Tenth Census*, p. 864; and U.S. Bureau of the Census, *Statistics of Women at Work*, p. 222.

[a] 1860 and 1880 figures include all workingwomen; 1900 figures include women 16 and over.

Note: Percentages may not add up to 100.0 because of rounding.

than was true for other groups. For Boston as a whole, a third of women over fifteen were employed in 1900; for black women, the comparable figure was 51.5 percent.[14] Second, black women remained confined to a very limited range of occupations: in 1860 more than 96 percent had been employed in domestic service and the needle trades; in 1900 that proportion remained at 81 percent. For all workingwomen, the proportion employed in these two sectors had declined by a third over the forty-year period; black women, however, continued to be largely confined to these low-paid occupations.[15]

The combination of high labor force participation and yet restricted employment opportunities evident for African American women in Boston reflected broader occupational patterns in northern cities at the turn of the century. In New York City, for instance, more than 31 percent of black married women in 1900 were employed compared with only 4 percent of white married women. Black married women commonly

14. *Twelfth Census of the United States*, vol. 2, *Population*, pt. 2, p. 124; and U.S. Bureau of the Census, *Statistics of Women at Work*, p. 226.

15. Elizabeth Hafkin Pleck, *Black Migration and Poverty: Boston, 1865–1900* (New York: Academic Press, 1979), table II-4, p. 40, confirms the perspective offered here with evidence on both male and female employment patterns. The Boston patterns were replicated across the urban United States around 1900. For a discussion of the national patterns and consideration of the cultural and economic factors responsible for the high levels of employment of married black women, see Elizabeth H. Pleck, "A Mother's Wages: Income Earning among Married Italian and Black Women, 1896–1911," in Michael Gordon, ed., *The American Family in Social Historical Perspective*, 2d ed. (New York: St. Martin's, 1978), pp. 490–510.

Table 7.4. Family status of Boston workingwomen, 1860–1900

Relation to head of household	1860	1900
Household head	9.2%	10.6%
Child	14.1	32.2
Spouse or other relative	3.2	13.0
Live-in or boarder	73.6	44.2
Total cases	16,849	68,799

Sources: 1860 federal manuscript census of Boston; and U.S. Bureau of the Census, *Statistics of Women at Work*, p. 222.

took in laundry or entered domestic service in white families to supplement the insufficient wages of their husbands. Fully 84 percent of black workingwomen in New York City in 1900 were domestic servants or laundresses; in Pennsylvania in 1890, the comparable proportion was 91 percent.[16] There was a basic similarity across northern cities in terms of the employment patterns of African American women.

Although African American women were largely denied the opportunity to move into the greater variety of occupations that white women enjoyed in 1900, all workingwomen in Boston increasingly lived in family settings. A comparison of residence patterns for Boston workingwomen in 1860 and 1900 shows this development quite clearly (see Table 7.4). The proportion of Boston workingwomen who were daughters living at home with parents more than doubled over the period, and the proportion of women workers boarding on their own or living with employers declined accordingly. This development had begun in the 1860–1880 period, as discussed in Chapter 5, but the shift accelerated in the final decades of the century. The evidence indicates that women's employment in Boston in 1900 was more fully integrated within a family wage economy than had been the case earlier in the century. Initially, at least, employment opportunities drew women out of their families. As the

16. David M. Katzman, *Seven Days a Week: Women and Domestic Service in Industrializing America* (New York: Oxford University Press, 1978), p. 219; and Isabel Eaton, "Special Report on Negro Domestic Service in the Seventh Ward, Philadelphia," in W. E. B. DuBois, *The Philadelphia Negro: A Social Study* (New York: Schocken, 1967; originally published in 1899), p. 428.

century progressed, the changing nature of female employment and the aging of the migrant population in the city permitted more working-women to live at home.

The change in the residence patterns of Boston workingwomen resulted in large part from a shift in the ethnic composition of the female work force. In 1860, immigrant women constituted more than 80 percent of female domestic servants and fully 64 percent of all working-women in the city. With some slowing of the intense Irish immigration of the famine years and the onset of childbearing for the immigrant generation, the share of immigrants in the city's population declined, though it remained substantial. In 1880 the proportion of immigrants among workingwomen stood at 45 percent, a figure that declined slightly further over the next twenty years.[17]

As the share of immigrants among workingwomen declined, daughters of immigrants entered the city's work force in large numbers and more than compensated for the relative slowdown in immigration. Daughters of immigrants constituted almost 55 percent of native-born domestic servants and garment workers in the 1880 samples and made up about two-thirds of all native-born Boston workingwomen in an 1883 study conducted by the Massachusetts Bureau of Statistics of Labor.[18] In 1900, native-born women of immigrant parentage accounted for almost 31 percent of workingwomen in Boston, whereas women of native-born parentage made up only 25.5 percent.[19] Taken together, women of foreign birth or parentage consistently constituted about three-fourths of all workingwomen in Boston after mid-century.

How did ethnicity influence the relationship of workingwomen in Boston to the family wage economy? The first year for which data address this issue is 1860. At that date a larger share of native-born than of immigrant women lived with their families while working (see Table 7.5). More than 34 percent of native-born workingwomen lived at home

17. Proportions for 1860 are based on analysis of all workingwomen recorded in the federal manuscript census of Boston; for 1880, see Carroll D. Wright, *The Working Girls of Boston* (Boston: Wright and Potter, 1889; originally published in 1884), pp. 14–15, and for 1900, U.S. Bureau of the Census, *Statistics of Women at Work*, pp. 224–28.

18. Wright, *Working Girls of Boston*, p. 33.

19. U.S. Bureau of the Census, *Statistics of Women at Work*, p. 224.

Table 7.5. Family status of Boston workingwomen, 1860,
by nativity

Family status	Native-born	Foreign-born
Household head	9.1%	9.2%
Child	21.9	9.7
Other relative	3.3	3.0
Live-in or boarder	65.6	78.1
Total cases	6,058	10,781

Source: Federal manuscript census of Boston, 1860.

Note: Percentages may not add up to 100.0 because of rounding.

compared with only 22 percent of immigrants.[20] The much larger proportion of immigrants employed in domestic service was the principal reason for the difference.

The 1860 evidence, however, blends together two quite distinct groups within the "native-born" population, including both daughters of native-born parents and daughters of immigrants. The census for 1860 did not record parental nativity, thus making it impossible to distinguish among native-born Boston workingwomen on the basis of their parentage.

Only in 1900 do published census reports provide evidence bearing on this question. For that year, the living arrangements of workingwomen are reported separately for the native-born of native parentage, the native-born of immigrant parentage, and immigrants. Table 7.6 summarizes the evidence on Boston's white workingwomen in these three groups.

Boston workingwomen in 1900 can be seen as distributed along a continuum. Most likely to be living at home contributing directly to the family wage economy were native-born women of immigrant parentage, 60 percent of whom lived at home with their parents, whereas less than 20 percent boarded in the city. At the other extreme, fully 60 percent of immigrant workingwomen in 1900 lived on their own or in the households of their employers, whereas only 16 percent lived at home with their parents. And in an intermediate position were native-born women of native-

20. Although there are differences between native-born white and black women, the overall proportions of workingwomen residing with their families—34.5 and 31.7 percent, respectively, for whites and blacks—are roughly comparable. Among family members, white women workers include a much larger proportion of children, whereas household heads outnumbered children more than two to one for blacks.

Table 7.6. Family status of white workingwomen in Boston,
1900, by nativity

Family Status	Native-born, native parentage	Native-born, foreign parentage	Foreign-born
Household head	12.3%	6.6%	11.7%
Child	28.6	60.1	16.0
Other relative	13.4	13.4	12.2
Live-in or boarder	45.7	19.9	60.1
Total cases	15,290	21,282	29,968

Source: U.S. Bureau of the Census, *Statistics of Women at Work*, pp. 224–26.

born parentage. Almost 46 percent of this last group boarded on their own, but a still substantial 28.6 percent lived at home with their parents.

Nativity and parentage account for much of the variation evident in the residence patterns of Boston workingwomen in 1900, but one group escapes our view in this analysis—Boston's black workingwomen. Numbering more than 2,200, blacks were 3.3 percent of Boston working-women in 1900, up from 1.3 percent forty years earlier. They stand out from other women workers in several respects. They were considerably older than other groups of workingwomen. Only 8.5 percent of black workingwomen lived at home with their parents, a figure that is less than a third and about a seventh of that for white women with native-born parents and white women with immigrant parents, respectively. Moreover, 21.5 percent of black workingwomen headed their own households, a proportion almost twice that for any other group. Although paid employment remained primarily confined to the years before marriage for white women in Boston in 1900, wage labor was evidently a lifelong experience for black women.[21]

Aggregate statistics reveal the unique employment profile of black women in late nineteenth-century Boston, but focusing on a concrete group of individuals provides a still sharper picture. Included in the 1880 sample of native-born Boston servants discussed earlier were thirty-six black women. Altogether, they made up just over 9 percent of all

21. That the Boston evidence is not atypical is indicated by aggregate census data for 1890. See Robert W. Smuts, *Women and Work in America* (New York: Columbia University Press, 1959), pp. 56–57.

servants in that sample. They were considerably older than the white women in the sample, averaging almost 33 years of age compared with only 26 for whites. Moreover, almost half the black servants in the sample—seventeen of thirty-six—were married, widowed, or divorced, a figure that stands in sharp contrast to the comparable proportion among native-born white servants of 13 percent. All in all, whether we examine citywide evidence for 1900 or a sample of domestic servants in 1880, it is clear that Boston black women found themselves confined to the very bottom of the female occupational ladder throughout the period between 1860 and 1900.[22]

White workingwomen in Boston in 1900 differed from one another primarily in terms of the relative shares that children and boarders made up of each group. Much of the difference in residence patterns was a function of patterns of migration and demographics. Most immigrants came to Boston in their teens or twenties, usually on their own.[23] Few of them had parents living in Boston with whom they might reside. Conversely, native-born women with immigrant parents were typically born in Boston, had living parents when they began work, and continued to reside at home and contribute to the family till. A lower proportion of native-born workingwomen with native-born parents had parents also living in Boston. Many were recent migrants to the city, and although they were not drawn in great numbers to domestic service, they nonetheless did fill the city's lodging and boardinghouses. A fair share, 28.6 percent, lived at home, but an even larger proportion lived on their own in the city. Structurally they were simply not so fully integrated within the family wage economy as was the case for the native-born women of immigrant parentage. The evidence for 1900 shows the clear existence of a family wage economy in Boston and depicts the differential place within that system of groups of women based on ethnicity. The picture that emerges is very different from that for mid-century, when domestic ser-

22. For a similar argument, see Pleck, *Black Migration and Poverty*, chap. 5, and "Mother's Wages." For comparable Philadelphia data at a slightly later date, see Eaton, "Special Report," p. 490.

23. Although separate Boston immigration data are not readily available, see Kerby A. Miller, *Emigrants and Exiles: Ireland and the Irish Exodus to North America* (New York: Oxford University Press, 1985), tables 11 and 12, p. 581, for confirming evidence for the immigrant Irish, a major component of Boston immigrants in this period.

Table 7.7. Occupations of Boston workingwomen in 1900,
by nativity, parentage, and race

| | Native-born whites | | | |
Occupation	Native parentage	Immigrant parentage	Foreign-born whites	Native-born blacks
Domestic service	15.3%	15.9%	56.2%	75.3%
Clothing trades	16.6	17.5	17.3	5.6
Teaching	9.0	4.0	0.8	0.4
Clerical, sales	28.6	29.3	7.3	1.3
Proprietors, professionals	12.3	5.4	7.8	1.9
Other occupations	18.2	28.0	10.6	15.5
Total cases	15,290	21,282	29,968	2,259

Sources: U.S. Bureau of the Census, *Statistics of Women at Work*, pp. 224, 226; and *Twelfth Census, Special Reports: Occupations*, p. 498.

Note: Percentages may not add up to 100.0 because of rounding.

vice dominated women's work in Boston and 47 percent of nonservants among workingwomen boarded away from home as well.

Just as ethnicity and parentage affected the residence of Boston workingwomen, so too did the occupations they held reflect these differences. By 1900, native-born women of native-born parentage had emerged as a distinct elite among all workingwomen. Roughly half of these women were employed as proprietors or professionals or in white-collar jobs by this date. A clear occupational hierarchy existed, with native-born women of immigrant parentage following them on the scale and with immigrants and then African Americans trailing far behind (see Table 7.7).

A good gauge of the employment opportunities for different groups among Boston's workingwomen in 1900 is the proportion of each group still employed in domestic service. Among native-born women—whether of native-born or immigrant parentage—less than a sixth were employed as servants in 1900. A majority of immigrants, by contrast, worked as servants, and among African Americans the proportion exceeded three-fourths.

At the turn of the twentieth century, employment in the needle trades accounted for about a sixth of women's wage work in Boston (see Figure 7.3). It did not vary greatly among ethnic groups, with roughly equal proportions of native-born and immigrant women finding employment in the city's garment industry in 1900. African Americans,

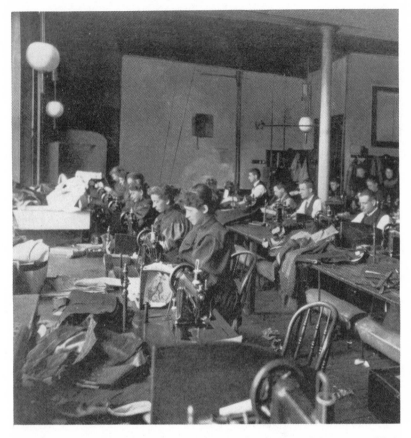

Figure 7.3. Boston garment workers, c. 1895, Macullar, Parker & Company, 400 Washington Street. Courtesy of the Bostonian Society.

concentrated as they were in domestic service occupations, were decidedly underrepresented in the city's needle trades.

The rapidly growing clerical and sales occupations were filled by different ethnic groups in proportions that contrasted sharply with those evident for domestic service. Contemporaries were sensitive to the unstated barriers that kept black Bostonians out of these higher-status occupations. One observer noted, "Of the thousands of clerks in Boston I do not know a single Negro behind the counter."[24] Census enumerators ac-

24. "The Race Problem in Boston," *Liberia: Bulletin*, no. 9, November 1896, 13; also quoted in Pleck, *Black Migration and Poverty*, p. 130.

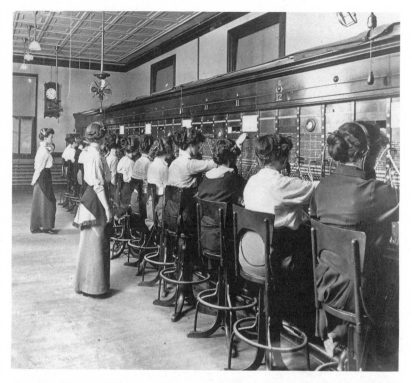

Figure 7.4. Boston telephone operators, 1915. Courtesy of Boston Public Library, Print Department.

tually found seven black saleswomen in the city, but the point was well taken. All told, only twenty-nine black women found employment in clerical or sales positions in 1900 in this metropolis of more than 560,000, and they constituted only 1.3 percent of black workingwomen in the city. Among the foreign-born, a scant 7 percent found employment in white-collar clerical or sales occupations. For the native-born, whether of native-born or immigrant parentage, about 29 percent enjoyed the better wages and working conditions of clerical and sales jobs (see Figures 7.4 and 7.5). By 1900 an ethnic occupational hierarchy had clearly emerged among Boston's workingwomen.[25]

25. For a parallel picture for black workingmen in Boston in the late nineteenth century, see Stephan Thernstrom, *The Other Bostonians: Poverty and Progress in the American Metropolis, 1880–1970* (Cambridge: Harvard University Press, 1973), pp. 184–94.

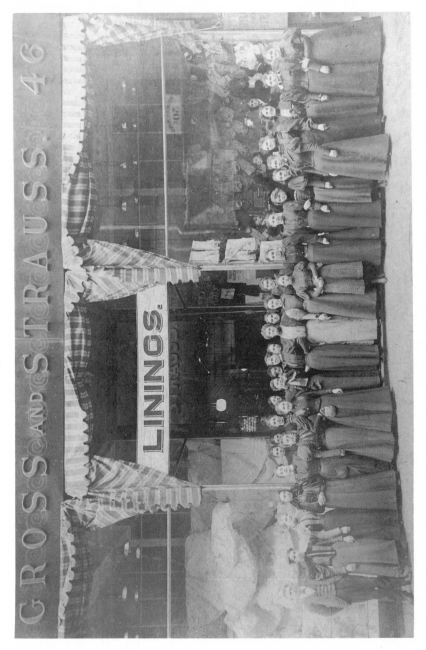

Figure 11. Boston saleswomen, Winter Street, c. 1890. Courtesy of Boston Public Library, Print Department.

Table 7.8. Occupations of rural workingwomen, 1860–1900

Occupation	1860	1880	1900
Textiles	36.5%	24.8%	20.1%
Teachers	35.8	19.1	11.0
Domestic service	14.6	41.9	31.2
Needle trades	10.9	3.5	4.5
Farming	0.7	5.7	19.5
Others	1.4	5.0	13.6
Total cases	137	141	154

Sources: 1860, 1880, and 1900 federal manuscript censuses of population for Boscawen, Canterbury, and Lyndeborough, N.H.

Note: Percentages may not add up to 100.0 because of rounding.

Just as the nature of women's paid employment in Boston was changing at the end of the century, so too were rural opportunities for women's wage work. Looking at the central New Hampshire communities of Boscawen, Canterbury, and Lyndeborough—the towns whose women teachers provided the focus for Chapter 6—offers a view of the dimensions of rural change in this period.[26]

Two major developments emerge in examining women's wage labor in these three New Hampshire communities over the years 1860–1900. First, workingwomen as a share of adult women in these communities rose steadily in this period. In 1860 less than 9 percent of women 15 and older were recorded as employed by census enumerators. This figure increased to 11 percent in 1880 and to more than 15 percent in 1900. Lower proportions of rural women were employed at each of these dates than of urban women. In Boston the overall proportion of wage-earning women stood at 33 percent in 1900. Still, the rates of increase were similar across urban and rural New England in these decades.

Second, over time there were shifts in the distribution of rural workingwomen among wage-earning occupations (see Table 7.8). As was true for New England generally, the proportion of textile workers among workingwomen in Boscawen, Canterbury, and Lyndeborough declined considerably over the forty-year period. Moreover, the percentage of women

26. See Appendix 7 for a discussion of the methods employed in recording occupations of rural women in the period 1860–1900.

employed in teaching declined even more sharply. The declining population of rural New England and the consolidation of one-room schoolhouses both undercut employment opportunities for women teachers.[27] Finally, the proportion of women engaged in farming appears to have increased substantially across these decades. This trend probably does not reflect a substantive change in women's employment patterns but rather a change in recording practices of census enumerators. In addition, it may not have represented an increase in women's wage work, as women employed in farming were most likely unpaid labor on family farms.

The profile of women recorded as employed in farming in the three towns in 1900 offers strong evidence of changing enumeration practices. More than 83 percent of these women were widows; their mean age was slightly above 58. They had been farmers' wives most of the last twenty years, but only when they became farmers' widows did the census record their employment. If anything, farming probably decreased as an employer of rural women as agriculture came to make up a declining share of the overall rural economy.[28] The evidence here may well reflect the growing outmigration of farmers' sons from these communities. Whereas in earlier years a farmer's widow would have continued to live in the household of an inheriting son, by 1900 she was more likely to operate the family farm and head her own household.[29]

Other developments are apparent in this period as well. The average age of workingwomen in the countryside increased from a mean of 28 in 1860 to 30 in 1880 to 37 in 1900.[30] This relative aging over time coin-

27. A contemporary writing in the Andover, N.H., *Annual Report*, 1872, p. 21, noted just this phenomenon: "It is a fact patent to all that the schools in our back districts grow less in numbers each year."

28. Among all employed men enumerated in the three towns, the proportion of farmers and farm laborers declined steadily after 1860, from 65.5 percent on the eve of the Civil War to 46.9 percent in 1900. This substantial decrease leads to the reasonable conclusion that the apparent simultaneous increase in employed women in agriculture reflects a shift in enumeration practices rather than a shift in work patterns.

29. If we limit our examination of women's occupations in the three towns between 1860 and 1900 to non-household heads, there is no longer a significant increase over time in the proportion of women employed in agriculture.

30. Even if we exclude women employed in farming, the mean age of wage-earning women increased from 28.1 to 31.5 years. The pattern of aging was not due entirely to the increased enumeration of widows in farming families.

Table 7.9. Relationships of rural workingwomen
to household heads, 1860–1900

Relation to head	1860	1880	1900
Head	6.6%	6.4%	21.4%
Spouse	0.7	5.7	2.6
Daughter	52.9	41.1	27.3
Other relative	8.1	9.2	8.4
Boarder	31.6	37.6	40.2
Total cases	136	141	154

Sources: 1860, 1880, and 1900 federal manuscript censuses of population for Boscawen, Canterbury, and Lyndeborough, N.H.

Note: Percentages may not add up to 100.0 because of rounding.

cided with a parallel shift in the family status of rural workingwomen. The share made up by daughters living at home declined from almost 53 percent to just over 27 percent during the period. The proportion of workingwomen who were heads of households, in turn, grew from 6.6 to 21.4 percent. Finally, the share consisting of boarders living away from family increased from 31.6 to 40.2 percent in the same period. Table 7.9 summarizes evidence for each of the three census years.

Developments in rural wage work paralleled some of the changes evident among urban women workers in these years, but interregional differences outweighed similarities. In both areas, workingwomen were aging, and married and widowed women made up growing shares of the female labor force. In the countryside, however, the proportion of daughters among workingwomen declined, whereas the share of women who boarded increased between 1860 and 1900. This shift was precisely opposite the patterns evident for workingwomen in Boston, Lowell, and Lynn in this period. Rural workingwomen were moving away from residence at home with their parents, whereas a growing share of urban women workers were daughters living at home. Moreover, the urban numbers overwhelmed the rural ones in these decades. In 1900, urban residents constituted more than 68 percent of New England's population.[31] Because urban women were twice as likely as rural women to be employed in wage labor, urban women probably accounted for more than

31. U.S. Bureau of the Census, *Historical Statistics of the United States: Colonial Times to 1970* (Washington: GPO, 1975), ser. A202 and A203, pp. 25–35.

five-sixths of workingwomen in the region in 1900. In other words, rural workingwomen proved the exception, rather than the rule, at the turn of the twentieth century, and the urban employment patterns of Boston, Lowell, and Lynn offer more representative evidence for women in the region as a whole.

Although rural women made up a small share of workingwomen in New England in 1900, they probably supplied a considerably greater proportion of teachers in the region. Women of foreign birth or parentage predominated among workingwomen generally, but fully 71 percent of New England teachers in 1900 were of native birth and parentage. Furthermore, although more than a third of all workingwomen were married, divorced, or widowed in 1900, less than 8 percent of women teachers fell within these groups.[32] As with rural workingwomen generally, teachers differed significantly from all New England women workers in terms of ethnicity and marital status.

Although the identity of teachers remained consistent over the last third of the nineteenth century, the profession underwent important change over time. Schools were in session more weeks during the year, thus permitting women teachers to earn far more in the first decade of the twentieth century than had been possible thirty years earlier. A 1911 national study of more than five thousand teachers found women teachers in rural areas earning $366 annually on average, whereas their urban counterparts earned $591. Such salaries stood in sharp contrast to the common annual earnings (for eleven weeks of teaching) of $48 in Lyndeborough, New Hampshire, between 1860 and 1880. Teaching enabled women to be self-supporting after the turn of the century in a way that had simply not been the case earlier.[33]

32. U.S. Bureau of the Census, *Statistics of Women at Work*, pp. 110, 117.

33. Lotus Delta Coffman, *The Social Composition of the Teaching Population* (New York: Teachers College, 1911), p. 39. For discussions of bias in this study, see John L. Rury, "Who Became Teachers?: The Social Characteristics of Teachers in American History," in Donald Warren, ed., *American Teachers: Histories of a Profession at Work* (New York: Macmillan, 1989), p. 31; and Joel Perlmann and Robert A. Margo, "Who Were America's Teachers? Toward a Social History and a Data Archive," *Historical Methods* 22 (1989): 73 n. 19.

Inflation was minimal between 1870 and 1910, amounting to either 5.5 or 0.6 percent depending on which price series we employ. Deflating 1911 figures by the higher of these two figures would reduce urban earnings only to $560 and rural earnings to $341. U.S. Bureau of the Census, *Historical Statistics of the United States*, ser. E183 and E184, pp. 211–12.

If women teachers could earn more in 1900, they likely needed the income more than ever. Evidence on the recruitment of teachers suggests that they no longer came from relatively wealthy rural families. Farmers were still comparably overrepresented among fathers of teachers, but by the early twentieth century, farmers' incomes were commonly below those of their neighbors. Elite women from the countryside had a greater range of options in 1900 than had been the case in 1860, and teaching no longer seemed quite as appealing as it had a generation earlier.[34] In terms of status, teaching no longer stood out particularly from the range of occupations open to women at the century's close.

These brief portraits of each of the major female occupational groups in late nineteenth-century New England reveal a number of broader patterns. Among urban workingwomen—textile, shoe, and garment workers and domestic servants—there was a distinct increase in the proportion of those living at home with their families and contributing to a family economy. Among Lowell, Lynn, and Boston workingwomen, there was a convergence in residence patterns: differences that had been substantial at mid-century were considerably muted by 1900. Moreover, by 1900, the range of employment opportunities open to women had widened, and we begin to see the appearance of a sharper hierarchy among workingwomen along lines of ethnicity. Native-born women in white-collar occupations, immigrant women in factory jobs, and African American women in domestic service epitomized the emerging segmentation of the female work force in New England in 1900.

The patterns evident for specific female occupational groups become sharper still when we examine the overall picture. Massachusetts women made up almost 60 percent of all New England workingwomen and provide a useful approximation of the region as a whole. What changes do we see for Massachusetts women workers in the last third of the nineteenth century?

The absolute number of workingwomen in Massachusetts grew dramatically, from about 128,000 in 1870 to 329,000 thirty years later. Moreover, the concentration of workingwomen in domestic service and manufacturing occupations declined as the proportion of women in sales and clerical occupations increased. Nonetheless, more than three-fourths of

---

34. Coffman, *Social Composition*, pp. 73–76.

Table 7.10. Occupations of Massachusetts workingwomen,
1870 and 1900

Sector	1870	1900
Agriculture	0.04%	0.6%
Professional	5.8	7.1
Domestic and personal service	37.4	32.3
Trade and transportation	1.6	13.6
Manufacturing	55.2	46.4
Total women employed	128,000	329,000

Sources: *Ninth Census*, vol. 1, p. 739; and U.S. Bureau of the Census, *Twelfth Census of the United States*, vol. 2, *Population*, pt. 2, p. 141.

Note: Data are for females 10 years of age and older.

women workers in Massachusetts in 1900 remained employed in domestic service or manufacturing (see Table 7.10).

As was true for Boston, the female occupational distribution for Massachusetts as a whole was a composite of quite distinct occupational patterns for different ethnic groups. Once again native-born women of native-born parentage enjoyed the greatest occupational diversity. Although manufacturing employed more than a third of this group and domestic service more than a fifth, substantial numbers of the workingwomen of native-born parentage (17.5 percent) found employment in professional occupations, especially teaching. Another 21 percent worked in trade and transportation, where white-collar work in clerical and sales occupations offered relatively high wages and shorter hours (see Table 7.11).

Among native-born women of immigrant parentage, manufacturing employment, particularly work in the textile and garment industries, predominated. Almost three-fifths of these women worked in manufacturing and mechanical occupations; another sixth worked in domestic and personal service, with almost a fourth working in professional, sales, and clerical occupations.

As in Boston, immigrant and black women in Massachusetts in 1900 found places at the bottom of the female occupational hierarchy. Immigrant women enjoyed fewer opportunities than either of the native-born groups, with domestic service and manufacturing employment accounting for more than 92 percent of immigrant workingwomen in the state. Black women fared even more poorly, with 87 percent employed in domestic

Table 7.11. Occupations of Massachusetts workingwomen, 1900,
by nativity, parentage, and race

| | Native-born whites | | | |
Sector	Native parentage	Immigrant parentage	Foreign-born whites	Native-born blacks
Agriculture	1.5%	0.1%	0.3%	0.1%
Professional	17.5	5.9	1.4	1.7
Domestic and personal service	24.2	16.4	46.9	87.2
Trade and transportation	21.6	18.4	5.5	1.7
Manufacturing	35.2	59.2	45.8	9.3
Total cases	87,464	100,403	135,378	5,747

Source: U.S. Bureau of the Census, *Occupations at the Twelfth Census: Special Reports: Occupations*, pp. 304, 306.

and personal service occupations and another 9 percent in manufacturing jobs. White-collar and professional occupations accounted for only 3 percent of black workingwomen and 7 percent of foreign-born whites, proportions far below those enjoyed by native-born women workers.

The evidence on the occupational distributions of workingwomen along racial and ethnic lines reveals the emergence of distinct working-class worlds for Massachusetts women in 1900. Yankee women—native-born women of native-born parentage—came from families with greater economic resources and cultural advantages relative to other workingwomen. Prospective employers felt the greatest cultural affinity to this group of job seekers. When Yankee women went into the labor market, they parlayed this advantage into relatively better jobs. Substantial numbers worked as teachers or clerical or sales workers in the growing white-collar sector of the early twentieth-century New England economy. Native-born daughters of immigrants most often found work in factories, whereas immigrant women divided their employment almost evenly between domestic service and factory work. Finally, at the very bottom of the female occupational hierarchy, native-born black women continued, even as late as 1900, to be confined almost exclusively to the domestic and personal service sector.

The emergence in New England in the second half of the nineteenth century of a female occupational hierarchy shaped by race and ethnicity was by no means a unique regional phenomenon; rather, this development

TRANSFORMING WOMEN'S WORK

reflected national patterns in the post–Civil War decades. Precisely the same occupational patterns existed for different ethnic groups nationally as within New England.[35] In these hierarchical employment patterns we see clear evidence of a development that remains characteristic of women's paid work today in the 1990s. Gender confines women to specific occupational niches within the broader American economy, while race and ethnicity largely determine the placement of different groups of women within the female occupational world.[36]

The years between the middle of the nineteenth century and 1900 saw dramatic changes in the nature of women's wage work in New England, with a shift from patterns associated with the first stages of industrialization to more mature patterns that anticipate those found in the United States today. With the decline of rural outwork and the movement of wage labor out of the home, textile factory work and urban domestic service principally occupied the female labor force. Young single women predominated, Yankee rural-urban migrants and Irish immigrants working primarily in the years before marriage. In this context women's wage work offered workingwomen an unprecedented social and economic independence. Although there is plenty of evidence of the emotional and economic bonds that linked migrant workingwomen to their families back home, it is also clear that the assistance they offered their families was voluntarily rendered. They were free to contribute or not to their families as circumstances dictated. They were generally also free to decide how long to continue working and (for the Yankees, at least) whether and when to return home.

Whether they were millhands in Lowell or domestic servants in Boston, native-born workingwomen typically came from propertied rural families, and there is no evidence of extreme poverty that would have meant daughters' contributions were required on a regular basis to meet

35. Joseph A. Hill, *Women in Gainful Occupations, 1870 to 1920* (Washington: GPO, 1929), chaps. 10–13.
36. For a penetrating analysis of the racial division of female employment, see Evelyn Nakano Glenn, "From Servitude to Service Work: Historical Continuities in the Racial Division of Paid Reproductive Labor," *Signs* 18 (1992): 1–43. For a broad analysis of women's changing labor force in the participation that focuses primarily on the twentieth century, see Claudia Goldin, *Understanding the Gender Gap: An Economic History of American Women* (New York: Oxford University Press, 1990).

everyday needs. Rather, daughters' earnings helped provide more extraordinary familial needs—marriage portions being probably the most obvious one. Earnings as mill operatives and domestic servants gave Yankee daughters a degree of independence from their families and freed their parents to divide their limited resources among the remaining children. Women's wages thus played a more important role in the long-term reproduction of the family than in its daily subsistence.

This picture had changed significantly by 1900. In Boston, Lowell, and Lynn, the shares of workingwomen made up by daughters of immigrants increased substantially in the last decades of the nineteenth century. For the families of immigrants living in Boston and Lowell and even for native-born families living in Lynn, daughters' earnings were needed in 1900 for more than simply the long-term reproduction of the family across generations. Those earnings played an increasingly important role in providing daily subsistence for families. The same held true with even greater force for black women, for whom wage work often continued after marriage. On a daily basis, New England women were much more integral to the family wage economy than had been urban Yankee migrants at mid-century.

Moreover, increasing numbers of married, widowed, and divorced women were earning wages in 1900 compared with earlier periods. In Massachusetts in 1900, for instance, married women accounted for almost 12 percent of all workingwomen and widowed and divorced women another 10 percent. These proportions stood in sharp contrast to earlier patterns. Among Yankee women workers in Lowell before 1850, typically no more than 5 percent of textile operatives were married, widowed, or divorced. Even in 1860, when the immigrant Irish predominated in the mills, only 7.5 percent of women operatives were married or widowed. Finally, among workingwomen in Boston in 1860, less than 9 percent were married, widowed, or divorced.[37]

All in all, wage-earning women in New England in 1900 were older, more likely to be married or widowed, and more integrated into a family wage economy than were workingwomen in 1850. They were also

37. Dublin, *Women at Work*, pp. 31, 168, 282 n. 23. The proportion for 1860 is not reported in *Women at Work* but is based on the 1860 female millhand sample analyzed in chapter 10. The 1860 Boston figure is based on all workingwomen enumerated in the federal manuscript census of that year.

more ethnically diverse and were employed across a broader range of occupations than had been the case earlier. Women workers were also distributed along an occupational hierarchy that reflected new diversity in terms of race, ethnicity, and parentage. Two generations of cultural and economic change separated the worlds of Yankee female migrants in Lowell and Boston at mid-century and the daughters of immigrants in those cities in 1900. Immigrants and the daughters of immigrants now predominated among workingwomen in New England, and women's wages were increasingly crucial for the daily subsistence of working-class families. The dependence and subordination of wage-earning women within their families so characteristic of women's secondary status in the United States economy in the twentieth century emerged steadily in New England across the second half of the nineteenth century.

This study has addressed substantive changes in women's wage work and family lives in nineteenth-century New England, but it also speaks to our understanding of the character of the industrial revolution in the United States. The industrial revolution led to a dramatic increase in wage labor for both men and women, but the overall impact of capitalist industrialization varied along lines of gender. For men, the shift was one from independent agricultural production and artisanal labor to urban wage labor. For women, the shift was more drawn out and occurred in two distinct steps. It entailed a movement from unwaged productive and reproductive labor in the home first to waged labor within the home and then to waged labor outside the home. Recall, after all, the importance of rural outwork and urban domestic service and needlework for women during the first decades of New England's industrial revolution. All these occupations were conducted primarily in private homes, either those of workers or of their employers. By 1900, factory work in textiles, boots and shoes, and garment manufacturing had expanded considerably but so also had women's work in white-collar clerical and sales occupations. Throughout these decades, "industrial" employment never accounted for a majority of women's wage-earning occupations. Bringing gender into the analysis of the industrial revolution underscores the diversity of employment prospects generated by capitalist industrialization. Without paying attention to gender, we might well limit our analysis to changes taking place in factories and workshops and thereby miss much of the breadth of the social change occurring in these years.

Similarly, women's familial roles were uniquely affected by the industrial revolution. Single men had far greater opportunities for wage labor than did single women, and within families married men exercised control over the family farm economy that predominated in the region in the early nineteenth century. Given the advantaged circumstances of men in the preindustrial economy, women particularly benefited from expanded wages during early industrialization. Thus, women enjoyed new opportunities to purchase store goods with the advent of outwork weaving and hat making, and urban textile work and domestic service gave Yankee women still greater economic independence.

As wage work for women expanded further in the last decades of the nineteenth century, however, the social and economic independence of workingwomen proved short-lived. The proportion of workingwomen who resided on their own while working declined significantly, and family needs and obligations increasingly determined the nature of women's wage work. Daughters living at home and contributing their wages to their families and married and widowed women with families to support came to predominate among workingwomen. Women's work and wages in New England were reintegrated within a patriarchal family wage economy by the turn of the twentieth century. The window of independence that had partially opened in the early industrial revolution remained open only briefly. Although the *feme covert* of the colonial era was a relic of the past, wage work in nineteenth-century New England had by no means opened up a world of individual opportunity for women.

These developments are of more than simply historical interest. In the transformation of women's paid employment in New England in these decades lie the origins of social practices that are very much a part of life in the United States today. The past fifty years have seen another revolution in the character of women's wage work fully as dramatic as the nineteenth-century transformation chronicled here. The proportion of adult women working, the range of occupations they have entered, and the timing of their employment in relation to women's life cycle have all undergone major shifts in recent decades.[38] Whether the dependence and subordination of workingwomen so evident in the first

38. For an optimistic summary of recent economic research, see Sylvia Nasar, "Women's Progress Stalled? Just Not So," *New York Times*, October 18, 1992, sec. 3, pp. 1, 10.

seven decades of the twentieth century will continue as the United States moves into the twenty-first century remains to be seen. Clearly the recent expansion of employment opportunities for women has been remarkable, and workingwomen have greater prospects for economic independence than at any previous time in American history. At the same time, the backlash against these gains is very real, as many Americans back away from fully accepting the egalitarian implications of this change. The tension between these recent developments creates uncertainty that only the ongoing historical process will resolve.

Appendix 1. *Sources and Methods in the Outwork Study*

The study of outwork networks in Richmond and Fitzwilliam rests on the reconstitution of the families of individuals holding accounts with outwork middlemen Silas Jillson, John Whittemore, and Dexter Whittemore.[1] The conclusions reached and comparisons with studies of outwork in other communities depend on methods adopted and assumptions made in the course of the research. It will be useful, then, to discuss the procedures followed in moving from the original manuscript records to the computer data sets analyzed here.

Silas Jillson kept records of the webs of yarn that he put out to weavers in the years between 1822 and 1829, an account aimed primarily at satisfying the Rhode Island spinning firms that supplied him with yarn. He noted at the top of a given page a date and the name of the firm supplying a particular shipment of yarn. Below, in the main body of the record, he numbered each web and noted the names of weavers (or, more accurate, of account holders), the weight and thickness of warp and filling yarn, the length of the piece of cloth returned, its price per yard, and the payment credited. On some pages, Jillson recorded the kind of cloth, but equally often he left out this information. On occasion, cloth seems never to have been returned, and twice Jillson noted that he did not credit particular weavers. Probably these cases involved weaving so poor that Jillson did not think it would be acceptable to the mill agent to whom he was responsible. In all, there were 2,041 completed transactions noted in just under seven years.

---

1. Silas Jillson Weaving Account, 1822–1829, MATH; John Whittemore & Son Ledger, 1821–1824, private collection of the late Joel Whittemore, photocopy in possession of author; and Dexter Whittemore & Son Collection, BL.

Once the transactions were coded and keyed into a computer file, I alphabetically sorted the names of account holders and created aggregate records for each individual. I excluded from subsequent analysis four accounts that were not simply those of outworkers—Jillson's accounts with himself; a middleman, Enoch Whipple; and two Fitzwilliam store-keepers, John Whittemore and Luke Richardson. With an alphabetized listing of 249 aggregate records, I began linkage in other sources.[2] Published genealogies in the *History of Richmond* provided the starting point, followed by genealogies of neighboring towns.[3] Genealogies gave the birth and marriage dates of account holders, family status in 1822, the number of living parents in the family in 1822, the ages in 1822 and sexes of all unmarried children in the family, and the likely town of residence. Where I found two or more possible links for an account holder in a given town genealogy, I did not make the linkage. Without positive information to favor one possible link over another, I refused to make a firm link. Genealogical linkage began in Richmond first and continued into neighboring towns when individuals could not be found in Richmond genealogies or where the information given was incomplete.

Once genealogical linkage was complete, I traced individuals in the 1830 federal manuscript census of Richmond and in an 1826 tax list of the community.[4] I separately coded all individuals enumerated in the census and tax list in order to be able to compare outwork and nonoutwork families. Where genealogical linkage had placed an individual in a neighboring town, I also searched in the 1830 federal manuscript census

2. The actual work was not quite as linear as the description here suggests. At any point in the linkage process, I might determine that what appeared at first to be "two" individuals were, in fact, a single person. Only at the end of the entire process did I know that I would be analyzing 249 Jillson account holders. For the sake of consistency, I will employ the first-person singular in the discussion of the work process. As noted in my acknowledgments, the work reported here (and in succeeding appendixes) was supported by numerous hard-working research assistants over the years.

3. William Bassett, *The History of the Town of Richmond, Cheshire County, New Hampshire* (Boston: C. W. Calkins, 1884); John F. Norton, *History of Fitzwilliam, New Hampshire* (New York: Burr, 1888); Albert Annett and Alice E. E. Lehtinen, *History of Jaffrey (Middle Monadnock) New Hampshire*, 2 vols. (Jaffrey: By the Town, 1937); M. T. Stone, *Historical Sketch of the Town of Troy . . . 1764–1897* (Keene, N.H.: Sentinel Press, 1897); and Benjamin Read, *The History of Swanzey, from 1734 to 1890* (Salem, Mass.: Salem Press, 1892).

4. Federal Manuscript Census of Population, 1830, Cheshire County, N.H., M19, roll 74; and 1826 Richmond Tax List, town hall.

of population for that community. Finally, I linked individuals residing in Fitzwilliam in an 1819 tax list of that town.[5]

A word on the coding of these additional sources will be helpful. Coding of the 1830 federal manuscript censuses for Richmond and Fitzwilliam was straightforward, as enumerators had recorded the names of household heads and the sex and age range of each household member. Tax lists required more care. First, I excluded entries for nonresidents and for estates listed in the names of guardians, administrators of estates, or "heirs of. . . ." Second, once I had completed coding of the tax lists, I linked them to the closest federal manuscript census to identify taxed individuals as either household heads or nonheads. This latter information proved important in comparisons of outworkers and nonoutworkers. Following record linkage, I added tax information to the records of Jillson account holders and also added to the computerized tax lists an indication of whether a given taxpayer had an outwork account with Silas Jillson. Similarly, I added census household information to the combined Jillson records and noted on census records whether a given household head did outwork weaving for Jillson.

I followed similar steps with Whittemore outworkers. The earliest of the Whittemore store accounts analyzed was an 1821–1824 ledger volume of John Whittemore.[6] Considerably more extensive than the Jillson weave book, this volume recorded credits and debits of Whittemore's customers in individual accounts. Because thousands of transactions were noted, I chose the individual account as the unit of analysis. For each account, I recorded the name of the account holder; first and last dates of transactions; the values of notes, cash, interest, and third-party payments debited; and the values of notes, cash, third-party payments, cloth, agricultural products, and miscellaneous items credited. What made analysis of the John Whittemore ledger particularly worthwhile was the fact that a fair number of Silas Jillson's outwork weavers left

5. Tax lists are found in the respective town halls and were chosen as the lists closest in time to dates of the account books to which they were being linked. My thanks to town officers who permitted me to microfilm or photocopy the original records.

6. In terms of the order of the work completed, I actually coded and analyzed the 1830 and 1850 Dexter Whittemore ledgers before the 1821–1824 John Whittemore volume. The issues addressed in the coding process were essentially the same, and it may prove clearer to keep the discussion here in the same order as the presentation in Chapter 2.

their work for him at the Whittemore store and received credit toward store purchases.

After coding account information and alphabetizing the names of account holders, I proceeded to link individuals with names of outworkers listed in Silas Jillson's weave book and of palm-leaf hat makers recorded in the 1830 Dexter Whittemore ledger.[7] Linkage continued in published genealogies of Fitzwilliam and neighboring towns and in an 1819 Fitzwilliam tax list and an 1826 Richmond tax list.[8] Finally, I linked account holders in the 1820 federal manuscript censuses of population for Richmond, Fitzwilliam, and neighboring towns.[9] As in the work with Richmond local records, I coded and made machine-readable the entire 1819 tax list and 1820 federal manuscript population census for Fitzwilliam. By noting the presence or absence of each of these individuals in the early Whittemore account book, I was able to compare the property holdings and household composition and family size of outworkers and nonoutworkers in Fitzwilliam. The linkage of account holders across the different sets of records proved particularly useful, permitting comparisons of Jillson and Whittemore outworkers, placing weaving outwork within the larger context of individuals' trading activities at the Whittemore store, and tracing the shift from outwork weaving to palm-leaf hat making over time.

As the Whittemore store established its palm hat outwork network in the late 1820s, its business expanded dramatically. So, too, did the surviving historical record. The Dexter Whittemore & Son Collection consists of more than ninety volumes and seven wooden crates of records. Covering a period of thirty years, the collection permits, even encourages, consideration of change over time. To facilitate such an approach, I selected two ledger volumes—one covering roughly 1829–1831; the other, 1850–1855—for coding and subsequent record linkage.[10]

---

7. Because genealogical and census linkage for 1821–1824 account holders followed similar work with the 1830 Whittemore ledger, I was able to draw on the earlier linkage. Of the 190 individuals listed in the 1821–1824 account, I found 79 who had been identified in genealogies in earlier linkage. This information was quite easily added to new records at the outset of the linkage step.

8. For published sources, see note 3 above.

9. Federal Manuscript Census of Population, 1820 Cheshire County, N.H., M33, roll 59.

10. Dexter Whittemore & Son Collection, vols. 44, 55.

The study population drawn from these ledgers consisted of all account holders who had one hat transaction or at least two non-hat transactions recorded in the ledgers. I excluded a limited number of individuals who worked as teamsters, leaf splitters, or clerks and whose accounts with Whittemore were really payrolls. These criteria led me to include 298 individual accounts from the 1830 ledger and 971 from 1850.

Once again, I recorded summary information on accounts, including names of account holders; dates of first and last transactions; the values of credits for agricultural goods, cloth, palm-leaf hats, miscellaneous goods and services; IOUs; cash payments; and payments by third parties. For a sample of 1830 account holders, I also recorded debits (largely for purchases) in a number of broad categories.[11]

I linked account holders in a variety of local sources. Published genealogies for Fitzwilliam and surrounding communities, surviving vital records, the 1830 and 1850 federal manuscript censuses of population, an 1850 Fitzwilliam tax list, and the 1850 federal manuscript census of agriculture for Fitzwilliam provided an extremely diverse body of supplementary sources.[12]

For the four distinct sets of data, record linkage proved to be quite complete. Typically, I was able to find more than three-fourths of account holders in local genealogies, more than half in tax lists, and more

11. Debit categories coded for the sample of 1830 account holders included split palm leaf; sewing goods; food items; household furnishings; finished clothing; agricultural implements and supplies; books, stationery, and similar supplies; sundries; third-party payments; cash; and notes. I chose a stratified sample of 1830 account holders in order to be certain of including a reasonable number of male and female household heads, wives, daughters, and sons in the analysis of store purchases.

12. Silas Cummings, "Deaths' Doings," in Silas Cummings Notebook, Fitzwilliam Town Hall, and "Deaths in Fitzwilliam," Fitzwilliam Town Hall. Federal Manuscript Census of Population, Cheshire County, N.H., 1830, M19, roll 74, and 1850, M432, rolls 427–28, Worcester County, Mass., 1830, M19, roll 68, and 1850, M432, rolls 340–45. Particularly valuable when tracing account holders in neighboring towns were the published indexes of the New Hampshire and Massachusetts censuses for 1830 and 1850 available from Accelerated Indexing Systems, Bountiful, Utah. The 1850 tax list is held in the town hall in Fitzwilliam, and volumes of the agricultural census are at the New Hampshire State Library in Concord. I did not link 1830 account holders in the 1819 Fitzwilliam tax list because I felt the eleven-year gap between store account and tax list made the latter a somewhat untrustworthy measure of family property holdings. Unfortunately, there appear to be no surviving Fitzwilliam tax lists closer to the date of the Whittemore ledger account.

Table A.1. Extent of linkage of outwork account holders
in local genealogies, tax lists, and censuses

Account	Genealogies	Tax lists	Censuses	Total cases
Silas Jillson	89.2%	55.8%	53.0%	249
John Whittemore	78.9	63.2	54.7	190
1830 Whittemore	80.9	a	71.5	298
1850 Whittemore	65.6	36.1	76.3	971

Sources: Silas Jillson Weaving Account, 1822–1829, MATH; John Whittemore &
Son Ledger, 1821–1824; Dexter Whittemore & Son Collection, account books, vols. 44
and 55, BL; 1830 and 1850 federal manuscript censuses; 1819 and 1850 Fitzwilliam
Tax Lists; 1826 Richmond tax list; and published genealogies of Richmond, Fitzwilliam, and surrounding towns.

aLinkage not carried out for this possible source.

than two-thirds in local censuses.[13] The extent of record linkage suggests that findings for linked individuals are unlikely to be subject to
significant distortion because of the existence of missing data on particular variables. The extent of record linkage in individual sources for
each of the studies is noted in Table A.1.

Part of the success of the record linkage stemmed from the systematic cross-checking that was made possible by the existence of four different study populations. Names were checked not only in the various
additional sources described here but between lists of account holders as
well. Information gathered, for instance, in the study of the 1830 palm
hat accounts was added to the records of 1821–1824 Whittemore account holders when subsequent record linkage indicated that individuals
were found in more than one set of ledger accounts. Similarly, the detailed record linkage for Silas Jillson's outwork weavers in Richmond
proved useful when an occasional Richmond resident turned up in the
Whittemore accounts. Similarities in the composition of account holders
or in patterns of outwork from one account book to another confirm and

13. The notable exception is tax list linkage for 1850 Whittemore account holders. The
lower proportion linked in the tax list for that year results from the fact that less than half of
individuals trading with Whittemore at that date resided in Fitzwilliam. The proportion of
Fitzwilliam account holders successfully traced to the tax list was comparable with those
recorded for earlier groups of outworkers.

reinforce the substantive conclusions reached here; the repeated efforts at record linkage also made the overall results more reliable than any single study would have been by itself.

In addition to reporting cross-sectional findings for each of the four sets of outwork accounts, I also report a certain amount of information based on tracing individual account holders in successive ledgers of Dexter Whittemore & Son. In this manner, I was able to analyze the hat making of women before and after their marriages and before and after their husbands' deaths. Because Whittemore kept an index for each ledger volume, it proved a relatively simple process to trace specific individuals, their parents, and their spouses through successive ledger accounts.[14] This work was necessarily dependent on knowledge of names of spouses and dates of marriage or death drawn from genealogical or vital record linkage. Tracing women's hat making in different phases of the life cycle provides evidence that simply could not have been extracted from cross-sectional data at a single point in time. The richness of these findings offers testimony to the utility of record linkage. Only by assembling data from disparate genealogical, vital, census, and tax records can we know enough about individual account holders to permit the kind of fine-tuned analysis of outwork that is presented here.

14. The major complication in tracing account holders was the fact that one Whittemore ledger volume is held by the Fitzwilliam Town Library. Otherwise, the ledgers employed in this tracing are in Dexter Whittemore & Son Collection, vols. 44–57.

Appendix 2. *The Samples and Populations of Women Wage Earners*

The analysis presented in Chapters 3–6 developed as a single coordinated effort to explore the work and family lives of New England women in five occupational groups. Because of the unique nature of records in different communities associated with different occupations, it was not possible (or even desirable) to use a uniform procedure for drawing the samples or populations for study. It made sense, where possible, to take advantage of unique possibilities as they presented themselves while still making every effort to assure comparability across occupational groups.

Putting together a population of Lowell millhands began with my research for *Women at Work*, in which I traced 175 women millhands from the Hamilton Manufacturing Company in Lowell back to their rural hometowns.[1] I analyzed the work experiences and family origins of women from the towns of Boscawen, Canterbury, and Sutton, New Hampshire, who were employed at the company between 1830 and 1850. These towns were chosen because they sent large numbers of women to work at Hamilton and had published genealogies. The initial results were suggestive, but at several points it became clear that including a larger number of women in the study population would permit a fuller analysis of the mill experience.

To expand the number of millhands required the selection of additional towns. Examination of published genealogies for New Hampshire towns led me to six towns as possible candidates. I then recorded all entrants into the Hamilton work force from these towns as noted in com-

---

1. Thomas Dublin, *Women at Work: The Transformation of Work and Community in Lowell, Massachusetts, 1826–1860* (New York: Columbia University Press, 1979), chap. 3 and app. 2.

pany register books for the period 1830–1850.[2] Four towns stood out in terms of the number of women employed at Hamilton in this period. Preliminary linkage of a small number of millhands from each of the towns to local genealogies led me to select the towns of Lyndeborough, Northfield, and Sanbornton for inclusion in the expanded sample. The new women from these towns selected from Hamilton registers for the years between 1830 and 1850 plus the women originally chosen from Boscawen, Canterbury, and Sutton resulted in the study population of 410 operatives discussed in Chapter 3.[3]

No comparable business records survive for any major shoemaking firm in Lynn, thus necessitating a different sampling strategy for women shoeworkers. The 1860 federal manuscript census was the first systematically to record women's occupations, and I began my work with that document. Preliminary examination of enumerations for Lynn revealed surprisingly few women with shoe occupations.[4] This development led me to explore the 1865 Massachusetts state census for Lynn. This latter census proved superior to the 1860 census in two respects. First, women workers were recorded in much larger numbers; second, for the three central working-class wards of the city, enumerators exceeded their instructions and recorded the actual towns of birth of virtually all residents.[5] Here was a record, then, that approximated the Hamilton

2. Hamilton Manufacturing Company Records, vols. 481–91, BL.

3. Published genealogies for the six towns are found in Charles Carleton Coffin, *The History of Boscawen and Webster, from 1733 to 1878* (Concord, N.H.: Republican Press Association, 1878); James Otis Lyford, *History of the Town of Canterbury, New Hampshire, 1727–1912* (Concord, N.H.: Rumford Press, 1912); Augusta Harvey Worthen, *The History of Sutton, New Hampshire* (Concord, N.H.: Republican Press Association, 1890); Lucy R. H. Cross, *History of the Town of Northfield, New Hampshire, 1780–1905* (Concord, N.H.: Rumford Press, 1905); Dennis Donovan and Jacob A. Woodward, *The History of the Town of Lyndeborough, New Hampshire, 1735–1905* (Lyndeborough: By the Town, 1906); and Moses T. Runnels, *History of the Town of Sanbornton, New Hampshire*, 2 vols. (Boston: Alfred Mudge, 1881).

4. My initial judgment here was subsequently confirmed by work by Mary H. Blewett, who found only 486 women shoeworkers enumerated in the 1860 federal manuscript census of Lynn out of a likely 2,800 women shoeworkers employed in the city at that date. See Blewett, *Men, Women, and Work: Class, Gender, and Protest in the New England Shoe Industry, 1780–1910* (Urbana: University of Illinois Press, 1988), pp. 329–31.

5. Mass. State Census of Population, 1865, Massachusetts State Archives, Lynn. Wards 3, 4, and 5 contain the additional information on towns of birth.

Company register volumes in permitting one to trace shoeworkers back to their specific hometowns in the countryside. Especially valuable was the differentiation between shoeworkers born in Lynn and those born elsewhere in Massachusetts, a distinction not possible to make with censuses noting only the state of birth.

I proceeded to code all women shoeworkers enumerated in Lynn wards 3, 4, and 5 born in specified Massachusetts, New Hampshire, and Maine hometowns. The native-born made up more than 85 percent of all Lynn residents in 1865 and probably an even greater share of female shoeworkers.[6] As in the examination of the origins of Hamilton Company millhands, this study addresses issues relevant to the overall female work force in Lynn. Although this procedure excluded foreign-born female shoeworkers, it made possible subsequent linkage with a broad range of other records and comparison with earlier findings for Lowell millhands. From a population of 810 female shoeworkers from known Massachusetts, New Hampshire, and Maine hometowns recorded in Lynn's central wards, I drew a random sample of 402 for subsequent record linkage and analysis.

The existence of published school reports that noted the names of teachers for most New Hampshire towns beginning in 1859 permitted the use of employment records rather than censuses for drawing a population of women teachers.[7] As my earlier research had entailed tracing Lowell operatives back to six New Hampshire hometowns, I looked initially at school reports for these communities. Only scattered records survived for the antebellum decades, which made it impossible to reconstruct the female teaching force in these towns in the same period for which Hamilton Company records exist. Complete runs of annual school reports for the towns of Boscawen, Canterbury, and Lyndeborough after 1859 led me to select those communities for further study. Recording the names (and often hometowns) of all women teachers in

6. Mass. Secretary of the Commonwealth, *Abstract of the Census of Massachusetts, 1865* (Boston: Wright & Potter, 1867), pp. 64–65; and U.S. Immigration Commission, *Reports of the Immigration Commission*, vol. 12, *Immigrants in Industries*, pt. 9, "Boot and Shoe Manufacturing" (Washington: GPO, 1911), pp. 367–68. Reworking Blewett's findings for an 1870 sample of female shoeworkers suggests that 15.5 percent were foreign-born at that date. See *Men, Women, and Work*, pp. 335–37.

7. See the NHHS for annual school reports for virtually all towns in the state.

these towns between 1860 and 1880, sorting and combining multiple teaching stints into records for individuals, and further consolidating entries that referred to the same person resulted in a population of 449 for analysis.

I chose to examine Boston records in the selection of samples of domestic servants and garment workers—the final occupational groups in the study. Once again, the lack of appropriate employment records led to the use of censuses as a starting point for sampling. The 1860 federal manuscript census was the first to record women's occupations; a brief examination of other state and federal censuses found that none provided more than state of birth. This being the case, I relied on the 1860 Boston census for drawing samples of native-born servants and garment workers.[8]

To permit the analysis of all workingwomen in Boston and thus place findings for servants and garment workers in a broader context, I began by recording a limited amount of information on all women listed in the census for whom enumerators noted an occupation. In all, 16,852 workingwomen resided in the city's twelve wards at this date. Of this number, more than 13,700 were employed in occupations I considered within the categories of domestic service and the needle trades.[9] I proceeded to draw random samples of about 400 native-born women from each of these larger populations of domestic servants and garment workers.[10]

The five separate studies provide information about 2,069 native-born workingwomen in New England between 1830 and 1880. They cover the range of occupations in which women earned wages—from domestic service at the bottom of the hierarchy through semiskilled work

8. Federal Manuscript Census of Population, 1860, Boston, M653, rolls 520–25.

9. I found ten occupations within domestic service and thirty within the needle trades. The leading occupations within domestic service were domestic, servant, waitress, cook, nurse, housekeeper, and laundress. I excluded from the domestic service category housekeepers who headed their own households and nurses residing in hospitals or boardinghouses associated with hospitals. Leading occupations in the needle trades included seamstress, dressmaker, milliner, and tailoress.

10. A desire to make the Boston samples roughly comparable with those for native-born women in the shoe, textile, and teacher groups led to this focus. As the vast majority of Boston women workers resided apart from their families, the two samples include large numbers of native-born daughters of immigrants. It was not possible to limit the samples at the outset to Yankee women. Ultimately, it proved useful to have both Yankee migrants from the countryside and Boston-born daughters of immigrants in the samples. A fuller understanding of work and family relations of women is possible with a comparison of these two groups.

in textile, shoe, and garment manufacturing in the middle to teaching, the leading white-collar occupation for women in the nineteenth century. Geographically, the samples also cover the range of locations in which women found employment in these decades. They include three New Hampshire rural communities, two middle-sized, single-industry towns in Massachusetts, and the commercial metropolis of Boston. Short of drawing an entirely random sample of all workingwomen—a mammoth undertaking—these five groups offer as representative a picture of native-born workingwomen in nineteenth-century New England as we are likely to find.

Appendix 3. *Methods of the Millhand Study*

With the selection of 410 Hamilton millhands from six New Hampshire towns, I began work on the tracing of millhands back to their families of origin, through their careers in the mills, and into their subsequent marriages.

For the millhands from Boscawen, Canterbury, and Sutton, much tracing had already been accomplished in the course of my research on *Women at Work*.[1] For the additional millhands from Lyndeborough, Northfield, and Sanbornton, the first step consisted of consolidating all the entrances, departures, and room changes into single records for each individual. With the assignment of unique identification numbers for each sample member, it was possible to combine the two groups of millhands so that the same procedures could be employed with all sample members.

Although they provided the starting point for the study, register book entries were often incomplete. They might note a starting date for a given millhand but fail to record her departure from the mill. At times, there were two millhands from the same hometown whose names were strikingly similar. To supplement data from register books, I examined the original Hamilton payroll records for those millhands with ambiguous register entries. Additional entry and departure dates were recorded and signatures checked to permit the consolidation of apparently separate cases. This work assured a greater accuracy to the records summarizing each individual's employment at the Hamilton Company.

At this point I alphabetized the records within hometowns and began linkage in published town genealogies and Massachusetts and New Hampshire state vital records. For each individual successfully linked,

---

1. See Thomas Dublin, *Women at Work: The Transformation of Work and Community in Lowell, Massachusetts, 1826–1860* (New York: Columbia University Press, 1979), app. 2, for a discussion of the initial record linkage.

birthdate, marriage date, death date, and parents' names and dates of death were recorded. In addition, I noted the number of sons and daughters in the family of origin and the millhand's birth order among all children and daughters. From genealogical or vital records, I added the name, occupation, and birthdate of husbands where that evidence was available. Indications from genealogies that parents, siblings, husband, or children resided in Lowell at any time were noted as well. Finally, places of marriage or death or any significant migration noted in genealogies were recorded to facilitate subsequent census linkage.

Initially I traced millhands in the published genealogies for their hometowns. With this step completed, I continued to look for unlinked individuals or to fill in missing linkage information in genealogies of neighboring towns. In addition, where I had a husband's name, I also looked for entries under his name in the genealogies of his hometown or neighboring towns. To expand family information, I searched church, town, and state vital records as well. These sources included cemetery inscriptions, town meeting records, and records of births, deaths, and marriages kept by local churches or ministers.

After this first round of linkage in local records, I traced individuals in the vital record registration system of New Hampshire for additional information. Initially, those unlinked in any source were traced in birth records. Because of the commonality of names, I required positive identification of the individual record with the appropriate hometown. Marriage and death records were searched in much the same way. Vital record linkage often provided information that was lacking in published genealogies, and partial information from earlier sources often assisted in making a positive link between a millhand and an incomplete vital record. Finally, published family genealogies proved useful in supplementing town and state genealogies and vital records.[2] Given the broad coverage of family genealogies, I required records drawn from these sources to connect the person to either Lowell or her hometown or to family members already identified in local sources.

Lowell and Massachusetts vital records provided the next sources for record linkage. Published volumes of births, marriages, and deaths in

2. It would be impossible to note all the family genealogies employed in the tracing. The largest collections of these sources are available at the New Hampshire Historical Society, the New England Historical Genealogical Society, and the Massachusetts State Library.

Lowell before 1849, manuscript records in the Lowell City Clerk's Office, and records of the state registration system in Boston all proved useful.[3] A fair number of operatives married, bore children, or died in Lowell (or elsewhere in Massachusetts), and I added this information to their records.

Census linkage provided the next major source of information on Lowell millhands and their families. Tracing began with census enumerations for Lowell and the six hometowns in 1850 and 1860, and I employed a coding scheme that permitted recording information on millhands and their parents, even if they resided in separate households.[4] The existence of published indexes to the 1850 federal manuscript censuses for Massachusetts and New Hampshire permitted linkage of millhands, husbands, and parents beyond the bounds of Lowell and their hometowns.[5]

Residence was only one of several pieces of information added through census linkage. Censuses often provided age data on the operative or her spouse that was unavailable elsewhere. Parents' deaths or the dates of the births of children might also be inferred from census listings. Occasionally the census provided evidence of a marriage not found in any surviving vital record. Most important, the census noted occupational and property data for husbands and fathers, which permitted the placing of operatives' families within the social and economic structure of their hometowns. This final step was greatly facilitated by recording the census enumerations of all household heads in 1850 and 1860 for the six New Hampshire towns. I noted data on the sex, age, property ownership, and

3. *Vital Records of Lowell, Massachusetts, to the End of the Year 1849*, 4 vols. (Salem, Mass.: Essex Institute, 1930); Lowell Vital Records, 1826–1860, City Clerk's Office; and Mass. Department of Vital Statistics, indexes of births, marriages, and deaths, Boston.

4. The censuses for 1830 and 1840 were closer to the dates that sample members entered employment at the Hamilton Company. Unfortunately, census enumerators recorded the names of heads of households only in those years, so those censuses do not permit linkage with sample members who were typically children living at home. For this reason, I concentrated linkage efforts on the 1850 and 1860 censuses. Federal Manuscript Census of Population, Lowell, 1850, M432, rolls 326–27, and 1860, M653, roll 507, and New Hampshire towns, 1850, M432, rolls 425, 433, and 436, and 1860, M676, rolls 666, 673, and 676.

5. Ronald Vern Jackson and Gary Ronald Teeples, eds., *Massachusetts 1850 Census Index* (Bountiful, Utah: Accelerated Indexing Systems, 1978), and *New Hampshire 1850 Census Index* (Bountiful, Utah: Accelerated Indexing Systems, 1978).

occupation of each household head and subsequently compared this information on the parents of millhands with evidence for the communities from which they came.

To permit analysis of the property ownership of the families of millhands before they entered employment at the Hamilton Company, I linked parents of millhands in surviving tax inventories of their hometowns. For five of the six towns, 1830 tax records were employed; for Sanbornton, the closest surviving record covered 1836. Data recorded included (with minor variations from town to town) the number of polls, value of livestock, value of improved and unimproved lands, value of personal estate, and total tax.[6] As in the analysis of tax lists for Fitzwilliam and Richmond in the outwork studies, some judgments had to be made in the course of this coding. I excluded nonresident taxpayers from the analysis as well as units of property designated in the names of heirs of an individual's estate. Occasionally the towns taxed individuals who rented land from someone else, usually a nonresident, and I excluded these holdings as well. Where two residents held property as partners, I attempted to identify the partners and to assign shares of the property to the appropriate individuals. Finally, I linked taxed individuals to enumerations of the 1830 federal manuscript census in the towns and added the sex and household status of each taxed person to the record. Together, the 1850 and 1860 property data and 1830 tax data permit the analysis of the parents and husbands of millhands within a broader context.

Additional tracing in Lowell records provided further useful information on millhands and their husbands. Linkage in an 1836 supplement to the Lowell City Directory permitted the updating in my computerized database of a millhand's employment at the Hamilton Company or another firm in Lowell.[7] In addition, each husband was traced in Lowell city directories for the two years before the date of marriage and until

6. State legislation set the ground rules for local tax assessments and assures comparability between towns. See *Laws of the State of New Hampshire . . . Published by Authority* (Hopkinton, N.H.: Isaac Long, Jr., 1830), pp. 551–59.

7. *Female Supplement to the Lowell Directory* (Lowell, Mass.: Leonard Huntress, 1836). Unfortunately, only in 1836 did compilers of the directory include names of female mill operatives. In other years, the only women recorded in directories were boardinghouse keepers or proprietors of shops.

he had disappeared from two successive directories or for at least two years after the date of marriage. I also traced husbands in Hamilton register books for evidence of possible employment.

The record linkage described here was completed with the assistance of computer-generated alphabetical printouts. Typically I prepared a list that summarized what information I already knew about a group of individuals before I began tracing in a new source, be it the 1850 census or New Hampshire state vital records. Lists utilized an individual's maiden or married name, whichever was appropriate for the particular linkage. I included considerable personal information in the lists to permit checking of evidence in the new source with what was already known about the individual. Thus, in carrying out linkage in death records, I had access to the names of a millhand's parents and husband, her birth and marriage dates, and whatever residence information I had already found. Humans made all linkage decisions (rather than a computer employing a weighting scheme), but computerization of the data files and repeated updating of printouts contributed dramatically to the success of record linkage. Although the discussion has suggested a linear sequence of steps in the process of record linkage, in fact the work had more of a circular character. With the additions and corrections made following one linkage step, I reexamined old sources to see whether new links could be made taking the new information into consideration. City directory and census linkage, for instance, were repeated numerous times as the number of marriage links increased, providing new husbands to be traced. Even when linkage appeared to be complete and computer analysis began, occasional inconsistencies in linkage data became apparent and required rechecking and new decisions. In the end, we will never be certain that all the information assembled in the linkage process is "correct" or that further investigation could not have increased the number of "good" links to various sources. Still, there are numerous checks in the process, and its iterative nature provides some assurance that on the whole the evidence that is ultimately analyzed is trustworthy and the results of that analysis reliable.

Appendix 4. *Methods of the Shoeworker Study*

The study of women shoeworkers began with a sample of 402 female shoeworkers from the 1865 Massachusetts state census of Lynn. The choice of that particular census was based on two factors. First, the 1860 federal manuscript census appeared to systematically underenumerate workingwomen in Lynn, particularly Maine- and New Hampshire–born migrants in the city.[1] Second, for three working-class wards in the city, enumerators for the 1865 state census exceeded their instructions and recorded hometowns as well as states of birth. This additional information clinched the decision and led to the coding of information on 810 women shoeworkers of known hometowns of birth in Massachusetts, Maine, and New Hampshire who resided in wards 3, 4, and 5 of Lynn in 1865. From this larger population, I then drew a random sample of 402 workingwomen for subsequent record linkage and analysis.

Tracing proceeded rather differently for shoeworkers than for millhands for several reasons. Shoeworkers came from numerous hometowns in Massachusetts, New Hampshire, and Maine rather than from six communities. For this reason, reliance on genealogies as a major source of information on families was not possible. The later date of the shoeworker sample, however—1865 compared with the 1830–1850 period for Lowell millhands—meant that censuses proved a richer source for record linkage. Federal manuscript censuses for 1850, 1860, 1870, and 1880 were particularly useful, and the Massachusetts state census

---

1. Mary Blewett estimates that based on comparison with manufacturing census figures, the 1860 population census recorded only 17 percent of Lynn female shoeworkers. She argues that the population census improved in succeeding years, recording more than 53 percent of female shoeworkers in Lynn in 1870 and 80 percent in 1880. Blewett, *Men, Women, and Work: Class, Gender, and Protest in the New England Shoe Industry, 1780–1910* (Urbana: University of Illinois Press, 1988), pp. 329–31, 334, and 338–39.

for 1855 yielded additional information. The fact that about half of the shoeworkers were born in Lynn meant that the Massachusetts registration system of vital records was an invaluable source of data.

The 1865 state census of Lynn provided the sample of shoeworkers in the first place and valuable information that assisted subsequent record linkage as well. Unlike the register book entries for the Hamilton Company, the census enumerations gave considerable information about the families of shoeworkers. Almost two-thirds of sample members lived with family in Lynn—either their families of origin or of marriage. Data collection began first by recording information about each sample member and also about co-resident family members. The availability of the names of parents, siblings, husbands, and children greatly facilitated subsequent linkage in other censuses and in state vital records.

Linkage in marriage records was the most important step in tracing shoeworkers because it provided former maiden names for married or widowed shoeworkers and new married names for single shoeworkers. The Massachusetts state registration system of vital records proved the most useful source. Linkage was particularly certain because the census gave the towns of birth and ages of all sample members and parents' names for a good share. Linkage for married women was assisted by knowledge of husbands' names, and only widowed shoeworkers were difficult to trace in marriage records. For this group, it was possible to begin by searching for deaths after 1865 and with maiden names drawn from death records to return to earlier marriage records. Published vital records for Lynn before 1850 were also a valuable source for linkage information on older members of the sample.[2] For single or widowed shoeworkers, I proceeded also to search for marriages in the post-1865 period. Exact dates of marriage and maiden and married names were especially important in modifying the alphabetical lists employed in census linkage. In making links in marriage records, I required confirmation of the hometowns of birth of sample members; Lynn residence and reasonable agreement on the age of the sample member were helpful but not absolutely required for linkage.

With the completion of the first rounds of marriage linkage in local Lynn and Massachusetts state records, I turned to linkage in the New

2. *Vital Records of Lynn, Massachusetts, to the End of the Year 1849*, 2 vols. (Salem, Mass.: Essex Institute, 1905–6).

Hampshire vital records system. Maine state records are especially un-even for the period before 1900, and the number of Maine-born in the sample was small enough that I did not feel a need to extend my search into that state's vital records.[3]

At this point, linkage in census records began. Because social mobil-ity studies had generally indicated high rates of turnover between cen-suses, it made sense to work backward one census at a time from the 1865 census.[4] I thus began with the 1860 federal manuscript census for Lynn, utilizing an alphabetical listing of sample members with accom-panying information about other family members. After completing link-age in Lynn, I used a much-reduced list to trace in surrounding Essex County towns, taking advantage of birthplace information noted in the 1865 census enumeration.

With the alphabetical listing updated to include new family infor-mation derived from 1860 census linkage, I began tracing in the 1855 Massachusetts state census of Lynn and surrounding towns. As with the 1860 linkage, name, age, town of birth, and names of family members provided variables to be checked in confirming possible linkages. Once Lynn tracing had been completed, linkage proceeded in surrounding Essex County towns.

After the completion of the 1860 census linkage and while the 1855 linkage was winding up, I began tracing in the 1850 federal manuscript census. As almost half of shoeworkers were born in Lynn and given the large number of 1860 and 1855 links to Lynn censuses, it made sense to begin first with that city. Using an alphabetical listing of shoeworkers—corrected with maiden names of those marrying between 1850 and 1865

3. The distribution of birthplaces for sample members as recorded in the 1865 census sug-gested that linkage in the Massachusetts and New Hampshire state registration systems would be adequate. Over 78 percent of sample members were born in named Massachusetts towns, another 10.0 percent in New Hampshire, and 11.7 percent in Maine.

4. Stephan Thernstrom, *Poverty and Progress: Social Mobility in a Nineteenth-Century City* (Cambridge: Harvard University Press, 1964); Peter R. Knights, *The Plain People of Boston, 1830–1860: A Study in City Growth* (New York: Oxford University Press, 1971); Stephan Thernstrom, *The Other Bostonians: Poverty and Progress in the American Metropolis* (Cam-bridge: Harvard University Press, 1973); and Howard M. Gitelman, *Workingmen of Waltham: Mobility in American Urban Industrial Development* (Baltimore: Johns Hopkins University Press, 1974).

and with added names of family members derived from the 1860 and 1855 censuses—I checked sample members in the published 1850 census index for Massachusetts.[5] Possible links were verified first in the Lynn census and then in other Massachusetts towns. Fair numbers of links were made in other Essex County towns and in nearby Middlesex County. After completion of linkage in Lynn and other Massachusetts towns, I first checked all still-unlinked New Hampshire– and Maine-born sample members in the 1850 census indexes for those states and then in the manuscript censuses themselves.[6] Once again, information on the specific hometowns of shoeworkers proved crucial in making links, especially for shoeworkers who had boarded by themselves in Lynn in 1865.

New information on the parents or husbands of shoeworkers found in the 1850 census linkage step was added to records utilized in subsequent linkage. These additions were particularly significant because the existence of census indexes permitted extensive linkage outside of Lynn and surrounding towns. This linkage often provided the first solid information on the names of parents of migrant shoeworkers and greatly facilitated ongoing tracing in Massachusetts or New Hampshire marriage records.

Linkage in the 1870 federal manuscript census drew on the progress made in tracing the marriages of sample members. Where Massachusetts or New Hampshire state vital records revealed a marriage between 1865 and 1870, I replaced shoeworkers' maiden names with married names and added husbands' names to the records to facilitate linkage. Because all sample members were living in Lynn in 1865 and there were no indexes for the 1870 census, linkage began with the city of Lynn for this year. After completion of linkage in Lynn, I used hometown information noted in the 1865 census to search for the remaining unlinked shoeworkers in surrounding Essex County towns and in selected towns in Maine and New Hampshire.

The final census linkage entailed tracing sample members in the 1880 federal manuscript census. Work began with the preparation of an

5. Ronald Vern Jackson and Gary Ronald Teeples, eds., *Massachusetts 1850 Census Index* (Bountiful, Utah: Accelerated Indexing Systems, 1978).

6. Ronald Vern Jackson and Gary Ronald Teeples, eds., *New Hampshire 1850 Census Index* (Bountiful, Utah: Accelerated Indexing Systems, 1978), and *Maine 1850 Census Index* (Bountiful, Utah: Accelerated Indexing Systems, 1978).

alphabetical listing of shoeworkers who were still alive at this date. Where sample members had married between 1865 and 1880, I changed surnames accordingly. This listing was checked against names enumerated in the censuses of Lynn and surrounding Essex County towns. With the completion of the first stage of tracing, I prepared a new list of those still unlinked in the census and traced these individuals in the 1880 Massachusetts soundex index. Possible links were checked out in the manuscript census listings of other Massachusetts towns. Finally, I traced those born in New Hampshire or Maine and still unlinked in the 1880 census in the soundex indexes and manuscript censuses of those states.[7]

The final major step in the process of record linkage required tracing for the deaths of sample members. Beginning with 1865, I utilized the five-year indexes of deaths compiled by the Massachusetts vital record registration system. Deaths before 1870 or 1880 permitted some reduction of the size of lists used in census linkage for those years. Linkage continued in the Massachusetts records through 1930, when all living sample members would have been in their eighties. Marital status at death was among the variables recorded, and where an individual died single, that was noted and used in determining the proportion of shoeworkers who never married. I traced New Hampshire–born shoeworkers in the death records of that state's office of vital records and added new dates and places of death to the records. Finally, family genealogies permitted some additional marriage and death linkage, and I employed information from those sources to update the computer records of sample members.

As with the tracing of Lowell millhands, work here took on a circular character. I used information derived from one linkage step to update records employed in successive steps. Census linkage was repeated numerous times, and each time the number of married names was somewhat larger and information on other family members somewhat fuller. Similarly, as marriage links rose in number, death linkage was repeated for those with new married names. The maintenance of a central computerized list of records on all individuals in the sample permitted frequent updating of linkage lists.

7. For a discussion of the use of the 1880 and 1900 soundex indexes in historical research, see Charles Stephenson, "The Methodology of Historical Census Record Linkage: A User's Guide to the Soundex," *Journal of Family History* 5 (1980): 112–15.

The determination of the date an individual first worked in shoe-making required inferences from contemporary records. The 1860 federal manuscript census of Lynn clearly underenumerated workingwomen, and the 1855 and 1850 censuses did not record women's occupations at all. These practices undermined my ability to determine a woman's first date of shoe employment and called for reasonable deductions on my part. When I found a sample member born outside Lynn residing in that city in 1850 or 1855 as a boarder, with another relative, or as a household head, and of an age when she might well have been working, I recorded her as employed in shoes. I did not make such conclusions for children or wives living at home. Boarders in Lynn provided the clearest case for making such inferences. The sample member had obviously made a decision to migrate alone from her hometown to Lynn and was residing there in, say, 1855. The most plausible reason for a woman to come to Lynn was to work in the stitching shops of the city, and I did have positive identification of these women as shoeworkers in 1865. The fact that census enumerators failed to record women's occupations seemed an inadequate reason to record this sample member as not employed in 1855. In all, I made employment inferences for twenty-five sample members, and the average length of women's work careers increased by 0.4 years as a result of the procedures described here.[8]

The logic of record linkage for the 1865 Lynn shoeworker sample was basically the same as that employed for the population of New Hampshire millhands who worked earlier at the Hamilton Company, but it is likely that reliance on a census sample has introduced bias. Although the 1865 state census had substantially fuller enumeration of women shoeworkers in Lynn than had the 1860 federal census, it was by no means complete. Recorded in June and July during one of the two slack periods in shoe production, the census undoubtedly missed a good number of transient shoeworkers who left the city as work declined. Thus a census sample may introduce bias into the analysis that would not be present for a population drawn from textile company employment records or New Hampshire town school reports.

Comparing statewide aggregate figures noted in the published Massachusetts state censuses of population and industry, I found that the

8. I made a similar inference for boarding domestic servants in Boston in 1850 and 1855; see Appendix 5.

1865 population census apparently recorded between a third and a half of female shoeworkers likely to have been employed in the state.[9] Part of this error may have been due to a failure to record occupations for women who worked only part-time on shoes; part may have resulted from the departure of migrant female shoeworkers from Lynn between the May 1 date of the census of industry and the enumeration of the population census, principally in June.

Because of underenumeration in the census of population, the analysis of the 1865 shoeworker sample is probably more reliable in terms of the evidence it offers on subgroups within the overall population than as an indicator of overall trends. We may not know with any certainty the actual proportions of migrant shoeworkers and permanent Lynn residents in the Lynn work force, but there is no reason to doubt the pictures that emerge for each of these groups.

9. Mass. Secretary of the Commonwealth, *Abstract of the Census of Massachusetts, 1865* (Boston: Wright & Potter, 1867), pp. 143, 166, and *Statistical Information Relating to Certain Branches of Industry in Massachusetts, for the Year Ending May 1, 1865* (Boston: Wright & Potter, 1866), p. 736.

Appendix 5. *Methods in Studying Servants and Garment Workers*

I began the study of servants and garment workers by recording a limited amount of information on all Boston women from these two occupational groups enumerated in the 1860 federal manuscript census of population. From this population of more than 13,700 women, I then drew random samples of about 400 native-born women for more detailed coding and analysis. Native-born women made up only 31 percent of this larger population, but I felt it important to draw a sample for Boston that was comparable with the textile operatives and shoeworkers already studied. Because those groups had been limited to New England–born women, I applied parallel criteria in drawing the Boston random samples. In successive steps I treated the two samples of servants and garment workers as a single group for linkage purposes. I traced them in federal and state manuscript censuses of Boston and in vital records without regard to their occupational status. I carried out the analyses of the findings separately, however, for each occupational group.

Once I had selected the members of the sample, I went back to the 1860 manuscript census to record additional information.[1] In particular, I added the names and ages of other family members to facilitate record linkage. For individuals who boarded (either as servants with their employers or simply as individuals living away from home), I noted the name of the household head as well. I took advantage of this coding step to record additional data concerning the numbers of servants or garment workers in the household, the number of apparently related co-boarders, the number of children in the family (when sample members lived at

---

1. Federal Manuscript Census of Population, 1860, M653, rolls 520–25.

home), the occupations of household heads, and other data of value in analyzing the living and working situations of sample members.

As the sample members all worked in Boston in 1860, census linkage began with the 1855 Massachusetts state census of Boston.[2] I prepared an alphabetical list of the names of sample members, along with relevant names of co-residents in 1860, for use in this work. Research assistants and I moved methodically through Boston's wards in the 1855 census, looking for links with the listing of sample members. I divided links into "good" links, where positive identification of co-residents supplemented basic consistency of the name, age, and birthplace of the sample member in the two censuses, and "plausible" links, where only consistent name, age, and birthplace provided connections between the two listings. As we worked through the census, we recorded all the links we could find, without regard to possible ones others might have found. In the end, "good" links were accepted over "plausible" ones, and where we had more than one "plausible" link, the possibilities were set aside and no definite linkage was made.

Record linkage for the Boston samples proved far more difficult than for millhands, shoeworkers, or teachers for a variety of reasons. Boston was much larger than any of the other cities or towns in which sample members were traced. The city ranged in population from 137,000 in 1850 to more than 363,000 in 1880, whereas neither Lowell nor Lynn ever exceeded 38,000 in the years examined.[3] Furthermore, workers in the other three samples were identified by specific hometowns, whereas Boston censuses provided only states of birth. Because more than 85 percent of native-born garment workers and servants were born in Massachusetts, this designation did not go very far in distinguishing among possible links. Moreover, very few of the sample members lived at home with family in Boston in 1860 so that names of other family members rarely assisted the linkage process. Finally, a large share of sample

2. Mass. State Census of Population, 1855, Boston, Massachusetts State Archives, Boston.
3. Peter R. Knights, *Plain People of Boston, 1830–1860: A Study in City Growth* (New York: Oxford University Press, 1971), p. 20; Stephan Thernstrom, *The Other Bostonians: Poverty and Progress in the American Metropolis, 1880–1970* (Cambridge: Harvard University Press, 1973), p. 11; Arthur L. Eno, Jr., ed., *Cotton Was King: A History of Lowell, Massachusetts* (N.p.: New Hampshire Publishing, 1976), p. 255; and Alan Dawley, *Class and Community: The Industrial Revolution in Lynn* (Cambridge: Harvard University Press, 1976), p. 245.

members—particularly among servants—appeared to be the native-born children of Irish immigrants with extremely common names. It was just as easy to get ten "plausible" links for an Ellen Sullivan as to get one, and in this situation I refused to make any linkage. Name commonality, then, was added to these other factors and hindered the process of linking sample members in various records. It is likely that fewer native-born daughters of the Irish were successfully traced in censuses and vital records than were Yankees, though one cannot estimate the extent of any resulting bias because parental nativity was not recorded in the 1860 census from which I drew the original samples.

After the completion of the 1855 linkage, I began tracing in the 1850 census index and in the 1850 federal manuscript census.[4] Where the 1860 census had provided parents' names, linkage was dramatically improved. Otherwise, it was simply a matter of looking up the names of sample members in the index and examining the multiple possibilities that emerged. Possibilities outside Boston were examined only when birthplace information (for the Vermont-, New Hampshire–, or Maine-born) suggested a reasonable prospect for linkage outside the city or where names of parents could be employed. Marriage linkage assisted considerably, because marriage records gave the names of parents and specific hometowns of birth and provided clues to migrants' former places of residence outside Boston. Where marriage records provided information on the parents or hometowns of sample members, the published census index provided possible links for further examination. Linkage in the 1850 census continued at all stages of the tracing; as new information from marriage or death records provided new leads on possible residences outside Boston for sample members, I repeated linkage in the appropriate 1850 census index.

As the vast majority of sample members were single when they were enumerated in the 1860 census, linkage in subsequent marriage records was crucial to the success of the study. Immediately after the sample members were selected and before linkage had proceeded very far in the 1855 census, I began searching for links in post-1860 marriage records

---

4. Ronald Vern Jackson and Gary Ronald Teeples, eds., *Massachusetts 1850 Census Index* (Bountiful, Utah: Accelerated Indexing Systems, 1978); see also companion volumes in series for Maine, New Hampshire, and Vermont. Federal Manuscript Census of Population, 1850, M432, rolls 334–39.

in the Massachusetts vital records office, moving through successive five-year indexes. Consistency of age and birthplace was necessary to make a link, but I also needed parents' names to feel that I had a solid link. Even more so than with the census linkage, multiple possibilities reduced the number of "good" links that I could make in this process. I employed information from marriage links in two ways in the census linkage process. New married names replaced maiden names for those who married after 1860 to permit linkage in the 1865, 1870, and 1880 censuses of Boston. In these cases, I added husbands' names to the records to facilitate subsequent linkage. In addition, I added hometowns of birth and names of parents to sample members' records to facilitate linkage in pre-1860 censuses.

Finally, where a sample member resided with an apparent brother or sister in the 1860 census but not with her parents, I also looked for the marriages of siblings in Boston vital records. These additional marriages often provided names of parents and rural hometowns that proved extremely useful in extending the linkage net out into the countryside.

With married names for at least a fraction of the sample members, I began linkage in censuses after 1860, starting with the 1865 Massachusetts state census.[5] Alphabetical lists with married names (where known) and names of husbands or parents provided the basic tool for this later linkage. Linkage proceeded through Boston's wards with the distinction being made once again between "good" links and "plausible" ones. As researchers worked independently, I deliberately tried to get multiple links for a sample member and compared one possible link with others before making a final decision. Where there was no basis to choose between alternative possibilities, no link was made.

Furthermore, a new form of checking was introduced at this stage of the record linkage—a consistency check across census years. Because a fair number of the links made in any given year appeared to be based on a relatively limited amount of consistent data, I made an effort to compare evidence (especially names of co-residents) found in the making of links in the new census listings. If, for instance, we found a sample member living at home with "new" parents in the 1855 census but with

5. Mass. State Census of Population, 1865, Boston, Massachusetts State Archives, Boston.

"different" parents in a possible 1850 census link, we dropped both possible links. The point here was to avoid making links based on flimsy evidence that introduced numerous discrepancies into the records associated with a given sample member. Where data is consistent from census to census or between a census link and a marriage record, the reliability of the evidence is increased. Where "soft" linkage standards permit discrepancies in linkage data, it seems better to accept a higher level of missing data and reject the links.

Linkage in the 1870 and 1880 federal manuscript censuses of Boston proceeded along the lines of the other tracing.[6] Because the number of links proved to be small and possibilities of omission quite real, linkage was repeated twice for each census year with updated lists used after the first pass through the census. For 1880, the soundex index provided an additional resource in completing linkage.[7] Once again an effort was made to check for contradictions between census links in different years, and this work further limited the number of links made (but hopefully improved their quality).

To improve linkage for servants in the Boston sample, I employed one additional set of procedures. Given the fact that household heads who employed servants were among the most prosperous residents of the city, I decided to trace this population for ten years before and after the 1860 census. I anticipated that household heads would be much more persistent than were servants. I had two purposes in mind here. First, I hoped to pick up additional linkages to servants who might have been missed by relying on census indexes and the scanning of the census microfilms themselves. Second, I planned to prepare additional data files on household heads employing servants in 1850, 1860, and 1870 to analyze servant employment patterns. Given the transience of servants, these additional data permitted fuller analysis of the structure of the labor market for servants in Boston.

Alphabetical listings of 1860 household heads and their servant sample members provided the basis for tracing in the 1850 and 1870 federal

6. Federal Manuscript Census of Population, Boston, 1870, M593, rolls 640–49, and 1880, T9, rolls 552–62.

7. 1880 Soundex Indexes, Massachusetts, T754, rolls 1–70, New Hampshire, T762, rolls 1–13, Maine, T752, rolls 1–29, and Vermont, T755, rolls 1–15.

manuscript censuses of population. Excluded from the tracing were household heads who worked in hotels or other institutions that employed
servants, which limited this linkage to heads of private households. The
1850 published census index greatly facilitated linkage of household
heads for that year; to facilitate 1870 linkage, I first linked household
heads in 1865 and 1870 Boston city directories. I proceeded to "map"
city directory links by ward and used this additional information to
focus the search in the 1870 manuscript census.[8] I coded linked households in 1850 and 1870 regardless of the presence of the 1860 servant in
my sample, recording a range of information useful in analyzing the size
and composition of the servant work force in each household. The
process also increased linkage on servants who had slipped through the
earlier tracing, and new information was added to their records based on
new links.[9] For instance, where I found a sample member residing in
the 1855 or 1850 household of the same person who employed her in
1860, I recorded the sample member as a servant at that earlier date.
Given the fact that the 1850 and 1855 censuses did not record women's
occupations, this seemed a reasonable inference to make.

As the census linkage proceeded for 1870 and 1880, tracing in Massachusetts death records began. I prepared an alphabetical listing of
sample members, with information on marital status and the names of
parents and husbands (where known) and their ages and birthplaces.
Five-year indexes provided entry into Massachusetts death records, and
tracing proceeded for the period 1860–1930. I traced New Hampshire–
born members of the sample unlinked in Massachusetts records in New
Hampshire indexes of vital records. Death linkage not only offered
additional information on sample members' occupations and places of

8. The concept of mapping an alphabetical city directory against a federal manuscript census for the same year was developed by Peter R. Knights, who was kind enough to share the
listings he had prepared for Boston in 1850. See Knights, *Plain People of Boston*, app. A.

9. One other procedure proved unhelpful, but is worth brief mention here. Anticipating
that many wealthy Boston households might have moved out to country homes by the time of
the census enumerations between June and August, I also searched for household heads in the
1850 censuses of selected towns on Boston's North and South Shores. Unfortunately, I added
no links to either household heads or servants. On the summering spots of Boston's elite, see
Joseph E. Garland, *Boston's Gold Coast: The North Shore, 1890–1929* (Boston: Little, Brown,
1981), and *Boston's North Shore: Being an Account of Life among the Noteworthy, Fashionable,
Wealthy, Eccentric, and Ordinary, 1823–1890* (Boston: Little, Brown, 1978).

Table A.2. Comparison of missing data on linkage for
different occupational groups traced

Category	Millhands	Shoeworkers	Teachers	Boston samples
Birthdate[a]	29.0%	—	11.4%	—
Marriage[b]	28.0	24.9%	27.6	65.4%
Death date	51.7	54.0	45.0	77.9
Census link[c]	58.5	15.2	17.6	42.8
Total cases	410	402	449	808

[a]The ages of shoeworkers and garment workers and servants in the Boston samples were known at the outset because these were census samples.

[b]Missing data here excludes individuals known to have never married.

[c]Percentages here refer to the share of group or sample members not linked to any census other than the one from which a given group or sample was drawn.

residence at their deaths but also provided evidence on places of birth and marriage that was extremely useful in extending linkage in decennial censuses.

Despite the enormous effort, record linkage for garment workers and domestic servants proved far less successful than for millhands, shoeworkers, or rural teachers. Table A.2 summarizes the situation by comparing missing data on a number of important variables for the different occupational groups traced in this study.

A glance at these figures indicates the difficulty of generalizing about Boston women workers solely from the longitudinal study of the samples of garment workers and servants. Death dates are known for less than a fourth of Boston sample members, and marriages are certain only for a third. With missing data outweighing good links on these two variables, one cannot place too much confidence in the findings based solely on study of the two samples. Fortunately, there is rich evidence available in a variety of other Boston sources, and Appendix 6 outlines the methods used in bringing that evidence to bear in the study.

Appendix 6. *Supplementary Studies*

The limitations of record linkage for the 1860 samples of garment workers and domestic servants led to the formulation of additional studies to examine the experiences of these groups over time. Two of the studies have already been referred to in the appendixes because they played roles in the selection of the Boston samples and in subsequent tracing over time—a study of all women workers enumerated in the 1860 federal manuscript census of Boston and the tracing of all household heads employing servants in the 1860 sample.

Recording of census data on all Boston workingwomen in 1860 proceeded in two distinct steps. I coded a small amount of information on all servants and garment workers enumerated in the census. This first round of work entailed coding the occupation, age, birthplace, marital status, and residence of 13,751 women employed in ten occupations for domestic servants and thirty occupations for garment workers. It was from this population that I drew the two random samples traced over time. As the tracing work drew to a close, however, I realized that it would not be a great deal more work (at least compared with the effort expended already) to record information about all Boston workingwomen. Therefore, I set about to code data on the remaining women workers not recorded in the preliminary round. Altogether, we found somewhat more than 3,000 additional women, bringing the total of workingwomen in Boston in 1860 to 16,852.[1]

The initial coding of 13,751 servants and garment workers had been intended to provide a population for the purpose of random sampling.

1. While coding women in additional occupations, I found a few more servants and garment workers who had eluded my net in earlier coding. I added these workingwomen to the study population, and citywide figures include all women in these two groups of occupations regardless of when they were added to the study population.

Therefore, I had recorded very minimal data concerning each working-woman. I had been particularly concerned with noting the ward and family number of each woman so that I might find her enumeration if she eventually became a member of one of the two samples. As I began coding all remaining Boston workingwomen, however, I decided to code considerably more information about each woman enumerated as employed. Because I knew I was not planning extensive study of any more samples, it made sense to get more data about these workers at the outset. Therefore, in this final coding of Boston workingwomen, I also recorded considerable information about heads of households and about the families or fellow boarders of workingwomen. Thus, in the discussion of Boston women workers offered in Chapter 5, there is occasionally a discrepancy between the range of data available on servants or garment workers citywide and that for other occupational groups. For the two groups I traced through successive censuses and studied in detail, I rely primarily on a close examination of the smaller samples. Still, analysis of the population of all Boston workingwomen provides a context within which to view the more detailed treatment of the samples of native-born servants and garment workers.

Because very few members of the two Boston samples were linked in Boston censuses in 1870 and 1880, I decided to draw additional samples to provide snapshots of workingwomen at a later date. Therefore, I drew two random samples of about four hundred native-born women each from among the domestic servants and garment workers enumerated in the 1880 federal manuscript census of Boston and coded a variety of variables about each worker and the household in which she lived.[2]

I took care to ensure that the 1880 samples included the same occupations as did the 1860 samples. The 1880 servant sample includes women recorded as servants, domestics, laundresses, waitresses, table

2. The samples were based on lists of random numbers. Utilizing published census information, I estimated the total number of workingwomen employed in domestic service and needle trades occupations. Next, I generated two sets of random numbers between one and a number considerably greater than the estimate for the number of workingwomen in each occupational group. Armed with these two sets of random numbers, a list of occupations to be included in the coding, and a guide to the variables to be recorded, research assistants proceeded to record the two samples from census microfilms. Federal Manuscript Census of Population, 1880, Boston, T9, rolls 552–62.

APPENDIX 6

girls, domestics in hotels and restaurants, cooks, ladies' maids, chambermaids, and governesses. Specifically excluded were housekeepers who
were household heads or daughters living with their families, for whom
I felt that "keeping house" more accurately described their nonwage
roles within their families. Nurses living in private households were included in the sample, but nurses living in hospitals or boarding with
other nurses in households near hospitals were excluded. Some ambigu-
ity obviously existed in occupational terms, but I attempted to apply
consistent principles across the two census years to permit comparison
over time.

Garment workers posed somewhat fewer problems in drawing the
samples. I included all women who appeared to be working—by hand
or by machine—in needle trades occupations. The major occupational
groupings for 1880 included tailoress, seamstress, and dressmaker. Individuals who stitched bags, carpets, or blankets were also included as
were women in ancillary occupations likely to be included in sewing
businesses such as cutter or shirt inspector. Specifically excluded were
women who worked with leather, lace, or feathers and workers in allied
occupations such as button makers, whalebone factory workers, glove
dyers, or makers of dress ornaments. Finally, I excluded from both
samples inmates in asylums or prisons and patients in hospitals (regardless of occupation).

The last two studies made to supplement the career tracing of workingwomen drew on federal manuscript censuses of manufacturing between 1850 and 1880. Several recent studies have indicated the utility of
the census of manufacturing for labor history.[3] The key limitation of evidence on garment workers in the manuscript population censuses stems
from the inability to determine the actual place of work. The population
census provides no clues as to whether an individual works at home or
in a shop or factory setting. The manufacturing census does not entirely
clear up the issue but does offer useful evidence on the capital investment and machinery employed by garment firms. To add this dimension to the study, I recorded information on all Boston garment firms

3. Bruce Laurie and Mark Schmitz, "Manufacture and Productivity: The Making of an Industrial Base, Philadelphia, 1850–1880" in Theodore Hershberg, ed., *Philadelphia: Work,
Space, Family, and Group Experience in Philadelphia in the Nineteenth Century* (New York: Oxford University Press, 1981), pp. 43–92.

listed in the federal manuscript censuses of manufacturing for 1850, 1860, 1870, and 1880.[4] Analysis of these data permits elaboration of the findings that emerge from the study of garment workers enumerated in the manuscript population schedules.

Finally, to explore similar questions concerning factory work and homework among women shoeworkers, I also recorded data on Lynn shoe firms found in the federal manuscript censuses of manufacturing between 1850 and 1880.[5] This material provided evidence that supplemented the analysis of the shoeworker sample in Chapter 4.

These additional studies proved useful at various points in the discussion of the nature of women's paid employment and changes in that work over time. Ultimately, there is no single approach that can provide all the answers we seek in studying wage-earning women in nineteenth-century New England. The historian must be open to a variety of approaches and utilize whichever appear most useful for a particular purpose. Theoretical clarity coupled with an empirical eclecticism suggest themselves as desired traits for anyone working in this field.

4. Federal Manuscript Census of Manufacturing, Boston (microfilm), T1204, 1850, roll 6; 1860, roll 15; 1870, roll 24; and 1880, roll 32.

5. Federal Manuscript Census of Manufacturing, Lynn (microfilm), T1204, 1860, roll 15; 1870, roll 21; 1880, roll 31. There are portions of the Lynn manufacturing censuses for 1870 and 1880 that are obviously missing from the microfilm; my thanks to Paul Faler, who checked the surviving manuscript volumes to determine that (unfortunately) the incompleteness of the microfilm copies is mirrored by the originals.

Appendix 7. *Methods in the Study of Teachers and Women's Rural Occupations*

Published school reports provided the starting point for the tracing of New Hampshire teachers. Utilizing reports from district prudential committees and tables printed in annual school reports, I recorded the town, the year of employment, the name of the teacher, the number of terms she taught, and (where noted) the hometown of the teacher. The latter was given for about half of the women teaching in Boscawen, Canterbury, and Lyndeborough and was useful as I moved to further record linkage.

After recording individual teacher information for the three towns over the period 1860–1880, I aggregated the annual references into individual records, alphabetized the entries, and assigned unique identification numbers to each person. As the process of record linkage proceeded, I periodically combined "two" people who proved to be the same person on further examination. Occasionally, teachers used their first name in one town and middle name in another or used a middle initial in one town but not in another, and these differences usually sorted themselves out over time. On a few occasions I found women teaching under both maiden and married names and combined these records. Undoubtedly, the 449 members of the population include a number of such multiples that have gone undetected because of the incompleteness of genealogical and vital record linkage.

With the initial population of teachers in hand, work began simultaneously in two directions. First, I traced women in published genealogies of these towns and of surrounding communities to determine their dates of birth, marriage, and death and to place them in their families. Second, I traced the women in school reports of surrounding communities to determine the extent of their careers as teachers.[1] In addition, I also examined school reports for Boscawen, Canterbury, and Lyndeborough before 1860 and after 1880 to extend the years of the women's teaching where appropriate. With preliminary information on their families and on their teaching careers, I traced the women in New Hampshire vital records to increase the number of marriage linkages and to add to my knowledge of birth and death dates. Where I had any genealogical information suggesting Massachusetts residence for a teacher at some point in her life, I also looked for marriages and deaths in the Massachusetts state system of vital records. Finally, where possible I explored published family genealogies to supplement the local and state sources.[2]

As family information built up, tracing shifted to the federal manuscript censuses of the three towns and of about twenty-five neighboring communities in the years between 1850 and 1880. I searched for women before and after their marriages and under maiden and married names. For the 1850 and 1880 censuses, indexes sped up the tracing and permitted me to extend the search beyond neighboring towns. Where additional census linkage might extend a lengthy career or provide new information on a husband's age or occupation, I also traced women in the 1900 soundex indexes for New Hampshire and Massachusetts and the corresponding manuscript census listings.[3] And because a fair number of teachers had either lived or taught in Concord, I searched the 1900 federal manuscript census of that city for additional links. By carrying the linkage through 1900, I added considerable information on the occupations of husbands and facilitated death linkage, which provided evidence on patterns of migration.

As census linkage moved beyond the 1880 census, I also tapped another set of sources that proved extremely valuable: catalogues and alumni records of private academies in or near Boscawen, Canterbury,

1. Towns examined systematically for additional teaching stints for members of the teacher group included Andover, Bradford, Concord, Francestown, Gilmanton, Greenfield, Hopkinton, Loudon, Milford, Mont Vernon, Nashua, New Boston, Peterborough, Salisbury, Sanbornton, Warner, Webster, and Wilton.

2. See note 3 to Appendix 2 above.

3. Charles Stephenson, "The Methodology of Historical Census Record Linkage: A User's Guide to the Soundex," *Journal of Family History* 5 (Spring 1980): 112–15. The 1850 census linkage drew on Ronald Vern Jackson and Gary Ronald Teeples, *New Hampshire 1850 Census Index* (Bountiful, Utah: Accelerated Indexing Systems, 1978).

and Lyndeborough.[4] In the mid-nineteenth century, rural academies provided what later became the basis of the high school curriculum. In some communities local authorities reached agreement with academy trustees and integrated the academy into the local public school system. In any event, private academies had something of a "public" character in the years before high schools were common in rural New Hampshire, and many teachers prepared for their work or supplemented their teaching with stints at a local academy. I searched for teachers among the lists of students recorded in the annual catalogues of local academies and in the subsequent reunion publications that appeared at the end of the century. Finally, one of the teachers in the study group kept a manuscript volume in which she recorded information on fellow alumnae in later years, and this record proved invaluable.[5] Listings in alumni directories often provided additional occupational information or marriage or death linkages and clues for further census linkage. In other words, academy tracing provided information not only on the education of women teachers but on their subsequent lives as well.

Finally, I made a systematic effort to determine date and place of death for members of the study. New Hampshire and Massachusetts vital records proved the most useful sources here, but local genealogies and vital records were helpful as well. This linkage was less complete than linkage for birth and marriage but gave important corroborating evidence at various points. In determining the proportion of women who never married, for instance, marital status at death provided a crucial link in the argument. Also, where women were employed at the time of death, this information helped extend my knowledge of women's careers.

Of all the occupational groups I studied, teachers proved to be the most easily traced. I have much higher rates of census linkage for teachers and generally higher linkage on births, marriages, and deaths as well. And tracing in neighboring towns led to a good number of links in school reports, making me confident that I know more about the employment

4. See catalogues and reunion publications, NHHS. The schools included the Appleton Academy, Boscawen Academy (Elmwood Institute), Francestown Academy, Gilmanton Academy, McCollum Academy, Sanbornton Academy, and Tilton Academy.

5. Martha A. Knowles, Scrapbook of teachers and students of the Elmwood Institute, 1857–1864, NHHS.

Table A.3. Extent of record linkage
for New Hampshire teachers

Birthdate	88.4%
Date of marriage	72.2[a]
Date of death	54.9
1860 census linkage	64.8
1870 census linkage	53.7[b]
1880 census linkage	49.0[b]
Linkage, any census	82.4
Father's occupation	61.9
Husband's occupation	42.7[c]

[a]Includes teachers linked to deaths as single women and concluded to have never married.

[b]Includes women who died before this census enumeration.

[c]Percentage based on the 225 women teachers known to have married, excluding those women who did not marry or for whom marriage linkage is missing.

of teachers than I do for the other occupational groups. Having an annual record of employment and records of numerous employers (in this case, towns) is a rare treat. The success of the various linkage efforts is summarized in Table A.3.[6]

As the teacher linkage was nearing completion, I realized the importance of recording women's occupations generally in these three New Hampshire towns in order to compare findings for teachers with those for other female occupational groups. The analysis of domestic servants and needle trades workers was enriched by evidence for all Boston workingwomen, so I felt that it made sense to place evidence for New Hampshire teachers within a broader context.

I coded all employed females recorded in the federal manuscript censuses of Boscawen, Canterbury, and Lyndeborough for the years 1860, 1880, and 1900. Variables recorded by enumerators differed somewhat from year to year, but I recorded age, marital status, relation to household head, occupation, and birthplace for workingwomen in each census year. I also coded age, occupation, and birthplace for all heads of households with an employed female.

6. For comparison of these results with those for the other occupational samples and populations, see Table A.2 above.

The occupation column of the census was used inconsistently by enumerators, thus requiring a number of exclusions on my part. I did not record women entered as "wife" in the occupation column or those wives who were noted to be "keeping house." In addition, I excluded from analysis women who were students or for whom "none" was recorded in the occupation column. Finally, in Lyndeborough in 1860 a great many daughters residing with their parents were recorded as domestics, though it seemed clear from the evidence that they were performing nonwage household duties in their own homes. These individuals were not coded, and the "domestic servant" occupation was restricted to women not residing in their own homes. Some servants may have been excluded by this distinction, but it seemed important to have consistency across census years, even when the practice of enumerators was not always consistent.[7]

The town of Canterbury included in this period a Shaker religious community with a large number of women residents enumerated as employed. In 1880, the census taker recorded each such woman as "house employee." There were also a fair number of deaconesses and ministers among women residents of the community. As the Shakers were an extremely atypical element in rural New England and enumerators were inconsistent in their treatment of Shaker occupations over the period, it seemed most sensible to exclude the Shakers from females recorded in each of the three census years.

A final small study that I conducted for comparative purposes led me to code information on the families of 168 husband-wife pairs in Boscawen, Canterbury, and Lyndeborough in 1880. Inclusion in this control group required that the wife be between 25 and 38 years of age (including the end points) and that she not be enumerated as a teacher or have been a member of the teacher sample. Women in these couples serve as a control group of married nonteachers in the three New Hampshire towns for comparison with married former teachers in terms of their age at marriage, age at first birth, and overall fertility. I chose this inclusive age range because it included the middle 75 percent of married former teachers linked in the 1880 federal manuscript census.

7. Marjorie Abel and Nancy Folbre, "A Methodology for Revising Estimates: Female Market Participation in the U.S. before 1940," *Historical Methods* 23 (Fall 1990): 167–76.

Selected Bibliography

Manuscript Sources

AAS American Antiquarian Society, Worcester, Mass.
Susan E. P. Brown Forbes Diary, January–September 1843.
Lizzie A. Wilson Goodenough Diaries, 1865–1875.
Caroline Barrett White Diaries, 1849–1915.

BL Baker Library, Harvard Graduate School of Business Administration, Boston, Mass.
R. G. Dun & Co. Collection.
Hamilton Manufacturing Company Records.
Register books and payrolls, 1830–1860.
Lawrence Manufacturing Company Records.
Payrolls.
Statistics of Lowell Manufactures, 1850, broadsides on microfilm.
Dexter Whittemore & Son Collection.
Daybooks, ledgers, inventories of stock, letterbooks, and unbound correspondence.

Duke University, Manuscript Department, William R. Perkins Library, Durham, N.C.
A. H. Jones Invoice Book, 1848–1849.
Henry Watson, Jr., Account Book, 1841–1844.

EI Essex Institute, Salem, Mass.
Martha Osborne Barrett Diary, 1848–1879.
Louisa Chapman Diary, 1848–1849.
Irena M. Knowlton Diaries, 1879–1888.
Larcom Family Collection.
Emeline Larcom Letters, 1840–1842.

Fitzwilliam, N.H., Town Library.
Dexter Whittemore Ledger #8.

Historical Society of Pennsylvania, Philadelphia.
Francis C. Rozier Collection, 1841–1857.

Huntington Library, San Marino, Calif.
　Anna Mason Letters, 1848–1857, Bronson Collection.

MHS　Massachusetts Historical Society, Boston.
　Mary E. Bradlee Diary, 1871–1876.
　Francis Cabot Lowell II Papers.
　　Lorenza Stevens Berbineau Diaries, 1851–1869.
　　Correspondence, between Lorenza Stevens Berbineau and the Lowells, 1842,
　　1850.
　　Mary Gardner Lowell Diaries, 1830–1853.
　Sanborn Family Papers.
　　Elizabeth Hodgdon Account, 1832–1839.

MATH　Museum of American Textile History, North Andover, Mass.
　Adams-Metcalf Letters, 1819–1857.
　Silas Jillson Weaving Account, 1822–1829.

NHHS　New Hampshire Historical Society, Concord.
　Mary Giddings Coult Diary, January–February 1851.
　"Deaths in Boscawen," Manuscript.
　Hodgdon Letters, 1830–1840.
　Martha A. Knowles, Scrapbook of teachers and students of the Elmwood Insti-
　tute, 1857–1864.
　Lizzie Piper Diary, November–December 1867.
　Helen A. Stewart Journal, 1880.

New Hampshire State Library, Concord.
　Tolford-Patten Collection, box 6.
　　Jane Stevens Letters, 1835–1841.

New York Public Library, New York.
　Fisher, Blashfield & Co., Accounts, 1845–1864.

Old Sturbridge Village, Sturbridge, Mass.
　Spaulding & Perkins, Ledger, 1830–1841.

Private Collections
　Jennison Letters, 1849–1861. In possession of Mary A. Dinmore, Cheshire, Conn.
　John Whittemore & Son Ledger, 1821–1824. Loaned by the late Joel Whitte-
　more; photocopy in possession of author.

Rhode Island Historical Society, Providence.
　Blackstone Manufacturing Company Records.

University of Connecticut, Urban Archives, Storrs.
　Jewett City Cotton Manufacturing Company Records.

University of Vermont Library, Special Collections, Burlington.
　Lucretia Wilson Dutton Papers, 1824–1855.

Bibliography

VHS   Vermont Historical Society, Montpelier.
Mary Paul Letters, 1845–1862.
Hazelton Rice Papers, 1839–1845.

Wheaton College, Marion B. Gebbie Archives and Special Collections, Norton, Mass. Larcom Collection.

GOVERNMENT RECORDS AND PUBLICATIONS

Local Records

Boscawen, N.H. 1830 Tax List.

Boscawen and Webster, N.H. Town Vital Records.

Canterbury, N.H. 1830 Tax List.

Curtis, Josiah. *Report of the Joint Special Committee on the Census of Boston, May, 1855, Including the Report of the Censors, with Analytical and Sanitary Observations.* Boston: Moore & Crosby, 1856.

Fitzwilliam, N.H. 1819, 1850 Tax Lists.

Lowell, Mass. Vital Records, 1826–1860. City Clerk's Office.

Lyndeborough, N.H. 1830 Tax List.

Merrimack, N.H. County Registry of Probate, Concord, N.H.

Northfield, N.H. 1830 Tax List.

Richmond, N.H. 1826 Tax List.

Sanbornton, N.H. 1836 Tax List.

Shattuck, Lemuel. *Report to the Committee of the City Council Appointed to Obtain the Census of Boston for the Year 1845.* Boston: John H. Eastburn, 1846.

Sutton, N.H. 1830 Tax List.

Vital Records of Lowell, Massachusetts, to the End of the Year 1849, 4 vols. Salem, Mass.: Essex Institute, 1930.

Vital Records of Lynn, Massachusetts, to the End of the Year 1849, 2 vols. Salem, Mass.: Essex Institute, 1905–1906.

State Records

Commonwealth of Massachusetts. *Report of a General Plan for the Promotion of Public and Personal Health, Devised, Prepared, and Recommended by the Commissioners Appointed under a Resolve of the Legislature of Massachusetts, Relating to a Sanitary Survey of the State.* Boston: Dutton & Wentworth, 1850.

Conn. Secretary of State. *Statistics of the Condition and Products of Certain Branches of Industry in Connecticut, for the Year Ending October 1, 1845.* Hartford: J. L. Boswell, 1846.

Dewitt, Francis. *Statistical Information Relating to Certain Branches of Industry in Massachusetts, for the Year Ending June 1, 1855.* Boston: William White, 1856.

Bibliography

Mass. Bureau of Statistics of Labor. *Annual Reports*, 1869–1910.

Mass. Department of Vital Statistics. Indexes of births, marriages, and deaths, Boston.

Mass. House Document no. 50, 1845.

Mass. Secretary of the Commonwealth. *Abstract of the Census of Massachusetts, 1865*. Boston: Wright & Potter, 1867.

——. *Statistical Information Relating to Certain Branches of Industry in Massachusetts, for the Year Ending May 1, 1865*. Boston: Wright & Potter, 1866.

——. *Statistical Tables Exhibiting the Condition and Products of Certain Branches of Industry in Massachusetts for the Year Ending April 1, 1837*. Boston: Dutton and Wentworth, 1838.

——. *Statistics of the Condition and Products of Certain Branches of Industry in Massachusetts for the Year Ending April 1, 1845*. Boston: Dutton and Wentworth, 1846.

Mass. State Censuses of Population, 1855, 1865. Boston and Lynn. Massachusetts State Archives, Boston.

N.H. Dept. of Vital Statistics. Indexes of births, marriages, and deaths. Concord, N.H.

R.I. Secretary of State. *Report upon the Census of Rhode Island, 1865*. Providence: Providence Press, 1867.

Wright, Carroll D. *The Census of Massachusetts: 1875*. 2 vols. Boston: Albert J. Wright, 1876.

——. *The Working Girls of Boston*. Boston: Wright and Potter, 1889; originally published in 1884.

Federal Records

DeBow, J. D. B. *Statistical View of the United States . . . Being a Compendium of the Seventh Census*. Washington: Beverly Tucker, 1854.

Federal Manuscript Census of Agriculture, 1850.
Boscawen and Fitzwilliam. New Hampshire Division of Records Management and Archives, Concord.

Federal Manuscript Census of Manufactures, 1820.
N.H. returns. Microfilm, Baker Library, Harvard Graduate School of Business Administration, Boston.

Federal Manuscript Census of Manufactures, 1850.
Boston, Mass.: T1204, roll 6.
Fitzwilliam. New Hampshire Division of Records Management and Archives, Concord.

Federal Manuscript Census of Manufactures, 1860.
Boston, Mass.: T1204, roll 15.
Lynn, Mass.: T1204, roll 15.

Federal Manuscript Census of Manufactures, 1870.

Boston, Mass.: T1204, roll 24.

Lynn, Mass.: T1204, roll 21.

Federal Manuscript Census of Manufactures, 1880.

Boston, Mass.: T1204, roll 32.

Lynn, Mass.: T1204, roll 31.

Federal Manuscript Census of Population, 1820.

Fitzwilliam and Richmond, N.H.

Federal Manuscript Census of Population, 1830.

Cheshire, Grafton, Hillsboro, and Merrimack Counties, N.H.

Federal Manuscript Census of Population, 1850.

Maine, Massachusetts, New Hampshire, and Vermont.

Federal Manuscript Census of Population, 1860.

Maine, Massachusetts, New Hampshire, and Vermont.

Federal Manuscript Census of Population, 1870.

Boston and Lynn, Mass.; Maine; New Hampshire; and Vermont.

Federal Manuscript Census of Population, 1880.

Boston, Hamilton, and Lynn, Mass.; Maine; New Hampshire; and Vermont.

Federal Manuscript Census of Population, 1900.

Boscawen, Canterbury, Concord, and Lyndeborough, N.H.

Fifth Census; or, Enumeration of the Inhabitants of the United States, as Corrected at the Department of State, 1830. Washington: Duff Green, 1832.

McLane, Louis. "Report of the Secretary of the Treasury, 1832." *Documents Relative to the Manufactures of the United States.* 2 vols. Washington: Duff Green, 1833.

Sumner, Helen. *History of Women in Industry in the United States.* Vol. 9 of *Report on the Condition of Woman and Child Wage Earners in the United States.* Washington: GPO, 1910.

U.S. Bureau of Statistics of Labor. "The Boot and Shoe Industry in Massachusetts as a Vocation for Women." Bulletin No. 180, October 1915.

U.S. Bureau of the Census. *Historical Statistics of the United States: Colonial Times to 1970.* Washington: GPO, 1975.

———. *Manufactures of the United States in 1860; Compiled from the Original Returns of the Eighth Census.* Washington: GPO, 1865.

———. *Occupations at the Twelfth Census: Special Reports.* Washington: GPO, 1904.

———. *Population of the United States in 1860.* Washington: GPO, 1864.

———. *Statistics of Women at Work.* Washington: GPO, 1907.

———. *Twelfth Census of the United States.* Vol. 7, *Manufactures*, pt. 1. Washington: U.S. Census Office, 1902.

———. *Twelfth Census of the United States.* Vol. 2, *Population*, pt. 2. Washington: U.S. Census Office, 1902.

U.S. Census Office. *Abstract of the Statistics of Manufactures According to the Returns of the Seventh Census.* Washington, 1859.

Bibliography

———. *Report of the Mortality and Vital Statistics of the United States as Returned at the Tenth Census*. Washington: GPO, 1886.

———. *Statistics of the Population of the United States at the Tenth Census*. Washington: GPO, 1883.

———. *The Statistics of the Population of the United States . . . from the Original Returns of the Ninth Census*. Washington: GPO, 1872.

U.S. Department of the Treasury. *Letter from the Secretary of the Treasury . . . on the Subject of American Manufactures*. Washington: Roger C. Weightman, 1810.

U.S. Immigration Commission (1907–1913). *Reports of the Immigration Commission*. Vol. 12, *Immigrants in Industries*, pt. 9, "Boot and Shoe Manufacturing." Washington: GPO, 1911.

CONTEMPORARY PUBLISHED SOURCES

Alcott, Louisa May. "How I Went Out to Service." *Independent*, June 4, 1874.

Appleton, Nathan. *Introduction of the Power Loom, and the Origin of Lowell*. Lowell, Mass.: B. H. Penhallow, 1858.

Bacon, Louisa Crowninshield. *Reminiscences*. Salem, Mass.: Privately Printed, 1922.

Bessie; or, Reminiscences of a Daughter of a New England Clergyman; Simple Facts, Simply Told by a Grandmother. New Haven, Conn.: J. H. Benham, 1861.

Boston, Mass. City Directories, 1850–1880.

Eaton, Isabel. "Special Report on Negro Domestic Service in the Seventh Ward, Philadelphia." In W. E. B. DuBois, *The Philadelphia Negro: A Social Study*. New York: Schocken, 1967; originally published in 1899.

Larcom, Lucy. *A New England Girlhood: Outlined from Memory*. Boston: Northeastern University Press, 1986; originally published in 1889.

Lowell, Mass. City Directories, 1833–1860.

Lowell Offering, 1840–1845.

Miles, Henry A. *Lowell as It Was and as It Is*. Lowell, Mass.: Powers and Bagley, 1845.

"Needle and Garden: The Story of a Seamstress Who Laid Down Her Needle and Became a Strawberry-Girl." *Atlantic Monthly*, January–October, 1865.

Rhode Island Society for the Encouragement of Domestic Industry. *Transactions*, 1861.

Robinson, Harriet H. *Loom and Spindle; or, Life among the Early Mill Girls*. Kailua, Hawaii: Press Pacifica, 1976; originally published in 1898.

Salmon, Lucy Maynard. *Domestic Service*. New York: Arno Press, 1972; originally published in 1897.

Thompson, Zadock. *A Gazetteer of the State of Vermont*. Montpelier: E. P. Walton, 1824.

Wilson, Harriet E. *Our Nig; or, Sketches from the Life of a Free Black*. Edited by Henry Louis Gates, Jr. New York: Random House, 1983; originally published in 1859.

Bibliography

SECONDARY SOURCES

Abel, Marjorie, and Nancy Folbre. "A Methodology for Revising Estimates: Female Market Participation in the U.S. before 1940." *Historical Methods* 23 (Fall 1990): 167–76.

Accampo, Elinor. *Industrialization, Family Life, and Class Relations: Saint Chamond, 1815–1914.* Berkeley: University of California Press, 1989.

Annett, Albert, and Alice E. E. Lehtinen. *History of Jaffrey (Middle Monadnock) New Hampshire.* 2 vols. Jaffrey: By the Town, 1937.

Bagnall, William R. *The Textile Industries of the United States.* Cambridge, Mass.: Riverside Press, 1893.

Baron, Ava, and Susan E. Klepp. "'If I Didn't Have My Sewing Machine . . .': Women and Sewing Machine Technology." In Joan M. Jensen and Sue Davidson, eds., *A Needle, a Bobbin, a Strike: Women Needleworkers in America*, pp. 20–59. Philadelphia: Temple University Press, 1982.

Baron, Ava, ed. *Work Engendered: Toward a New History of American Labor.* Ithaca: Cornell University Press, 1991.

Basch, Norma. *In the Eyes of the Law: Women, Marriage, and Property in Nineteenth-Century New York.* Ithaca: Cornell University Press, 1982.

Bassett, William. *The History of the Town of Richmond, Cheshire County, New Hampshire.* Boston: C. W. Calkins, 1884.

Benson, Sue. "The 1920's through the Looking Glass of Gender: A Response to David Montgomery." *International Labor and Working-Class History*, no. 32 (Fall 1987): 25–30.

Berg, Maxine, Pat Hudson, and Michael Sonenscher, eds. *Manufacture in Town and Country before the Factory.* Cambridge: Cambridge University Press, 1983.

Bernard, Richard M., and Maris Vinovskis. "The Female School Teacher in Antebellum Massachusetts." *Journal of Social History* 10 (Spring 1977): 332–45.

Bidwell, Percy. "The Agricultural Revolution in New England." In L. B. Schmidt and E. A. Ross, eds., *Readings in the Economic History of American Agriculture.* New York: Macmillan, 1925.

Biklen, Sari Knopp. "Confiding Woman: A Nineteenth-Century Teacher's Diary." *History of Education Review* 19, no. 2 (1990): 24–35.

Blake, Francis, comp. *History of the Town of Princeton . . . Massachusetts.* Princeton, Mass.: By the Town, 1915.

Blewett, Mary H. *Men, Women, and Work: Class, Gender, and Protest in the New England Shoe Industry, 1780–1910.* Urbana: University of Illinois Press, 1988.

———. *We Will Rise in Our Might: Workingwomen's Voices in Nineteenth-Century New England.* Ithaca: Cornell University Press, 1991.

———. "Women Shoeworkers and Domestic Ideology: Rural Outwork in Early Nineteenth-Century Essex County." *New England Quarterly* 60 (1987): 403–28.

Bibliography

——. "Work, Gender, and the Artisan Tradition in New England Shoemaking, 1780–1860." *Journal of Social History* 17 (Winter 1983): 221–48.

——, ed. *Caught between Two Worlds: The Diary of a Lowell Mill Girl, Susan Brown of Epson, New Hampshire.* Lowell, Mass.: Lowell Museum, 1984.

Blouin, Francis X., Jr. *The Boston Region, 1810–1850: A Study of Urbanization.* Ann Arbor, Mich.: UMI Research Press, 1980.

Boris, Eileen, and Cynthia R. Daniels, eds. *Homework: Historical and Contemporary Perspectives on Paid Labor at Home.* Urbana: University of Illinois Press, 1989.

Boris, Eileen, and Nelson Lichtenstein, eds. *Major Problems in the History of American Workers.* Lexington, Mass.: D. C. Heath, 1991.

Boydston, Jeanne. *Home and Work: Housework, Wages, and the Ideology of Labor in the Early Republic.* New York: Oxford University Press, 1990.

Brewer, Priscilla J. *The Queen of Inventions: Sewing Machines in American Homes and Factories, 1850–1920.* Pawtucket, R.I.: Slater Mill Historic Site, 1986.

Brigham, Loriman, ed. "An Independent Voice: A Mill Girl from Vermont Speaks Her Mind." *Vermont History* 41 (1973): 142–46.

Bryant, Blanche Brown, and Gertrude Elaine Baker, eds. *The Diaries of Sally and Pamela Brown.* Springfield, Vt.: William L. Bryant Foundation, 1970.

Chambers-Schiller, Lee Virginia. *Liberty, a Better Husband: Single Women in America: The Generations of 1780–1840.* New Haven: Yale University Press, 1984.

Clark, Christopher. *The Roots of Rural Capitalism: Western Massachusetts, 1780–1860.* Ithaca: Cornell University Press, 1990.

Clark, Victor S. *History of Manufactures in the United States,* vol. 1. New York: Peter Smith, 1949; originally published in 1916.

Clark-Lewis, Elizabeth. "'This Work Had a End': African-American Domestic Workers in Washington, D.C., 1910–1940." In Carol Groneman and Mary Beth Norton, eds., *"To Toil the Livelong Day": America's Working Women, 1780–1980.* Ithaca: Cornell University Press, 1987.

Coffin, Charles Carleton. *The History of Boscawen and Webster, from 1733 to 1878.* Concord, N.H.: Republican Press Association, 1878.

Coffman, Lotus Delta. *The Social Composition of the Teaching Population.* New York: Teachers College, 1911.

Coleman, D. C. "Proto-Industrialization: A Concept Too Many." *Economic History Review,* 2d ser., 36 (1983): 435–48.

Coleman, Peter J. "Rhode Island Cotton Manufacturing: A Study in Economic Conservatism." *Rhode Island History* 23 (July 1964): 65–80.

Conk, Margo. *The United States Census and Labor Force Change: A History of Occupation Statistics, 1870–1940.* Ann Arbor, Mich.: UMI Research Press, 1980.

Creamer, Daniel, and Charles W. Coulter. *Labor and the Shut-Down of the Amoskeag Textile Mills.* Philadelphia: Works Projects Administration, 1939.

Bibliography

Cross, Lucy R. H. *History of the Town of Northfield, New Hampshire, 1780–1905.* Concord, N.H.: Rumford Press, 1905.

Cumbler, John Taylor, ed. *A Moral Response to Industrialism: The Lectures of Reverend Cook in Lynn, Massachusetts.* Albany: State University of New York Press, 1982.

Dalzell, Robert F., Jr. *Enterprising Elite: The Boston Associates and the World They Made.* Cambridge: Harvard University Press, 1987.

Daniel, Robert L. *American Women in the 20th Century: The Festival of Life.* San Diego: Harcourt Brace Jovanovich, 1987.

Daniels, John. *In Freedom's Birthplace: A Study of the Boston Negroes.* Boston: Houghton Mifflin, 1914.

Dawley, Alan. *Class and Community: The Industrial Revolution in Lynn.* Cambridge: Harvard University Press, 1976.

Degler, Carl N. "Labor in the Economy and Politics of New York City, 1850–1860: A Study of the Impact of Early Industrialism." Ph.D. diss., Columbia University, 1952.

Diner, Hasia R. *Erin's Daughters in America: Irish Immigrant Women in the Nineteenth Century.* Baltimore: Johns Hopkins University Press, 1983.

Donovan, Dennis, and Jacob A. Woodward. *The History of the Town of Lyndeborough, New Hampshire, 1735–1905.* Lyndeborough: By the Town, 1906.

Dublin, Thomas. "The Mill Letters of Emeline Larcom, 1840–1842." *Essex Institute Historical Collections* 127 (July 1991): 211–39.

——. "Rural Putting-Out Work in Early Nineteenth-Century New England: Women and the Transition to Capitalism in the Countryside," *The New England Quarterly* 64 (1991): 531–73.

——. "Rural-Urban Migrants in Industrial New England: The Case of Lynn, Massachusetts, in the Mid-Nineteenth Century." *Journal of American History* 73 (1986): 623–44.

——. "Women and Outwork in a Nineteenth-Century New England Town: Fitzwilliam, New Hampshire, 1830–1850." In Steven Hahn and Jonathan Prude, eds., *The Countryside in the Age of Capitalist Transformation: Essays in the Social History of Rural America.* Chapel Hill: University of North Carolina Press, 1985.

——. *Women at Work: The Transformation of Work and Community in Lowell, Massachusetts, 1826–1860.* New York: Columbia University Press, 1979.

——. "Women's Work and the Family Economy: Textiles and Palm Leaf Hatmaking in New England, 1830–1850." *Tocqueville Review* 5 (1983): 297–316.

——, ed. *Farm to Factory: Women's Letters, 1830–1860.* 2d ed., 1993. New York: Columbia University Press, 1981.

Dudden, Faye E. *Serving Women: Household Service in Nineteenth-Century America.* Middletown, Conn.: Wesleyan University Press, 1983.

Earle, Alice Morse. *Home Life in Colonial Days.* New York: Macmillan, 1898.

Bibliography

Early, Frances H. "The French-Canadian Family Economy and Standard-of-Living in Lowell, Massachusetts, 1870." *Journal of Family History* 7 (Summer 1982): 180–99.

———. "Mobility Potential and the Quality of Life in Working-Class Lowell, Massachusetts: The French-Canadians, ca. 1870." *Labour/Le Travailleur* 2 (Fall 1977): 214–28.

Emery, Sarah Anne. *Reminiscences of a Newburyport Nonagenarian.* Newburyport, Mass.: William H. Huse, 1879.

Eno, Arthur L., ed. *Cotton Was King: A History of Lowell, Massachusetts.* N.p.: New Hampshire Publishing, 1976.

Ernst, Robert. *Immigrant Life in New York City, 1825–1863.* Port Washington, N.Y.: Ira J. Freeman, 1965; originally published in 1949.

Faler, Paul G. *Mechanics and Manufacturers in the Early Industrial Revolution: Lynn, Massachusetts, 1780–1860.* Albany: State University of New York Press, 1981.

Fowler, Gail. "Rhode Island Handloom Weavers and the Effects of Technological Change, 1780–1840." Ph.D. diss., University of Pennsylvania, 1984.

Freeman, Charles. *Luton and the Hat Industry.* Luton, Eng.: Luton Museum, 1953.

Gamber, Wendy. "The Female Economy: The Millinery and Dressmaking Trades, 1860–1930." Ph.D. diss., Brandeis University, 1990.

———. "A Precarious Independence: Milliners and Dressmakers in Boston, 1860–1890." *Journal of Women's History* 4 (1992): 60–88.

Garland, Joseph E. *Boston's Gold Coast: The North Shore, 1890–1929.* Boston: Little, Brown, 1981.

———. *Boston's North Shore: Being an Account of Life among the Noteworthy, Fashionable, Wealthy, Eccentric, and Ordinary, 1823–1890.* Boston: Little, Brown, 1978.

Gersuny, Carl. "'A Devil in Petticoats' and Just Cause: Patterns of Punishment in Two New England Factories." *Business History Review* 50 (Summer 1976), 131–52.

Gitelman, Howard M. *Workingmen of Waltham: Mobility in American Urban Industrial Development.* Baltimore: Johns Hopkins University Press, 1974.

Glenn, Evelyn Nakano. "From Servitude to Service Work: Historical Continuities in the Racial Division of Paid Reproductive Labor." *Signs* 18 (1992): 1–43.

Goldin, Claudia. *Understanding the Gender Gap: An Economic History of American Women.* New York: Oxford University Press, 1990.

Groneman, Carol. "'She Earns as a Child; She Pays as a Man': Women Workers in a Mid-Nineteenth-Century New York City Community." In Milton Cantor and Bruce Laurie, eds., *Class, Sex, and the Woman Worker.* Westport, Conn.: Greenwood Press, 1977.

Gullickson, Gay L. "Agriculture and Cottage Industry: Redefining the Causes of Proto-Industrialization." *Journal of Economic History* 43 (December 1983): 831–50.

Gutman, Herbert G. "Work, Culture, and Society in Industrializing America, 1815–1919." *American Historical Review* 78 (1973): 531–68.

Bibliography

——. *Work, Culture, and Society in Industrializing America: Essays in American Working-Class and Social History*. New York: Pantheon, 1977.

Gutmann, Myron P., and René Leboutte. "Rethinking Protoindustrialization and the Family." *Journal of Interdisciplinary History* 14 (Winter 1984): 587–607.

Handlin, Oscar. *Boston's Immigrants: A Study in Acculturation*. Rev. ed. New York: Atheneum, 1968; originally published in 1941.

Hareven, Tamara K. *Family Time and Industrial Time: The Relationship between the Family and Work in a New England Industrial Community*. Cambridge: Cambridge University Press, 1982.

Harris, Marc. "A Demographic Study of Concord, Massachusetts, 1750–1850." Undergraduate honors thesis, Brandeis University, 1973.

Hazard, Blanche Evans. *The Organization of the Boot and Shoe Industry in Massachusetts before 1875*. Cambridge: Harvard University Press, 1921.

Hershberg, Theodore, ed. *Philadelphia: Work, Space, Family, and Group Experience in Philadelphia in the Nineteenth Century*. New York: Oxford University Press, 1981.

Hill, Joseph A. *Women in Gainful Occupations, 1870 to 1920*. Washington: GPO, 1929.

Hobsbawm, E. J. *Industry and Empire: The Making of Modern English Society*. Vol. 2, *1750 to the Present Day*. New York: Pantheon, 1968.

Horowitz, Daniel. *The Morality of Spending: Attitudes toward the Consumer Society in America, 1875–1940*. Baltimore: Johns Hopkins University Press, 1985.

Horton, James Oliver, and Lois E. Horton. *Black Bostonians: Family Life and Community Struggle in the Antebellum North*. New York: Holmes & Meier, 1979.

Jensen, Joan M. *Loosening the Bonds: Mid-Atlantic Farm Women, 1750–1850*. New Haven: Yale University Press, 1986.

Jillson, David. *Genealogy of the Gillson and Jilson Family*. Central Falls, R.I.: E. L. Freeman, 1876.

Joyce, Patrick. *Work, Society, and Politics: The Culture of the Factory in Later Victorian England*. New Brunswick, N.J.: Rutgers University Press, 1980.

Kaestle, Carl F. *Pillars of the Republic: Common Schools and American Society, 1780–1860*. New York: Hill and Wang, 1983.

Kaestle, Carl F., and Maris A. Vinovskis. *Education and Social Change in Nineteenth-Century Massachusetts*. Cambridge: Cambridge University Press, 1980.

Katzman, David M. *Seven Days a Week: Women and Domestic Service in Industrializing America*. New York: Oxford University Press, 1978.

Kelly, Joan. *Women, History, and Theory: The Essays of Joan Kelly*. Chicago: University of Chicago Press, 1984; originally published in 1977.

Kennedy, Lawrence W. *Planning the City upon a Hill: Boston since 1630*. Amherst: University of Massachusetts Press, 1992.

Kenngott, George F. *The Record of a City: A Social Survey of Lowell, Massachusetts*. New York: Macmillan, 1912.

Bibliography

Kimball, Gertrude S. *Pictures of Rhode Island in the Past, 1642–1833.* Providence: Preston and Rounds, 1900.

Kitteringham, Jennie. "Country Work Girls in Nineteenth-Century England." In Raphael Samuel, ed., *Village Life and Labour*, pp. 119–21. London: Routledge & Kegan Paul, 1975.

Knights, Peter R. *Plain People of Boston, 1830–1860: A Study in City Growth.* New York: Oxford University Press, 1971.

——. *Yankee Destinies: The Lives of Ordinary Nineteenth-Century Bostonians.* Chapel Hill: University of North Carolina Press, 1991.

Kulik, Gary, Roger Parks, and Theodore Z. Penn, eds. *The New England Mill Village, 1790–1860.* Cambridge: MIT Press, 1982.

Kull, Nell, ed. "'I Can Never Be Happy There in among So Many Mountains'—The Letters of Sally Rice." *Vermont History* 38 (1970): 49–57.

Lasser, Carol. "The Domestic Balance of Power: Relations between Mistress and Maid in Nineteenth-Century New England." *Labor History* 28 (Winter 1987): 5–22.

Lasser, Carol S. "Mistress, Maid, and Market: The Transformation of Domestic Service in New England." Ph.D. diss., Harvard University, 1983.

Laurie, Bruce. *Working People of Philadelphia, 1800–1850.* Philadelphia: Temple University Press, 1980.

Laurie, Bruce, Theodore Hershberg, and George Alter. "Immigrants and Industry: The Philadelphia Experience, 1850–1880." In Theodore Hershberg, ed., *Philadelphia: Work, Space, Family, and Group Experience in Philadelphia in the Nineteenth Century.* New York: Oxford University Press, 1981.

Laurie, Bruce, and Mark Schmitz. "Manufacture and Productivity: The Making of an Industrial Base, Philadelphia, 1850–1880." In Theodore Hershberg, ed., *Philadelphia: Work, Space, Family, and Group Experience in Philadelphia in the Nineteenth Century.* New York: Oxford University Press, 1981.

Layer, Robert G. "Wages, Earnings, and Output of Four Cotton Textile Companies in New England, 1825–1860." Ph.D. diss., Harvard University, 1952.

Lebergott, Stanley. *Manpower in Economic Growth: The American Record since 1800.* New York: McGraw-Hill, 1964.

Leighton, Perley M., comp. *A Leighton Genealogy: Descendents of Thomas Leighton of Dover, New Hampshire.* Boston: New England Historic Genealogical Society, 1989.

Lerner, Gerda. *The Majority Finds Its Past: Placing Women in History.* New York: Oxford University Press, 1979.

Levine, David. *Family Formation in an Age of Nascent Capitalism.* New York: Academic Press, 1977.

Long, Clarence D. *Wages and Earnings in the United States, 1860–1890.* Princeton: Princeton University Press, 1960.

Lown, Judy. *Women and Industrialization: Gender at Work in Nineteenth-Century England.* Cambridge: Polity Press, 1990.

Bibliography

Lyford, James Otis. *History of the Town of Canterbury, New Hampshire, 1727–1912*, 2 vols. Concord, N.H.: Rumford Press, 1912.

MacLean, Annie Marion. *Wage-Earning Women.* New York: Macmillan, 1910.

Marchalonis, Shirley. *The Worlds of Lucy Larcom, 1824–1893.* Athens: University of Georgia Press, 1989.

Martin, Edgar W. *The Standard of Living in 1860: American Consumption on the Eve of the Civil War.* Chicago: University of Chicago Press, 1942.

Medick, Hans. "The Proto-Industrial Family Economy: The Structural Function of Household and Family during the Transition from Peasant Society to Industrial Capitalism." *Social History* 3 (1976): 291–315.

Mendels, Franklin. "Proto-Industrialization: The First Phase of the Industrialization Process." *Journal of Economic History* 32 (1972): 241–61.

Miller, Kerby A. *Emigrants and Exiles: Ireland and the Irish Exodus to North America.* New York: Oxford University Press, 1985.

Modell, John. "Patterns of Consumption, Acculturation, and Family Income Strategies in Late Nineteenth-Century America." In Tamara K. Hareven and Maris A. Vinovskis, eds., *Family and Population in Nineteenth-Century America.* Princeton: Princeton University Press, 1978.

Mohanty, Gail Fowler. "Experimentation in Textile Technology, 1788–1790, and Its Impact on Handloom Weaving and Weavers in Rhode Island." *Technology and Culture* 29 (1988): 1–31.

——. "Handloom Outwork and Outwork Weaving in Rural Rhode Island." *American Studies* 30 (1989): 41–68.

——. "Putting Up with Putting-Out: Power Loom Diffusion and Outwork for Rhode Island Mills." *Journal of the Early Republic* 9 (Summer 1989): 191–216.

Monahan, Thomas. *The Pattern of Age at First Marriage in the United States.* 2 vols. Philadelphia: By the Author, 1951.

Montgomery, David. *The Fall of the House of Labor: The Workplace, the State, and American Labor Activism, 1865–1925.* Cambridge: Cambridge University Press, 1987.

Nelson, Margaret K. "Vermont Female Schoolteachers in the Nineteenth Century." *Vermont History* 49 (1981): 5–30.

Nobles, Gregory H. "Commerce and Community: A Case Study of the Rural Broommaking Business in Antebellum Massachusetts." *Journal of the Early Republic* 4 (Fall 1984): 287–308.

Norton, John F. *History of Fitzwilliam, New Hampshire.* New York: Burr, 1888.

Oppenheimer, Valerie Kincade. *The Female Labor Force in the United States: Demographic and Economic Factors Governing Its Growth and Changing Composition.* Westport, Conn.: Greenwood Press, 1976; originally published in 1970.

Osterud, Nancy Grey. *Bonds of Community: The Lives of Farm Women in Nineteenth-Century New York.* Ithaca: Cornell University Press, 1991.

Bibliography

Osterud, Nancy, and John Fulton. "Family Limitation and Age at Marriage: Fertility Decline in Sturbridge, Massachusetts, 1730–1850." *Population Studies* 30 (1976): 481–94.

Pease, Jane H., and William H. Pease. *Ladies, Women, and Wenches: Choice and Constraint in Antebellum Charleston and Boston*. Chapel Hill: University of North Carolina Press, 1990.

Peiss, Kathy. *Cheap Amusements: Working Women and Leisure in Turn-of-the-Century New York*. Philadelphia: Temple University Press, 1986.

Perlmann, Joel, and Robert A. Margo. "Towards a Social and Economic History of American Teachers: Some Preliminary Findings, 1860–1910." Paper presented at the annual meeting of the Social Science History Association, Washington, D.C., November 1989.

——. "Who Were America's Teachers? Toward a Social History and a Data Archive." *Historical Methods* 22 (1989): 68–73.

Phillips, Daniel L. *Griswold—A History; Being a History of the Town of Griswold, Connecticut, from the Earliest Times to the Entrance of Our Country into the World War in 1917*. New Haven: Tuttle, Morehouse, & Taylor, 1929.

Pleck, Elizabeth Hafkin. *Black Migration and Poverty: Boston, 1865–1900*. New York: Academic Press, 1979.

——. "A Mother's Wages: Income Earning among Married Italian and Black Women, 1896–1911." In Michael Gordon, ed., *The American Family in Social Historical Perspective*. 2d ed. New York: St. Martin's, 1978.

Preston, Jo Anne. "Learning a Trade in Industrializing New England: The Expedition of Hannah and Mary Adams to Nashua, New Hampshire, 1833–1834." *Historical New Hampshire* 30 (Spring/Summer 1984): 24–44.

——. "'To Learn Me the Whole of the Trade': Conflict between a Female Apprentice and a Merchant Tailor in Antebellum New England." *Labor History* 24 (Spring 1983): 259–73.

Prude, Jonathan. *The Coming of Industrial Order: Town and Factory Life in Rural Massachusetts, 1810–1860*. Cambridge: Cambridge University Press, 1983.

Quataert, Jean. "A New View of Industrialization: 'Protoindustry' or the Role of Small-Scale, Labor-Intensive Manufacture in the Capitalist Environment." *International Labor and Working-Class History*, no. 33 (Spring 1988): 3–22.

Read, Benjamin. *The History of Swanzey, from 1734 to 1890*. Salem, Mass.: Salem Press, 1892.

Richards, Peter John. "The French Canadians of Lowell: 1880–1900." M.A. thesis, Northeastern University, 1986.

Rix, Sarah E., ed. *The American Woman, 1990–91: A Status Report*. New York: W. W. Norton, 1990.

Runnels, Moses T. *History of the Town of Sanbornton, New Hampshire*. 2 vols. Boston: Alfred Mudge, 1881.

Bibliography

Rury, John L. "Who Became Teachers? The Social Characteristics of Teachers in American History." In Donald Warren, ed., *American Teachers: Histories of a Profession at Work*. New York: Macmillan, 1989.

Samuel, Raphael. "Workshop of the World: Steam Power and Hand Technology in Mid-Victorian Britain." *History Workshop*, no. 3 (Spring 1977): 6–72.

Schreiber, Henry Marcus. "The Working People of Boston in the Middle of the Nineteenth Century." Ph.D. diss., Boston University, 1950.

Scott, Joan Wallach. *Gender and the Politics of History*. New York: Columbia University Press, 1988.

Scott, Joan W., and Louise A. Tilly. "Women's Work and the Family in Nineteenth-Century Europe." *Comparative Studies in Society and History* 17 (1975): 36–64.

Sen, Amartya. "Gender and Cooperative Conflicts." In Irene Tinker, ed., *Persistent Inequalities: Women and World Development*, pp. 123–49. New York: Oxford University Press, 1990.

Shelton, Cynthia J. *The Mills of Manayunk: Industrialization and Social Conflict in the Philadelphia Region, 1787–1837*. Baltimore: Johns Hopkins University Press, 1986.

Shorter, Edward. "Female Emancipation, Birth Control, and Fertility in European History." *American Historical Review* 78 (1973): 605–40.

Sloat, Caroline. "'A Great Help to Many Families': Strawbraiding in Massachusetts before 1825." In Peter Benes, ed., *House and Home*, Proceedings of the Dublin Seminar for New England Folklore, Dublin, N.H. Boston: Boston University, 1988, pp. 89–100.

Smith, Daniel Scott. "Parental Power and Marriage Patterns: An Analysis of Historical Trends in Hingham, Massachusetts." *Journal of Marriage and the Family* 35 (1973): 419–28.

Smuts, Robert W. *Women and Work in America*. New York: Columbia University Press, 1959.

Stansell, Christine. *City of Women: Sex and Class in New York, 1789–1860*. New York: Alfred A. Knopf, 1986.

——. "The Origins of the Sweatshop: Women and Early Industrialization in New York City." In Michael H. Frisch and Daniel J. Walkowitz, eds., *Working-Class America: Essays on Labor, Community, and American Society*. Urbana: University of Illinois Press, 1983.

Stephenson, Charles. "The Methodology of Historical Census Record Linkage: A User's Guide to the Soundex." *Journal of Family History* 5 (Spring 1980): 112–15.

Stone, M. T. *Historical Sketch of the Town of Troy . . . 1764–1897*. Keene, N.H.: Sentinel Press, 1897.

Sutherland, Daniel E. *Americans and Their Servants: Domestic Service in the United States from 1800 to 1920*. Baton Rouge: Louisiana State University Press, 1981.

Bibliography

Taylor, George Rogers. *The Transportation Revolution, 1815–1860*. New York: Rinehart, 1951.

Taylor, P. A. M. "A Beacon Hill Domestic: The Diary of Lorenza Stevens Berbineau." *Proceedings of the Massachusetts Historical Society* 98 (1986): 90–115.

———. *More Than Common Powers of Perception: The Diary of Elizabeth Rogers Mason Cabot*. Boston: Beacon Press, 1991.

———. "A New England Gentleman: Theodore Lyman III, 1833–1897." *Journal of American Studies* 17 (1983): 367–390.

Tentler, Leslie Woodcock. *Wage-Earning Women: Industrial Work and Family Life in the United States, 1900–1930*. New York: Oxford University Press, 1979.

Thernstrom, Stephan. *The Other Bostonians: Poverty and Progress in the American Metropolis, 1880–1970*. Cambridge: Harvard University Press, 1973.

———. *Poverty and Progress: Social Mobility in a Nineteenth-Century City*. Cambridge: Harvard University Press, 1964.

Thompson, E. P. *The Making of the English Working Class*. New York: Pantheon, 1966.

Thomson, Ross. *The Path to Mechanized Shoe Production in the United States*. Chapel Hill: University of North Carolina Press, 1989.

Tilly, Louise A., and Joan W. Scott. *Women, Work, and Family*. New York: Holt, Rinehart, and Winston, 1978.

Tilly, Louise A., Joan W. Scott, and Miriam Cohen. "Women's Work and European Fertility Patterns." *Journal of Interdisciplinary History* 6 (1976): 447–76.

Tucker, Barbara. *Samuel Slater and the Origins of the American Textile Industry*. Ithaca: Cornell University Press, 1984.

Uhlenberg, Peter R. "A Study of Cohort Life Cycles: Cohorts of Native Born Massachusetts Women, 1830–1920." *Population Studies* 23 (November 1969): 411–20.

Ulrich, Laurel Thatcher. "Housewife and Gadder: Themes of Self-Sufficiency and Community in Eighteenth-Century New England." In Carol Groneman and Mary Beth Norton, eds., *"To Toil the Livelong Day": America's Women at Work, 1780–1980*. Ithaca: Cornell University Press, 1987.

———. "Martha Ballard and Her Girls: Women's Work in Eighteenth-Century Maine." In Stephen Innes, ed., *Work and Labor in Early America*. Chapel Hill: University of North Carolina Press, 1988.

———. *A Midwife's Tale: The Life of Martha Ballard, Based on Her Diary, 1785–1812*. New York: Alfred A. Knopf, 1990.

Ware, Caroline F. *The Early New England Cotton Manufacture: A Study in Industrial Beginnings*. New York: Russell & Russell, 1966; originally published in 1931.

Webster History Committee, *Webster, New Hampshire, 1933–1983: History*. Webster: Webster Publishing Committee, 1984.

Whitehill, Walter Muir. *Boston: A Topographical History*. Cambridge: Harvard University Press, 1959.

Wilentz, Sean. *Chants Democratic: New York City and the Rise of the American Working Class, 1788–1850*. New York: Oxford University Press, 1984.

Williamson, Jeffrey G. "Consumer Behavior in the Nineteenth Century: Carroll D. Wright's Massachusetts Workers in 1875." *Explorations in Entrepreneurial History*, 2d ser., 4 (1967): 98–135.

Worthen, Augusta Harvey, comp. *The History of Sutton, New Hampshire*. 2 vols. Concord, N.H.: Republican Press Association, 1890.

Yans-McLaughlin, Virginia. *Family and Community: Italian Immigrants in Buffalo, 1880–1930*. Ithaca: Cornell University Press, 1977.

Yasuba, Yasukichi. *Birth Rates of the White Population of the United States, 1800–1860: An Economic Study*. Baltimore: Johns Hopkins University Press, 1962.

Zevin, Robert Brooke. "The Growth of Textile Production after 1815." In Robert Fogel and Stanley Engerman, eds., *The Reinterpretation of American Economic History*. New York: Harper & Row, 1971.

Zonderman, David A. "From Mill Village to Industrial City: Letters from Vermont Factory Operatives." *Labor History* 27 (Spring 1986): 265–85.

Index

Index

Framework knitting, 114–15, 148
French Canadians, 109

Garment workers. *See* Needle trades
Genealogies, 260, 263, 266–67, 272, 276, 294
Griswold, Conn., 38
Groneman, Carol, 10
Gutman, Herbert, 2

Hale, Sarah Josepha, 45–46, 144
Hallowell, Maine, 38
Hamilton Manufacturing Company, 5, 79–93, 118, 130, 208, 266–69, 271–74
    employee register books, 79–81, 208
    See also Textile industry; Textile operatives
Handloom weaving, 31, 33, 45
    decline of, 31, 33, 48
    handloom rentals, 45n
    wages for, 48
    See also Weaving
Hareven, Tamara, 10–12, 109
Hat braiding, 20, 21n, 26, 32–34
    wages for, 35n
    See also Palm-leaf hat making
Haverhill, Mass., 34
Hobsbawm, E. J., 1
Home manufactures, 4, 142, 172
Hotels, women working in, 156, 161
Housing
    in boardinghouses, 108, 130, 154, 231–32
    of teachers, 217, 221, 224
    of textile operatives, 108, 231–32
    See also Residence patterns

Immigrants, 154
    in Boston work force, 154, 158–59, 184–85, 193, 200, 203–4
    family wage economy and, 181, 239–41
    French Canadian, 10–11, 230–32
    Greek, 230–32
    Irish, 10, 81, 121, 143, 196, 230–31, 254
    Italian, 10, 230
    in needle trades, 176–77, 243
    outwork and, 176–77
    Polish, 230
    Portuguese, 230
    shoemaking and, 233

Immigrants, children of, 154, 177–78, 180–81, 184–85, 201–3
    in domestic service, 201
    economic independence of, 182
    family wage economy and, 242–43
    increasing numbers in workplace, 200–201, 238–39
    in needle trades, 180, 243
    residence patterns of, 203, 238–42
Immigration, 26
    See also Ethnicity; Immigrants; Immigrants, children of
Independence, economic
    of dressmakers, 166
    of immigrant daughters, 182
    inability to achieve, 224, 227
    of milliners, 173
    of rural outworkers, 36–37
    of schoolteachers, 220–21
    of textile mill workers, 94–103
Individualism, 12, 198
Industrial capitalism
    gendered nature of, 256–58
    historiography of, 2–3, 7–9
    See also Industrialization
Industrialization, 1–19, 29, 230, 256
Inheritance, 5–6
Irish, 10, 81, 121, 143, 178–79, 196, 254

Jillson, Silas, 41–44, 259–64

Kin networks
    among shoemakers, 150
    among textile operatives, 107–9
    See also Family wage economy

Labor discipline, 81
Labor force
    occupational distribution, 20–24, 153, 156–60, 200–201, 236, 247–48
    women, participation rates of, 35, 50, 119, 120, 130, 156, 200–201, 207–8, 235–37, 247, 251–54
Labor turnover
    in domestic households, 195
    in textile mills, 106–7
    See also Employment, length of
Larcom, Lucy, 97
Larcom family, 96–97, 108

Index

Motivations for employment (*cont.*)
domestic service, 183–84
needle trades, 181
rural outworkers, 42–48, 54–62
schoolteachers, 205, 220–23
textile operatives, 87, 94–105
widows and married women, 143

Native-born. *See* Yankees
Nativity, 19, 25–26, 239, 242–43, 252–53,
  255
of domestic servants, 159, 161, 202, 243
of needleworkers, 159, 202, 243
of shoe stitchers, 121, 126, 134–37, 233
of textile operatives, 81–84, 88, 121,
  230–32
See also Residence patterns
Needle trades, 21, 22–24, 243–44
African Americans in, 243–44
background of workers, 185
compared with domestic servants, 187–93
decline of women in, 236
duration of employment, 190–93
female proprietors, 175–76
growth of, 173–75
importance of, 155–56, 158
inside workers, 169–72, 174
major occupations within, 164
mechanization of, 171–72
methods of researching, 269, 283–93
outwork and, 168–69, 173–74, 176–77
seasonal work, 170–71
wages in, 166–71
New Hampshire, 31, 35, 38, 71, 79, 81–
  82, 126, 134–37, 209–27, 229,
  294–98
New Ipswich, N.H., 38
New York, N.Y., 12–14, 18, 36, 49, 157–58,
  161n, 237–38
Northfield, N.H., 16, 84, 267, 271

Occupational mobility, 191–92, 220, 236–38
Outwork, 15
decline of, 20–21, 174–75
distribution of supplies for, 37–39, 46, 49,
  53
factory production vs., 36
family size and, 44–46, 63

family wealth and, 44–46, 63
farming and, 46
growth of, 33, 50, 54
immigrants and, 176–77
impact on rural communities, 71–72
middlemen, 39, 41, 51–53
predominance of, 20, 32
rural, 29–75
rural vs. urban, 36–37
transitional nature of, 72–75
urban, 168–69
See also Hat braiding; Needle trades;
  Weaving

Palm-leaf hat making, 20, 26, 32–33, 34n,
  48–71
centrality of women in, 57–59, 65–67
decline of, 20
distribution of supplies for, 49–53
methods of researching, 259–65
middlemen, 51–53
seasonal nature of, 49
wages for, 21, 53–54, 59, 69–70
weaving vs., 70–71
See also Hat braiding
Patriarchy, 30
See also Family wage economy
Paul, Mary, 77–79
Pawtucket, R.I., 35
Pease, Jane and William, 197
Peiss, Kathy, 182
Philadelphia, Pa., 14, 18, 31, 49, 157–58,
  181, 238
Piece wages, 39, 48, 131
Population growth, 121, 155
Power loom weaving, 31, 33, 41n, 48
See also Mechanization; Weaving
Productivity
hat braiders, 33–34, 49, 59–61
during life cycle, 68–70
of outwork, 36
of shoemaking, 123–25
weavers, 40–42
worker control over, 36–37
Property ownership
of domestic servants, 163, 183–84
of dressmakers, 165–66
of factory operatives' families, 90–94,
  135–37

Index